KU-515-250

Imponderables

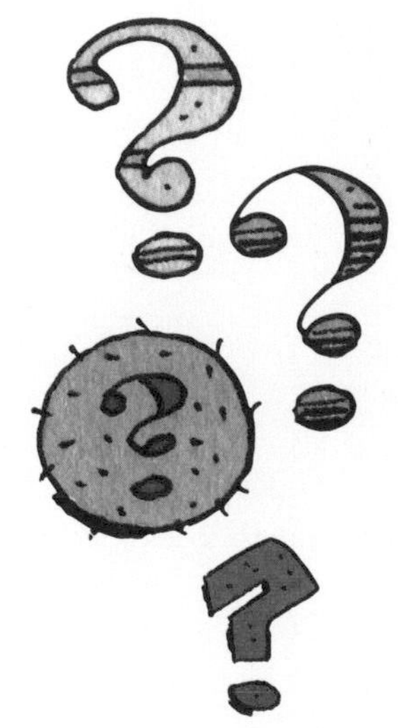

Imponderables

David Feldman

Answers to the most perplexing and amusing mysteries of everyday life

Reader's Digest

cont

ents

The never-ending quest to answer life's little questions

Have you ever wondered why dogs eat standing up but cats eat sitting down? Or why power lines hum? Or where Old Zealand is?

Some people can enjoy a perfectly happy life without finding the answers to these mysteries. Unfortunately, I'm not one of them. Since early childhood, I annoyed anyone within earshot with questions that started with the dreaded 'Why?'

On a Saturday afternoon more than 20 years ago, I was in the cereal section of a supermarket. I was on a diet and wanted to find a low-calorie cereal, but I realised I had never read the cereal boxes' nutritional panels carefully. To my surprise, I found that most cereals were between 350 and 400 kilocalories per 100 g. How, I wondered, could Kellogg's Corn Flakes and Kellogg's Frosties, for instance, have almost the same number of calories?

On the way home from the supermarket, the word 'Imponderables' popped into my mind to describe these little mysteries of everyday life that drive us nuts. We never find the answers because we don't know where to look or because we become preoccupied with other annoying things, like going to school or doing our jobs. I vowed to compile these Imponderables, mysteries that weren't discussed in standard reference books, and to find the answers by consulting experts in these fields. My goal was nothing less than eradicating Imponderability.

I learned an important lesson in searching out the answer to my breakfast cereal conundrum, and that is that the answers are often simpler than you'd think, and more interesting than you'd expect. In the case of breakfast cereal, the answer proved almost embarrassingly easy. (For the record, here it is: equal weights of all carbohydrates and proteins contain exactly the same amount of kilocalories: 4 kcal per gram. It doesn't matter whether it is a simple carbohydrate, like refined sugar, or the most healthy whole grain on the planet – in terms of kilocalories, they are equal.)

When I published my first book, I ended it with a page that asked readers to send in their own Imponderables. Ever since, I've been answering the

introd

mysteries of my readers. The people who have bought my books tend to fall into two camps: those who cannot sleep at night until their own Imponderables are solved; and those who hope my books will keep their loved ones from harassing them with their Imponderable obsessions. (If you fall into the first group and have any Imponderables you'd like solved, please send them to me at feldman@imponderables.com. If you are the first person to submit an Imponderable that we use in a future volume, we'll send you a complimentary copy, and give you an acknowledgement in the book.)

The fun part of my job is talking to experts in every conceivable field – from police officers to teddy bear designers; from neurologists to the world's foremost experts on pirates. These people, who are so generous with their time, are the backbone of my work.

I've long since given up on the fantasy of eliminating Imponderability. As soon as one mystery is solved, two more rear their ugly heads. But I'm resigned to fighting the good fight. Each new Imponderable is a challenge.

And after more than two decades of Imponderable-busting, I've learned that some refuse to go quietly – research findings and expert opinions emerge that throw a new light on the original questions. In my most recent book, *Why Do Pirates Love Parrots?*, I included updates on several previously published Imponderables. Many of them are included in this volume, at the end of the original Imponderables.

If you're itching to find the solution to any of the Imponderables I've posed in this introduction (all of which are answered in the volume you're reading), I think you'll discover what I have concluded: as long as you are curious, you'll never be bored.

–David Feldman

peo

Sometimes just being a person is confusing. Why do tiny paper cuts hurt so much? Why don't we get goose bumps on our faces? Why does our skin itch? Why does heat make us sleepy during the day, then keep us awake at night? Be prepared – the answers are often stranger than the questions.

people

Why does your whole body ache when you get a cold or flu?

When a virus enters your bloodstream, it releases several compounds that mount your body's defence against infection. Interferon, interleukin and prostaglandins are among the body's most valuable compounds. They raise a fever, shift the metabolism, and increase blood flow to areas of the body that need it.

Frank Davidoff, of the American College of Physicians, suggests that although science hasn't yet precisely defined their function, there is evidence to suggest that these compounds are responsible for the aching feeling that accompanies colds and flu. More of the compounds are usually found in the bloodstream during the aching phase than before symptoms start. And when doctors inject a purified form of each compound into a patient, many of the symptoms of a virus, including fever, sweating and aching, occur without causing the entire illness.

These compounds are effective without anyone knowing precisely how they work, but there are logical explanations for why they work. As Davidoff says:

> ‘The aching and other symptoms seem to be the “price” that's paid for mounting a defence against the infection. Whether the price is inseparable from the defence isn't clear. On the one hand, the symptoms might actually be a holdover from some mechanism that was important earlier in evolution but that is unnecessary now in more complex creatures. On the other hand, symptoms like aching may be part and parcel of the defence.’

What does it mean when we have 20–20 or 20–40 vision?

The first number in your visual acuity grade is always 20. That's because the 20 is a reference to the distance, in feet, you are standing or sitting from the eye chart. The distance is not a coincidence. Rays of light are just about parallel 20 feet (about 6 m) from the eye chart, so that the muscle controlling the shape of the lens in a normal eye is in a state of relative rest when viewing the chart. Ideally, your eyes should be operating under optimal conditions during the eye test.

The second number represents the distance at which a normal eye should be able to see the letters on that line. The third from the bottom line on most eye charts is the 20–20 line. If you can see the letters on that line, you have 20–20 ('normal') vision. A higher second number indicates your vision is subnormal. If you have 20–50 vision, you can discern letters that 'normal' observers could see from more than twice as far away, 50 feet (15 m). If you achieve the highest score on the acuity test, a 20–10, you can spot letters that a normal person could detect only if he were 50 per cent closer.

We also got the answer to another Imponderable about the vision test: are you allowed to miss one letter on a line and still get 'credit' for it? Yes, all you need to do is identify a majority of the letters on a line to get credit for reading it.

Who put E on top of the eye chart? And why?

Hermann Snellen, a Dutch professor of ophthalmology, put the E on top of the eye chart in 1862. Although his very first chart was headed by an A, Snellen quickly composed another chart with E on top.

Snellen succeeded Dr Frans Cornelis Donders as Director of the Netherlands Hospital for Eye Patients. Donders was then the world's foremost authority on geometric optics. Snellen was trying to standardise a test to diagnose visual acuity, to measure how small an image an eye can accept while still detecting the detail of that image.

Donders's complicated formulas were based on three parallel lines; of all the letters of the alphabet, the capital E most closely resembled the lines that Donders had studied so intensively. Because Donders had earlier determined how the eye perceives the E, Snellen based much of his mathematical work on the fifth letter.

The three horizontal limbs of the E are separated by an equal amount of white space. In Snellen's original chart, there was a one-to-one ratio between the height and width of the letters, and the gaps and bars were all the same length (in some modern eye charts, the middle bar is shorter).

Louanne Gould of Cambridge Instruments says that the E, unlike more open letters like L or U, forces the observer to distinguish between white and black, an important constituent of good vision. Without this ability, Es begin to look like Bs, Fs, Ps or many other letters.

Of course, Snellen couldn't make an eye chart full of only Es, or else all his patients would have 20-10 vision. But Snellen realised that it was important to use the same letters many times on the eye charts, to ensure that the failure of an observer to identify a letter was based on a visual problem rather than the relative difficulty of a set of letters. Ian Bailey, Professor of Optometry and Director of the Low Vision Clinic at the University of California at Berkeley, says that it isn't so important whether an eye chart uses the easiest or most difficult letters. Most eye charts incorporate only ten different letters, ones that have the smallest range of difficulty.

Today, many eye charts do not start with an E – and there is no technical reason why they have to – but most still do. Dr Stephen C Miller of the American Optometric Association suggests that the desire of optical companies to have a standardised approach to the production of eye charts probably accounts for the preponderance of E charts.

And we're happy about it. It's a nice feeling to know that even if our vision is failing us miserably, we'll always get the top row right.

What causes floaters, or spots, in the eyes?

The innermost part of the eye is a large cavity filled with a jellylike fluid known as vitreous humour. Floaters are small flecks of protein, pigment or embryonic remnants (trapped in the cavity during the formation of the eye) that are suspended in the vitreous humour.

The small specks appear to be in front of the eye because the semitransparent floaters are visible only when they fall within the line of sight. Most people might have specks trapped in the vitreous humour from time to time but not notice them. Eyes have a way of adjusting to imperfections, as any glasses wearer with dirty lenses could tell you. Floaters are most likely to be noticed when one is looking at a plain background, such as a blackboard, a bare wall or the sky.

What should one do about floaters? An occasional spot is usually harmless, although sometimes floaters can be precursors of retinal damage. Most often, a home remedy will keep floaters from bothering you. The American Academy of Ophthalmology suggests:

> 'If a floater appears directly in your line of vision, the best thing to do is to move your eye around, which will cause the inside fluid to swirl and allow the floater to move out of the way. We are most accustomed to moving our eyes back and forth, but

> looking up and down will cause different currents within the eye and may be more effective in getting the floaters out of the way. ’

Although you may be aware of their presence, it is often surprisingly difficult to isolate floaters in your line of vision. Because the floaters are actually within the eye, they move as your eyes move and seem to dart away whenever you try to focus on looking at them directly.

Why do your eyes hurt when you are tired?

Couch potatoes are busier than you might think. While lying on the sofa perusing a magazine or studying the impact of television violence on children by watching Bugs Bunny cartoons, they are actually exercising what ophthalmologist James P McCulley calls 'among the most active muscles in the body'.

Actually, your eyes contain three sets of muscle groups:

- Each eye has six extraocular muscles attached to the outside of the eyeball, which turn the eyes in all directions. The extraocular muscles must coordinate their movements so that both eyes look in the same direction at the same time.
- The sphincter and dilatory muscles open or close the pupils, defining how much light is allowed into the eye.
- The ciliary muscles attach to the lens inside the eye. When these muscles contract or relax, they change the shape of the lens, altering its focus.

Concentrated reading or close work provides a workout for these muscle groups strenuous enough to make your aerobics instructor proud. Unfortunately, as in all aerobic programs, the saying 'no pain, no gain' applies, as optometrist Steven Mintz explains:

> ‘ The human eye is designed so that, if perfectly formed, it will form a clear image on the retina (at the back of the eye) of any distant object without having to use any of the muscles. In order to see closer objects clearly, however, each set of muscles has to work. The extraocular muscles must turn each eye inwards; the sphincter muscles must work to make the pupil smaller; and the ciliary muscles must contract to allow the lens to change to a shape that will produce a clearer image.

This minimal muscular effort is significant in itself. However, no human eye is perfectly formed and these imperfections will increase the amount of effort required. For instance, people who are farsighted must exert more than the normal amount of effort on the part of the ciliary muscles. Many people have extraocular muscle imbalances that force them to work harder. Virtually every person, as [he or she] approaches or passes the age of 40, suffers from a stiffening of the lens inside the eye, which forces those ciliary muscles to work even harder. Reading under poor light (either too much or too little) will cause the sphincter and dilatory muscles to work excessively.

Just like doing 100 press-ups can cause the arm muscles to ache, so can the muscular effort described above cause sore eyes. Add to this that after several hours of close work, all of your body's muscles are going to be more tired, your level of tolerance or your pain threshold for sore eyes will be less than when you are fresh. ’

Ophthalmologists we consulted speculated that much of the eyestrain attributed to tiredness is in reality caused by dryness. Dr Ronald Schachar, of the Association for the Advancement of Ophthalmology, notes that when one is tired, the blink rate slows down and the eyes are not properly lubricated. Close work also slows down the blink rate. Eye specialists are finding that people who work on computers experience decreased blinking. This is one reason most consultants recommend stepping away from the computer at least once an hour. While most of us are more than happy to rest our muscles after doing a few press-ups, we expose our eyes to a marathon just about every day.

What causes bags under the eyes?

Let us count the ways, in descending order of frequency:

1 **Heredity.** That's right. It wasn't that night on the town that makes you look like a raccoon in the morning. It's all your parents' and grandparents' fault. Some people are born with excess fatty tissue and liquid around the eyes.

2 **Fluid retention.** The eyelids are the thinnest and softest skin in the entire body, four times as thin as 'average' skin. Fluid tends to pool in thin

In what direction do our eyes face when we are asleep?

Upwards, usually. Our eye muscles relax when we are asleep, and the natural tendency, known as Bell's Phenomenon, is for the eyes to roll back above their usual position. Of course, when we experience rapid eye movements during sleep, our eyes dart back and forth.

portions of the skin. What causes the fluid retention? Among the culprits are drugs, kidney or liver problems, salt intake and, very commonly, allergies. Cosmetics drum up more business for dermatologists and allergists than just about anything else. Allergic reactions to mascara and eyeliner are the usual culprits.

3 **Ageing.** The skin of the face, particularly around the eyes, loosens with age. Age is more likely to cause bags than mere sleepiness or fatigue.

4 **Too many smiles and frowns.** They not only can build crow's feet but bags.

A less fascinating explanation for many sightings of bags under the eyes was noted by Dr Tom Meek of the American Academy of Dermatology in *The New York Times*: 'The circles are probably caused by shadows cast from overhead lighting.'

Why do we 'see stars' when we bump our head?

Want to see stars? We heartily recommend going to the countryside, where there are few lights, and looking up, especially on a cloudless night. As Gerry Goffin and Carole King so eloquently phrased it in their song 'Up on the Roof', 'At night the stars put on a show for free.'

If looking up in the sky isn't edgy enough for you, you can try conking your cranium. It costs nothing to bump your head, but a knock on the noggin isn't as reliable as gazing skywards or visiting the local observatory – you may or may not see stars. And then there's the little matter of the ensuing headache. We consulted with several neuro-ophthalmologists as we weren't sure whether we saw stars because of damage to the eye or damage to the brain. As it turns out, there is a bit of controversy on the subject, but most agree that most of the time the 'eyes have it'.

Lenworth Johnson, a neuro-ophthalmologist at the Mason Eye Institute at the University of Missouri, Columbia, wrote to us that when you bump your head, you shake the vitreous humour, the transparent, colourless jelly that fills the eyeball. The vitreous, which is stuck to the underlying retina, then 'jiggles the retina'. The retina is the sensing element of the eye that sends information to the brain about light, colour and brightness. This jiggling sends the signal of stars to the brain. 'This is equivalent to having your skin squeezed and reporting pain or other sensation because of the nerves in the skull sensing the touch,' Johnson says.

The jostling of the retina doesn't translate to pain, though, as Scott Forman, Associate Professor of Ophthalmology, Neurology and Neurosurgery at New York Medical College, explains:

> Seeing stars after a head injury probably refers to what is known in the profession as "Moore's lightning streaks". A gentleman by that name coined the term to refer to the visual disturbances arising from sudden acceleration/deceleration of the eyeball (that accompanies a blow to the head). This produces a gravitational force exerted on the vitreous body, or vitreous humour.
>
> When the vitreous tugs on the retina, as it would if a sudden force is applied to it, the retina wrinkles ever so slightly. The mechanical deformation of the retina is not felt as pain, since there are no pain fibres in the retina. However, it sets off, most likely, a wave of depolarisation, a change in the electrical charge or electrical activity of the photoreceptor layers, those layers of the retina containing the elements that receive light from our environment. The mechanical deformation has the same effect as light entering the retina. That is, it sends a signal to the optic nerve and hence the visual brain (the occipital lobe, eventually, and other visual "association areas" in the brain) that we interpret as spots of light, sparkles, lightning or whatever.

If you want to see *someone else* see stars, your best shot is a Warner Brothers' cartoon – many an occipital lobe has been banged by a hammer in cartoons. But athletes, accident victims and crime sufferers who undergo concussions (the soft brain knocking against the hard surface of the skull) also often see stars. One study indicated that nearly 30 per cent of athletes who suffered head injuries from direct impact saw stars or unusual colours. Epileptics sometimes see stars during seizures, and sometimes after them.

So you can see stars by disturbing the brain directly and leaving out the 'middle man' (the retina), but chances are that, unlike bunnies in a cartoon, any knock on the head that is strong enough to make you see stars is sufficient to send you to A&E.

What are dimples? And why do only some people have them?

Dimples are a generic name for indentations of the skin. They are produced when muscle fibres are attached to the deep surface of the skin, such as in the cheek or chin, or where the skin is attached to bones by fibrous bands, such as the elbow, shoulder and back.

Dimples are most likely to appear where the skin is most tightly attached to the underlying bone. Dr William Jollie, Professor and Chairman of Anatomy at the Medical College of Virginia, says 'dimples probably are due to some developmental fault in the connective tissue that binds skin to bone'. So those dimples we've long envied are actually an anatomical flaw! And the tendency towards dimples seems to be hereditary. You have your father to blame, Michael Douglas.

What purpose do wisdom teeth serve?

They serve a powerful purpose for dentists, who are paid to extract them. Otherwise, wisdom teeth are commonly regarded as being useless to modern man. But because nature rarely provides us with useless body parts, a little investigation yields a more satisfying answer.

Primitive man ate meats so tough that they make beef jerky feel like mashed potatoes in comparison. The extra molars in the back of the mouth, now known as wisdom teeth, undoubtedly aided in our ancestors' mastication.

As humans have evolved, their brains have become progressively larger and the face position has moved downwards and inwards. About the time that primitive man started walking in an upright position, other changes in the facial structure occurred. The protruding jawbone gradually moved backwards, making the jaw itself shorter and leaving no room for the wisdom teeth. Most people's jaws no longer have the capacity to accommodate these now superfluous teeth.

What is the purpose of the little indentation in the centre of our upper lips?

You'll be proud to know that we have a groove running down our upper lip for absolutely no good reason, as William P Jollie, of the Medical College of Virginia, explains:

> The indentation in the centre of our upper lip is a groove, or raphe, that forms embryonically by merging paired right and left processes that make up our upper jaw.
>
> It has no function, just as many such midline merger marks, or raphes, have no function. We have quite a few merger-lines on our bodies: a raphe down the upper surface of our tongues; a grooved notch under the point of our chins; and a raphe in the midline of our palates. There are also several in the genital area, both male and female.
>
> Anatomically, the raphe on our upper lip is called the philtrum, an interesting word derived from the Greek word *philter*, which even in English means a love potion. I confess I don't see a connection, but many anatomical terms are peculiar in origin, if not downright funny.

Why do we have lips?

We have lips to stop our mouths from fraying. That's what the old joke says, anyway, and it raises a valid point. What purpose do human lips serve? Surely the mouth could carry out all of its vital functions – articulating speech, controlling breath, ingesting food – without the decorative pink piping round the edges?

There is a straightforward physiological explanation for the redness of lips. Their ruby hue is due to the fact that the skin around the mouth is extraordinarily thin – so much so that they are effectively transparent. The redness of lips is a glimpse of the tightly woven mesh of blood vessels that lies beneath the surface of our skins.

The skin is so amazingly sheer at the edge of our mouths because this area is a transitional zone between two types of body surface. Lips are the halfway house between the outside and the inside of our bodies. The 'mucous membrane' that lines the inside of our mouths has to be thin and porous enough to secrete and absorb moisture, whereas the stretchy hide that covers the rest of the body has to be tough, hard to tear or puncture, and utterly waterproof. The lips have some characteristics of both. They are dry, like the skin, but crammed with nerve endings, like the tongue. Consequently, they are very good at 'frisking' everything we put into our mouths. They are, so to speak, the customs officers at the main port of entry into our bodies. If we were about to eat something sharp or otherwise dangerous, our lips would be likely to detect it before it got inside our mouths where it could do harm.

So the lips have a practical, biological function. But, as so often is the case, homo sapiens has learned to make use of an incidental physical trait in subtle, social ways. For one thing, the lips highlight the mouth, and so make it easier for us to read clearly the facial expressions of others. Thanks to the lips, we can easily distinguish a smile from a snarl at some distance, and so we can tell in advance whether we are about to be hugged or punched. This would have been a handy early-warning system in our caveman days.

More subtly still, the lips themselves give out signals about the individual to whom they belong. Our lips are considerably plumper when we are young, so in a woman generous lips are a sign that she is likely to still be of child-bearing age. This, in turn, is what makes full lips so attractive to men – it's another legacy from our pre-history. This is also the explanation for the sexy movie-star pout (think of Marilyn Monroe posing for the photographers), for the longstanding popularity of lipstick, and for the modern fad for injecting Botox, collagen and other substances into the lips to accentuate them. They are all strategies for emphasising or enhancing the fullness of the lips, and so sending out positive sexual signals to the male of the species.

It would really be rather remiss of us to discuss lips without giving a mention to the other task at which they excel: kissing.

Lips are the perfect tool for this happy work. The extreme sensitivity of the lips means that touching another human being with this part of the body (so long as it is the right person, of course!) gives a sensual thrill out of all proportion to the surface area involved. As the author and physiologist Daniel McNeill has memorably written, the lips are 'twin pleasure puffs, rich with touch sensors'. Consciously or not, we garner a great deal of information about a person when we kiss them. It is reasonable to assume that the kissing evolved to help us make judgments as to whether the kissee is someone we might want as a mate.

You might say that all of us are programmed to read the lips of others; and that our lips, whatever they are doing, speak volumes.

Do we really need to put thermometers under our tongues? Couldn't we put them above our tongues if our mouths were closed?

Anyone who has ever seen a child fidgeting, desperately struggling to keep a thermometer under the tongue, has probably wondered, 'Why do doctors want to take our temperature in the most inconvenient places?'

No, there is nothing intrinsically important about the temperature under the tongue or, for that matter, in your rectum. The goal is to determine the 'core temperature', the temperature of the interior of the body.

The rectum and tongue are the most accessible parts of the body that are at the core temperature. Occasionally the armpit will be used, but the armpit is more exposed to the ambient air, and tends to give colder readings. Of course, drinking a hot beverage, as many schoolchildren have learned, is effective in raising one's temperature. But barring tricks, the area under the tongue, full of blood vessels, is almost as accurate as the rectal area, and a lot more pleasant place to use.

So what are the advantages of putting the thermometer under the tongue as opposed to over it? Let us count the ways:

1 **Accuracy.** Placing the thermometer under the tongue insulates the area from outside influence, such as air and food. As Dr E Wilson Griffin told *Imponderables*, 'Moving air would evaporate moisture in the mouth and on the thermometer and falsely lower the temperature. It is important to

have the thermometer under the tongue rather than just banging around loose inside the mouth because a mercury thermometer responds most accurately to the temperature of liquids or solids in direct contact with it.'

2 **Speed.** The soft tissues and blood vessels that make up our tongues create the ideal resting spots for a thermometer. Dr Frank Davidoff, Associate Executive Vice-President of the American College of Physicians, says that compared to the skin of the armpit, which is thick and nonvascular, the 'soft, unprotected tissues under the tongue wrap tightly around the thermometer, improving the speed and completeness of heat transfer.'

3 **Comfort.** Although you may not believe it, keeping the thermometer above the tongue would not be as comfortable. The hard thermometer, instead of being embraced by the soft tissue below the tongue, would inevitably scrape against the much harder tissues of the hard palate (the roof of your mouth). Something would have to give – and it wouldn't be the thermometer.

Davidoff concedes that, in a pinch, placing the thermometer above the tongue might not be a total disaster:

> 'In principle, you could get a reasonably accurate temperature reading with a thermometer above your tongue *if* you hadn't recently been mouth breathing or hadn't recently eaten or drunk anything, *if* you held the thermometer reasonably firmly between your tongue and the roof of your mouth, and *if* you kept it there long enough.'

Why does your voice sound higher and funny when you ingest helium?

The kiddie equivalent of the drunken partygoer putting a lampshade on his head is ingesting helium and speaking like a chipmunk with a caffeine problem. Many *Imponderables* readers want to know the answer to this question, so we contacted several chemists and physicists. They replied with unanimity. Perhaps the most complete explanation came from George B Kauffman:

> Sound is the sensation produced by stimulation of the organs of hearing by vibrations transmitted through the air or other mediums. Low-frequency sound is heard as low pitch and higher frequencies as correspondingly higher pitch. The frequency (pitch) of sound depends on the density of the medium through which the vibrations are transmitted; the less dense the medium, the greater the rate (frequency) of vibration, and hence the higher the pitch of the sound.
>
> The densities of gases are directly proportional to their molecular weights [mol. wt.]. Because the density of helium (mol. wt. 4) is much less than that of air, a mixture of about 78 per cent nitrogen (mol. wt. 28) and about 20 per cent oxygen (mol. wt. 32), the vocal cords vibrate much faster (at a higher frequency) in helium than in air, and therefore the voice is perceived as having a higher pitch.
>
> The effect is more readily perceived with male voices, which have a lower pitch than female voices. The pitch of the voice [can] be lowered by inhaling a member of the noble (inert) gas family (to which helium belongs) that is heavier than air ...

Brian Bigley, a chemist at Systech Environmental Corporation, told *Imponderables* that helium mixtures are used to treat asthma and other types of respiratory ailments. Patients with breathing problems can process a helium mixture more easily than normal air, and the muscles of the lungs don't have to work as hard as they do to inhale the same volume of oxygen.

Why does a hair in our mouth make us gag?

Our correspondent, Ilona Savastano, was passionate in her need for an answer to this burning Imponderable:

> How are we able to swallow just about any type of food, at times very large mouthfuls of it, with no problem, and yet we nearly gag to death if we get a tiny little hair in our mouth? I feel even one piece of fur in our mouth doesn't quite bring the same "yucky" reaction.

Why do women tend to have higher voices than men? Why do short people tend to have higher voices than tall people?

Daniel Boone, a University of Arizona professor and expert on vocal mechanisms, provides the answer: 'Fundamental frequency or voice pitch level is directly related to the length and thickness of the individual's vocal folds [or vocal cords].' The average man's vocal-fold length is approximately 18 mm; the average woman's is 10 mm. The tall person of either gender is likely to have longer vocal cords than a shorter person of the same sex.

We flew the question by our dental experts, who are used to patients gagging (sometimes even before they find out much all that dental work is going to cost). Their first reaction was to emphasise the sensitivity of the mouth. Dentist Ike House amplifies:

> 'Our mouths are the most sensitive parts of our bodies, especially at birth and in childhood. Children use their mouths for food (nursing), comfort (thumb-sucking or dummy), pleasure (witness the random exploration of children with their hands in their mouths) and exploration (children put a foreign object in their mouths to determine what it is). Because of our pattern of oral stimulation and exploration from an early age, the mouth is very sensitive.'

Now that we have established how sensitive our mouths are, we might ask whether there is anything particularly nasty about the hair itself that might cause particular problems if found in the mouth. Yes, indeed, insist our experts. Dentist Barnet Orenstein, of the New York University David B Kriser Dental Center, explains:

> 'Physically, a hair has two sharp ends capable of stimulating the very sensitive mucous membrane lining the oral cavity. Furthermore, the fine diameter and convoluted shape of a hair enable it to adhere to the mucosa. Dislodgement with the tip of the tongue is virtually impossible.'

The gag reflex isn't necessarily more likely to occur when the mouth is full than when it contains one lonely hair. We can be tickled more easily by the light touch of a feather on the neck than by a hard rubbing of a bulkier object.

But the main culprit in hair-gagging is well above the throat. All of our dental experts think that the main cause of hair-gagging is psychological.

Dr House reports that he has often been able to decrease or eliminate a patient's gag reflex simply by talking to him or her about the problem. And he opines that the nature of a foreign body determines our reaction to it:

> ‘For example, spaghetti would not feel much different in our mouth than worms (assuming you had some GREAT sauce and the worms were already dead and not wiggling around), but most people would choke at the thought. Hair is perceived as being dirty by most people, witness the displeasure people have with finding a hair in their food. During lovemaking, however, touching your partner's hair with your mouth might be enjoyable.’

So buck up, Ilona. Sure, you may not be able to control your gag on a single strand of hair, but blame the messenger, not the message. Gagging can be good for you, as Dr Orenstein explains:

> ‘The gag reflex is one of the many defence mechanisms nature has so miraculously endowed us with. Even infants will react violently to tickling of the soft palate. If it were not for this mechanism, many of us would expire by having the airway shut off by some foreign body lodged in our throat.’

Why don't people get goose bumps on their faces?

Be proud of the fact that you don't get goose bumps on your face. It's one of the few things that separate you from chimps.

We get goose bumps only on parts of our bodies that have hair. The purpose of body hair is to protect us from the cold. But when our hair doesn't provide enough insulation, the small muscles at the bottom of each hair tighten, so that the hair stands up.

In animals covered with fur, this means that a protective nest of hairs is formed. Cold air is trapped in the hair instead of bouncing against delicate skin. The hair thus insulates the animals against the cold.

Although humans have lost most of their body hair, the same muscular contractions occur to defend against the cold. Instead of a mat of hair, all we have to face the elements are a few wispy tufts and a multitude of mounds of skin. When a male lion gets goose bumps, his erect hair makes him ferocious; our goose bumps only make us look vulnerable.

Why do our noses run in cold weather?

Otolaryngologist Dr Steven C Marks, on behalf of the American Rhinologic Society, explains the physiology:

> 'The nose and sinuses are lined by a mucous membrane that contains both mucus-secreting glands and small cells called goblet cells, which also secrete a component of mucus. This mucus is produced in normal mucous membranes and in those that are infected or inflamed.'

Many medical problems, such as viral or bacterial infections or allergies, can cause your nose to run. But, Marks says, the nose's response to cold is different:

> 'The nasal and sinus mucous membranes are innervated [stimulated] by nerves which control, to some extent, the rate of mucus secretion. The response of the nose to cold air is in part a reflex mediated by these nerves. The cold air is sensed by the mucosa [mucous membrane], which then sends a signal back to the brain, which then sends a signal back to the mucosa: the result is a secretion of mucus.'

What good does a runny nose do anyone but Kleenex? Keith Holmes, an ear, nose and throat specialist, believes that it is 'a natural physiologic phenomenon of the organ to protect the warm lining of the nose', as cold irritates the mucous membrane. Marks speculates that 'the increased mucus flow may be necessary to improve the humidification and cleaning of the air in the cold environment'.

What causes the ringing sound you get in your ears?

Unless you are listening to a bell, a ringing sensation means you are suffering from tinnitus. Someone with tinnitus receives auditory sensations without any external auditory source. It is a chronic problem for millions of people.

Tinnitus is a symptom, not a disease in itself. Virtually anything that might disturb the auditory nerve is capable of causing tinnitus. Because the function of the auditory nerve is to carry sound, when the nerve is irritated for any reason the brain interprets the impulse as noise.

Some of the most common causes for temporary tinnitus are:

1 Reaction to a loud noise.
2 Vascular distress after a physical or mental trauma.
3 Allergic reaction to medication. (Many people who take more than 20 aspirin per day are subject to tinnitus attacks.) Luckily, the symptoms usually disappear upon discontinuance of the drug.

Causes of more chronic tinnitus conditions are myriad. Here are some of the most common: clogging of the external ear with earwax; inflammation of any part of the ear; drug overdoses; excessive use of the telephone; vertigo attacks; nutritional deficiencies (particularly a lack of trace minerals); muscle spasms in the ear; infections; allergies.

Chronic tinnitus sufferers have to live not only with annoying buzzing, but usually with accompanying hearing loss. Unfortunately, there is no simple cure for the condition. Much research is being conducted on the role of nutrition in helping treat tinnitus, but for now, the emphasis is on teaching sufferers how to live with the problem.

Why do other people hear our voices differently than we do?

We have probably all had this experience. We listen to a tape recording of ourselves talking with some friends. We insist that the tape doesn't sound at all like our voice, but everyone else's sounds reasonably accurate. 'Au contraire,' the friend retorts. 'Yours sounds right, but I don't sound like that.' According to speech therapist Dr Mike D'Asaro, there is a universal pattern of rejection of one's own voice. Is there a medical explanation?

Yes. Speech begins at the larynx, where the vibration emanates. Part of the vibration is conducted through the air – this is what your friends (and the tape recorder) hear when you speak. Another part of the vibration is directed through the fluids and solids of the head. Our inner and middle ears are parts of caverns hollowed out by bone – the hardest bone of the skull. The inner ear contains fluid; the middle ear contains air; and the two press against each other. The larynx is also surrounded by soft tissue full of liquid. Sound transmits differently through the air than through solids and liquids, and this difference accounts for almost all of the tonal differences we hear on a recording of own voice.

When we speak, we are not hearing our voice solely with our ears, but also through internal hearing, a mostly liquid transmission through a series of bodily organs. During an electric guitar solo, who hears the 'real' sound? The audience, listening to amplified, distorted sound? The guitarist, hearing a combination of the distortion and the pre-distorted sound? Or would a tape recorder located inside the guitar itself hear the 'real' music? The question is moot. There are three different sounds being made by the guitarist at any one time, and the principle is the same for the human voice. We can't say that either the tape recorder or the speaker hears the 'right' voice, only that the voices are indeed different.

Dr D'Asaro points out that we have an internal memory of our voice in our brain, and the memory is invariably richer than what we hear in a tape recorder playback. Indeed, listening to a recording of our own voice is like listening to a favourite symphony on a bad transistor radio – the sound is recognisable but a pale imitation of the real thing.

Do earlobes serve any particular function?

Our authorities answered as one: yes, earlobes do serve a particular function. They are an ideal place to hang earrings.

Of course, there are theories. Ear, nose, and throat specialist Dr Ben Jenkins remembers reading about a speculation that when our predecessors walked on four feet, our earlobes were larger 'and that they fell in[wards] to protect the ear canal'. Biologist John F Hertner, of Kearney State College, recounts another anthropological theory: that earlobes served as 'an ornament of interest in sexual selection'.

Doctors and biologists we confront with questions like these about seemingly unimportant anatomical features are quick to shrug their shoulders. They are quite comfortable with the notion that not every organ in our body is essential to our wellbeing and not every obsolete feature of our anatomy is eliminated as soon as it becomes unnecessary.

Actually, the opposite is closer to the truth. Anatomical features of earlier humankind tend to stick around unless they are an obvious detriment. As Professor Hertner puts it, 'Nature tends to conserve genetic information unless there is selection pressure against a particular feature. Our bodies serve in some respect as museums of our evolutionary heritage.'

Why are our fingers different lengths?

If you ask an authority, such as Dr William P Jollie, Chairman of the Anatomy Department at the Medical College of Virginia, about this Imponderable, you get an evolutionary approach:

> ... anatomically, fingers are digits (our other digits are toes), and people, like all four-legged vertebrate animals, have digits characteristic both for the large group to which they belong (called a class: amphibians, reptiles, mammals) and for a smaller group within the class (called an order: rodents, carnivores, primates). So we have five fingers of a length that is characteristic for the hands of primate mammals.

Of course, there is variation among different species and even variation among individual members of the same species. Some people have ring fingers noticeably longer than their index fingers; in others, the fingers are the same length. We once knew a woman whose second toe was considerably longer than her 'big' toe.

But is there any rhyme or reason for the relative size of our digits? Dr Duane Anderson, of the Dayton Museum of Natural History, was the only source that we contacted who emphasised the role of the fingers (and hands) in grabbing objects:

> Pick up a tennis ball and you will see the fingers are all the same length. Length is an adaptation to swinging in trees initially, and then picking things up. An "even hand" would

> be less versatile. A long little finger, for example, would get smashed more often.

Biologist John Hertner says that two characteristics of the digits of higher vertebrates reflect possible reasons for the unequal lengths. First, there is evidence that we can move around more effectively with smaller outer toes. Second, over time, many higher vertebrates have a tendency to lose some structures altogether (for example, horses have lost all but one toe).

Might humans lose a digit or two in the next few hundred million years? Unfortunately, none of us will be around to find out.

What is the purpose of the white half-moons on the base of our fingernails and toenails? Why don't they grow out with the nails?

Those white half-moons are called lunulae. The lunula, usually most prominent on the thumb, is the only visible portion of the nail matrix, which produces the nail itself. The matrix, and the lunulae, never move, but new nails continually push forward, away from the matrix.

Why does a lunula appear white? Dermatologist Harry Arnold explains:

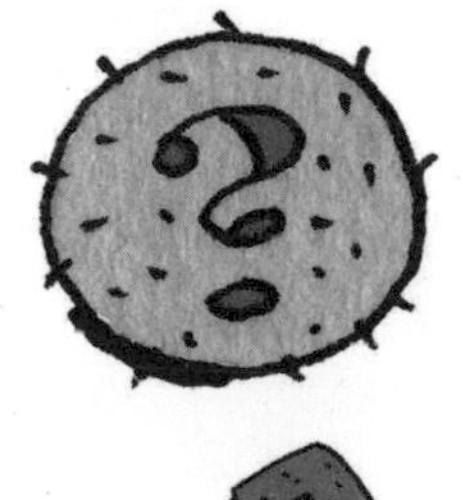

> The nail beds distal to [away from] the lunulae look pink because capillaries with blood in them immediately underlie the nail plate. The lunulae look white because the thin, modified epidermis of the nail bed is three or four times thicker there, being the busy factory where nail plate is manufactured. The lunula is avascular [without blood vessels], so it looks white.

Why do fingernails grow faster than toenails?

This is not the kind of question whose solution wins Nobel Prizes for scientists or garners prestigious grants for research institutions, yet the answer is not obvious. The average severed fingernail takes four to six months to grow back to its normal length. The average toenail takes nine to 12 months.

Dermatologist Dr Fred Feldman says that although nobody knows for sure why toenails lag behind fingernails in growth, there are many possible explanations:

1 Trauma makes nails grow faster. Dermatologists have found that if a patient bites a nail down or loses it altogether, the traumatised nail will grow faster than on one left alone. Fingernails, in constant contact with many hard or sharp objects, are much more likely to be traumatised in everyday life than toenails. Even nonpainful contact can cause some trauma to nails. Because we use our fingers much more often than our toes, toenails do not tend to get the stimulation that fingernails do.
2 All nails grow faster in the summer than the winter, which suggests that the sun promotes nail growth. Even during the summer, most people cover their toenails with socks and shoes.
3 Circulation is much more sluggish in the feet than in the hands.

Why do people seem to be immune to their own body odour?

How can so many otherwise sensitive people expose others to their body odours? Surely, they must not know that they (or their clothes) are foul-smelling, or they would do something about it. Right?

Right. Compared to most animals, humans don't have an acutely developed sense of smell. According to Dr Pat Barelli, Secretary of the American Rhinologic Society, 'The olfactory nerve easily becomes "fatigued" in areas where there are odours.' In order not to be overloaded with information, your nervous system decides not to even try being 'bothered' by your body odour unless it changes dramatically. Whether you usually smell like a spring bouquet or like last night's table scraps, you're unlikely to notice – even if you're sensitive to the body odour of other people.

Dr Morley Kare, Director of the Monell Institute at the University of Pennsylvania, adds that this fatigue principle applies to many of the senses. Workers at automobile factories must learn to block out the sounds of machinery or risk being driven insane.

And students often can't discriminate the taste of different dishes that are served in their school cafeteria. Of course, this phenomenon might be explained by the fact that all the cafeteria dishes do taste alike, but we would need a government grant to confirm the thesis.

Why do women put perfume on their wrists?

When we pass through the cosmetics counters of department stores, we see women applying perfume to their wrists and then sniffing intently. Why not on their fingers? The back of their hands? Their arms? Their underarms? What do they know that men don't know?

A cursory poll of some females indicated that most of them had no idea why they put perfume on their wrists. But there is a method to their madness. Irene L Malbin, of the Cosmetic, Toiletry and Fragrance Association, explains:

> Women put perfume on their wrists because there is a pulse point there. Pulse points are located wherever the pulse of the heartbeat is closest to the surface of the skin. The heat generated by the pulse point will intensify a perfume's impact.

Malbin lists other pulse points: behind the ears, the nape of the neck, the bosom, the crook of the elbows, behind the knees and at the ankles. Obviously, it is easier for a consumer to apply perfume to the wrist than the back of the knee.

All of this makes perfect sense. But then why don't men apply cologne to their wrists? Or do they?

Why did men thrust their right hand into their jacket in old photographs?

Most of the photo historians we contacted discounted what we considered to be the most likely answer: these subjects were merely imitating Napoleon and what came to be known as the Napoleonic pose.

Instead, the experts reasoned that just as subjects couldn't easily maintain a sincere smile during long exposure times, trying to keep their hands still was also a challenge. Frank Calandra, Secretary and Treasurer of the Photographic Historical Society, wrote to *Imponderables*:

> The hand was placed in the jacket or a pocket or resting on a fixed object so that the subject wouldn't move it [or his

other hand] and cause a blurred image. Try holding your hands at your sides motionless for 15 minutes or so – it's not easy. ’

Grant Romer, Director of Education at the George Eastman House's International Museum of Photography, adds that this gesture not only solved the problem of blurring and what to do with the subject's hands while striking a pose but forced the subject to hold his body in a more elegant manner.

Still, if these technical concerns were the only problem, why not thrust both hands into the jacket? Or pose the hands in front of the subject, with fingers intertwined?

John Husinak, Professor of Art History at Middlebury College, assured us that this particular piece of body language was part of a trend that was bigger and more wide-ranging than simply an imitation of Napoleon.

Early portrait photographers understood the significance of particular gestures to the point where they were codified in many journals and manuals about photography. Some specific examples are cited in an article by William E Parker in *After Image*, an analysis of the work of early photographer Everett A Scholfield. Parker cites some specific examples: two men shaking hands or touching each other's shoulders 'connoted familial relationship or particular comradeship'; if a subject's head was tilted up with the eyes open or down with eyes closed, the photographer meant 'to suggest speculative or contemplative moods'.

Harry Amdur of the American Photographic Historical Society told us that early photographers tried to be 'painterly' because they wanted to gain respect as fine artists. Any survey of the portrait paintings of the early and mid-nineteenth century indicates that the 'hand-in-jacket' pose was a common one for many prominent men besides Napoleon.

Another boon to the Napoleonic pose was the invention of the *carte de visite*, a photographic calling card. Developed in France in the 1850s, small portraits were mounted on a card about the size of today's business card. Royalty and many affluent commoners had their visages immortalised on *cartes*. In France, prominent figures actually sold their *cartes* – ordinary citizens collected them.

These photos were far from candid shots. Indeed, Roy McJunkin, Curator of the California Museum of Photography at the University of California, Berkeley, told *Imponderables* that *carte de visite* studios in the United States used theatrical sets, and that subjects invariably dressed in their Sunday best. The hand-in-jacket pose was only one of many staged poses, including holding a letter or Bible, holding a gun as if the subject were shooting, or pointing to an unseen (and usually nonexistent) point or object.

Why don't people in old photographs smile?

Sometimes, the more you delve into an Imponderable, the murkier it becomes. We asked about 20 experts in photography and photographic history, and the early responses were fairly consistent: the subjects in old photographs weren't all depressed; the slowness of the exposure time was the culprit. In some cases, the exposure time in early daguerreotypes was up to 10 minutes. As Frank Calandra, of the Photographic Historical Society, put it:

> Nineteenth-century photographic materials were nowhere near as light-sensitive as today's films. This meant that instead of the fractional second exposure times we take for granted, the pioneer photographers needed several minutes to properly set an image on a sensitised plate. While this was fine for landscapes, buildings and other still lifes, portraits called for many tricks to help subjects hold perfectly still while the shutter was open. (The first cameras had no shutter. A cap was placed over the lens and the photographer would remove it to begin the exposure and replace it when time was up.)
>
> Holding a smile for that length of time can be uncomfortable; that's why you see the same sombre look on early portraits. That's what a relaxed face looks like.

If that's so, Frank, we'll look jittery, any time.

Of course, the problem with trying to hold a smile for a long period of time isn't only that it is difficult. The problem is that the smile looks false. Photographer Wilton Wong told *Imponderables* that even today:

> A good portraitist will not ask subjects to smile and have them hold it even for more than a few seconds, as the smile starts looking forced. With the long exposures of old, the smiles would look phony and detract from the photo. Look at yourself in the mirror with a 30-second smile on your face!

The stationery of the Photographic Historical Society depicts a head clamp, which, although it looks like an instrument of torture, was used during the early days of photography to prevent a subject's head from moving while being photographed. In order to avoid blurring, subjects were forced to fix their gaze during the entire session. Iron braces were also used to keep the neck and bodies of subjects from moving.

In his book *The History of Photography from 1839 to the Present*, Beaumont Newhall recounts many anecdotes about the hardships caused by long exposure times. American inventor Samuel Morse, who was sent an early prototype by Daguerre (the French artist who pioneered photography), sat his wife and daughter down 'from 10 to 20 minutes' for each photograph. Newhall also describes the travails of an anonymous 'victim' who suffered through an excruciating single shot:

> ‘... he sat for eight minutes, with the strong sunlight shining on his face and tears trickling down his cheeks while the operator promenaded the room with watch in hand, calling out the time every five seconds, till the fountains of his eyes were dry.’

We were satisfied with this technological explanation for unsmiling subjects until we heard from some dissenters. Perhaps the most vehement is Grant Romer, of the George Eastman House's International Museum of Photography. Romer told us that the details of the daguerreotype process were announced to the public on August 19, 1839, and that only immediately after this announcement were exposures this long. By 1845, exposure time was down to six seconds. Yes, Romer admits, often photographers did utilise longer exposure times, but the technology was already in place to dramatically shorten the statuelike posing of subjects.

So could we find alternative explanations for the moroseness of early photographic subjects? We certainly could. Here are some plausible theories:

1 **Photographs were once serious business.** Joe Struble, Assistant Archivist at the George Eastman House, told us that the opportunity to have a photographic portrait was thought of as a once-in-a-lifetime opportunity. And it isn't as if the Victorian era was one where fooling about was prized. Roy McJunkin, of the California Museum of Photography at the University of California, Berkeley, feels that the serious expressions embody a 'Victorian notion of dignity – a cultural inclination to be seen as a serious, hardworking individual'.

2 **Early subjects were imitating the subjects of portrait painters.** Daguerre was a painter, and early photographers saw themselves as fine artists. Jim Schreier, a military historian, notes that subjects in this era did not smile in paintings.

3 **'Technology and social history are intimately interwoven.'** This comment, by Roy McJunkin, indicates his strong feeling that George Eastman's invention of roll film and the candid camera (which could be carried under a shirt or in a purse), both before the end of the nineteenth century, eventually forced the dour expressions of early photographic subjects to turn into smiles. The conventions of the early portrait pictures were changed forever once families owned their own cameras.

In the 1850s, according to McJunkin, the average person might have sat for a photographic portrait a few times in his or her life. With roll film, it became possible for someone oblivious to the techniques of photography to shoot pictures in informal settings and without great expense.

4 **Early photographs were consciously intended for posterity.** When he was asked why people didn't smile in old photographs, Grant Romer responded, 'Because they didn't want to.' Romer was not being facetious. Photographic sessions were 'serious business' not only because of their rarity and expense, but because the photographs were meant to create documents to record oneself for posterity. Rather, he emphasises that until the invention of the candid camera, photographers might have asked subjects to assume a pleasant expression, but the baring of teeth or grinning was not considered the proper way to record one's countenance for future generations.

5 **Who wants to bare bad teeth?** Grant Romer does not discount the poor dental condition of the citizenry as a solid reason to keep the mouth closed. As photographer Kevin Newsome put it: 'Baking soda was the toothpaste of the elite. Just imagine what the middle class used, if anything at all.'

6 **Historical and psychological explanations.** As compelling as all of these theories are, we still feel there are psychological, historical and sociological implications to the expressions of the subjects in old photographs. In 'The Photography of History', a fascinating article in *After Image*, Michael Lesy discusses the severe economic depression that began in 1836 and lasted six years. Photography was brought to the United States in the thick of it. Lesy observes that early American photographers were not seen as craftsmen or artists but as mesmerists and phrenologists (belief in both was rampant):

> ‘The daguerreotypists were called “professor” and were believed to practise a character magic that trapped light and used the dark to reveal the truth of a soul that shone through a face.

> These men may have been opportunists, but they moved through a population that lived in the midst of a commercial, political and spiritual crisis that lasted a generation that ended with carnage and assassination. The craft they practised and the pictures they made were the result not only of the conventional rationalism of an applied technology, but of irrational needs that must be understood psychologically. ’

In other words, this was not a period when photographers enticed subjects to yell 'cheese' or make a V sign over the heads of other subjects.

By the time George Eastman introduced the roll camera, Victorian morality was waning. At the turn of the century, there was a new middle class, eager to buy 'cutting edge' technology. As a benchmark, Roy McJunkin asks us to compare photographs of Queen Victoria and US President Andrew McKinley with those of Teddy Roosevelt, who consciously smiled for the camera: 'He was the first media president – he understood what a photo opportunity was and took advantage of it.' The politics of joy was born, and with it a new conviction that even the average worker had a right not only to the pursuit of happiness but to happiness itself.

We have one confession to make. Our research has indicated that smiles in old photographs, while uncommon, did exist. Dennis Stacey told us that more than a few existing Victorian photographs show the sitter 'grinning or smiling, usually with the mouth closed'. Grant Romer has an 1854 daguerreotype at the Eastman House of a woman standing on her head in a chair, smiling.

Romer admits that she was clearly defying the conventions of the period. But then, a little smile made Mona Lisa daring in her day too.

What are those twitches and jerks that occasionally wake us just as we are falling asleep?

It has probably happened to you. You are nestled snugly under the covers. You aren't quite asleep but you're not quite awake. Just as your brain waves start to slow, and as you fantasise about owning that Mercedes Benz convertible, you are jolted awake by an unaccountable spasm, usually in a leg.

You have been a victim of what is called a 'hypnic jerk', a phenomenon explained in David Bodanis's marvellous *The Body Book*:

> They occur when nerve fibres leading to the leg, in a bundle nearly as thick as a pencil, suddenly fire in unison. Each tiny nerve in the bundle produces a harsh tightening of a tiny portion of muscle fibre that is linked to it down in the leg, and when they all fire together the leg twitches as a whole.

Sleep specialists haven't pinned down what causes hypnic jerks or why they occur only at the onset of sleep. Although some people experience them more often than others, their appearance is unpredictable, unlike myoclonic jerks, spasms that occur at regular intervals during deep sleep.

Why does heat make us sleepy in the afternoon when we're trying to work but restless when we're trying to sleep at night?

Fewer experiences are more physically draining than sitting in an overheated library in the winter (why are all libraries overheated in the winter?) trying to work. You can be reading the most fascinating book in the world, and yet you would kill for a spot on a vacant bed rather than remaining on your hardback chair. So you trudge home, eventually, to your overheated house and try to get a good night's sleep. Yet the very heat that sent your body into a mortal craving for lassitude now turns you into a twisting and turning repository of frustration. You can't fall asleep. Why?

There is no doubt that heat saps us of energy. Many Latin American, Asian and Mediterranean cultures routinely allow their workforce to take siestas during the hottest portions of the day, aware both that productivity would slacken during the early afternoon without a siesta and that workers are refreshed after a nap.

Yet all of the sleep experts we consulted agreed with the declaration of the Better Sleep Council's Caroline Jones: 'Heat is not what makes us sleepy in the afternoon. Researchers have documented a universal dip in energy levels that occurs in the pm regardless of the temperature.' These daily fluctuations of sleepiness within our body are known as 'circadian rhythms'. David L Hopper, President of the American Academy of

Somnology, told *Imponderables* that late evening and early afternoon are the 'two periods during the 24-hour cycle when sleep is possible or likely to occur under normal conditions'.

Some sleep specialists believe that circadian rhythms indicate humans have an inborn predisposition to nap. But somnologists seem to agree that the natural sleepiness most of us feel in the afternoon, when it happens to be hottest outside, has little or nothing to do with the enervating effects heat has upon us.

Environmental temperatures do affect our sleep patterns, though. Most people sleep better in cool environments, which is why many of us have trouble sleeping in hot rooms even when we are exhausted at night. And if the temperature changes while we are asleep, it can cause us to wake up, as Hopper explains:

> 'Our body temperature is lowest in the early morning hours and highest in the evening. During deep NREM and REM sleep, we lose our ability to effectively regulate body temperature, so if the outside temperature is too warm or too cold, we must arouse somewhat in order to regulate our body temperature more effectively.'

Why do we dream more profusely when we nap than we do overnight?

According to the experts we consulted, we dream just as much at night as we do when we take a nap. However, we recall our afternoon-nap dreams much more easily than our dreams at night.

While we are dreaming, our long-term memory faculties are suppressed. During the night, our sleep is likely to go undisturbed. We tend to forget dreams we experience in the early stages of sleep. The sooner that we wake up after having our dreams, the more likely we are to remember them.

Any situation that wakes us up just after or during a dream will make the sleeper perceive that he or she has been dreaming profusely. Dr Robert McCarley, the Executive Secretary of the Sleep Research Society, told *Imponderables* that women in advanced stages of pregnancy often report that they are dreaming more frequently. Dr McCarley believes that the perceived increase in dreaming activity of pregnant women is prompted not by psychological factors but because their sleep is constantly interrupted by physical discomforts.

Why do we sometimes wake up in the morning with really bad breath?

Most bad breath is caused by sulphur-bearing compounds in the mouth. How do they get there? And why is the problem worse in the morning?

Micro-organisms in the mouth aren't fussy about what they eat. They attack:

- Food left in the mouth.
- Plaque.
- Saliva found in the spaces between teeth, the gum and on the tongue.
- Dead tissue that is being shed by the mouth, gums and tongue.

The micro-organisms convert this food into amino acids and peptides, which in turn break down into compounds with a pungent sulphur odour.

Brushing the teeth helps rid the mouth of all of these food sources of the micro-organisms. But the best defence is a regular salivary flow, the type you get by talking, chewing or swallowing – things that most of us do only when awake.

Eliminating cavities is not the only reason to floss. The longer food particles stay in the mouth, the more fetid the breath will be, so those hours of sleep are the perfect breeding time for bacteria and a threat to sensitive noses everywhere.

Why does warmth alleviate pain?

We had no idea of the answer to this Imponderable, but it was surprising that so many doctors we spoke to didn't know the answer either.

We finally got the solution from Daniel N Hooker, PhD, Coordinator of Physical Therapy/Athletic Training at the University of North Carolina at Chapel Hill. His answer included plenty of expressions like 'receptors', 'external stimuli' and 'pain sensors'. So let's use an analogy to simplify Hooker's explanation.

If a pneumatic drill is making a noise outside your window, you have a few choices. One is to do nothing, which won't accomplish much until the drill stops. But another option is to go to your CD player and put on something heavy at full blast. The pneumatic drill is still just as loud – you may still even be able to hear it. But the music will certainly distract you (and for that matter, your next-door neighbours as well), so the drilling doesn't seem as loud.

Hooker emphasises that most of us associate warmth with pleasant experiences from our youth. When we place heat on the area that hurts, sensory receptors tell our brain that there has been a temperature change. This doesn't eliminate the pain, but the distraction makes us less aware of it. As our body accommodates to the high temperature, we need fresh doses of warmth to dampen the pain. When we receive the renewed heat treatment, we expect to feel better, so we do.

Why are humans most comfortable at 22°C? Why not at 37°C?

We feel most comfortable when we maintain our body temperature of 37°C, so why don't we feel most comfortable when it is 37°C in the ambient air? We would – if we were nudists.

But most of us cling to the habit of wearing clothes. Clothing helps us retain body heat, some of which must be dissipated in order for us to feel comfortable in warm environments. Uncovered parts of our body usually radiate enough heat to meet the ambient air temperature halfway. If we are fully clothed at 22°C, the uncovered hands, ears and face will radiate only a small portion of our heat, but enough to make us feel comfortable. Nude at 22°C, we would feel cold, for our bodies would give off too much heat.

Humidity and wind also affect our comfort level. The more humid the air, the greater ability it has to absorb heat. Wind can also wreak havoc with our comfort level. It hastens the flow of the heat we radiate and then constantly moves the air away and allows slightly cooler air to replace it.

What exactly is happening physiologically when your stomach rumbles?

You've got gas in your stomach even when you, and others, aren't aware of it. You swallow gas as you eat and drink, and as you continuously swallow saliva. Also, some gases land in your stomach through bacterial fermentation.

Imagine your stomach and intestines as a front-loading washing machine. Instead of clothes, water and detergent whooshing around, there are solid foods, liquids from your diet, water, digestive fluids and gas constantly churning and contracting, even when you are not aware of it. This churning kneads and mixes the food and enzymes, making it easier for the stomach and intestines to digest and absorb the food.

But just as the excess water and suds must be eliminated from the washer, so must the food left in the stomach. These contractions enable the residue to move to the lower gut, where it is formed into faeces. Dr Frank Davidoff, of the American College of Physicians, describes the travels of gas in the stomach:

> ‘Now when bubbles of gas and liquid are mixed together in a hollow, muscular tube and the tube contracts in waves, massaging the contents along the way, pushing portions of the mixture through narrow, contracted gut segments, the result is gurgling, splashing and squeaking of all kinds – borborygmi, growls, rumblings – whatever you want to call them.
>
> Your stomach seems to growl more when you're hungry because part of the physiological condition of hunger is an increased muscular activity of your gut, as though it were anticipating the incoming meal, getting ready to move it along.’

Of course, the washing machine metaphor breaks down as this point. The washing machine doesn't particularly care whether it continues to get fed, and unlike our stomachs, we're not constantly stuffing clothes, water and detergent down its throat while it is still trying to work off its current load.

What use is the appendix to us? What use are our tonsils to us?

The fact that this Imponderable was first posed to us by a doctor indicates that the answer is far from obvious. We asked Dr Liberato John DiDio this question, and he called the appendix the 'tonsils of the intestines'. We wondered if this meant merely that the appendix is the organ in the stomach most likely to be extracted by a surgeon. What good are organs like tonsils and the appendix when we don't seem to miss them once they've been extracted?

Actually, tonsils and the appendix do have much in common. They are both lymphoid organs that manufacture white blood cells. William P Jollie,

Professor and Chairman of the Department of Anatomy at the Medical College of Virginia at Virginia Commonwealth University, explains the potential importance of the appendix:

> ‘One type of white blood cell is the lymphocyte; it produces antibodies, proteins that distinguish between our own body proteins and foreign proteins, called antigens. Antibodies, produced by lymphocytes, deactivate antigens.
>
> Lymphocytes come in two types: B-lymphocytes and T-lymphocytes. T-lymphocytes originate in the thymus. There is some evidence to suggest that B-lymphocytes originate in the appendix, although there is also evidence that bone marrow serves this purpose.’

If our appendix is so important in fighting infections, how can we sustain its loss? Luckily, other organs, such as the spleen, also manufacture sufficient white blood cells to take up the slack.

Some doctors, including Dr DiDio, even suggest that the purpose of the appendix (and the tonsils) might be to serve as a lightning rod and actually attract infections. By doing so, the theory goes, infections are localised in one spot that isn't critically important to the functioning of the body. This lightning-rod theory is supported, of course, by the sheer numbers of people who encounter problems with their appendix and tonsils compared to surrounding organs.

Accounts vary on whether patients with extracted tonsils and/or appendix are any worse off than those lugging them around. It seems that medical opinion on whether it is proper to extract tonsils for mild cases of tonsillitis in children varies as much and as often as hemlines on women's skirts. Patients in the throes of an appendicitis attack do not have the luxury of contemplation.

Why do superficial paper cuts tend to hurt more than deeper cuts?

Perhaps paper cuts hurt more because they are so emotionally maddening. How can such a trivial little cut, sometimes without a hint of blood, cause such pain?

The sensory nerve endings are located close to the skin surface, and the hands, where most paper cuts occur, contain more nerve endings than almost any other area of the body. Dr John Cook, of the Georgia Dermatology and Skin Cancer Clinic, adds that a trivial laceration such as a paper cut creates the worst of both worlds: 'It irritates these nerve endings but doesn't damage them very much.' Damaged nerve endings can lead to more serious complications, but sometimes to less pain than paper cuts.

Dr Cook and Dr Elliot, of the American Dermatological Association, also mentioned that most patients tend not to treat paper cuts as they would deeper cuts. After any kind of cut, the skin starts drying and pulling apart, exposing nerve endings.

Cuts are also exposed to foreign substances, such as soap, liquids, perspiration and dirt. Putting a bandage over a paper cut will not make it heal faster, necessarily, but if the cut stays moist, it won't hurt as much.

Why does the skin on the extremities wrinkle after a bath? And why only the extremities?

Despite its appearance, your skin isn't shrivelling after your bath. Actually, it is expanding. The skin on the fingers, palms, toes and soles wrinkles only after it is saturated with water (a prolonged stay underwater in the swimming pool will create the same effect). The stratum corneum – the thick, dead layer of the skin that protects us from the environment and that makes the skin on our hands and

Why do we feel drowsy after a big meal?

After we eat a big meal, the blood supply concentrates around the digestive organs and intestinal system, reducing the blood supply for other activities. We tend to slow down metabolically and in our ambitions. ('Fine, why not have a fourteenth cup of coffee? They won't miss us at the office.') Equally important, during digestion, foods are broken down into many chemicals, including amino acids such as 1-tryptophan, which help induce sleep. Serotonins, which constrict the blood vessels, also make us drowsy. Alcohol, if consumed with your meal, often produces sleepiness as well.

feet tougher and thicker than that on our stomachs or faces – expands when it soaks up water. This expansion causes the wrinkling effect.

So why doesn't the skin on other parts of the body also wrinkle when saturated? Actually, it does, but there is more room for the moisture to be absorbed in these less densely packed areas before it will show. One doctor we contacted said that soldiers whose feet are submerged in soggy boots for a long period will exhibit wrinkling all over the covered area.

Why do we itch?

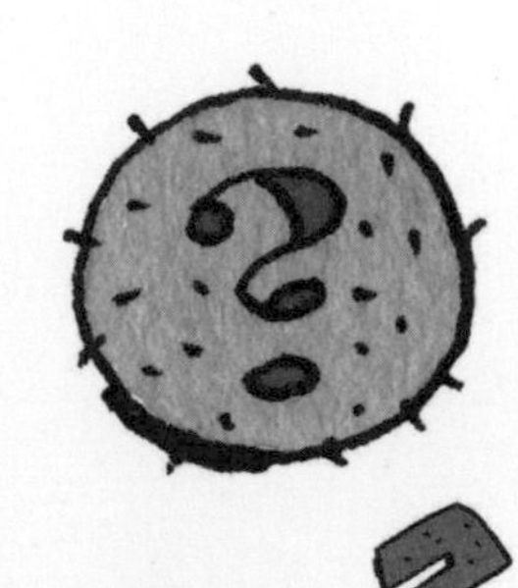

The short answer is: we don't know.

Here's the long answer. Itching is an enigmatic phenomenon. If a patient complains to a doctor that she has horrible itching and the doctor finds hives on the surface of the skin, the doctor can treat the hives and alleviate the itching symptoms. But a lot of itching has no obvious cause and is not associated with any accompanying illness.

Scientists can induce itching by heating the skin too close to the pain threshold or giving subjects certain chemicals, especially histamines (thus explaining why doctors prescribe antihistamines as a treatment for itching), but the ability to induce itching doesn't mean that doctors know its etiology.

This much is known. There are sensory receptors just below the surface of the skin that send messages to the brain. The itch sensation seems to flow along the same pathways of the nervous system as pain sensations.

According to Dr George F Odland, Professor of Dermatology at the University of Washington Medical School, the vast majority of sensory receptors are 'free' nerve terminals. These 'free' terminals do not seem to be designed for any specialised or particular function, but they carry both pain and itch sensations to the brain. These pain receptors are the most common in our nervous systems. When they operate at a low level of activity, they seem to signal itchiness rather than pain.

Many scientists have speculated about the function of itching. Some believe that itching exists in order to warn us of impending pain if action is not taken. Others speculate about the usefulness of itching in letting primitive man know it was time to pluck the vermin and maggots out of his skin and hair. Itchiness can also be an early symptom of more serious illnesses, including diabetes and Hodgkin's disease.

Itching sensations are distinct from ticklishness, which at least some people find pleasurable. Itching is rarely pleasurable; in fact, most people tolerate itching less well than pain. Patients with severe itching are invariably more than willing to break the skin, including pain and bleeding, in order to remove the itch.

How do astronauts scratch an itch when they have space suits on?

Most of the time, an itch presents no problem for an astronaut in space. If an itch is annoying, the astronaut reaches to the offending nerve endings and scratches. If the itch is in an 'unfortunate' place, perhaps the astronaut will look around the cabin, make sure no one is looking and then scratch. Still, no problem.

That's because most of the time when an astronaut is in space, he or she is in street clothes – typically comfortable trousers or shorts and a polo shirt. There are only three times when the space suit conspires to foil an itch: upon launch, during re-entry and during 'extravehicular activity' in space, such as a space walk.

During launch and re-entry, astronauts wear an 'LES' (launch-and-entry suit), the bright orange garb we see the astronauts wear when boarding the shuttle. These are 'partial pressure' suits, designed to pressurise in case the cabin has a sudden loss of pressure during launch or entry and are not unlike the suits worn by jet fighter pilots. Of course, a helmet is an essential component of the LES.

The 'EVA' (extravehicular activity) suit is far bulkier and designed to withstand the rigours of outer space. This is the 'big white uniform' that we associate with astronauts and with space walks, and that dominated the imagery in the film *Apollo 13.* But even back in the Apollo days, astronauts rid themselves of the bulky suits once they were in orbit. Today, space shuttle astronauts wear EVAs while doing repair work in space on satellites or other pieces of equipment.

While EVAs are more flexible than the old Apollo suits, they are hardly a model of comfort. An astronaut first dons a bodysuit, akin to long underwear, made of thin fabric. Over this go layers of insulation and life-support equipment, including tubes carrying liquid and gas. Then the 'HUT' (hard upper torso), a stiff upper suit, is placed over all the layers. The suit proper ends at the neck, with a hard metal locking ring, which clamps the helmet. Once the suit is pressurised, it puffs up, making it difficult to move freely. The helmet is locked rigidly at the neck clamp. If an astronaut swivels their head to the left, the helmet doesn't turn with them. If they want to see something they have to turn their whole body in that direction.

In the Apollo days, suits were individually constructed for each astronaut. Now, they come 'off the peg' in pretty standard sizes. They are sized 'small, medium and large', with some allowances for long and short limbs.

By all accounts, the LES suits are more comfortable than the EVA suits. Astronauts are normally in these suits for at least 90 minutes prior to launch. With delays, they can however be stuck, unable to move freely, for up to four or five hours: plenty of time to contemplate itchiness, and what they are going to do about it. But once the launch takes place, the shuttle is in orbit within eight and a half minutes; at that point, they can put on street clothes and scratch to their heart's (or other body part's) content.

So, is itchiness a burning issue among astronauts? Have they come up with inventive solutions to this intractable problem? To find out, we assembled five leading experts:

1 **Wendy Lawrence,** a former naval aviator and astronaut, who flew on shuttle flight STS-67, a historic 16-day mission, which was the second flight of the ASTRO observatory.
2 **G David Low,** who retired in 1996 after a 10-year career as an astronaut. Dave flew on three space shuttle missions and performed a six-hour space walk.
3 **Mike Lounge,** a former astronaut, veteran of three space shuttle flights, who trained for space walks but never did one.
4 **Glenn Lutz,** a NASA project manager, who has specialised in the design of space suits.
5 **James Hartsfield,** a former NASA public affairs director.

We asked the three astronauts if itching bothered them, particularly when wearing the stiff EVA suits. They all agreed that the biggest problem was with facial itches, particularly on the nose. Luckily for them, that is one of the few parts of the anatomy that the space suit is equipped to help – but not because NASA was concerned about itching!

Built into the side of an EVA helmet is a V-shaped object called a 'Valsalva device', which is designed to relieve earaches created by pressure changes in the cabin. To execute the 'Valsalva manoeuvre', you hold your nose shut and blow through your nose to equalise pressure in the middle ear and clear the Eustachian tubes. Obviously, an astronaut can't 'hold his nose' (there's that awkward little problem of the helmet being in the way), so instead the astronauts rest their heads on the 'V' of the Valsalva device and blow. The Valsalva device is built into the side of the helmet, so astronauts can simply turn their heads and place their proboscises right on it.

Ingenious astronauts discovered that they seldom needed the device for ear problems; they more frequently could use it for itch problems! In his funny and informative book, *How Do You Go to the Bathroom in Space?*, ex-astronaut William R Pogue addresses this issue directly:

> Not only did my nose itch occasionally, but also my ears. Because a scratch is almost an involuntary reaction, I frequently reached up to scratch my nose and hit my helmet – which can make you feel really dumb. I scratched my nose by rubbing it on a little nose pincher device we used to clear our ears [the Valsalva device]. If our ears itched, we just had to tolerate it. I usually tried rubbing the side of my head against the inside of the helmet, but it didn't help much. The best thing to do was to think of something else.

Some of our astronauts had their own workarounds:

> **LAWRENCE:** On an EVA you don't have direct access to your face. Hopefully you can wiggle your nose to satisfy it. You just try to move your nose around, maybe see if you can get your nose down to the base of the mounting ring on the inside – you see if that'll work.
>
> **LOUNGE:** The Valsalva device can help you with your nose. If you get an itch [elsewhere] on your face, you kind of move your head around and find something inside the helmet to rub against it.

Astronaut David Low had a hate relationship with the Valsalva device that turned into love:

> I had hundreds of hours in EVA training. I'd probably used that Valsalva device only a few times on a couple of different training runs. It always got in my way. In fact, a lot of times when just moving my head around, I'd bump into it, and it became somewhat of a pain to me. I found I could always clear my ears by just moving my jaw around.

Why don't you feel or see a mosquito bite until after it begins to itch?

We would like to think that the reason we don't feel the mosquito biting us is that Mother Nature is merciful. If we were aware that the mosquito was in the process of sinking its mouth into our flesh, we might panic, especially because a simple mosquito bite takes a lot longer than we suspected.

A female mosquito doesn't believe in a casual 'slam bam, thank you, ma'am'. On the contrary, mosquitoes will usually rest on all six legs on human skin for at least a minute or so before starting to bite. Mosquitoes are so light and their biting technique so skilful that most humans cannot feel them, even though the insect may be resting on their skin for five minutes or more.

When the mosquito decides to finally make her move and press her lancets into a nice, juicy capillary, the insertion takes about a minute. She lubricates her mouthparts with her own saliva and proceeds to suck the blood for up to three minutes until her stomach is literally about to burst. She withdraws her lancets in a few seconds and flies off to deposit her eggs, assuring the world that the mosquito will not soon make the endangered species list.

A few sensitive souls feel a mosquito's bite immediately. But most of us are aware of itching (or in some cases, pain) only after the mosquito is long gone, not because of the bite or the loss of blood but because of the saliva left behind. The mosquito's saliva acts not only as a lubricant in the biting process but as an anaesthetic to the bitee. Unfortunately, it also contains anticoagulant components that cause allergic reactions in many people. This allergic reaction, not the bite itself, is what causes the little lumps and itchy sensations that make us wonder why mosquitoes exist in this otherwise often wonderful world.

In training, I never used it for what it was intended for. I was considering asking them to remove it from my helmet for the mission. But for some reason, about two weeks before flight, I was sitting in my office one day and I thought, What if I have to use the Valsalva device on my real space walk? I called our support guy and asked if they could make sure that there was a Valsalva device on my helmet.

It turns out that I had the worst ear block I've ever had in my life when I was coming back in from my space walk and repressurising. If you've ever had one of those, they're very uncomfortable and you can have a lot of pain. Nothing you can do about it. You can't get your hands in there to blow your nose. I was so happy that I had that Valsalva device. '

Included on every EVA helmet is a straw, leading to a water pouch, and a food bar. Dehydration is a problem during space walks, so astronauts are encouraged to drink. Although it is possible to try to satisfy itches with these two devices, James Hartsfield indicates it isn't wise:

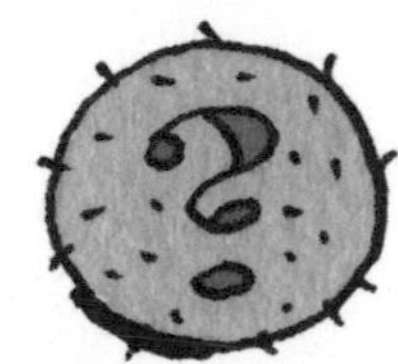

' The water straw is within reach of your mouth. You can get a drink by just bending your head down to get your lips onto the straw. There's also a food bar. But you don't want to use them to scratch facial itches ... they might come loose.

LUTZ: On an EVA, it's possible to scratch a facial itch with the water straw and/or the food bar. But because both those things are going to be ingested, you probably want to avoid as much body contact with them as you can. Most of the guys eat that food bar before they get outside or quickly because the EVA is usually pretty task-intensive and they don't want to be messing around eating things. '

The prognosis for nasty facial itches in the LES suit is much more favourable, because the visor is flexible:

' LOW: You can raise the visor on the helmet of an LES suit. For most of the ride uphill and downhill, we leave the visor open. We close them for the first two minutes of each launch, until solid rocket booster separation occurs. After that, we raise the visor. So when the visor is open, you can easily scratch a face itch. But if the orbiter lost pressurisation, you'd have to leave the visor down. '

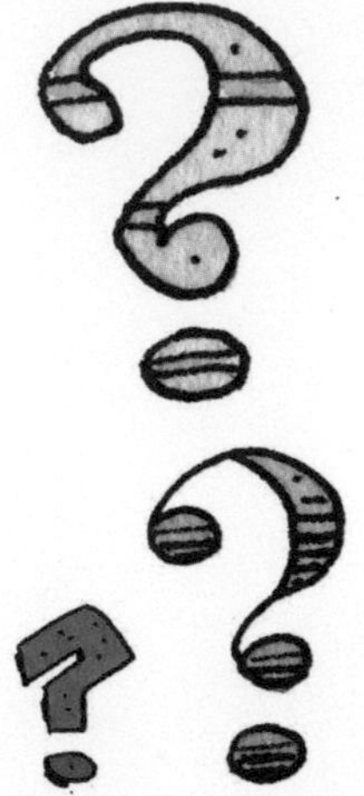

What about body itches? In some cases, the space suit is as unforgiving as the helmet. David Low said it was difficult to work in an EVA suit: 'It's hard to move in the things. They are pressurised and they balloon up. It wants to stay in the same, blown-up state. Any time you bend it, it pops back to that original state.'

Our experts had slight disagreements about how easy it was to scratch an itch in the EVA suits:

' **LOUNGE:** The EVA suits are pressurised enough that you can't feel sensation if you try to scratch from the outside. It's not like a soft garment; it's like a hard shell. The tips of the gloves are rubber. You can move your fingers, but you don't have a good tactile sense.

LUTZ: When the suit's not fully pressurised, that is, before you go out the door as you're getting ready for the space walk, if you get an itch on the soft part of the suit, like your arms, for instance, you can sort of compress it a little bit. You do that by squeezing with your arms from the outside of the suit.

However, once it's pressurised and you're on the space walk, the suit makes a pretty rigid balloon. It's feasible to rub your body against the inside of the suit. We're trying to make the suits as close as we can to a snug fit, but there is enough free volume that you can move around some. You can often get enough friction to scratch a bit.

LOW: It depends where the itch is. You can feel certain skin parts from the inside. The space suit is fairly tight. It looks bulky, but there are enough layers on the inside that you're almost touching something everywhere. You can just bend your leg or elbow [if you had an itch there]. You also typically have a little bit of room inside the chest cavity. If your shoulder itched, you could just contort yourself around there and scratch it the best you can.

HARTSFIELD: I've asked the suit technicians about this. The best you can do is try to rub against some part of the suit that might be close by. If you can't do that, you're out of luck. You just grin and bear it. [Where did we hear that line before?]

If your leg itched, you couldn't scratch it. That is, you wouldn't feel it through the suit at all if you reached there with your hand. Externally, you can't scratch through the outside of the suit. The pressure in the suit is such that, for instance, if you work with your hands and you have to make a grip, it's like trying to squeeze a balloon. If you push your leg, the pressure would go somewhere else. There are just too many layers to go through. In fact, once you're in the suit, you wouldn't even try – it's obvious that it isn't going to work.

If you were lucky enough to have an itch somewhere close by some part of the suit you could feel on the skin, you could try to scratch it up and down, but that would still be hard to do because you're wearing a liquid cooling vent garment, like a pair of long underwear. You'd have to try to scratch through that by rubbing your leg against some part of the suit.

LES space suits, much to the relief of the astronauts, are much more forgiving. Barring an emergency, they are not inflated, so they are not as stiff as EVA suits:

LAWRENCE: For the most part, the suits are comfortable. What makes it uncomfortable is if there's a launch delay – you're lying on your back maybe four hours, strapped to a seat. That's the uncomfortable part. But if you had an itch, you could scratch it through the outside of the suit.

This is a substantial improvement from the earlier Apollo days. In his book *Liftoff*, astronaut Michael Collins talks about the exigencies of itches and other physical discomforts during the Gemini era:

Inside the suit were other odds and ends, such as biomedical sensors taped to the chest with wires running to electronic amplifiers placed in pockets in the underwear. Finally, there was a "motorman's friend", a triangular urine bag with a condomlike device into which the astronaut inserted his penis before donning the suit. Once you're locked inside the suit, none of this gear could be adjusted, nor could an eye be rubbed, a nose blown, or an itch scratched. Some of the most fundamental amenities that we take for granted on Earth are difficult or impossible for an extravehicular astronaut.

To be honest, we were surprised that itching wasn't more of a complaint or concern. But look at it this way: when the astronauts are performing a space walk or about to launch, they might actually have other things on their minds. Hartsfield, who has worked with so many astronauts, comments: 'Most astronauts, when they do a space walk, are so enthralled by the experience that their mind doesn't wander to small things like this.'

And it's not as if astronauts lean towards the wimpy or whiny. Many astronauts have a military background, and even those that don't tend to share the stiff-upper-lip demeanor depicted in *The Right Stuff* and *Apollo 13.* Perhaps astronaut Wendy Lawrence put it best:

You just deal with it. My background is that of a navy pilot. If you get an itch when you are in military formation and standing in ranks, you just can't scratch it. You do what you can to alleviate the discomfort, but at the same time you realise that you have to stay at attention. You come up with ways to work around the problem and try to alleviate it, but you can't get out of your main responsibility.

But let me tell you. When the engines are on, and you're on solid rocket boosters, it's a nit! I was so wrapped in what was going on with the launch, and all my responsibilities with the launch, I didn't even notice any of that stuff.

Since blood is red, why do veins look blue?

We'll let one of our favourite medical authorities, Dr Frank Davidoff, Associate Executive Vice-President of the American College of Physicians, take the floor:

Veins look blue because they are fairly large blood vessels, full of blood that has been stripped of its oxygen load, and close enough to the surface of your skin to see the blue colour of this blood. Inside the red blood cells that make up about 40 per cent of your blood volume is the oxygen-carrying pigment haemoglobin. As the red cells pass through your lungs, the haemoglobin picks up oxygen and binds it, turning bright red in the process. The oxygen-haemoglobin combination is called "oxyhaemoglobin". This oxyhaemoglobin is pumped on out of your heart under pressure through the large muscular blood vessels called arteries.

In the tissues, red cells with their oxyhaemoglobin ultimately pass on through tiny blood vessels called capillaries, where they give up their oxygen to cells for use in metabolism. (The skin is rich in capillaries, which is why healthy, nonpigmented skin is pink; a sudden rush of extra oxyhaemoglobin into dilated blood vessels in skin causes the phenomenon of blushing.)

As haemoglobin loses its oxygen, it turns a dark purplish blue – deoxyhaemoglobin – which collects in larger and larger veins on its way back to the heart. While the biggest veins are deep in the tissues (they tend to run paired with the largest arteries), some fairly large veins lie just under the skin, where you can appreciate their blueness if there isn't too much brown skin pigment (melanin) to hide the colour. ’

Why are tattoos usually blue (with an occasional touch of red)?

Most tattoos are not blue. The pigment, made from carbon, is actually jet black. Since the pigment is lodged underneath the skin, tattoos appear blue because of the juxtaposition of black against the yellowish to brown skin of most Caucasians. Although red is the second most popular colour, many other shades are readily available; in fact, most tattoo artists buy many different ready-made colourings.

We spoke to Spider Webb, leader of the Tattoo Club of America, about the prevalence of black pigment in tattoos. He felt that most clients, once they decide to take the plunge, want to show off their tattoos: black is by far the strongest and most visible colour. Webb added that in the case of one client, albino guitarist Johnny Winter, a black tattoo does appear to be black and not blue.

How can amputees feel sensations in limbs that have been severed?

Most amputees experience 'phantom limb' sensations. Many patients report feelings as vivid and sensitive in the severed limb as the real counterpart. A patient, for example, with an arm amputated at the elbow might feel she could wave her hand, make a fist or raise a finger. The phantom limb may feel hot, cold, wet, itchy or painful. The most common report is that the amputee feels a mild tingling sensation or tightness in the phantom.

In most cases, phantoms start when the patient regains consciousness after surgery, but the duration of phantom limbs varies. While some patients lose feeling in their phantom limbs in a matter of months, others never lose theirs, although in most cases phantom limb sensations become less distinct over time. Sensations in the proximal parts (e.g. upper arm, thigh) tend to disappear first, with the extremities (fingers and toes) tending to linger. The amputee often perceives the (phantom) extremities moving closer to his or her stump.

Phantom limbs can occur with other forms of amputation. Some women experience phantoms after mastectomy; plastic surgeons report an occasional phantom after removal of fat or even after nose jobs.

There are both physical and psychological explanations for the phantom limb phenomenon, with very few practitioners doubting the importance of either factor. The best argument for the organic etiology of the phantom limb is that its existence is almost universal among amputees and that there is no evidence that sufferers of phantom limb have any different psychological profile than those who don't experience it.

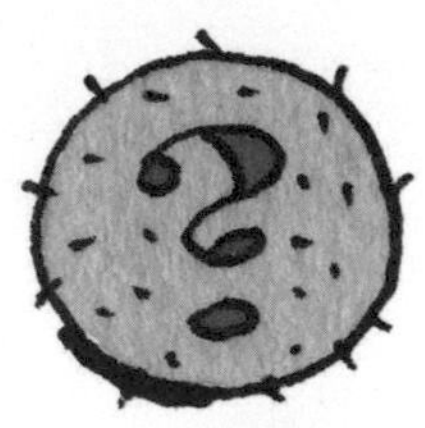

Most theories attribute phantoms to the sensory cerebral cortex. There is ample evidence for this supposition. The parts of the phantom most vividly felt by amputees are the digits of the hands and feet (particularly the big toe and thumb), the areas with the most representation in the cerebral cortex. The proximal areas of phantom limbs, such as thighs and upper arms, with the least representation in the cerebral cortex, not only evoke the least feeling in the amputee, but tend to have their symptoms disappear first.

One approach, the 'peripheral theory', ascribes phantom limb sensation to irritants in the nerves of the stump. The 'central theory' assumes that neighbouring cortical areas stimulate the part of the brain, the sensory homunculus of the cerebral cortex, that once affected the phantom limb. Physicians agree that the brain can send physical sensations to the stump. In other words, phantom limb sufferers are not just imagining these sensations.

Psychological theories about phantom limbs tend to acknowledge the organic origins of the phenomenon, but they stress that amputation is a traumatic event for most individuals and that most patients are forced to redefine their self-image after surgery. Many amputees, after surgery, feel that they are less than a whole person and feel both anger and shame about their stump. Psychiatrist Thomas Szasz stresses the individual's need to preserve the 'integrity of body image' and sees the phantom limb as both a form of denial and a means of recognising the transition that must be faced by the recent amputee. The sensations are a way to focus attention upon the loss, and as a way of denying it ('If I feel it, it can't be missing').

Although the mere appearance of the phantom limb does not indicate any psychopathology, most psychologists feel that painful phantom limbs, not uncommon, tend to be a symptom of depression. Painful stumps are often symbols of anger, as well as grief, directed inwardly. Several psychologists have had much success healing painful phantom limbs by treating the patient as if he were 'simply' a depressive.

Biofeedback has also worked in some settings, perhaps corroborating Szasz's theory that recovering patients need to focus on the stump in order to relieve anxieties about their self-image. Another clue to the supposition that problem phantoms might have at least a partly psychological base is the observation that many amputees forget about their phantoms for long periods of time but are immediately able to feel them when prompted by another person.

Why have humans lost most of their body hair?

Anthropologists have debated this issue for a long time. Hair on most creatures is an important means of maintaining heat in the body, so the reasons for humans losing this valuable form of insulation are unlikely to be trivial. Here are some of the more logical theories advanced about why hair loss made sense for humans, along with the opinions of Desmond Morris, whose book *The Naked Ape* derives its title from this very Imponderable.

1 Hair loss allowed primitive people to cope better with the myriad skin parasites, such as ticks, mites and vermin, that bothered them. Parasites were more than a nuisance; they spread many potentially fatal infectious diseases. Although this theory makes sense, it doesn't explain why other relatives of man, equally bothered by parasites, have not evolved similarly.

2 Naked skin could have been a social rather than a functional change. Most species have a few arbitrarily selected characteristics that differentiate them from other species – what Desmond Morris calls 'recognition marks'. Morris doubts the validity of the 'recognition mark theory', for hair loss is a far more drastic step than is necessary to differentiate humans from other primates.

3 Hair loss might have had a sexual and reproductive basis. Male mammals generally are hairier than their female counterparts. This type of sex-based physiological difference helps make one sex more attractive to the other. Morris also mentions that hair loss served to heighten the excitement of sex – there is simply more tactile sensation without fur. With ongoing efforts to slow escalating birth rates in many parts of the world, it is easy to forget that nature has built into our species characteristics to help increase our numbers.

4 Some anthropologists believe that before humans became hunting animals, stalking the savannas of East Africa, they went through a phase as an aquatic animal, seeking food at tropical seashores rather than on the more arid open plains. Without hairy bodies, humans became more streamlined in the water, able to swim and wade effectively. This is also a possible explanation for our hair being so plentiful on the head: if we spent much of our time wading in the water, only the top of the head needed to be covered, as protection against the sun. According to this theory, humans left the water only after they developed the tools necessary to hunt.

5 Even if the aquatic phase never existed, hair loss helped humans regulate their body temperature after they moved from the forests to a plains-based hunting culture. Morris questions this theory. After all, other mammals, such as lions and jackals, made a similar switch of terrains without accompanying hair loss. Furthermore, the loss of body hair had a negative effect in that it subjected humans to dangerous ultraviolet radiation from the sun.

6 Hair loss kept primitive humans from overheating during the chase when hunting. This is Morris's pet theory. When our ancestors became hunters, their level of physical activity increased enormously. By losing their heavy coat of hair, and by increasing the number of fat and sweat glands all over the body, humans could cool off faster and more efficiently. Sweat glands could not deliver their cooling effect nearly as effectively if fur trapped perspiration.

As divorced as we are from the problems of our primate forebears, Desmond Morris believes that human genetics will always countermand our attempts to elevate our culture. '[Man's] genes will lag behind, and he will be constantly reminded that, for all his environment-moulding achievements, he is still at heart a very naked ape.'

Why is pubic hair curly?

If you want to know the anatomical reason why pubic hair is curly, we can help you. Dr Joseph P Bark, of the American Board of Dermatology, explains:

> 'Pubic hair is curly because it is genetically made in a flat shape rather than in a round shape. Perfectly round hair, such as the hair seen on the scalps of Native Americans, is straight and has no tendency to curl. However, ribbonlike hair on the scalps of African Americans is seen to curl because it is oval in construction. The same is true with pubic hair.'

But answering what function curly pubic hair serves is a much trickier proposition. Some, such as dermatologist Samuel T Selden, speculate that pubic hair might be curly because if it grew out straight and stiff, it might rub against adjacent areas and cause discomfort. (Dermatologist Jerome Z Litt, who has been confronted with the question of why pubic and axillary hair doesn't grow as fast as scalp hair, facetiously suggests that 'not only wouldn't it look sporty in the shower room, but we'd all be tripping over it.')

Before we get carried away with our theories, though, we might keep in mind a salient fact – not all pubic hair is curly. Early in

Why can't hair grow on a vaccination mark?

A vaccination mark is nothing more than scar tissue. A vaccination causes an inflammation intense enough to destroy the hair follicles in its vicinity. Any deep injury to the skin will destroy hair follicles and cause hair loss. One can transplant hair onto a vaccination mark, but one can never bring a dead hair follicle back to life.

puberty, it is soft and straight. And Selden points out that this Imponderable likely would never have been posed in Japan or China. The pubic hair of Asians tends to be sparser and much straighter than that of whites or blacks.

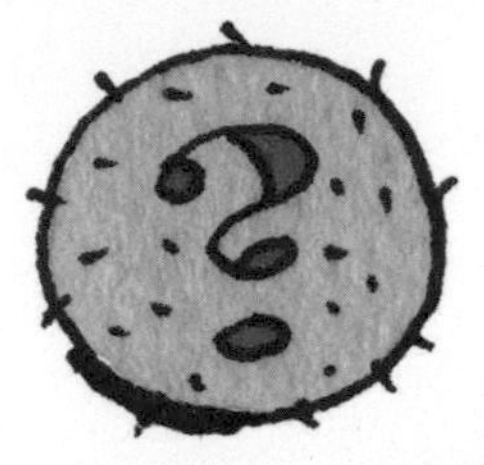

Why are some parts of our bodies more ticklish than others?

The experts who tackled this Imponderable focused on serious benefits that ticklishness might bestow on us mortals, all agreeing that what we now consider a benign tingling sensation at one time in our evolution might have warned us against serious trauma.

Biophysicist Joe Doyle notes that some parts of our body are more richly endowed with nerves than others – including such tickling meccas as the bottom of the feet, the underarms, and the hands and fingers. Evolutionists, notes Neil Harvey of the International Academy for Child Brain Development, 'would say that the reason for the heavier concentration may be whatever survival benefits we derive from being more sensitive in those places'.

How could, say, the armpit possibly be necessary to survival? 'The axilla warns of a touch that might progress to a wound of the brachial plexus, which could paralyse an arm,' answers University of Chicago neurosurgeon Sean F Mullan. Other sensitive sites, such as the nostrils, ear canals and eye sockets, are all subject to invasion by foreign objects or creeping or flying insects.

What about the underside of the foot, then? Mullan is slightly more tentative:

> 'The role of the foot is more perplexing. Is it a warning against the snake that crawled up the tree when we lived in its branches? Is it a hypersensitivity resulting from the removal of the thicker skin of our soles, which was normal before we began to wear shoes? I prefer the former explanation.'

Why do your feet swell up so much in planes?

We talked to two specialists in aviation medicine who assured us that there is no reason why atmospheric changes when you fly would cause feet to swell. Both assured us that the reason your feet swell up on a plane is the same reason they swell up on the ground – inactivity.

Your heart is not the only organ in the body that acts as a pump; so do the muscles of the legs. Walking or flexing a leg muscle assists the pumping effect. On a plane, you are not only confined in movement but sitting with the legs perpendicular to the floor. If you sit for prolonged periods without muscular activity, blood and other fluids collect in the foot with the assistance of gravity.

It doesn't really matter whether you leave your shoes on or off during periods of inactivity. If left on, they will provide external support, but they will inhibit circulation, feel tight – and, in any case, will not prevent feet from swelling. If you take your shoes off, you will feel more comfortable, but you'll have a tough time putting your shoes back on.

The pooling of fluids in the feet can happen just as easily in a bus, a train or an office. Most people's feet swell during the day, which is why podiatrists often recommend buying shoes during the middle of the afternoon. Many people require a shoe a half size to a full size larger in the afternoon than when they wake up.

If your feet swelling becomes a problem, consider aeroplane aerobics. A few laps around a wide-body plane will do wonders for your feet – and build up your appetite for the in-flight meal.

Why is it more tiring to stand than to walk? Why is it hard to stand still on two legs?

We're quite fond of moving as little as possible. But we've noticed the same phenomenon as our readers. When forced to stand still for prolonged periods, we feel as fidgety as three-year-olds who have drunk too much juice and can't get to a toilet.

While there might be some psychological elements at play, the physiological forces are probably dominant. When we stand, gravity pulls the fluid in our body down. The fluid can then pool in the legs and feet, putting pressure on the muscles and, eventually, even pain.

When we move, the contraction of the muscles pushes the fluids back up, and the veins contribute by sending blood back to the heart.

Walking increases the circulation not just to your heart, but all over your body, including to not-insignificant organs, such as your brain.

Even sitting for a long time can cause circulation problems. Swelling feet (oedema) can be traced to passengers' lack of movement and sedentary state on planes. In extreme circumstances, passengers can suffer from DVT (deep vein thrombosis), when a blood clot develops. That's why most doctors recommend walking around a bit on long flights, or at least stretching your calves periodically – which might be safer than dodging the service trolley in the aisle.

Airline seats force your legs to be perpendicular to the floor, so it's easy for fluid to build up, still another reason why we're fidgety on flights. To the extent that restlessness while standing or sitting straight causes us to fidget or move, our discomfort is serving an evolutionary advantage.

During a hernia examination, why does the doctor say, 'Turn your head and cough'? Why is the cough necessary? Is the head turn necessary?

Although a doctor may ask you to cough when listening to your lungs, the dreaded 'Turn your head and cough' is heard when the doctor is checking for hernias, weaknesses or gaps in the structure of what should be a firm body wall.

According to Dr Frank Davidoff, of the American College of Physicians, these gaps are most frequently found in the inguinal area in men, 'the area where the tube (duct) that connects each testicle to the structures inside the body passes through the body wall'. Some men are born with fairly large gaps to begin with. The danger, Davidoff says, is that:

> ‘repeated increases in the pressure inside the abdomen, as from repeated and chronic coughing, lifting heavy weights, etc., can push abdominal contents into the gap, stretching a slightly enlarged opening into an even bigger one, and leading ultimately to a permanent bulge in contents out through the hernia opening.
>
> Inguinal hernias are obvious and can be disfiguring when they are large and contain a sizable amount of abdominal contents, such as pads of fat or loops of intestine. However, hernias are actually more dangerous when they are small, because a loop of bowel is likely to get pinched, hence obstructed, if caught in a small hernia opening, while a large hernia opening tends to

allow a loop of bowel to slide freely in and out of the hernia "sac" without getting caught or twisted. Doctors are therefore particularly concerned about detecting inguinal hernias when they are small, exactly the situation in which they have not been obvious to the patient. A small inguinal hernia may not bulge at all when the pressure inside the abdomen is normal.

Most small hernias would go undetected unless the patient increased the pressure inside the abdomen, thus causing the hernia sac to bulge outwards, where it can be felt by the doctor's examining finger pushed up into the scrotum. And the fastest, simplest way for the patient to increase the intra-abdominal pressure is to cough, since coughing pushes up the diaphragm, squeezes the lungs and forces air out past the vocal cords. By forcing all the abdominal muscles to contract together, coughing creates the necessary increase in pressure. ’

If the doctor can't feel a bulge beneath the examining finger during the cough, he or she assumes the patient is hernia-free.

And why do you have to turn your head when coughing? Dr E Wilson Griffin, a family doctor, provided the most concise answer: 'So that the patient doesn't cough his yucky germs all over the doctor.'

Why don't women faint as much as they used to?

The most common cause of fainting is a lack of sufficient blood flow to the brain because of a sudden drop in blood pressure. Serious heart problems, including arrhythmia and ventricular tachycardia, can also be the culprit as well as, less frequently, neurological irregularities. Some phobics truly do faint at the sight of blood or a coiling snake, but this is the result of a sudden loss of blood pressure.

None of these medical conditions has been eradicated, so it's always a shock to pick up a Victorian novel and find damsels fainting when they are frightened, fainting when they are ecstatic, fainting when their heart is heavy, and most of all, fainting when it is convenient to their purposes. Whatever happened to swooning?

The most often cited faint-inducer in the past was a torture device known as the corset, an undergarment so tight that, according to Lynda Stretton's essay 'A Mini-History of the Corset':

> By the time they were teenagers, the girls were unable to sit or stand for any length of time without the aid of a heavy canvas corset reinforced with whalebone or steel. The corset deformed the internal organs, making it impossible to draw a deep breath, in or out of a corset. Because of this, Victorian women were always fainting and getting the vapours.

What was the purpose of this torture? The mark of a beautiful woman was thought to be the thinnest possible waist. Stretton reports that although the literature refers to corseted waists as small as 30 to 45 cm in adult women, most of these figures were probably fantasies:

> Measurements of corsets in museum collections indicate that most corsets of the period 1860 to 1910 measured from 20 to 22 inches [50 to 55 cm]. Furthermore, those sizes do not indicate how tightly the corsets were laced. They could easily have been laced out by several inches, and probably were, because it was prestigious to buy small corsets.

Even so, trying to cinch in a waist 15 or 20 cm tighter than nature intended could do damage to the circulatory system.

Corsets, with certain Madonna-like exceptions, are no longer a fashion rage. Has fainting stopped? Nope. As Louis E Rentz, Executive Director of the American College of Neuropsychiatrists, wrote that fainting 'is one of the most common complaints that present to a physician's office and certainly one of the most common things neurologists and cardiologists see. It is common at all ages.'

Two US studies of more than 5000 healthy people indicate that somewhere between three and six per cent of the population report at least one fainting episode over an extended period of time (10 years in one study, 26 in another). One statistic popped out on all of the research about fainting we consulted: men fainted almost as much as women. Could all the reports of female swooning in the nineteenth century be inaccurate? Exaggerated?

Upper-crust society in England, the subject of most of the Victorian novels we read in English class, were living in times when women were considered to be delicate creatures. Corsets were thought not only to make women look more attractive, but to help them medically (children as little as three or four wore corsets, in the mistaken belief that such support would help strengthen their posture and musculature).

Even more bizarre were the beliefs about the 'delicate sensibilities' of ladies. The Society for the Reformation of Manners, founded in London in 1690, first started fighting against prostitution and drunkenness, but by the nineteenth century became preoccupied with 'cleaning up' the language. *Bloody* became a taboo word, and no host would serve a woman a rare cut of beef for fear that the sight of blood would send a delicate lady to the fainting couch for a swoon. In her review of etiquette books of the period, *The Best Behavior*, Esther B Aresty notes that not only sticks and stones but words were believed to be able to hurt Victorian females:

> Well-bred English people never spoke of going to bed; they retired. Even a bureau could not have "drawers". To refer to a female as a "woman" was insulting and a foreigner might cause a fainting spell if he said "woman" to a lady's face ... Delicacy was, in fact, being carried to such extremes that Lady Gough's *Etiquette* ruled that even *books* by male and female authors should "be properly separated on bookshelves. Their proximity unless they happen to be married should not be tolerated."

Women in the nineteenth century lived in a culture in which fainting was seen as a badge of femininity. When Alexis de Tocqueville came to the United States as a young man in the 1830s, he observed that European women were 'seductive and imperfect beings ... [who] almost consider it a privilege that they are entitled to show themselves futile, feeble and timid ... The women of America claim no such privileges.'

In this environment, who could blame a woman for timing a swoon so that it coincided with the approach of her intended? If you wanted to avoid a nasty confrontation, why not faint instead?

Our theory is that fainting was largely a cultural phenomenon, a benign form of mass hysteria. No doubt, tight corsets constricted blood flow and caused fainting, especially in women with low blood pressure. But Victorian society rewarded fainting – it was considered feminine and attractive behaviour. The faint became an all-purpose excuse for ducking difficult obligations, the nineteenth-century equivalent of 'the dog ate my homework', with the added benefit of garnering sympathy.

Why is yawning contagious?

After the publication of the first *Imponderables* book, this question quickly became our most frequently asked Imponderable. And after years of research, it became one of our most nagging ones as well. We couldn't find anyone who studied yawning, so we asked our readers for help.

As usual, our readers were bursting with answers – unfortunately, conflicting answers. They fell into three classes.

1. The physiological theory. Proponents of this theory stated that science has proven that we yawn to get more oxygen into our system or to rid ourselves of excess carbon dioxide. Yawning is contagious because everybody in any given room is likely to be short of fresh air at the same time.
2. The boredom theory. If everyone hears a boring speech, why shouldn't everyone yawn at approximately the same time, wonders this group.
3. The evolutionary theory. Many readers analogised contagious yawning in humans to animals displaying their teeth as a sign of intimidation and territoriality. Larry Rose argued that yawning might have originally been a challenge to others, but has lost its fangs as an aggressive manoeuvre as we have become more 'civilised'.

Several readers pointed us in the direction of Dr Robert Provine, of the University of Maryland at Baltimore County, who somehow had eluded us. You can imagine our excitement when we learned that Dr Provine, a psychologist specialising in psychobiology, is not only the world's foremost authority on yawning, but has a special interest in why yawning is contagious! In one fell swoop, we had found someone who not only might be able to answer our question but a fellow researcher whose work was almost as weird as ours.

Dr Provine turned out to be an exceedingly interesting and generous source, and all the following material is a distillation of his work. As usual, experts are much less likely to profess certainty about answers to Imponderables than are laymen. In fact, Provine confesses that we still don't know much about yawning; what we do know is in large part due to his research.

Provine defines yawning as the gaping of the mouth accompanied by a long inspiration followed by a shorter expiration. This definition seems to support the thinking of some who believe the purpose of a yawn is to draw more oxygen into the system, but Provine disagrees. He conducted an experiment in which he taped the mouths of his subjects shut. Although they could yawn without opening their mouths, they felt unsatisfied, as if they weren't really yawning, even though their noses were clear and were capable of drawing in as much oxygen as if their mouths were open. From this experiment, Provine concludes that the function of yawning is not related to respiration.

In other experiments, Provine has proven that yawning has nothing to do with oxygen or carbon dioxide intake. When he pumped pure oxygen into subjects, for example, their frequency of yawning did not change.

Provine's research also supports the relationship between boredom and yawning. Considerably more subjects yawned while watching a 30-minute test pattern than while watching 30 minutes of rock videos (although he didn't poll the subjects to find out which viewing experience was more bearable – we wouldn't yawn while watching and listening to 30 minutes of fingernails dragged across a blackboard, either). Did the subjects yawn for psychological reasons (they were bored) or for physiological reasons (boredom made them sleepy)?

When Provine asked his students to fill out diaries recording their every yawn, certain patterns were clear. Yawning was most frequent the hour before sleep and especially the hour after waking. And there was an unmistakable link between yawning and stretching. People usually yawn when stretching, although most people don't stretch every time they yawn.

Yawning is found throughout the animal kingdom. Birds yawn. Primates yawn. And, when they're not sleeping, fish yawn. Even human fetuses have been observed yawning as early as 11 weeks after conception. The child psychologist Piaget noted that children seemed susceptible to yawning contagion by the age of two. It was clear to Provine that yawning was an example of 'stereotyped action pattern', in which an activity once started runs out in a predictable pattern. But what's the purpose of this activity?

Although Provine is far from committing himself to an answer of why we yawn, he speculates that yawning and stretching may have been part of the same reflex at one point (one could think of yawning as a stretch of the face). Bolstering this theory is the fact that the same drugs that induce yawning also induce stretching.

The ubiquity of yawning epidemics was obvious to all the people who sent in this Imponderable. Provine told us, 'Virtually anything having to do with a yawn can trigger a yawn', and he has compiled data to back up the contention:

- Fifty-five per cent of subjects watching a five-minute series of 30 yawns yawned within five minutes of the first yawn, compared to the 21 per cent yawn rate of those who viewed a five-minute tape of a man smiling 30 times.
- Blind people yawn more frequently when listening to a recording of yawns.
- People who read about yawning start yawning. People who even think about yawning start yawning. Heck, the writer of this sentence is yawning as this sentence is being written.

If we are so sensitive to these cues, Provine concludes that there must be some reason for our built-in neurological yawn detectors. He concludes that yawning is not only a stereotyped action pattern in itself, but also a 'releasing stimulus' that triggers another consistently patterned activity (i.e. another yawn) in other individuals. Yawns have the power to synchronise some of the physiological functions of a group, to alter the blood pressure and heart rate (which can rise 30 per cent during a yawn).

Earlier in our evolution, the yawn might have been the paralinguistic signal for members of a clan to prepare for sleep. Provine cites a passage in Dr Eibl-Eibesfeldt's *Ethology*, in which a European visitor to the Bakairi of Central Brazil quickly noted how yawns were accepted behaviour:

> ‘If they seemed to have had enough of all the talk, they began to yawn unabashedly and without placing their hands before their mouths. That the pleasant reflex was contagious could not be denied. One after the other got up and left until I remained.’

Yet, Provine is not willing to rule out our evolutionary theory either. Perhaps at one time, the baring of teeth sometimes apparent in yawning could have been an aggressive act. Or more likely, combined with stretching, it could have prepared a group for the rigours of work or battle. When bored or sleepy, a good yawn might have revivified ancient cavemen or warriors.

Update

Robert Provine was just about the only person studying the contagiousness of yawning when we first explored this Imponderable. In the last few years, though, there has been an explosion of research on yawning contagion, in particular from cognitive researchers. Drexel University psychologist Dr Steven Platek and his team of researchers have tried to figure out what brain and neural pathways are involved in contagious yawning. They hooked up volunteers to an MRI to compare how subjects' brain substrates behaved when exhibiting contagious yawning as opposed to laughing and a 'neutral expressive condition'.

Platek and team administered several psychological tests and found that those subjects who did exhibit contagious yawning showed lower levels of schizotypal symptoms and higher levels of 'mental state attribution', which Platek defines as 'the ability to inferentially model the mental states of others'. Contagious yawners could recognise their own faces faster when their images were flashed on a computer monitor. Yawners also demonstrated more empathy for others.

Although their most recent study published in 2005 in *Cognitive Brain Research* isn't exactly beach reading ('This contrast revealed significant [FDR-corrected P<0.01] activation in bilateral posterior cingulated [BA 31] and precuneus [BA 23] and bilateral thalamus and parahippocampal gyrus [BA 30] ... '), the conclusion was clear that parts of the brain definitely acted differently when yawning spontaneously. The superior face-recognition skills of the yawners might be explained by the activation of the posterior cingulate/precuneus region of the brain, which helps process our personal memories.

Platek and his colleagues hypothesise that contagious yawning may be a primitive way for us to model our behaviour on others, albeit a totally unconscious one. Certainly, other types of animals engage in this kind of modelling behaviour. When one bird of a resting flock suddenly takes wing, and the others follow, it's likely that they don't know the cause of the threat that alarmed the first bird – but imitation is a valuable survival tactic in this case. Schizophrenics and autistics, who often lack the ability to pick up social clues and score low on empathy scales, rarely yawn contagiously. Babies, who any parent can tell you, have – to put it kindly – undeveloped powers of empathy, resist yawning contagiously.

While some psychologists are poking and prodding humans, other scientists are exploring yawning behaviour in other animals. Many other species of mammals, birds, fish, amphibians and reptiles yawn. But as far as we know, the chimpanzee is the only other creature that participates in human-like contagious yawning. James Anderson, a psychologist from the University of Stirling, in Scotland, along with two Japanese colleagues, showed six female adult chimpanzees videotapes of other chimps yawning as well as other videos of chimps with open mouths who were not yawning. Two of the six subjects yawned significantly more (more than double the amount) when shown yawning videos (none yawned more when seeing videos of non-yawners). Although obviously a small sample, the one-third 'success' rate is in line with – and only slightly less than – the percentage of humans that Provine and Platek found were contagious yawners. In another respect, chimps proved to be like humans: three infants were with their mothers, and none of them yawned, even though they were watching the same videos and saw their mothers yawning.

The chimp studies excite researchers in the field because none of the other primates exhibit contagious yawning, and so far, only the chimpanzee has displayed what psychologists would describe as empathetic behaviour. (Primatologist Frans de Waal's book *Good Natured: The Origins of Right and Wrong in Humans and Other Animals* is a good place to start when exploring this topic.) Who knows? Maybe some day, this research into contagious yawning might unlock the mysteries, or at least the neurological underpinning, of empathetic and cooperative behaviour.

Information about yawning is exploding on the web. Although it is a French site, Le Baillement ('The Yawn') at http://baillement.com has a plethora of excellent articles in English. And to view more 'Gaping Maws' in the animal kingdom than you can imagine, surf thee over to www.gapingmaws.com.

Why do pregnant women get strange food cravings? And why do they suddenly start hating foods they used to love?

Is there something specific about being in the family way that produces a sudden passion for a pickle sundae? A pork-and-banana sandwich? Or biscuits with a dollop of mustard?

A few social scientists subscribe to the notion that cravings are 'all in pregnant women's heads', but the nutritionists and medical experts we consulted dissent. Food cravings are prevalent all over the world: we found scores of studies that found at least some food cravings in one-half to more than 90 per cent of pregnant women, with most falling in the 65 to 75 per cent range.

Cravings are likely a result of hormonal changes that alter taste perception. One strong argument for hormones as the culprit is that women tend also to undergo strong food cravings (and aversions) during menopause, another period when hormones are raging and changing. Janet Pope, Associate Professor of

Nutrition and Dietetics at Louisiana Tech University, told *Imponderables* that pregnant women evaluate flavour differently, so they may try different foods or combinations of foods to find foods that will now satisfy them.

And then there is the indisputable fact that the little fetus is draining some nutrition from the mother. 'You are now eating for two,' so the cliché goes. But most nutritionists believe the average female need consume only 1250 extra kilojoules a day of a well-balanced diet to compensate for the other life she is carrying. It would seem logical to assume that the fetus is taking in nutrients unevenly, and that is the reason for weird cravings and aversions. Ethiopian women believe that their sudden aversion to usual staples can be explained by their babies' distaste for that particular food. But biologists and nutritionists still can't explain the unpredictability in food preferences during pregnancy.

Some cravings are relatively easy to explain on a strictly nutritional basis. For example, a woman who craves olives or pickles might be low in sodium. A newfound peanut butter fanatic might need additional protein, fat, or B vitamins. But sodium can be obtained from cracker biscuits or pretzels too. Protein, fat and B vitamins are contained in fish or meat as well.

Cross-cultural studies indicate that most mothers crave nutritious items that are not part of their regular diet. In the West, many expectant mothers swear off meat; where meat is prized but scarce, it is among the most common cravings. Unusual food cravings may also be, in part, an attempt to find new food combinations to stave off some of the unpleasant symptoms of pregnancy, such as morning sickness.

Almost as many women experience food aversions as strong cravings, often from foods and drinks that they enjoyed before pregnancy. One theory is that aversions are nature's way of assuring the fetus obtains good nutrition by diversifying the diet of the mother. This might explain why in developing countries, poor women often experience aversions to staple grains – normal diets often contain too much cereal and starch, and not enough protein and fat.

Others contend that food aversions are a way of safeguarding the fetus by making dangerous substances unpalatable to the mother. Some chain-smoking, coffee-sipping, booze-guzzling females find it remarkably easy to shed their vices when pregnant. They might maintain that their sudden upgrading of habits is done out of altruism, but studies indicate that these were among the most common aversions even before their potential damage to the fetus was known. Likewise, many women find themselves nauseated at even the thought of consuming raw meat, sushi or soft cheeses, substances that are usually safe to consume but do offer increased health risks if prepared inadequately.

But some cravings have no conceivable nutritional advantage. Perhaps the most popular craving of pregnant women is ice: ice, not water or a soft drink. Ella Lacey, a nutritionist at Southern Illinois University's medical school, says that nobody understands why women often crave foods that offer few, if any nutrients, let alone the particular nutrients she might lack. She theorises that it may be some form of addictive behaviour, where there is a drive to gain satisfaction, even if the outcome doesn't fulfil the deficiency.

The most aberrant addictive craving is pica, a condition most prevalent in the south of the United States and in Central America, in which people crave and eat non-food substances, often dirt, clay, chalk, dishwasher detergent and, least scary, ice chips. Pregnant women comprise the largest, but by no means only, group of pica practitioners, but in most, the desire goes away once the baby is born.

Pica is more prevalent among poor people, many of whom have nutritional deficiencies, leading some nutritionists to believe that pica, and especially geophagy (eating of dirt and clay), is a response to an iron or calcium deficiency. The more affluent woman is likely to detect such a deficiency by consulting a doctor or nutritionist, and once diagnosed, more likely to turn to spinach and liver than the garden for a remedy.

All of a sudden, that pickle sundae is starting to sound awfully tempting.

Why do babies sleep so much? Why do they sleep so much more soundly than adults or older children?

This is Mother Nature's way of preserving the sanity of parents.

And there's an alternative, less cosmic, explanation. Dr David Hopper, President of the American Academy of Somnology, told *Imponderables* that sleep is crucial to the brain development of infants. After birth, the average infant spends 16 to 18 hours asleep per day. Up to 60 per cent of that time is spent in REM (rapid eye movement) sleep, more than twice the percentage of adults. What is the significance of their greater proportion of REM sleep? Dr Hopper explains:

> REM sleep is the stage of sleep that dreams are associated with. Brainwave activity is very active during this stage and closely resembles an awake state. It is sometimes called paradoxical

> sleep because the brain is very active as if awake but the individual is deeply asleep. By one year of age, the brains of babies are sufficiently developed to begin cycling of four distinct NREM (non-rapid eye movement) sleep stages with REM sleep. ’

Although sleep researchers still do not understand precisely how this works, REM sleep seems crucial to the development of the central nervous system of infants. The NREM 'quiet sleep' is far from a waste of time, though, for the pituitary hormones, crucial for growth, are released during this phase of sleep.

Parents will be glad to inform anyone willing to listen that their babies don't always sleep soundly, yet the cliché persists that anyone who can withstand interference from sound or light while snoozing is sleeping 'like a baby'. The solution to this paradox lies in the unique sleep cycle of newborns. The reason babies sleep like a log much of the time, as we learned above, is because they are in REM sleep 50 to 60 per cent of the time. It can be difficult to rouse an infant during REM sleep; yet the same baby might awaken quite easily when in any stage of NREM sleep.

The proportion of REM to NREM sleep gradually decreases during the first year of life, and babies sleep for longer periods at a stretch. Still, they may be fussier and wake up more easily, especially if they are being weaned from breast milk, which studies show truly does help babies 'sleep like a baby'.

Why do babies blink less often than adults?

Babies blink a lot less than adults – many babies blink only once or twice a minute. The purpose of blinking is to spread tears over the surface of the eyes. Adults vary widely in their blink frequency, and such exigencies and circumstances as corneal touching, irritation, drying, foreign matter entering the eye and emotional distress or excitement can all cause the blinking rate to rise dramatically.

Ophthalmologists we contacted are full of theories but not a definitive answer. James P McCulley, of the Association of University Professors of Ophthalmology, points out that the nerve structure of the infant's eye is much less well developed than its adult counterpart. Babies don't even manufacture tears during their first month of birth, so they clearly seem immune to the pain of dry eyes that would afflict adults who don't blink more often.

Ophthalmologist Samuel Salamon muses over other possible explanations:

> It is puzzling to us as to why babies' eyes don't simply dry out. Of course, they don't spend that much time with their eyes open and the tiny bit of mucus that the eyes manufacture is usually enough to keep the front surface of the eye, the cornea, moistened sufficiently. Babies probably do not need to blink as often as adults because their fissures are much smaller. That is, much less of their front eye surface is exposed to the environment both because of the shape of their skulls and because their eyelid openings are very small. Thus, the eyes dry out much more slowly and need lubrication much less often.

Some ophthalmologists we contacted also speculated that babies' blinking rates may not be caused as much by emotional components as adults' are. Perhaps, but any parent who has had a baby cry for hours for totally unexplained reasons may hesitate to believe that stress isn't a major part of the infant's ecosystem.

Why does Caucasian babies' and children's hair get darker as they age?

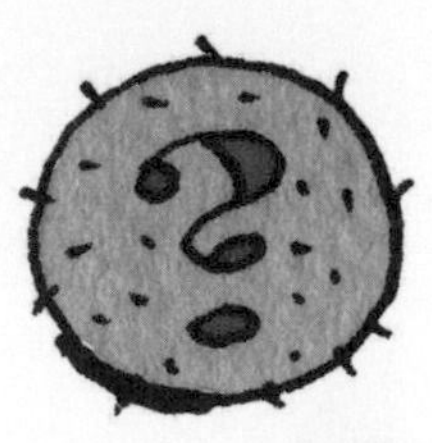

Our hair colour is determined by genetics, but in some cases Mother Nature chooses to not reveal our ultimate hair colour until well into adolescence. During infancy, the melanocytes, skin cells that mark and deposit pigment, are not fully active and don't function in many children until sometime during adolescence.

Scientists still don't understand exactly why hair darkening occurs in fits and starts throughout childhood and adolescence. Dermatologist Joseph Bark, author of *Skin Secrets: A Complete Guide to Skin Care for the Entire Family*, wrote that the eventual darkening of hair colour seems to be a 'slow maturation process rather than a hormonally controlled process associated with the "juices of puberty", which causes so much else to happen to the skin of kids'.

As is often the case with medical questions that are curious but have no practical application, the definitive solution to this Imponderable is likely to remain elusive. As dermatologist Samuel Selden celebrates: 'I don't believe that much study has been made of this, and until that is done, it means that armchair speculators like myself can have a field day with answering questions like this.'

Why do we close our eyes when we sneeze?

We thought we'd get off easy with this mystery. Of course, a true Imponderable can't be answered by a standard reference work, but would a poke in a few medical texts do our readers any harm? We shouldn't have bothered. We understand now that a sneeze is usually a physiological response to an irritant of some sort. We learned that there is a fancy term for sneezing (the 'sternutatory reflex') and that almost all animals sneeze. But what exactly happens when we sneeze? Here's a short excerpt from one textbook:

> When an irritant contacts the nasal mucosa, the trigeminal nerve provides the affect limb for impulses to the pons, and medullai Preganglionic efferent fibres leave these latter two structures via the intermediate nerve, through geniculate ganglion to the greater petrosal nerve, through the vividian nerve and then synapse at the sphenopalatine ganglion ...

Huh? Until someone publishes *Rhinology for Dummies*, we'll go to humans for the answers. Our rhinologist friend, Dr Pat Barelli, managed to read those textbooks and still writes like a human being. He explains that the sneeze reflex is a protective phenomenon:

> The sneeze clears the nose and head and injects [oxygen] into the cells of the body, provoking much the same physiological effect as sniffing snuff or cocaine. When a person sneezes, all body functions cease. Tremendous stress is put on the body by the sneeze, especially the eyes.

As Dr GH Drumheller of the International Rhinological Society put it, 'We close our eyes when sneezing to keep the eyes from extruding.' There is more than a grain of truth to the folk wisdom that closing your eyes when you sneeze keeps them from popping out, but probably not more than three or four grains.

Why does patting on the back make babies burp?

When babies get hungry, they want milk and they want it yesterday. Inevitably, overeager babies, especially those fed on the bottle, ingest air along with milk, and they experience the same windy feeling as adults who ingest too much fizzy soft drink or beer at once.

There are only two ways for the baby to get rid of the air bubbles. Air can escape with the food from the stomach into the small intestine, but the passageway is closed right after a meal, nature's way of making sure we digest our food sufficiently before it rides through the gut. The second alternative is for the air to come back up, through the oesophagus, back to the mouth. A valve at the entrance of the stomach tries to block food from coming back up, but if there is sufficient gas, the valve bursts open and baby emits a burp or what we hoity-toity people call an eructation.

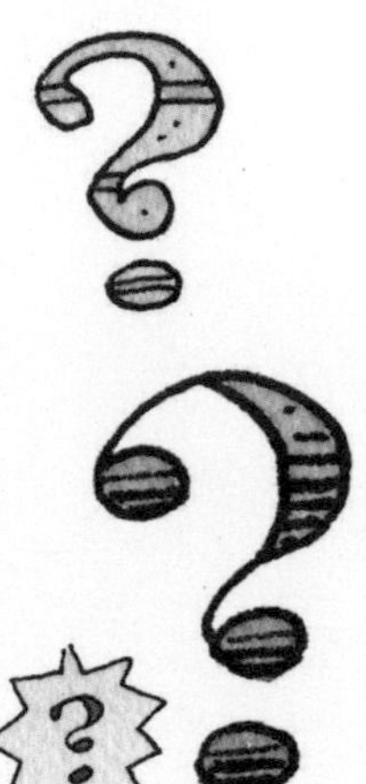

Most adults have figured out methods to force a burp, but babies need a little help. Paediatrician Don Schiff told *Imponderables* that gentle pats are usually sufficient to dislodge air bubbles that are trapped along the oesophagus or in the stomach of the baby (and adults too). Once the bubbles have been jolted free, the air rises and we are treated to that sound which is cute when babies do it but we get yelled at for emitting. (Some drakes even use burps as mating calls, not unlike their male human counterparts, albeit with much more luck.)

Back patting isn't just useful for humans, either. While researching this Imponderable, we stumbled upon a web site that instructed how to burp a bottle-fed raccoon ('You must assist with burping by laying the baby across your lap and patting the upper back gently'). That begs the question of whether raccoon parents are giving their progeny such attention, although come to think of it, they are probably not giving their offspring bottled milk.

Do identical twins have identical fingerprints?

Let's put it this way: if identical twins had identical fingerprints, do you really think *CSI: Crime Scene Investigation* or one of its spin-offs wouldn't have fashioned a murder mystery about it on one of its shows?

Scientists corroborate our TV-based evidence. Identical twins result when a fertilised egg splits and the mother carries two separate embryos to term. The key to the creation of identical twins is that the split occurs after fertilisation.

The twins come from the same sperm and egg – and thus have the same DNA, the identical genetic makeup.

Because their DNA is an exact match, identical twins will always be the same sex, have the same eye colour and share the same blood type. 'Fraternal twins', on the other hand, are born when two separate eggs are fertilised by two different sperms. Their DNA will be no more of a match than any other pair of siblings from the same parents. Not only do fraternal twins not necessarily look that much alike, but they can be of the opposite sex and may possess different blood types.

Even though identical twins share the same DNA, however, they aren't carbon copies. Parents and close friends can usually tell one identical twin from the other without much difficulty. Their personalities may differ radically. And their fingerprints differ. If genetics doesn't account for these differences, what does? Why aren't the fingerprints of identical twins, er, identical?

The environment of the developing embryo in the womb has a hand in determining a fingerprint. That's why geneticists make the distinction between 'genotypes' (the set of genes that a person inherits, the DNA) and 'phenotypes' (the characteristics that make up a person after the DNA is exposed to the environment). Identical twins will always have the same genotype, but their phenotypes will differ because their experience in the womb will diverge.

Edward Richards, the Director of the Program in Law, Science and Public Health at Louisiana State University, writes:

> 'In the case of fingerprints, the genes determine the general characteristics of the patterns that are used for fingerprint classification. As the skin on the fingertip differentiates, it expresses these general characteristics. However, as a surface tissue, it is also in contact with other parts of the fetus and the uterus, and their position in relation to uterus and the fetal body changes as the fetus moves on its own and in response to positional changes of the mother.
>
> Thus the microenvironment of the growing cells on the fingertip is in flux, and is always slightly different from hand to hand and finger to finger. It is this microenvironment that determines the fine detail of the fingerprint structure. While the differences in the microenvironment between fingers are small and subtle, their effect is amplified by the differentiating cells and produces the macroscopic differences that enable the fingerprints of twins to be differentiated.'

Influences as disparate as the nutrition of the mother, position in the womb and individual blood pressure can all contribute to different fingerprints of identical twins. Richards notes that the physical differences between twins widen as they age: 'In middle and old age [identical twins] will look more like non-identical twins.'

About two per cent of all births are twins, and only one third of those are identical twins. But twins' fingerprints are like snowflakes – they may look alike at first blush, but get them under a microscope, and the differences emerge.

Why do kids get more runny noses than adults?

The most common causes of runny noses are nasal infections, allergies and the common cold. Kids tend to suffer from these conditions more than adults. As ear, nose and throat (ENT) specialist Keith M Holmes wrote: 'Perhaps it is safe to say that children are more susceptible to nasal infections. This susceptibility gradually clears as the child ages.' Stephen C Marks, of the American Rhinologic Society, notes that research shows that:

> ‘the average child contracts up to six colds per year, while the average adult has only two colds per year. The reason for this may be that children have a less well developed immune system than adults. Alternatively, it may be that each time a person gets a cold, he or she develops some degree of immunity towards a subsequent infection by the same virus. Therefore, as time goes on, the immunity to different viruses becomes greater and greater, leading to fewer episodes of infection. A third possibility is that due to the close interpersonal relationships of children compared with adults, viral infections tend to be passed from child to child more readily.’

Dr Ben Jenkins, an ENT specialist, notes that many serial runny nosers suffer from problems with adenoids, an affliction adults are spared.

But we cast our lot with osteopath Richard O'Brien, who observes that children don't have the same obsessions about hygiene and aesthetics that their elders do. Although he concedes all the foregoing, he reminds us that kids have less awareness of their runny noses than adults. Smaller kids haven't learned that they are supposed to blow their noses when they start running. And children, who are prone to assorted high jinks and hyperactivity, often don't feel the drip on their faces. Or they do feel the drip, and they just don't care.

When you have a cold, why does only one nostril at a time tend to get clogged? Why do we need two nostrils in the first place?

The shifting of clogged nostrils is a protective effort of your nasal reflex system. Although the nose was probably most important to prehistoric man as a smelling organ, the sense of smell of modern humans has steadily decreased over time. The nose is now much more important in respiration, breathing in oxygen to the nose, trachea, bronchi, heart and blood, and ultimately in the exchange of oxygen and carbon dioxide. As rhinologist Dr Pat Barelli explains:

> ‘A fantastic system of reflexes that originate in the inner nose sends impulses to the heart and indirectly to every cell in the body. These reflexes, coupled with the resistance of the nose, increase the efficiency of the lungs and improve the effectiveness of the heart action.’

The most common cause of clogged nostril switching is sleep. When we sleep, our body functions at a much reduced rate. The heart beats more slowly and the lungs need less air. As rhinologist Dr Zanzibar notes:

> ‘Patients commonly complain that at night when they lie on one side, the dependent side of the nose becomes obstructed and they find it necessary to roll over in bed to make that side open. Then the other side gets obstructed, and they roll over again.’

When the head is turned to one side during sleep, the 'upper nose' has the entire load of breathing and can get tired. According to Dr Pat Barelli:

> ‘One nostril during solo duty can tire in as little as one to three hours, and internal pressures cause the sleeper to

change his head position to the opposite side. The body naturally follows this movement. And so, the whole body, nose, chest, abdomen, neck and extremities rest one side at a time. ’

Bet you didn't know your nose was so clever. Our motto is: 'One nostril stuffed is better than two.'

Why do we cry at happy endings?

Eureka! There is actually a conclusion upon which psychologists agree: there is no such thing as 'tears of happiness'. We cry not because we are happy but because unpleasant feelings are stirred up at the occasion of a happy ending.

Most adults are capable of repressing the urge to cry, but not without exerting psychic energy. When a happy ending indicates that our grief is no longer merited, the energy used to inhibit our tears is discharged, sometimes in the form of laughter, but more often in an expression of the repressed sadness – tears.

Many people sit stoically through a tearjerker like *Camille* and then sob at a 'heartwarming' 30-second TV ad. Happy endings often conjure up an idealised world of kindness and love that we once, as children, believed was possible to attain in our own lives. Children rarely cry at happy endings because they are not yet disillusioned about their own possibilities.

For the adult, the happy ending is a temporary return to the innocence of childhood – the tears stem from the recognition that one must return to the tougher 'real' world. The child, without comprehension of the permanence of death, sees the happy ending as confirmation of the limitless possibilities of life.

The tendency to cry at happy endings is not restricted to stories. In real life, it is common for relatives of a critically ill patient to cry not before or during surgery, but after the operation is successful. The happy ending enables the loved one to feel safe in unleashing all of the repressed sadness and anxiety.

Psychologists even dispute the idea that the tears shed at rites of passage such as weddings and graduations are tears of joy. Precisely because these ceremonies symbolise transitions in young people's lives, rituals stir up repressed anxieties in loved ones about the past ('Why wasn't my wedding as joyous?'), insecurities about the present ('Why haven't I found true love?') and fear about the future ('How will I survive when my children leave home?'). In our emotional world, we are needy, selfish and demanding. We cry for ourselves at happy endings, not for others, but this does not mean we are incapable of feeling joy in others' happiness. Crying at the happy ending reveals our idealistic side, the part that yearns for the simplicity and love we once thought possible and the part of us that mourns its unattainability.

Why do we feel warm or hot when we blush?

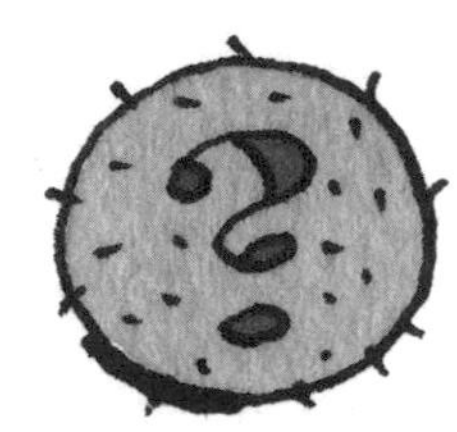

We blush – usually due to an emotional response such as embarrassment – because the blood vessels in the skin have dilated. More blood flows to the surface of the body, where the affected areas turn red.

We associate blushing with the face, but blood is also sent to the neck and upper torso. According to John Hertner, Professor of Biology at Kearney State College:

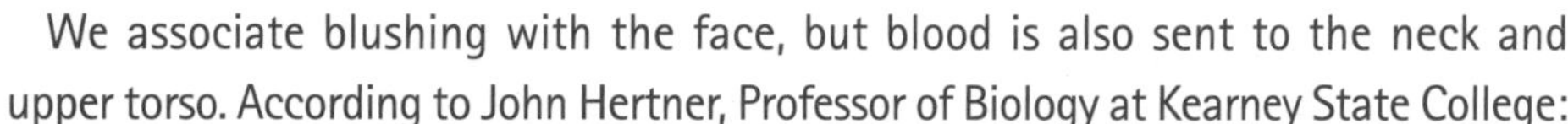

> 'This increased flow carries body core heat to the surface, where it is perceived by the nerve receptors. In reality, though, the warmth is perceived by the brain in response to the information supplied by the receptors located in the skin.'

Because of the link between the receptors and the brain, we feel warmth precisely where our skin turns red.

Why do people look up when thinking?

Doctors have a nasty little habit. You pose them a particularly tough Imponderable and they answer, 'I don't know.' Most medical and scientific research is done on topics that seem likely to yield results that can actually help clinicians with everyday problems. Determining why people look up when thinking doesn't seem to be a matter of earth-shattering priority.

Ironically, some serious psychologists have decided that this question is important, have found what they think is a solution to the Imponderable and, most amazingly, found a very practical application for this information. These psychologists are known as neurolinguists.

Neurolinguists believe that many of our problems in human interaction stem from listeners not understanding the frame of reference of the people speaking to them. Neurolinguists have found that most people tend to view life largely through one dominant sense – usually sight, hearing or touching. There are many clues to the sensory orientation of a person, the most obvious being his or her choice of words in explaining thoughts and feelings.

People with varying sensory orientations might use different verbs, adjectives and adverbs to describe exactly the same meaning. For example, a hearing-oriented person might say, 'I hear what you're saying, but I don't like the sound of your voice.' The visually oriented person would be more likely to say, 'I see what you mean, but I think your real attitude is crystal clear.' The touch-dominant person (neurolinguists call them kinaesthetics) might say, 'I feel good about what you are saying, but your words seem out of touch with your real attitude.'

Neurolinguistically trained psychologists have found that they can better understand and assist clients once they have determined the client's dominant sense (what they call the client's representational system). All three of the above quotes meant the same thing: 'I understand you, but your words belie your true emotions.' Neurolinguists adapt their choice of words to the representational system of the client, and they have found that it has been a boon to establishing client trust and to creating a verbal shorthand between psychologist and patient. Any feeling that can be expressed visually can be expressed kinaesthetically or auditorily as well, so the psychologist merely comes to the patient rather than having the patient come to the psychologist – it helps eliminate language itself as a barrier to communication.

When grappling with finding the answer to a question, most people use one of the three dominant senses to seek the solution. If you ask people what their phone number was when they were 12 years old, three different people might use the three dominant senses of vision, hearing and feeling. One might try to picture an image of the phone dial; one might try to remember the sound of the seven digits, as learned by rote as a small child; and the last may try to recall the feeling of dialling that phone number. Notice that all three people were trying to remember an image, sound or feeling from the past.

But some thoughts involve creating new images, sounds or feelings. Neurolinguists found they could determine both the operative representational system of their clients and whether they were constructing new images or remembering old ones before the clients even opened their mouth – by observing their eye movements.

These eye movements have now been codified. There are seven basic types of eye movements, each of which corresponds to the use of a particular sensory apparatus. Please note that these 'visual accessing cues' are for the average right-handed person; left-handers' eyes usually move to the opposite side. Also, 'left-right' designations indicate the direction from the point of view of the observer.

Direction	**Thought Process**
up-right	visually remembered images
up-left	visually constructed new images
straight-right	auditorily remembered sounds or words
straight-left	auditorily constructed new sounds or words
down-right	auditorily sounds or words (often what is called an 'inner dialogue')
down-left	kinaesthetic feelings (which can include smell or taste)

There is one more type of movement, or better, nonmovement. You may ask someone a question and he will look straight ahead with no movement and with eyes glazed and defocused. This means that he is visually accessing information.

Try this on your friends. It works. There are more exceptions and complications, and this is an admittedly simplistic summary of the neurolinguists' methodology. For example, if you ask someone to describe his first bicycle, you would expect an upwards-right movement as the person tries to remember how the bike looked. If, however, the person imagined the bike as sitting in the restaurant where you are now sitting, the eyes might move up-left, as your friend is constructing a new image with an old object. The best way to find out is to ask your friend how he tried to conjure up the answer.

Neurolinguistics is still a new and largely untested field, but it is fascinating. Most of the information in this chapter was borrowed from the work of Richard Bandler and John Grinder. If you'd like to learn more about the subject, we'd recommend their book *Frogs Into Princes.*

To get back to the original Imponderable – why do people tend to look up when thinking? The answer seems to be that most of us, a good part of the time, try to answer questions by visualising the answers.

Did we say people are confusing? Our apologies – what we really meant to say was cats. And dogs. Cows too – and elephants, lizards, penguins and lobsters. We love our pets, and wild animals as well, but they do the strangest things. They can't tell us why, but we've worked out a few answers.

animals

When did wild poodles roam the earth?

The thought of wild poodles roaming the earth and contending with the forbidding elements of nature makes us shudder. It's hard to imagine any type of poodle surviving torrential rainstorms or blistering droughts in the desert, or slaughtering prey for its dinner (unless its prey was canned dog food). Or even getting its haircut messed up.

For that matter, what animal would make a poodle its prey in the wild? We have our doubts that it would be a status symbol for one lion to approach another predator and boast, 'Guess what? I bagged myself a poodle today.'

If something seems wrong with this picture of poodles in the wild, you're on the right track. We posed our Imponderable to the biology department of the University of California, Los Angeles, and received the following response from Nancy Purtill, an administrative assistant:

> ‘The general feeling is that, while there is no such thing as a stupid question, this one comes very close. Poodles never did live in the wild, any more than did packs of roving Chihuahuas. The present breeds of dogs were derived from selective breeding of dogs descended from the original wild dogs.’

Sally Kinne, Secretary of the Poodle Club of America, Inc., was a little less testy:

> ‘I don't think poodles ever did live in the wild! They evolved long after dogs were domesticated. Although their exact beginnings are unknown, they are in European paintings from the fifteenth century [the works of German artist Albrecht Dürer] on to modern times. It has been a long, LONG time since poodles evolved from dogs that evolved from the wolf.’

Bas-reliefs indicate that poodles might date from the time of Christ, but most researchers believe that they were originally bred to be water retrievers much later in Germany. (Their name is a derivation of the German word *pudel* or *pudelin*, meaning 'drenched' or 'dripping wet'.) German soldiers probably brought the dogs to France, where they have traditionally been treated more kindly than *Homo sapiens*. Poodles were also used to hunt for truffles, often in tandem with dachshunds. Poodles would locate the truffles and then the low-set dachshunds would dig out the overpriced fungus.

Dog experts agree that all domestic dogs are descendants of wolves, with whom they can and do still mate. One of the reasons it is difficult to trace the history of wild dogs is that it is hard to discriminate, from fossils alone, between dogs and wolves. Most of the sources we contacted believe that domesticated dogs existed over much of Europe and the Middle East by the Mesolithic period of the Stone Age, but estimates have ranged widely – from 10,000 to 25,000 AD.

Long before there were any 'man-made' breeds, wild dogs did roam the earth. How did these dogs, who may date back millions of years, become domesticated? In her book, *The Life, History and Magic of the Dog*, Fernand Mery speculates that when hunting and fishing tribes became sedentary during the Neolithic Age (around 5000 AD), the exteriors of inhabited caves were like landfills from hell – full of garbage, animal bones, shells and other debris. But what seemed like waste to humans was an all-you-can-eat buffet table to wild dogs.

Humans, with abundant alternatives, didn't consider dogs as a source of food. Once dogs realised that humans were not going to kill them, they could coexist as friends. Indeed, dogs could even help humans, and not just as companions – their barking signalled danger to their two-legged patrons inside the cave.

This natural interdependence, born first of convenience and later affection, may be unique in the animal kingdom. Mery claims our relationship to dogs is fundamentally different from that of any other pet – all other animals that have been domesticated have, at first, been captured and taken by force:

> ‘The prehistoric dog followed man from afar, just as the domesticated dog has always followed armies on the march. It became accustomed to living nearer and nearer to this being who did not hunt it.
>
> Finding with him security and stability, and being able to feed off the remains of man's prey, for a long time it stayed near his dwellings, whether they were caves or huts. One day the dog crossed the threshold. Man did not chase him out. The treaty of alliance had been signed.’

Once dogs were allowed 'in the house', it became natural to breed dogs to share in other human tasks, such as hunting, fighting and farming. It's hard to imagine a poodle as a retriever, capturing dead ducks in its mouth, but not nearly as hard as imagining poodles contending with the dinosaurs and pterodactyls, or fighting marauding packs of Chihuahuas.

Why do dogs have black lips?

You would prefer mauve, perhaps? Obviously dogs' lips have to be some colour, and black makes more sense than most.

According to vet Dr Peter Ihrke, pigmentation helps protect animals against solar radiation damage. Because dogs don't have as much hair around their mouths as on most parts of their bodies, pigmentation plays a particularly important role in shielding dogs against the ravages of the sun.

According to Dr Kathleen J Kovacs, of the American Veterinary Medical Association, the gene for black pigment is dominant over the genes for all other pigments, so the presence of black lips is attributable to hereditary factors. If two purebred dogs with black lips breed, one can predict with confidence that their puppies will have black lips too.

Not all dogs have black lips, though. Some breeds have non-pigmented lips and oral cavities. James D Conroy, a veterinary pathologist affiliated with Mississippi State University, told *Imponderables* that some dogs have a piebald pattern of nonpigmented areas alternating with pigmented areas. The only breed with an unusual lip colour is the chow-chow, which has a blue colour. Conroy says that 'the blue appearance of the lips and oral cavity is related to the depth of the pigment cells within the oral tissue'.

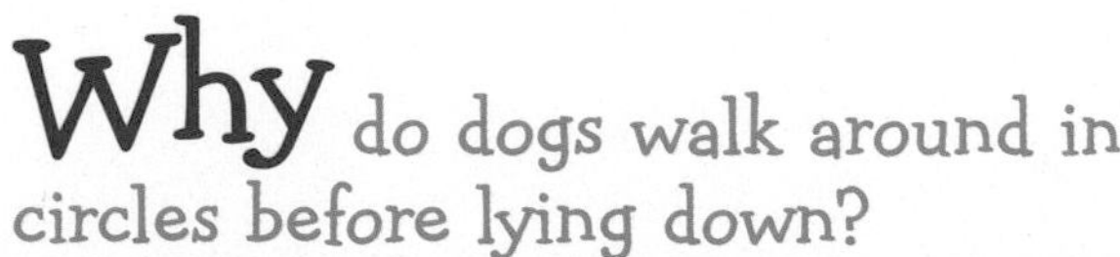

Why do dogs walk around in circles before lying down?

The most common and logical explanation for the phenomenon is that in the wild, circling was a method of preparing a sleeping area or bed, particularly when it was necessary to flatten down an area among tall grass, leaves and rocks. Some experts also believe that circling is a way for dogs to map territory, to define an area of power. Dog writer Elizabeth Crosby Metz explains the habit this way:

> I believe it also has to do with spreading their proprietary scent around their nesting site, to say: "Keep away, this is MY nest!"
>
> In fact, as a breeder I know that mother dogs will circle many times before lying down to feed their sightless, deaf newborns as a way of spreading her scent and indicating to them exactly where she is and how far they have to go to reach her. Think about it: how else can blind, deaf newborns so surely find the milk bar?

Why do dogs love to put their heads out the windows of moving cars, but then hate to have their ears blown into?

Most of the people who have asked this Imponderable connect these two questions, wondering why a dog loves speeding down a motorway at 100 km/h (with its head totally exposed to the wind) when it balks at a little playful ear blowing. But dog authorities insisted the two Imponderables we were talking about mixed apples and oranges.

Of course, nobody has been able to interview canines on the subject, but the consensus is that dogs like to put their heads out of car windows because they are visually curious. Many dogs are not tall enough to have an unobstructed view of the outside world from the front seat, and most dogs are too short to have any forward or rearward view from the back seat. Poking their head out of the window is a good way to check out their surroundings and enjoy a nice, cool breeze at the same time.

But blowing in a dog's ear, even gently, can hurt it, not because of the softness of the skin or the sensitivity of the nerves, but because of the sound of the blowing. Veterinarian Ben Klein told *Imponderables* that one of the ways a dog is tested for deafness is by the vet blowing into the ear through a funnel; if the dog doesn't get upset, it's an indication of deafness.

So while we may associate blowing into the ear of a dog as playfulness, to the dog it is the canine equivalent of scratching a blackboard with fingernails. The frequency of the sound drives them nuts.

Dr William E Monroe, of the American College of Veterinary Internal Medicine, adds that the external ears of dogs are full of sensory nerves that help to prevent trauma injuries and preserve hearing: 'By preventing debris (sand, dirt, etc.) from entering the ear canal, damage to the ear and hearing is prevented. Thus, avoiding air in the ear could have survival advantage.'

The ear can't trap all the debris a dog must contend with. In fact, Dr Klein mentioned that sticking their heads out of car windows is one of the major causes of ear infections in dogs.

Next thing we know, we'll have to install seat belts for dogs.

Why do dogs have wet noses?

To tell you the truth, we committed to this Imponderable as the title of a book before we had a definitive answer to it. When the deadline for the title faced us, we called some friends, Tom and Leslie Rugg, who have a large reference library about dogs, and asked them if there was any information in their books about dogs and wet noses. 'Sure', they replied. They found several books that talked about sweat glands in dogs' noses that secrete fluid. The moisture of the nose evaporates as air is exhaled from the nostrils, thus cooling off the dog.

Sounded good to us. Our title Imponderable was answerable.

An ethical dilemma nagged at us, though. We always claim that Imponderables are questions you can't easily find an answer to in books. And we like to find experts to answer our mysteries. Were we really going to allow our title Imponderable to be answered by other books? So we decided to confirm the answers supplied by the Ruggs's books.

Now we know where the phrase 'Let sleeping dogs lie' comes from. The next month involved calls to numerous vets, dog anatomists, zoologists, canine histologists and even canine respiratory specialists. Without exception, they were gracious, knowledgeable and interesting. But we have one serious complaint about dog experts, and scientists in general. They refuse to BS.

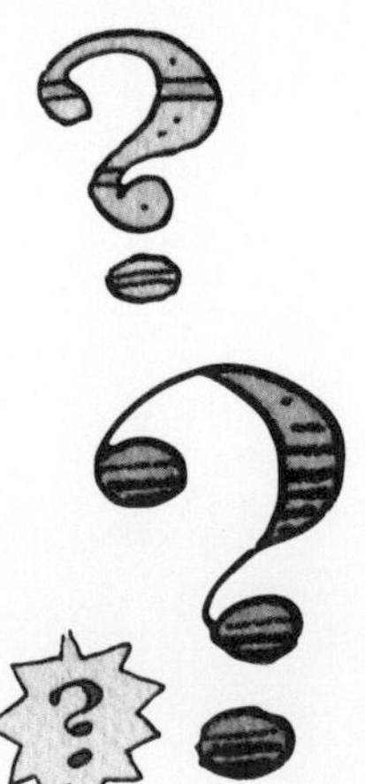

How we long for the experts in the humanities and the social sciences, who have theories about everything and never let a lack of evidence get in the way of their pronouncements. But dog researchers insisted that we are closer to cloning human beings than we are to having a definitive answer to this Imponderable.

Here's what we do know. Most healthy dogs have wet noses most of the time. If a dog has a dry nose, it might just mean it has slept in a heated room or buried its nose between its paws for an extended period. But it might also mean that the dog is dehydrated, often an early warning sign of illness. What causes the wetness in the first place? We heard three main theories:

1 The lateral nasal glands in a dog's nose secrete a fluid. Some of these glands are near the opening of the nostril and may be responsible for most of the moisture, but no one has proven how these secretions get to the tip of a dog's nose (there are no glands on the exterior of the nose).
2 Dr Howard Evans, of Cornell University, believes that the wetness is probably a combination of secretions of the lateral nasal glands and the (nasal) vestibular glands.
3 Dr Don Adams, a specialist in the respiratory system of canines at Iowa State University, adds that dogs often lick their noses with their tongues. Much of what we perceive to be secretions on a dog's nose might actually be saliva.

So what function might a wet nose serve? Several theories here too:

1 Most likely, the secretions of the nasal glands help the dog dissipate heat. Dogs do not sweat the way humans do. They dissipate most of their heat by panting with their tongues hanging out, evaporating from the moist surface of the tongue. While they pant, most of the air enters through their nose, which is more efficient than the mouth in evaporating water vapour. In his book *How Animals Work*, zoologist Knut Schmidt-Nielsen reported that:

> In the dogs we tested, on the average about a quarter of the air inhaled through the nose was exhaled again through the nose, the remaining three-quarters being exhaled through the mouth. The amounts could vary a great deal, however, and at any given moment from zero to 100 per cent of the inhaled air volume could be exhaled through the nose.

Schmidt-Nielsen's study indicated that exhaling through the mouth doubled dogs' heat loss, but when they were only slightly overheated, some dogs didn't pant at all. Schmidt-Nielsen indicated that the sole function of the nasal glands might be to provide moisture for heat exchange.
2 Lateral nasal glands contain odorant-binding particles that help dogs smell. Dr Dieter Dellman, of Cornell University, told us that all animals can smell better when odours are picked up from a moist surface. Whether or not moisture on the *exterior* of a dog's nose actually aids in olfactory functions is not well established.
3 Dr Adams thinks that the lateral nasal glands might be connected with salivary functions. He told us about a personal experience. Adams was measuring lateral nasal gland secretions one day (we thought we had a weird job!) and felt sorry for the poor dog stuck wearing an Elizabethan

collar. Secretions were coming in a steady trickle, until Adams decided to reward the dog with some sausage. All of a sudden, the lateral nasal glands sprung a leak. Adams doesn't claim to understand what the connection is yet, but such accidental discoveries explain why scientists aren't apt to offer definitive answers until they can prove the veracity of the theory.

4 The wetness is a cosmic joke meant only to spoil the life of anyone who writes about it. This, of course, is our theory.

So, dear readers. If you should see us on television or hear us speaking on the radio and the host asks this Imponderable, please be advised that though our answer might be short and glib and we appear to be carefree, don't let our glad expression give you the wrong impression. We are really shedding the tears of a clown. Every time we provide the simple, 10-second sound bite that the host craves but doesn't really answer this Imponderable with the complexity it deserves, we are being paid back for premature title selection.

Why don't dogs develop laryngitis, sore throats, voice changes or great discomfort after barking continuously?

A caller on a chat show hit us with this Imponderable. The dog next door, left alone by his master, had been barking, continuously, for hours. Why didn't it hurt the dog's throat at least as much as the caller's ears?

We approached several vets and stumped some, but the consensus answer was best expressed by William E Monroe, DVM, Diplomate, of the American College of Veterinary Internal Medicine:

> Dogs do occasionally get laryngitis and voice changes from excessive barking. It is not as common in dogs as in people because the motor control of the canine larynx (voice box) is not as refined as that of humans for sound production. Therefore, the voice range is narrower and subsequent stress from phonation is probably not as severe.
>
> Since barking is not much a part of daily living for most pet dogs as speaking is for people, laryngitis manifested as a voice change is also not as frequently observed in dogs, even though it may be present.

Why do **dogs** eat standing up, while **cats** often **eat** sitting down?

No dog or cat would volunteer to answer this Imponderable, so we were forced to consult human experts. All agreed that the answer goes back to the ancestors of our pets, who lived in the wild.

Our most interesting response came from Dr James Vondruska, Research Veterinarian and Senior Developmental Scientist for the US pet food giant Quaker Oats Company. Vondruska reminds us that dogs are by nature pack animals. In the wild, they hunted in packs. In homes, they adopt the household as their pack and their owners as dominant members:

> ‘In their prehistoric years, dogs lived with others of their type, and hunted or scavenged for food together ... Scavenging dogs must compete with the pack members for their food, which often leads to fighting. For this reason, dogs will eat standing up, so that they can better protect their food. Even though they usually don’t have to fight over their food any more, the behaviour persists in modern dogs.’

Most cats, on the other hand, are hunters rather than scavengers. Susie Page of the American Cat Association compares the eating posture of cats to that of other hunting predators who 'hunch' over their prey while devouring it.

With the exception of African lions, who live in prides, cats rarely had to contend with eating companions/rivals in the wild. This probably explains not only why cats today would feel secure eating in a more relaxed crouched or sitting position but also why cats eat languorously, while dogs eat at a pace that suggests that any meal might be their last.

Of course, cats as well as dogs often eat standing up, even while eating in comfortable surroundings from a bowl. Vondruska points out one big advantage to eating in a crouched position for both cats and dogs: 'This is the only way in which they can use their paws to hold their food, and this is sometimes necessary when chewing bones.'

Why do dogs wiggle their rear legs when scratched on their belly or chest?

Maybe there is a labrador retriever out there writing a book of canine Imponderables, trying to answer the mystery: why do humans kick their legs up when you tap the area below their kneecaps? The leg wiggling of dogs is called the scratch reflex, the doggy equivalent of our involuntary knee-jerk reflex.

Anatomist Robert E Habel, of Cornell University's College of Veterinary Medicine, wrote to *Imponderables* that the scratch reflex allows vets to diagnose neurological problems in dogs:

> Because the same spinal nerves pass all the way down to the midline of the chest and abdomen, you can stimulate the scratch reflex anywhere from the saddle region to the ventral midline. You can test the sensory function of many spinal nerves and the motor function of the nerves to the hind limb (they don't wiggle their forelimbs). If the dog moves the hind limb it means the spinal cord is not severed between the origin of the nerve stimulated and the origins of the lumbar through first sacral nerves, but the cord may be injured above the level stimulated.

A dog is not necessarily injured if it doesn't exhibit the scratch reflex. In fact, Dr Habel reports that his hound doesn't respond at all.

What function does the scratch reflex serve? Nobody knows for sure, but that doesn't stop dog experts from theorising. Breeder and lecturer Fred Lanting believes that the wiggling might be a 'feeble or partial attempt' to reach the area where you are scratching. Just as scratching ourselves sometimes causes the itch to migrate to other parts of the body, Lanting believes that scratching a dog may cause itchiness in other regions.

Dog expert and biology instructor Jeanette Hayhurst advances an even more fascinating theory, which is that the scratch reflex might help dogs survive. The movement of the back legs during the scratch reflex resembles the frantic movements of a puppy learning to swim. The scratch reflex might be an instinctive reaction to pressure on the abdomen, the method nature provides for a puppy to survive when thrown into the water. Newborn pups also need to pump their back legs in order to crawl to reach their mother's teat.

We'd like to think that our human knee-jerk reflex might also have a practical purpose, but we'll leave it to the dogs to solve this particular mystery.

Why do dogs smell funny when they get wet?

Having once owned an old beaver coat that smelled like a men's locker room when it got wet, we assumed that the answer to this Imponderable would have to do with fur. But all of the experts we spoke to agreed: the funny smell is more likely the result of dogs' skin problems.

First of all, not all dogs do smell funny when they get wet. Shirlee Kalstone, who has written many books on the care and grooming of dogs, says that certain breeds are, let us say, outstanding for their contribution to body odour among canines. Cocker spaniels and terriers (especially Scotties) lead the field, largely because of their propensity for skin conditions. (Cockers, for example, are prone to seborrhea.)

Jeffrey Reynolds, of the US National Dog Groomers Association, adds that simple rashes and skin irritations are a common cause of canine body odour, and that water exacerbates the smell. In his experience, schnauzers are particularly susceptible to dermatological irritations.

Of course, dogs occasionally smell when they get wet because they have been rolling in something that smells foul. Gamy smells are usually caused by lawn fertiliser, for example.

Regular grooming and baths can usually solve the odour problem, according to Kalstone. Don't blame the water, in other words – blame the owner.

There are many miniature dogs. Why aren't there any miniature house cats?

Our correspondent, Elizabeth Frenchman, quite rightly points out that there are legitimate breeds of dogs that resemble rodents more than canines. If poodles can be so easily downsized, why can't Siamese cats? If dogs can range in size from the pygmyesque Pekingese or a sausage-like dachshund to a nearly metre-high borzoi or a hulking Saint Bernard, why is the size variation so small in cats?

According to Enid Bergström, editor of *Dog World*, the answer is in the genes. Bergstrom says that dogs are the most genetically variable mammals, the easiest to breed for desired characteristics. The genes of cats, on the other hand, are much less plastic. If you try to mix two different breeds of cats, the tendency is for the offspring to look like an Oriental tabby. Of course, as dog breeder Fred Lanting points out, domestic breeds are miniature cats of sorts, the descendants of the big cats found in zoos.

Helen Cherry, of the US Cat Fanciers Federation, told *Imponderables* that felines could be reduced somewhat in size by interbreeding small cats, but she, as well as all of the cat experts we spoke to, insisted that they had never heard of any interest expressed in trying to miniaturise cats. A representative of the American Cat Association remarked that a cat is small enough already.

Cat associations and federations are conservative by nature. Helen Cherry predicted that miniature cats would not be allowed to register or show or be 'acknowledged in any way'. It isn't easy being small.

Update

When we answered this Imponderable almost 15 years ago, we noted that cats are much less 'plastic' genetically – it was far harder to change the size and shape of cats through selective breeding than dogs. We also quoted cat fanciers who claimed that there was little demand for miniature cats.

Times have changed. While it's sometimes hard to believe that a Saint Bernard and a chihuahua are both from the same planet, let alone relatives, the variances between average-sized and 'miniature' cats is relatively small. Perhaps the most popular of the novelty breeds is the 'munchkin'. A Louisiana woman, Sandra Hochenedel, found a female cat with extremely short legs living under her van in the early 1980s. Hochenedel discovered that the cat, whom she named Blackberry, was pregnant, and in her first and subsequent litters, Blackberry passed along the short-legged trait to about half of her offspring. Munchkins seem able to run and climb adequately but don't have the jumping ability of their long-legged peers.

Another natural breed is the Singapura, known as a 'drain cat' in its native land (they lived in the culverts of Singapore) – healthy female Singapuras grow to only 2 to 3 kg.

Several American breeders specialise in 'downsizing' standard popular breeds, such as Persians and Siamese.

We aren't yet at the stage where Paris Hilton is carrying a 'teacup cat' into nightclubs, but in another 15 years, we're betting that a profusion of miniature cats is more likely than Paris Hilton still gracing magazine covers.

Does catnip 'work' on big cats like lions and tigers?

Catnip (or *Nepeta cataria*, as scientists so eloquently call it) is a perennial herb that drives many house cats wild with delight. It was probably first noticed as an attractant when big cats swarmed around withered or bruised plants in the wild.

A full response to catnip involves four actions, usually in this order:

1 Sniffing.
2 Licking and chewing with head shaking.
3 Chin and cheek rubbing.
4 Head-over rolling and body rubbing.

The full cycle usually lasts less than 15 minutes. Some cats will also vocalise after the head-over rolling, presumably a response to hallucinations. Although the cats exposed to catnip mimic their behaviour when in heat, catnip does not increase sexual interest or activity and doesn't seem to affect cats in heat more.

Scientists know quite a bit about how domestic cats react to catnip. Most cats do not begin responding to it until they are six to eight weeks of age, and some may not respond until they are three months of age. All of the research provided by the Cornell Feline Health Center indicates that cats' reaction to catnip is independent of sex or neutering status. Susceptibility is inherited as an autosomal dominant trait – about a third of domestic cats have no reaction to catnip.

Two-legged mammals have not been immune to the charms of catnip. Vet Jeff Grognet cites the historical use of catnip by humans; the versatile herb was used to make tea, juice, tinctures, poultices and infusions. Catnip was also smoked and chewed for its reputed therapeutic, hallucinogenic or euphoria-inducing properties.

Scientists, like our reader, have been curious about the effect of catnip on other cats and other types of animals. In the largest study of catnip's effect on a wide range of animals, Dr NB Todd's conclusion was clear: although a few individual animals of almost every type reacted in some way to catnip, cats responded most often and most intensely.

Out of 16 lions tested, 14 had full household cat-type responses. Almost half of 23 tigers tested had no response at all, but many had incomplete responses: some sniffed; fewer licked; only a couple chin-rubbed; and none exhibited head-over rolling. But young tigers had violently strong reactions to catnip. Most leopards, jaguars and snow leopards had strong, full-cycle reactions to catnip. We know that bobcats and lynx love catnip, for the herb is sold commercially to lure these cats for trapping purposes.

Noncats, such as civets and mongooses, were mostly indifferent to catnip, although a few exhibited sniffing reactions. An earlier study that predates Todd's concluded that dogs, rabbits, mice, rats, guinea pigs and fowls were indifferent to a powdered form of catnip that seduced domestic cats. Yet many dog owners report that their pets respond to catnip.

For some anecdotal evidence, we contacted several zoos to see if they exposed their big cats to catnip. We found cat keepers almost as curious about catnip as the cats themselves. 'They like it,' one cat keeper who fed jaguars catnip directly told us. But the same keeper reported that a snow leopard wasn't interested. Another keeper reported that tigers responded 'to some extent'.

Rick Barongi, Director of the Children's Zoo at the San Diego Zoo, reports that although most pet owners usually spray catnip scent on a favourite toy of their cat, zoo keepers cannot. A jaguar or lion will simply rip apart and then eat the toy, so instead they spray a piece of wood or a log that a big cat can claw or scratch. Barongi shares the belief that all cats respond to catnip to some extent but that younger cats respond more than older cats, and that all cats react more on first exposure to catnip than in subsequent encounters.

Why don't cats like to swim?

Many people think that cats are afraid of water. They're not. Occasionally, one can see a cat pounce spontaneously into the water. Nature documentary fans can attest to the fact that many of cats' larger relatives, such as tigers and jaguars, love to swim. Jaguars are even known to dive into rivers and streams and attack alligators. Abandoned house cats will dive into water to do a little fishing.

So why isn't your cat likely to stick a paw into the garden pond? For the same reasons your cat drives you nuts: it has a cleanliness fetish, and it's lazy. Your cat, unlike your dog, refuses to have a good time and pay the piper. It won't get wet because it thinks that it isn't worth the effort needed to dry and clean itself with its tongue to enjoy something as superficial as a marine frolic. Unless you starve it and stock your pool with fish, your cat is likely to remain landlocked.

Why do rabbits wiggle their noses all the time?

Rabbits don't wiggle their noses all the time, but enough to make one wonder if they have a cocaine habit or a bad allergy. Little did we suspect that this charming idiosyncrasy is a key to the workings of the rabbit's respiratory system. There are at least four reasons why rabbits' noses twitch away:

1 The movement activates the sebaceous gland (located on the mucous membranes) and creates moisture to keep the membranes damp and strong. Like other animals (including, ahem, dogs), rabbits can smell better off a wet surface.

2 Frequent wiggling expands the nasal orifices, or nares, so that the rabbit can inhale more air. According to Dr TE Reed, of the American Rabbit Breeders Association, nose wiggling helps rabbits cool themselves on hot days:

> The only method of cooling themselves is by expiring the superheated air from the respiratory tract to the environment and through the convection of heat from the ears ... The inhalation ... of a voluminous amount of air is extremely important.
>
> The normal respiratory rate in the domestic rabbit is approximately 120 breaths per minute. However, during extremely hot weather, it is not uncommon for the respiratory rate to approach 300 to 350 breaths per minute.
>
> The nares [control] the amount of air rabbits can inhale. In order to increase the volume of air that is inhaled, the rabbit will twitch its nose by activating the various types of muscles surrounding each of the nostrils to increase the orifice size.

3 When a rabbit's whiskers are touched, the muscles surrounding the nostrils expand and contract in order to sharpen the animal's olfactory abilities.

4 If a rabbit continuously wiggling its nose appears to be nervous, Dr Reed reminds us that it might be:

> When a rabbit is calm and unattended, each of the nostrils usually will remain in a stationary position. However, if the rabbit gets excited, the rabbit's pulse rate and respiratory rate increase and there is a nervous intervention to the nose that causes a constriction and relaxation of the paranasal muscle – the "wiggle" that most lay individuals observe.

Some readers have speculated that the 'wiggle' is caused by the continual growth of the incisor teeth, but the rabbit experts we spoke to disputed the claim.

Why do pet rodents drink water out of bottles instead of dishes or bowls?

Because we offer them bottles. Rats or guinea pigs would be more than happy to drink out of bowls or dishes as well. After all, in the wild, rodents have to fend for themselves, gathering water from lakes or ponds if they have easy access. More likely, their search for water will be more labour-intensive, involving extracting moisture from succulent plants or dew drops on greenery, or stumbling upon opportunistic puddles (the natural equivalent of a water bowl).

David M Moore, Virginia Tech University's Veterinarian and Director of the Office of Animal Resources, says the practice of using water bottles with sipper tubes was developed by researchers to promote the health of laboratory animals. When a rodent soiled the water in a bowl, bacteria grew and caused illness. On the other hand, rats cannot defecate or urinate into a water bottle with a sipper tube.

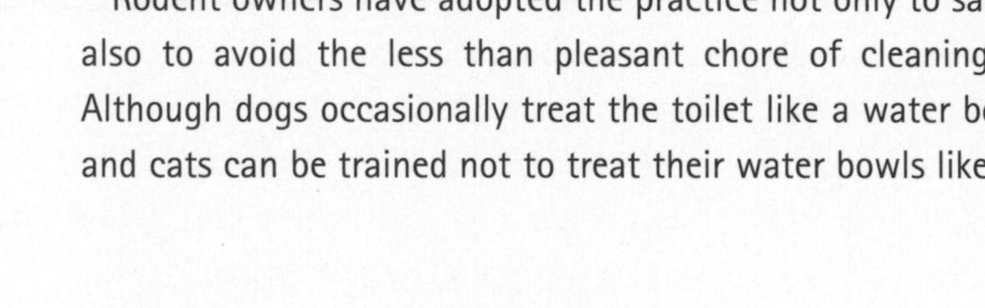

Rodent owners have adopted the practice not only to safeguard their pets but also to avoid the less than pleasant chore of cleaning soiled water bowls. Although dogs occasionally treat the toilet like a water bowl, luckily both dogs and cats can be trained not to treat their water bowls like a toilet.

How and why do horses sleep standing up?

Horses have a system of interlocking ligaments and bones in their legs, which serves as a sling to suspend their body weight without strain while their muscles are completely relaxed. Thus, horses don't have to exert any energy consciously to remain standing – their legs are locked in the proper position during sleep.

Most horses do most of their sleeping while standing, but patterns differ. Vets we spoke to said it was not unusual for horses to stand continuously for as long as a month or more. Because horses are heavy but have relatively fragile bones, lying in one position for a long time can cause muscle cramps.

While one can only speculate about why the horse's body evolved this way, most experts believe that wild horses slept while standing for defensive purposes.

Wayne O Kester, DVM, Executive Director of the American Association of Equine Practitioners, told us that in the wild, the horse's chief means of protection and escape from predators was its speed: 'They were much less vulnerable while standing and much less apt to be caught by surprise than when lying down.'

Update

It turns out we might have overstated how universal this phenomenon is. Yes, horses have the physiological equipment to sleep standing up and, in the wild, sleeping on all fours could provide for a quick getaway.

But new research indicates that horses lie down more often than we suggested. Most horse owners and researchers have observed their horses standing while sleeping. But when horses enter REM (rapid eye movement) deep sleep, their legs often buckle. In the middle of the night, horses usually catch their REM sleep and lie down on their sides for two to four hours at a stretch. If they cannot spread out completely to sleep, a common affliction in stables, horses often lean against a wall or any sturdy object nearby.

The New York Times Q&A column tackled this Imponderable several years ago and quoted Dr Katherine A Houpt, a physiologist at the Cornell University College of Veterinary Medicine. Although conceding that horses sleep less in the wild, she's not so sure that they stand for defensive purposes, proposing that it 'is more likely due to the fact that they eat day and night at times of year when less feed is available. In summer [when food is more abundant] they lie down a fair amount.' According to Houpt, when wild horses do lie down, a single horse stays on all fours as a sentry, allowing its compatriots to get their REM sleep.

Why are horses' heights measured to the shoulder rather than to the top of the head?

David Moore, of Virginia Tech's Office of Animal Resources, compares measuring a horse to trying to measure a squirming child. At least you can back a child up to a wall. If the child's legs, back and neck are straight, the measurement will be reasonably accurate:

> ‘But with a horse, whose spinal column is parallel to the ground (rather than perpendicular, as with humans), there is no simple

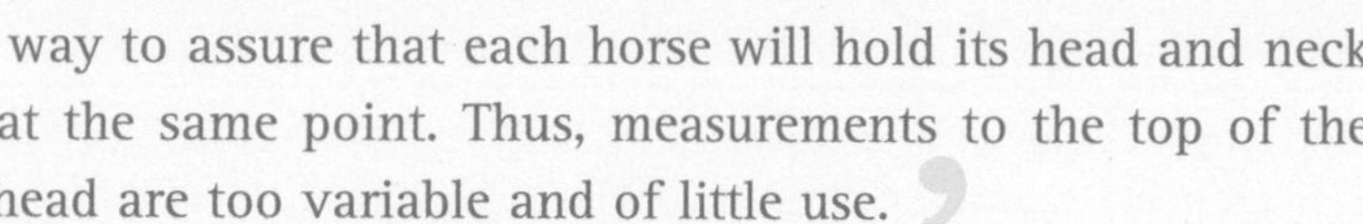

way to assure that each horse will hold its head and neck at the same point. Thus, measurements to the top of the head are too variable and of little use.'

Dr Wayne O Kester, of the American Association of Equine Practitioners, told *Imponderables* that when a horse is standing squarely on all four feet, the top of the withers (the highest point on the backbone above the shoulder) is always the same fixed distance above the ground, thus providing a consistent measurement for height. Kester estimates that 'head counts' could vary as much as 60 to 180 cm.

Who got the idea of making horseshoes? Why are horseshoes necessary? What would happen if horses weren't shod?

If horses weren't shod, they would probably have trouble getting served at fast-food establishments. Maybe they can get away with wearing no shirts. But no shoes? We don't think so.

But seriously, horses have the Romans to blame for the end of their barefoot existence. Horses were perfectly happy galloping around without shoes until the leaders of the Roman Empire decided that it would be a good idea to build paved roads. Without support, horses' hooves would split and crack on the hard surface.

The paving of roadways hastened the time when horses, used to riding the range in the wild, were domesticated and forced to carry loads and pull heavy carts. These added burdens put strain on horses' feet, so the Romans used straw pads as the first horseshoes.

Karen L Glaske, Executive Secretary of the United Professional Horsemen's Association, says that although evolution has bred out some of the toughness of horses' feet, many can still live a barefoot life:

'Shoes are not essential to a horse that is left to pasture or used only as an occasional trail mount. However, the stresses which horses' feet endure when jumping, racing, showing or driving make it necessary for the conscientious owner to shoe the animal. It is a protective measure.'

Why do cows stick their tongues up their nostrils?

We were tempted to say, 'Because they can!' But in our relentless quest for truth we asked several cattle experts about this unsightly habit. Our serious guess was that the tongue was the easiest way to lubricate the dreaded 'dry nose' condition that we assumed plagued our bovine friends. Wrong. Cows stick their tongues up their nostrils for two distinct reasons.

Cows have nasolabial glands located in the dermis (just under the epidermis of the skin) that produce a watery secretion that helps keep their noses moist. Cows and other ruminants use these secretions to digest their food, as Michael T Smith, of the National Cattlemen's Association, explains:

> They frequently thrust their muzzles into the feed and, during rumination, run their tongues into the nostril and over the muzzle, thus bringing the secretion into the mouth. The chemical properties of nasolabial secretions are similar to saliva and aid in the digestive process.

Smith adds that buffalo exhibit the same behaviour as their bovine cousins.

Cows frequently endure respiratory infections that involve involuntary nasal discharges, sometimes quite heavy. Dr Harold Amstutz, of the American Association of Bovine Practitioners, told *Imponderables* that these discharges are quite irritating and need to be expelled. But 'cows don't have handkerchiefs or fingers'. So they use their tongues to remove the irritant instead.

Do elephants jump?

We talked to a group of elephant experts and none of them has ever seen an elephant jump. Most think it is physiologically impossible for a mature elephant to jump, although baby elephants have been known to do so, if provoked. Not only do mature elephants weigh too much to support landing on all fours, but their legs are designed for strength rather than leaping ability. Mark Grunwald, of the Philadelphia Zoo, notes that elephants' bone structure makes it difficult for them to bend their legs sufficiently to derive enough force to propel themselves up.

Yet there are a few sightings of elephants jumping in the wild. Vet Judy Provo found two books in her university library that illustrate the discrepancy.

SK Ettingham's *Elephant* lays out the conventional thinking: 'Because of its great weight, an elephant cannot jump or even run in the accepted sense since it must keep one foot on the ground at all times.' But an account in JH Williams's *Elephant Bill* describes a cow elephant jumping a deep ravine 'like a chaser over a brook'.

Animals that are fast runners or possess great leaping ability have usually evolved these skills as a way of evading attackers. Elephants don't have any natural predators, according to the San Diego Wild Animal Park's manager of animals, Alan Rooscroft: 'Only men kill elephants. The only other thing that could kill an elephant is a 14-tonne tiger.'

Most of the experts agree with zoologist Richard Landesman of the University of Vermont that there is little reason for an elephant to jump in its natural habitat. Indeed, Mike Zulak, an elephant curator at the San Diego Zoo, observes that pachyderms are rather awkward walkers, and can lose their balance easily, so they tend to be conservative in their movements.

But that doesn't mean that elephants are pushovers. In India, trenching has been the traditional way of trying to control movements of elephants. Vet Myron Hinrichs notes that the traditional trench has to be at least 2 m deep, 2 m across at the top, and 1.5 m across at the bottom to serve as a barrier for elephants:

> 'But these trenches have a high failure rate, for elephants can fill them in, especially in the rainy season, and then walk across the trough they have made. And larger bull elephants can go down through and up even a trench that size.'

Why leap when you can trudge?

Why do deer stand transfixed by the headlights of oncoming cars?

Although no zoologist has ever interviewed a deer, particularly a squashed one, we can assume that no animal has a death wish. In fact, instinct drives all animals to survive. We asked quite a few animal experts about this Imponderable, and we received three different theories, none of which directly contradicts the others.

1 The behaviour is a fear response. University of Vermont zoologist Richard Landesman's position was typical:

> 'Many mammals, including humans, demonstrate a fear response, which initially results in their remaining perfectly still for a few seconds after being frightened. During this time, the hormones of the fear response take over and the animal or person then decides whether to fight or run away. Unfortunately, many animals remain in place too long and the car hits them.'

The self-defeating mechanism of the fear response is perpetuated because, as Landesman puts it, 'these animals don't know that they are going to die as a result of standing still and there is no mechanism for them to teach other deer about that fact'.

2 Standing still isn't so much a fear response as a reaction to being blinded. Deer are more likely to be blinded than smaller animals, such as dogs and cats, because they are much taller and vulnerable to the angle of the headlight beams. If you were blinded and heard a car approaching at high speed, would you think it was safer to run than to stand still?

3 The freeze behaviour is an extension of deer's natural response to any danger. We were bothered by the first two theories insofar as they failed to explain why deer, out of all disproportion to animals of their size, tend to be felled by cars. So we prevailed upon our favourite naturalist, Larry Prussin, who has worked in Yosemite National Park for more than a decade. He reports that deer and squirrels are killed by cars far more than any other animals, and he has a theory to explain why.

What do these two animals have in common? In the wild, they are prey rather than predators. Ill-equipped to fight with their stalkers, they freeze to avoid detection by the predator; they will run away only when they are confident that the predator has sighted them and there is no alternative. Defenceless fawns won't even run when being attacked by predators.

The prey's strategy forces the predator to flush them out, while the prey attempts to fade into its natural environment. Hunters similarly need to rouse rabbits, deer and many birds with noises or sudden movements.

Although deer may not be genetically programmed to react one way or the other to oncoming headlights, their natural predisposition dooms them from the start.

Do skunks think skunks stink?

Skunks can dish out a foul scent. But can they take it?

If, like us, most of our education about skunks comes from animated cartoons, you might be surprised to learn that skunks don't spray their noxious scent cavalierly. According to Skunks Scentral's counsellor Nina Simone:

> Skunks only spray as a form of defence. It is the last action they will take when frightened. Each skunk has its own level of what degree of fear will trigger a spray. Some will stomp three times as a warning before "firing", which will give the "perpetrator" a chance to depart.

What exactly happens when a skunk sprays? We asked Jerry Dragoo, interim Curator of Mammals at the Museum of Southwestern Biology in Albuquerque, New Mexico, who is quite the mephitologist (an expert on bad smells):

> A skunk's scent glands are at the base of the tail on either side of the rectum. The glands are covered by a smooth muscle layer that is controlled by a direct nerve connection to the brain. The decision to spray is a conscious one. The smooth muscle makes a slight contraction to force the liquid through ducts connected to nipples just inside the anal sphincter, which is everted [turned inside out] to expose the nipples. The nipples can be aimed towards the target.
>
> When a skunk is being chased by a "predator" and is not exactly sure where the pursuer is located, the skunk, while running away will emit a cloud of spray in an atomised mist. The mist is light and takes a while to settle to the ground. A predator would run through this cloud and pick up the scent and usually stop pursuit. I call this the "shotgun approach". When the skunk is cornered or knows exactly where the predator is located, it emits the liquid in a stream that usually is directed towards the face. This intense spray will sting and temporarily blind the predator. I call this the ".357 Magnum approach".

Perhaps cartoons aren't so far off the mark. Dragoo's description of the 'shotgun approach' is not unlike Pépé Le Pew's 'cloud of stink bomb' method of foiling his enemies. But does the spray repulse other skunks? Our experts agree: 'Yes.' Simone mentioned that when other skunks smell a whiff, they become agitated. It is unclear whether this is a chemical reaction to the smell or if it signals danger to them. She compared skunks' uneasy behaviour when they smell other skunks' sprays to 'a dog before an earthquake'.

Considering that skunks don't like the smell of other skunks, it's surprising that they don't use their 'weapon' more often during 'intramural' battles. One skunk expert e-mailed us:

> Skunks actually don't like the smell of skunk, either, and unless one is accidentally in the line of fire, it would never get sprayed by another skunk. It's kind of like a skunk pact that they won't spray each other.

If only humans were as accommodating!

But seriously, we must delve into the seamier side of skunk behaviour, for internecine spraying isn't that unusual. The most common perpetrators of skunk-on-skunk abuse are juveniles. Janis Grant, Vice President of North Alabama Wildlife Rehabilitators, wrote that:

> The only situation in which I have observed skunks exchanging liquid insults has been when I have mixed different litters of young skunks together. They proceed to have a "fire-at-will stink-off" for about four to six minutes, including growls, chirps and foot stomping, then gradually settle down to cohabitation. I can't say if this is to establish alpha status or just to make everybody smell the same, but none of them runs away from the encounters – they just spray a few times, retire to their corners and let it go.

Dragoo notes that just as juveniles display the stomp, chirp and spray behaviour, sometimes a weaker skunk will spray a stronger young rival 'if it feels it is being bullied'. But they have been known to spray unknown adult skunks, too, 'because adult males are known to kill young skunks'.

Dragoo describes skunks' reaction to being sprayed as 'the same behaviour as other animals when they are sprayed ... They will slide their face on the ground to attempt to wipe the odour off. They will also groom themselves [lick hands and rub face] to help remove the odour.'

Are skunks, like humans, more tolerant of their own stench than others? According to Dragoo, skunks are not as egocentric:

> The skunk can spray without getting a drop on itself. Skunks are actually clean-smelling animals. It is what they hit that smells, well, like "skunk". If a skunk is in a situation where it would get its own spray on itself, the skunk's chances of survival are usually low. An animal hit by a car will often get the liquid on itself, but usually after death. If a skunk is caught by a predator and in the midst of a fight, it can get some of the liquid on itself. But in those situations the predator likely has already been sprayed and has not been deterred. The skunk will spray to defend itself even if it gets spray on itself.
>
> The chemical composition of the spray is the same from one animal to another with some potential individual variation, but the "smelly" components are the same. Their own spray is as offensive as another's. The difference is that they are likely not to get their own spray near their face, whereas they would aim for the face of a "rival".
>
> I have approached live, trapped animals and covered the trap with a plastic bag. This usually keeps the animal calm. However, on a few occasions, I have approached high-strung animals that spray multiple times at the bag. They are then covered by the same bag. They are still agitated when covered, but this may be a result of their already being wired.
>
> On one occasion, I peeked under the bag and did observe the animal rubbing its face along the bottom of the trap as if it were trying to "get the odour off". Then it sprayed me ... in the face.

Do penguins have knees?

They certainly do, although they are discreetly hidden underneath their feathers. Anatomically, all birds' legs are pretty much alike, although the dimensions of individual bones vary a great deal among species.

Penguins, like other birds, have legs divided into three segments. The upper segment, the equivalent of our thigh, and the middle segment, the equivalent of our shinbone, or the drumstick of a chicken, are both quite short in penguins.

When we see flamingos, or other birds with long legs, they appear to possess a knee turned backwards, but these are not the equivalent of a human knee. Penguins, flamingos and other birds do have knees, with patellas (knee caps) that bend and function much like their human counterparts.

We spoke to Dr Don Bruning, Curator of Ornithology at the New York Zoological Park (better known as the Bronx Zoo), who told us that the backwards joint that we perceive as a knee in flamingos actually separates the bird equivalent of the ankle from the bones of the upper foot. The area below the backwards joint is not the lower leg but the upper areas of the foot. In other words, penguins (and other birds) stand on their toes, like ballet dancers.

Penguins are birds, of course, but their element is water rather than sky. Penguins may waddle on land, but their legs help make them swimming machines. Penguins use their wings as propellers in the water and their elongated feet act as rudders.

So rest assured. Even if you can't see them, penguins have legs (with knees). And they know how to use them.

Why don't penguins in the Antarctic get frostbite on their feet?

The yellow-necked emperor penguin, the largest species of penguin, spends its entire life resting on snow or swimming in water at a below-freezing temperature. A penguin's dense feathers obviously provide insulation and protection from the cold, but how can it withstand the cold on its feet, when humans won't put their limbs into the ocean when the water is 15°C?

Penguins' feet are remarkable creations. They are set back much farther than other birds' feet, so that penguins walk upright, but this conformation's main attribute is to help them swim. Next to the dolphin, the penguin is the fastest swimmer in the ocean. When swimming, a penguin's foot trails behind in the water, acting as a rudder and a brake.

During their hatching season, mother and father alternate diving into the ocean for food. *Encyclopaedia Britannica* estimates that the cooling power of the sea water to which they are exposed is the equivalent to the temperature of -20°C with a wind of 110 km/h. Add the 15 or 30 km/h speed at which the penguin typically swims, and you have rather uncomfortable conditions. The penguin's skin is protected by a layer of air trapped under its feathers – only the feet directly touch the water.

When the penguin finds food, returns to the mate, sits on the chick and watches the mate leave to find more food, it has gone from the frigid water to standing directly on snow that is, needless to say, freezing temperature. How can the feet withstand such punishment?

Penguins' feet do get very cold. They have been measured at exactly freezing, in fact. If their feet stayed at a warmer temperature, they would lose heat through convection or conduction.

The low temperature is maintained by penguins' unique circulatory system. As arteries carry warm blood towards the toes, penguins have veins right next to them carrying cold blood back in the opposite direction. In effect, the two bloodstreams exchange heat so that the circulation level can remain low enough to conserve heat and just high enough to prevent tissue damage and frostbite. Penguins' feet have very few muscles. Instead, their feet possess a vast network of tendons, which do not become as painful as muscles when cold.

Of course, there is another explanation for why penguins don't exhibit foot pain. They are not crybabies, and they are tougher than humans.

Do birds sweat?

No – not even when they are nervous.

Birds don't have sweat glands, so they can't sweat. But they have plenty of methods to cool themselves off. Birds are warm-blooded, like we are, and their normal body temperature is actually a little higher than ours.

Although you may have never heard it, birds also pant, just like dogs, and can cool themselves off in this way. And when birds fluff up their feathers, it isn't just to show off – fluffing allows air close to the skin so that even more evaporation occurs. These are the two most common ways that birds eliminate excess heat.

Birds are so active, and burn off so many kilojoules while they fly about looking for food (including migrations that, for some birds, can require thousands of kilometres of flying), that it is a constant struggle for them to maintain the proper temperature. Hypothermia is a serious danger, so some species have developed specialised mechanisms to regulate their body temperature.

Have you ever seen the fleshy part of a bird's bill vibrate? Herons do this most visibly, but many other species, such as pelicans and cormorants, regulate their temperatures by this 'gular fluttering'. By vibrating the hyoid muscles and bones in their throat, gular fluttering achieves the same cooling effect as panting.

Many other birds in warm climates use their feet to cool off. Martha Fischer, of the Cornell Lab of Ornithology, explains:

> ‘Herons and gulls can also lose a large percentage of heat through their feet. The veins and arteries in birds' legs and feet are intertwined and the blood flowing out to the extremities in arteries is cooled by blood flowing back to the body in veins. This is called countercurrent exchange (and is the reason ducks can stand on the ice without freezing their feet).’

Fischer adds that birds are believed to have evolved from reptiles, which also do not sweat: 'In their evolution to their present state, selection has favoured physiological and morphological changes that enhance light-weightedness.'

Dinosaurs would tend to agree.

Why don't migrating birds get jet lag, or do they?

No, birds don't seem to suffer from jet lag. But then again they don't suffer from airport delays, crowded seating, inedible airline food or lost luggage either.

Human jet lag seems to be bound inextricably to passing rapidly through time zones. Birds usually migrate from north to south, often not encountering any time change.

Vet Robert B Altman speculates that if you put a bird on a plane going east to west, it might feel jet lag.

But birds, unlike humans, don't try to fly from New York to Australia in one day. Some migrations can take weeks. Birds don't stretch their physical limits unless they have to (such as when flying over a large body of water). If they are tired, birds stop flying and go to sleep, while their human counterparts on a plane choose between being kept awake by a screaming baby or the one film they have assiduously avoided seeing.

Humans are particularly susceptible to jet lag when they travel at night. As a rule, migration doesn't upset birds' natural sleeping patterns. They sleep when it is dark and awaken when it is light. On planes, humans fall asleep only immediately preceding the meal service or the captain's latest announcement of the natural wonders on the ground.

When not flying, why do some birds walk and others hop?

Birds are one of the few vertebrates that are built for both walking and flying. Physiologically, flying is much more taxing on the body than walking. Usually a bird without fear of attack by predators in its native habitat will eventually become flightless. New Zealand, an oceanic island with few predators, has flightless cormorants, grebes, wrens and even a flightless owl parrot. As Joel Carl Welty states in *The Life of Birds*:

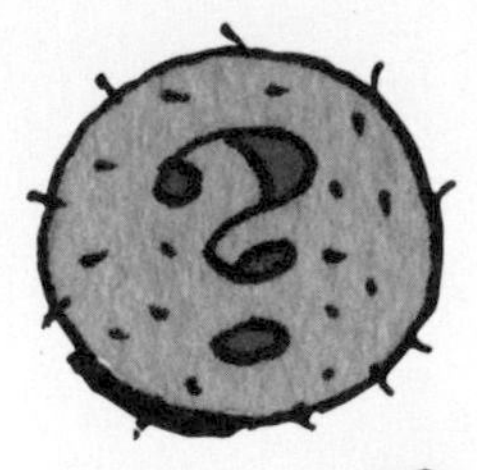

> Why maintain splendid wings if the legs can do an adequate job? This principle may well explain why birds who are good runners fly poorly or not at all. And some of the best fliers, such as swifts, hummingbirds and swallows, are all but helpless on their feet.
>
> More birds are hoppers than walkers. Birds that walk or run characteristically possess long legs and live in wide open spaces. While the typical tree dweller has four toes on each foot, many walkers have only two or three. Most tree-dwelling birds are hoppers, because it is easier to navigate from branch to branch by hopping than by walking. Most birds that hop in trees will hop on the ground. Although each hop covers more ground than a step would, the hop is more physically taxing.

Vet Robert Altman points out that some birds will hop or walk depending on the amount of ground they plan to cover: 'For a few steps, it might be easier for a bird to hop from place to place as he would from perch to perch in trees. To cover longer distances, the bird would walk or run.'

Why do pigeons make a whistling sound when they take off in flight?

Those aren't pigeons' voices but rather their wings you are hearing. Bob Phillips, of the American Racing Pigeon Union, told *Imponderables* that we are hearing the sound of air passing through feathers that are spread wide for acceleration, beating faster for lift and spread wide for take-off.

Although we tend to associate this kind of high-frequency noise with hummingbirds, many birds produce similar tones, not unlike the sound of the wind whistling through the branches of trees.

Why do roosters crow in the morning?

Because there are humans around to be awakened, of course. Does anyone really believe that roosters crow when they are by themselves? No way! Actually, they speak perfectly good English.

Ornithologists don't go for our commonsense answer. They insist that crowing 'maps territory' (a euphemism for 'Get the hell out of my way and don't mess with my women – this is my coop'). In the spirit of fair play, we'll give the last word to one of those nasty ornithologist types (but don't believe a word she says), Janet Hinshaw of the Wilson Ornithological Society:

> 'Most of the crowing takes place in the morning, as does most singing, because that is when the birds are most active, and most of the territorial advertising takes place then. Many of the other vocalisations heard throughout the day are for other types of communication, including flocking calls, which serve to keep members of a flock together and in touch if they are out of sight from one another.'

Why don't birds tip over when they sleep on a telephone wire?

A telephone wire is only a substitute for a tree branch. Most birds perch in trees and sleep without fear of falling even during extremely windy conditions.

The secret to birds' built-in security system is their specialised tendons that control their toes. The tendons are located in front of the knee joint and behind the ankle joint. As it sits on its perch, the bird's weight stretches the tendons so that the toes flex, move forward and lock around the perch.

Other tendons, located under the toe bones, guarantee that a sleeping bird doesn't accidentally tip over. On the bottom of each tendon are hundreds of little projections. These fit perfectly into other ratchet-like sheaths. The body weight of the bird pressing against the telephone wire (or tree branch) guarantees that the projections will stay tightly locked within the sheaths.

Barbara Linton, of the National Audubon Society, adds that while this mechanism is most highly developed in perching birds and songbirds, many other birds do not perch to sleep. They snooze on the ground or while floating on water.

Why do birds tend to stand on one foot while sleeping? Why do birds tend to bury their heads under their wings while sleeping?

Thanks to the amazing locking mechanism of birds' toes, they can perch just as easily while standing on only one leg. Since they can balance as easily on one leg as two, one of the main reasons for perching on one leg (whether or not they are sleeping) is simply to give the other leg a rest. But birds also seek warmth, and perching on one foot gives them a 'leg up' on the situation, as Nancy Martin, naturalist at the Vermont Institute of Natural Science, explains:

> 'Since birds' feet are not covered with feathers, they can lose significant amounts of body heat through their feet, especially when standing on ice or in cold water. With their high metabolic rates, birds usually try to conserve as much energy as possible, hence the habit of standing on one leg.'

A corollary: birds also stick their head under their feathers to preserve heat.

Why don't we ever see dead birds?

We see hundreds of birds on an average day, and occasionally spot one run over by a car, but why don't we ever see one dead from natural causes? Don't they ever keel over in flight? Do birds go somewhere special to die?

Surprisingly, birds don't fly anywhere particular to die. The reason we don't see dead birds is that they are quickly scavenged by other animals. Although this sounds like a cruel fate, bird expert Starr Saphir views it differently, marvelling at the efficiency of the natural world. The moment a bird can no longer function, it is used as valuable fuel. Birds are eaten by cats, dogs, rats, small insects and even bacteria.

Saphir told us that she has led birdwatching walks and seen the intact but dead body of a bird on the ground on the first leg of the walk; on the way back, an hour later, the majority of the body was already scavenged. Within 24 hours, the remains of most birds, in the wild or in an urban area, would presumably become only a pile of feathers.

Richard C Banks, Vice-President of the US Ornithologist's Union, told *Imponderables* that a few birds might actually die in flight (although he had not personally ever seen this happen). The most likely candidates would be migrating birds flying over the ocean, far away from food sources and without convenient landing spots to fight off exhaustion. Sick birds generally don't take wing in the first place.

Why don't we ever see baby pigeons?

Pigeons, or rock doves, as your school biology teacher would more properly call them, are known in the birding trade as ledge nesters. In the wild, they build nests on cliffs, canyons and rocky terrains. But pigeons are just as comfortable using man-made structures such as bridges and ledges of buildings. You won't find pigeon nests in trees.

Baby pigeons have an extremely high metabolism, eating a large proportion of their body weight every day. They grow so fast that by the time their mothers kick them out of the house (usually within one month of birth), baby pigeons, like all birds, are close to or have already achieved full size. When you think you see babies loitering with their parents, you are probably spotting two different species of birds.

The only way to distinguish between an immature and mature pigeon is to examine its plumage. Younger birds tend to have raggedy feathers, especially at the ends of their tail feathers. Although pigeons have varying colourations, mature birds tend to have brighter feathers.

Why do parrots and other birds mimic human speech and other sounds?

Wouldn't it be cool to be lost in the jungles of Belize and have a yellow-headed parrot assist us with a timely: 'Turn left!'?

Cool? Yes. Likely? No way. As far as we know, birds, even chatty ones like parrots and mynahs, do not mimic human speech in the wild, but they do imitate other sounds, and especially other birds.

In the wild, birds mimic for a variety of reasons. Depending upon the circumstances, birds feigning the songs of other species can attract members of the opposite sex, fool predators into misidentifying the species of the singer or ward off competitors for food or territory.

Since humans are usually capable of differentiating between the song of a mimic from the song of the bird the mimic is imitating, it's likely that the impersonation isn't fooling other birds (whose hearing is much more sensitive than ours) either. But, like humans, birds would rather avoid confrontation or competition than face it head on – mimicking clearly works.

Birds are flock creatures. Closeness within its species is crucial to a parrot's survival: while one parrot focuses on foraging, others look for predators. When taken out of the wild and into a household, birds will imprint with their human owners. Mimicking seems to be a way to foster closeness with their human 'flockmates'. As Todd Lee Etzel, an officer of The Society of Parrot Breeders and Exhibitors, told *Imponderables*:

Hello! Bonjour! Ello-hay

> The pet bird becomes imprinted with human vocalisations and hence mimicking takes place due to the bird's desire to be part of the "flock", even though it is not a natural one. Keep in mind that most species of parrots are highly social and the need for social interaction is so strong that innate behaviour is modified to fit the situation.

If pet birds are motivated by social interaction, why do they tend to mimic at least as much when their owners leave the room? Animal behaviourist WH Thorpe offers a theory:

> As they develop a social attachment to their human keepers, they learn that vocalisations on their part tend to retain and increase the attention they get, and as a result vocal production, and particularly vocal imitation, is quickly rewarded by social contact. This seems an obvious explanation of the fact that a parrot when learning will tend to talk more when its owner is out of the room or just after he has gone out – as if he is attempting, by his talking, to bring him back.

Thorpe's theory advances the notion that bird psychology differs little from infant psychology, which isn't farfetched in the least. Dr Irene Pepperberg, a research scientist at MIT and a professor at Brandeis University, has studied and written about the abilities of African grey parrots, particularly her oldest bird, Alex. Just as other scientists have proven that primates are capable of complex communication, so Pepperberg has shown that parrots can do far more than mimic. If shown two blocks that are identical except for their hue, and is asked what is different about them, Alex will answer, 'Colour.' He has mastered numbers, shapes, locations and the names of objects, and has learned to ask for, or more accurately, demand them. 'If he says that he wants a grape and you give him a banana, you are going to end up wearing the banana,' Pepperberg says. She estimates that Alex's cognitive ability is comparable to a four- to six-year-old child, with the emotional maturity of a two-year-old.

Pepperberg plays a version of the shell game with Alex and other parrots, hiding nuts below one of three cups. Alex usually spots the nut, except when the experimenter doesn't play fair. Sometimes, the scientists will deceive the parrot by sneaking the nut under another cup while distracting him from the subterfuge:

> So Alex goes over to where he expects the item to be, picks up the cup and finds that the nut is not there; he starts banging his beak on the table and throwing the cups around. Such behaviour shows that Alex knew that the object was supposed to be there, that it's not, and he's giving very clear evidence that he perceived something, and that his awareness and his expectations were violated.

Why do birds' eggs tend to have a round end and a pointy end?

Any ornithologist will tell you that the pointiest eggs tend to be laid by birds that nest high up. That fact contains the vital clue to egg design. A pointed egg, when it moves, will roll in a tight circle and so is less likely to fall out of the nest. If eggs were square, they would be even less likely to fall and break – but then laying them would be too eye-watering an experience for mother birds.

In the wild, parrots use their wits to evade predators and find food and mates. The need to solve problems might be as innate in a parrot as its mimicking skills. If a parrot's cognitive skills are as great as Alex has exhibited, Pepperberg implores pet owners to provide the proper stimulation:

> I try to convince them that you can't just lock it in a cage for eight hours a day without any kind of interaction. I don't mean just interpersonal interaction, or having other birds around; parrots have to be intellectually challenged.

Etzel thinks that parrots and other birds mimic our language and other sounds in their environment 'simply because they are able to do so. It might even be a form of entertainment for them.' Indeed, parrots might be musing about us while we are 'training them': 'Doesn't my owner look silly constantly repeating "Polly wanna biscuit?" Oh well, might as well go through the drill if it's going to end up with some tasty carbs down my gullet.'

Why do male birds tend to be more colourful than females? Is there any evolutionary advantage?

'Sexual dimorphism' is the scientific term used to describe different appearances of male and female members of the same species. Charles Darwin wrestled with this topic in his theory of sexual selection. Darwin argued that some physical attributes of birds evolved solely to act as attractants to the opposite sex. As Kathleen Etchpare, Associate Editor of the magazine *Bird Talk*, put it: 'As far as an evolutionary advantage goes, the mere number of birds in the world today speaks for itself.'

Sure, but there are plenty of cockroaches around today, too, and they have managed to perpetuate themselves quite nicely without the benefit of colourful males. Many ornithologists believe that the main purpose of sexual dimorphism is to send a visual message to predators. When females are nesting, they are ill-equipped to fend off the attacks of an enemy. 'It behoves the female to be dully coloured so that when she sits in the nest she is less conspicuous to predators,' says Michele Ball, of the National Audubon Society.

Conversely, the bright plumage of many male birds illustrates the principle of 'the best offence is a good defence'. Male birds, without the responsibility of nesting, and generally larger in size than their female counterparts, are better suited to stave off predators. The purpose of their bright colouring might be to warn predators that they will not be easy prey; most ornithologists believe that birds are intelligent enough to register the dimorphic patterns of other birds.

And most animals are as lazy as humans. Given a choice, predators will always choose the easy kill. If a predator can't find a dully coloured female and fears the brightly coloured male, perhaps the predator will pick on another species.

Why don't lizards get sunburned? Why don't other animals get sunburned?

Look down on lizards if you want, but you must admit that they certainly know how to cope with the sun better than we do. We stay out too long at the beach and our skin starts peeling and falling off. Next thing we know, our bodies look like a television weather map (and not on a sunny day). All mammals shed skin as soon as their outer layer of skin (epidermis) dies.

But reptiles can hang out on rocks all day, basking in the sun. Reptiles, clearly, are different. As Dr Norman J Scott, Jr, Past-President of the Society for the Study of Amphibians and Reptiles, told *Imponderables*: 'Reptiles keep the outer layer of dead cells on their skin until the next layer is ready. Then it is shed.' Scott also points out that a lizard's epidermis, both the living and dead layers, is thick and cornified, making it far harder for ultraviolet rays to penetrate.

And, as in humans, the pigment melanin helps protect lizards from harmful rays. Dr R Anderson of the American College of Veterinary Dermatology notes that heavily pigmented animals are protected from the sun, much as darker complected humans are partially safeguarded. But many animals do exhibit ill effects from the sun, even ones with fur.

Just like us, many animals are subject to skin cancer. Dogs can and do get carcinomas, even ones with heavy fur. White-eared cats often develop carcinomas at the ends of the ears. 'For some reason,' Anderson observes, 'bull terriers seem to love to sunbathe and can contract solar-induced lesions on their undersides.'

Are we sensing a potentially booming market for 'Sunblock for Pets'?

Why do snakes dart out their tongues?

Although snake watchers at zoos love to see the reptiles flick their tongues, imagining they are getting ready to pounce on unsuspecting prey, the tongues are perfectly harmless. Snakes don't sting or use their forked tongues as weapons.

The tongue is actually an invaluable sensory organ for the snake. It enables the reptile to troll for food (just as a fisherman sticks his line out in the water and hopes for the best), while feeling its way over the ground. It does this by bringing in bits of organic matter that it can smell or taste, alerting it to a potential food source. Some evidence suggests that a snake's tongue is equally sensitive to sound vibrations, warning it of potential prey or predators.

Do snakes sneeze?

Norman J Scott, Jr, of the Society for the Study of Amphibians and Reptiles, told *Imponderables*: 'As far as I know, snakes don't sneeze with their mouths shut, but they do clear fluid from their throat with an explosive blast of air from the lungs.'

Snakes don't sneeze very often, though. In fact, a few herpetologists we contacted denied that snakes sneeze at all. But John E Simmons, of the American Society of Ichthyologists and Herpetologists Information Committee, insisted otherwise:

> Snakes sneeze for the same reason as other vertebrates – to clear their respiratory passages. Snakes rarely sneeze, however, and people who keep them in captivity know

that sneezing in snakes is usually a sign of respiratory illness resulting in fluid in the air passage.

Why do frogs close their eyes when swallowing?

There is a downside to those big, beautiful frog eyes. While they may attract the admiration of their beady-eyed human counterparts, frog eyes bulge not only on the outside but on the inside of their faces. The underside of their eyeball is covered by a sheet of tissue and protrudes into the mouth cavity. Frogs literally cannot swallow unless they use their eyes to push the food down their stomach. Richard Landesman, zoologist at the University of Vermont, amplifies:

> In order for frogs to swallow, they must be able to push material in the mouth backwards into the oesophagus. Humans use their tongue to accomplish this task; however, frogs use their eyes. By depressing their eyes, food can be pushed posteriorly in the mouth. Frogs also use this same mechanism to breathe, since they lack a diaphragm.

If we ate what frogs eat, we might close our eyes when swallowing too.

Why do bees buzz? Do they buzz to communicate with one another?

Most of the bee buzzing that we hear is nothing other than the vibrations of their flapping wings during flight. When bees are flying, their wings are usually cycling more than 200 times per second. Entomologist Lynn Kimsey of the Bohart Museum of Entomology in Berkeley, California, notes:

> In my experience, even a bee flying slowly makes a buzzing sound. However, many bees are small enough that the human ear simply isn't capable of hearing the sound they generate. The speed that a bee is flying does alter the sound quality to the human ear to some extent.

> The buzzing sound in bees is generated by the architecture and deformation of the thorax by the flight muscles. Because of this, larger bees produce a lower-pitched sound than smaller ones.

Before we generalise about bees, entomologists tend to get a tad waspish when the term is thrown around indiscriminately. The 'bee' is actually a member of a superfamily (Apoidea) of the order that includes many other insects, including wasps. Only approximately 500 species of the 20,000 or so bees are the social bees (e.g. honeybees, bumblebees) that form colonies and seem to have a 50/50 chance of being followed by camera crews from documentary nature shows. As Kimsey puts it:

> You have to realise that 90 per cent of the bee species are solitary and have no reason to communicate with other individuals except to find a mate. Only the social bees (honeybees, stingless bees and bumblebees) need any kind of specialised communications among individuals. In all bees, mating "communication" is done either using visual or olfactory cues.

Leslie Saul-Gershenz, Insect Zoo Director at the San Francisco Zoological Society, says bees are also capable of other forms of nonvocal communication, including creating vibrations by tapping a substrate, and touch or tactile signals (honeybees use their antennae to communicate with one another).

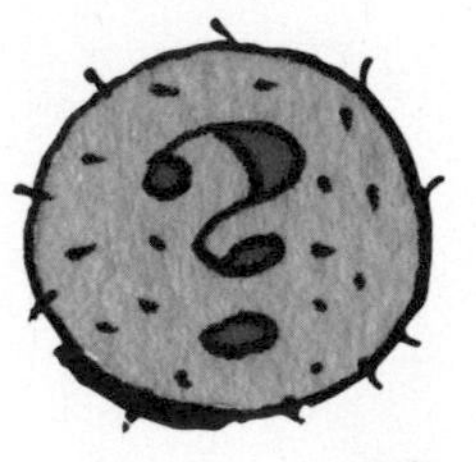

Bees can't hear the way we do (if they could, they'd probably knock off that annoying buzzing) for one simple reason – they don't have ears. They detect sound by 'feeling' the vibration through their antennae or feet.

Nowhere is the bees' potential for using vibrations from buzzing to communicate more evident than in their 'waggle dance'. In 1973, Karl von Frisch won the Nobel Prize for unlocking the mystery of how worker honeybees 'tell' their companions at the hive about nectar sources. Frisch discovered that bees perform two distinct dances. One is a 'circle dance', which seems to indicate a food discovery, but not its specific location; and a tail-wagging dance, which pinpoints the treasure. While the dancer is tail-wagging, the bee is also madly beating its wings, generating a distinctive buzzing sound.

Although the other bees can't hear the buzz, they can feel the vibration through their feet. Successors to von Frisch have confirmed the validity of his discovery by creating a 'robot bee' that is capable of transmitting information that other bees can successfully interpret. Kimsey reports that the vibrating wings of the dancer also help to disperse the aroma of the flowers visited by the worker, which helps the other bees locate the same resource.

According to Mark Winston, Associate Professor of Biological Sciences at Simon Fraser University, the beating of the wings during the waggle dance is considerably slower than during flight, so the buzz would be at a much lower pitch, more like a 'low-pitched drone': 'The tone would be comparable to that produced by the lowest notes on a piano. Most of the bee buzzing that we hear is certainly at much higher tones.'

The other most common form of buzzing is what Doug Yanega, of the Illinois Natural History Survey, refers to as 'body-buzzing'. Unlike wing-buzzing, body-buzzing is executed with the wings folded, with the bees using their thoracic muscles to produce the vibrations. Whereas wing-buzzing seems to be merely a coincident by-product of flight (although it might, possibly, scare off potential non-bee predators), body-buzzing, according to Yanega:

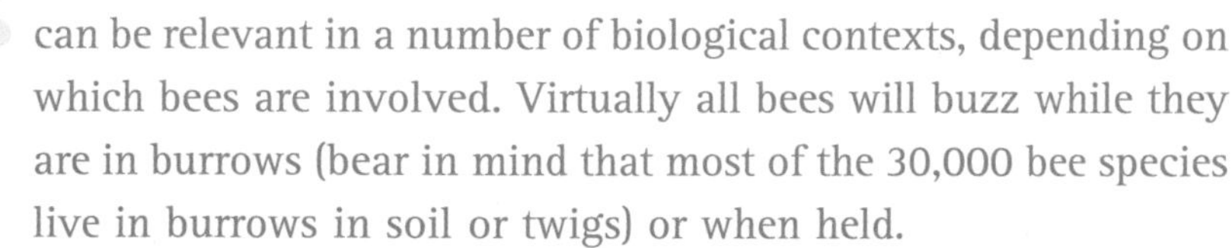

> 'can be relevant in a number of biological contexts, depending on which bees are involved. Virtually all bees will buzz while they are in burrows (bear in mind that most of the 30,000 bee species live in burrows in soil or twigs) or when held.
>
> Bumblebees will buzz to warm up their bodies and to produce heat to warm young brood. Male bees of many species will vibrate during mating, and presumably the buzzing is part of the ritual, performed in a species-specific manner.'

We have heard of only one other use of buzzing in bees. Pia Bergquist, a graduate student in chemical ecology at Göteborg University in Sweden, is currently researching bumblebees and pollination. Bergquist told *Imponderables* that while most flowers' anthers (the part of the stamen that contains pollen) open longitudinally and are relatively easy for bees to extract nectar from, some flowers have only tiny holes or channels. Bees have found an extraordinary way, though, to bring home their equivalent of the bacon:

> 'In these flowers, the bees can't just brush and groom to get pollen, so they use the buzzing technique. Usually, the bees hang from the flower holding on to the anther with all six legs. While hanging like this, the bee buzzes. This causes vibrations, which sonicate the flower and cause the pollen to fall out from the anther and onto the bee's belly.'

Why do some insects fly in a straight line, while others tend to zigzag?

As entomologist Randy Morgan of the Cincinnati Insectarium puts it, 'Flight behaviour is an optimisation of the need to avoid predators while searching for food and mates.' If Morgan just eliminated the word 'flight' and changed the word 'predators' to 'creditors', he'd be describing our lives.

Notwithstanding the cheap joke, Morgan describes the problems of evaluating the flight patterns of insects. An insect might zigzag because it is trying to avoid an enemy or because it doesn't have an accurate sighting of a potential food source. A predatory insect might be flying in a straight line because it is unafraid of other predators or because it is trying to 'make time' when migrating; the same insect in search of food might zigzag if its target wasn't yet selected.

Leslie Saul-Gershenz, the Insect Zoo Director at the San Francisco Zoological Society, told *Imponderables* that the observable flying patterns of different insects can vary dramatically:

> ‘Flight paths are usually determined by visual, auditory or olfactory stimulation. For example, bees and butterflies orient to the colour and size of flowers; dragonflies orient to their prey items; moths orient to a wind carrying a specific smell, usually a "pheromone".’

When a fly alights on the ceiling, does it perform a loop or a roll in order to get upside down?

The problem, as David Bodanis states it in *The Secret House*, is that: 'Flies, like most airplanes, lose their lift when they try to go through the air bottom-side up and become not flies, but sinks.'

We would not venture an uninformed opinion on such a weighty subject. When confronted with a fly question, we of course immediately think of contacting the Canada Biting Fly Centre. Its director, Dr MM Galloway, is bold enough to offer a definitive answer: 'A fly lands by raising the forelegs above its head, making contact with the ceiling and then bringing its second and hind legs forward and up to the ceiling. The fly thus flips with a landing.' Bodanis points out the extraordinary efficiency of this technique:

> As soon as these two front legs contact the ceiling, the fly will acrobatically tuck up the rest of its body and let momentum rotate it to the ceiling. The manoeuvre leaves the fly's body suspended upside down, without it ever having had to do a full roll, a remarkable piece of topological extrication.

Can a spider get caught in the web of another spider? And would it be able to navigate with the skill of the spinner?

Yes, spiders get caught in the webs of other spiders frequently. And it isn't usually a pleasant experience for them. Theoretically, they might well be able to navigate another spider's web skilfully, but they are rarely given the choice. Spiders attack other spiders, and, if anything, spiders from the same species are more likely to attack each other than spiders of other species.

Most commonly, a spider will grasp and bite its intended victim and inject venom. Karen Yoder, of the Entomological Society of America, explains, 'Paralysis from the bite causes them to be unable to defend themselves and eventually they succumb to or become a meal!'

Different species tend to use specialised strategies to capture their prey. Yoder cites the example of the Mimetidae, or pirate spiders:

> They prey exclusively on other spiders. The invading pirate spider attacks other spiders by luring the owner of the web by tugging at some of the threads. The spider then bites one of the victim's extremities, sucks the spider at the bite and ingests it whole. The cryptic jumping spider will capture other salticids or jumping spiders and tackle large orb weavers in their webs. This is called web robbery.

Other spiders will capture prey by grasping, biting and then wrapping the victim with silk. Leslie Saul-Gershenz, Insect Zoo Director at the San Francisco Zoo, cites other examples:

> 'Others use webbing to alert them of the presence of prey. Others still have sticky strands such as the spiders in the family Araneidae. Araneidae spiders have catching threads with glue droplets. The catching threads of Uloborid spiders are made of a very fine mesh ("hackel band"). *Dinopis* throws a rectangular catching web over its prey item, and the prey becomes entangled in the hackle threads.'

Saul-Gershenz summarises by quoting Rainer F Foelix, author of *Biology of Spiders*: 'The main enemies of spiders are spiders themselves.'

Not all spiders attack their own. According to Saul-Gershenz, there are about 20 species of social spiders that live together peacefully in colonies.

Why do only female mosquitoes eat human blood? What do male mosquitoes eat?

No, the mosquito menfolk aren't out eating steak and chips while the females are busy feasting on the blood of unwitting humans. Actually, the main food of both male and female mosquitoes is nectar from flowers. The nectar is converted to glycogen, a fuel potent enough to provide their muscles with energy to fly within minutes of consuming the nectar. Mosquitoes also possess an organ, known as the fat-body, that can store sugar for conversion to flight fuel.

Male mosquitoes can exist quite happily on a diet of only nectar, and nature makes certain that they are content – males don't have a biting mouth part capable of piercing the skin of a human. But females have been anatomically equipped to bite because they have an important job to do: lay eggs. In some species, female mosquitoes are not capable of laying any eggs unless they eat a nutritional supplement of some tasty, fresh blood. Their organs convert the lipids in blood into iron and protein that can greatly increase their fecundity.

A mosquito that would lay five or 10 eggs without the supplement can lay as many as 200 with a dash of Type O. Although we don't miss the blood sucked out of us, this is quite a feast for the mosquito; many times, she consumes more than her own body weight in blood.

But let's not take it personally. Some studies have indicated that, given a choice, mosquitoes prefer the blood of cows to humans, and in the jungle are just as likely to try to bite a monkey or a bird as a human.

Why do mosquitoes seem to like some people more than others?

Our correspondent was gracious enough to state her Imponderable delicately. She really meant: 'Why do mosquitoes *bite* some people more than others?' and, unless we're mistaken, even 'Why do mosquitoes bite *me* more than others?'

It occurred to us that perhaps differences in human blood types might play a factor in mosquitoes' culinary preferences. Dr Steven Schutz, of the University of California's Mosquito Control Research Laboratory, wrote to us that although it was once believed that blood types were an important factor in varying attraction rates, this theory has been discredited. He continued:

> Almost everyone who lives or works with mosquitoes has noticed that they seem to bite some people more than others. In part, this may be due to the fact that individual sensitivity to mosquito bites varies among individuals, so some people notice bites more than others.
>
> However, it has been scientifically demonstrated that certain individuals are consistently more attractive to mosquitoes than others ... If you put two people in two different huts, one may consistently attract more mosquitoes than the other, and this pattern holds up in repeated trials. This does not necessarily mean the more attractive person will be bitten more; there are also preferences for biting different individuals, which may be independent of their long-range attractiveness.

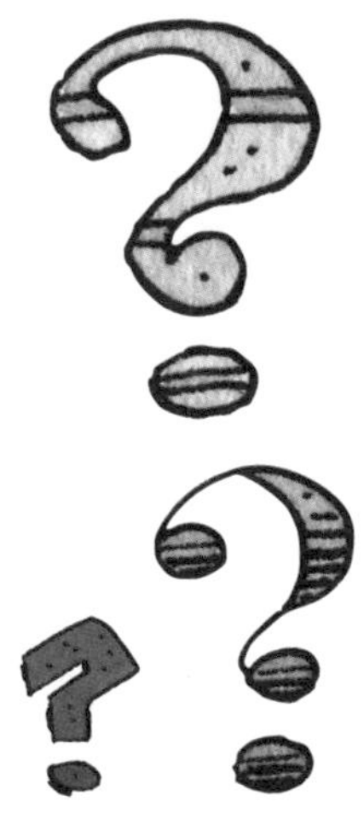

The entomologists we contacted indicated that two of the factors that might influence biting behaviour are heat and visual differentiation, as hard as they are to quantify. For example, Leslie Saul-Gershenz, Insect Zoo Director of the San Francisco Zoological Society, says that *Aedes* mosquitoes seem to be attracted to warm bodies only when the temperature is below 15°C.

But almost certainly, the dominant factor in attracting mosquitoes is how you smell. We know that most mosquitoes are attracted to the odour of carbon dioxide, but all of us exude CO_2 every time we exhale, so that wouldn't explain why mosquitoes are attracted to particular individuals. Other smells are probably the determinants, possibly including lactic acid and octenol, two other chemicals that we know attract mosquitoes. And perhaps mosquitoes are just as opinionated and arbitrary as we are, as Saul-Gershenz explains:

> 'We all smell a bit different, depending on our individual body chemistry. Just as we like some smells more than others, mosquitoes have very good chemoreception (sense of smell) and can detect these differences and express their preferences by feeding on some people more than others.'

Schutz indicates that it is difficult to isolate particular components of insect attraction, and the solution to this mystery would be of help to more than authors of *Imponderables* books. It might lead to better repellents and an ability to identify those most susceptible to mosquito-borne diseases, such as malaria.

Most insect repellents used by humans work on the principle of either masking odours that might attract mosquitoes or by creating smells that are repulsive. Randy Morgan, Entomologist and Head Keeper of the Insectarium at the Cincinnati Zoo, reports that 'regular intake of some materials (such as yeast), which ultimately are exuded through one's pores, change our smell and have proven effective in deterring mosquito bites'.

On a personal and ironic note, Morgan reports he, an entomologist, is far less attractive to mosquitoes than his wife, Kathy, who is a naturalist. He attributes this to her being 'sweeter' than he is, but at best we're not sure this would bear the brunt of scientific rigour, and at worst this is a blatant attempt to butter up his spouse. And even though mosquitoes 'reject' him, he can't take it personally: 'My wife gets larger and more irritated welts from mosquitoes than I do.'

Update

Although pointing to ambient temperature and visual cues as minor factors, all of the sources we cited above agreed that mosquitoes were attracted to humans whose fragrance attracted them. In early 2005, Rothamsted Research, in Hertfordshire, announced that its researchers found that bad smells can drive out good.

Some people are lucky enough to give off more than 10 separate chemical compounds, 'masking odours', that either repel mosquitoes or prevent them from detecting the human smell that they ordinarily like so much.

This research confirms previous research on cattle. By taking individual cows with masking odours away from the herd, scientists found that mosquitoes would flock to the remaining cattle in greater numbers. We've known some humans who can clear a room of other humans with their odour, but mosquitoes and humans don't seem to share the same taste in fragrances.

If moths are attracted to light, why don't they fly towards the sun?

There is one little flaw in the premise of this Imponderable. Even if they were tempted to fly towards the sun, they wouldn't have the opportunity – the vast majority of moths are nocturnal animals. When's the last time you saw one flitting by in daylight? Actually, though, the premise of this question isn't as absurd as it may appear. For details, see the Imponderable below.

Why are moths attracted to light? And what are they trying to do when they fly around light bulbs?

Moths, not unlike humans, spend much of their time sleeping, looking for food and looking for mates. Most moths sleep during the day. Their search for dinner and procreation takes place at night. Unlike us, though, moths are not provided with maps, street signs or web sites to guide them to the best places for feeding or mating.

Over centuries of evolution, moths have come to use starlight, and particularly moonlight, for navigation. By maintaining a constant angle in reference to the light source, the moth 'knows' where to fly. Unfortunately for the insects, however, humans introduce artificial light sources that lull the moths into assuming that a light bulb is actually their natural reference point.

English biologist RR Baker developed the hypothesis that when a moth chooses an artificial light source as its reference point, and tries keeping a constant angle to it, it ends up flying around the light in ever-smaller concentric circles, until it literally settles on the light source. Baker even speculates that moths hover on or near the light because they are attempting to roost, believing that it is daytime, their regular hours. Moths have been known to burn themselves by resting on light bulbs. Others become so disoriented, they can't escape until the light is turned off or sunlight appears.

So don't assume that moths are genuinely attracted by the light. Sad as their fate may be, chances are what the moth 'is trying to do' isn't to hover around a porch light – the only reason the moth is there is because it has confused a soft white bulb with the moon. The moth would far rather be cruising around looking for food and cute moths of the opposite sex.

Where do flies go in winter?

To heaven, usually. Some flies manage to survive winter, but only under extremely favourable conditions, when they can take shelter in barns or human residences where they can find enough organic matter and warmth to allow them to eat and breed.

Even under the best of circumstances, the normal life-span of a housefly north of the equator is approximately seven to twenty-one days. The most important variable in the longevity of these insects is the ambient temperature – they die off in droves when it falls below freezing or becomes excessively hot.

Although they actually live longest in cool temperatures, because they are less active, flies breed most prolifically when temperatures are warm, food is abundant and humidity is moderate. Winter tends to deprive them of all of these favourable conditions, so that they not only die off themselves, but do so without having been able to breed successfully.

So how can they regenerate the species? Most people believe that flies hibernate or become dormant, like some other insects, but this theory has proved to be untrue. The few flies that we find in the spring are mainly the descendants of the adult flies that managed to find good hiding places during the previous winter. These spring flies breed their little wings off, just in time to harass you on your picnics when the weather gets good.

Some of the flies that survive winter are not adults, but rather flies in their earlier developmental stages. Fly eggs are usually deposited in the ground, in crevices, in wood or in a particular favourite – cow pats. These eggs hatch in a few hours and turn into larvae, a phase that can last anywhere from one to four days. Larvae feed on decaying plants or animals (such as other insect larvae). As the fly larva grows, it undergoes pupation, a phase that lasts about five days, in which the fly rests as its larval features are transformed into adult ones. Many entomologists used to answer the Imponderable by speculating that most flies that survive the winter do so in the form of larvae or pupae, but scientists now believe that adult flies have a much better chance of surviving the winter than their younger brethren, who have a hard time coping with cold weather. Still, some larvae and pupae do stay alive during the very end of winter and develop into adults in the spring.

The fecundity of the *Musca domestica* is truly awesome. One scientist estimated that a single mating pair of houseflies could generate as many as 325,923,200,000,000 offspring in one summer. One-sixth of a cubic foot of soil taken in India revealed 4,024 *surviving* flies. Maybe the Imponderable should read: why isn't the entire world overcome with flies?

Any notion that flies migrate south during the winter is easily dispelled. The average flight range of a housefly is a measly one-quarter of a mile. Scientists have tracked the flight of flies: they rarely go beyond a ten-mile radius of their birthplace during their whole lifetime.

Why do bugs seem to suddenly appear in flour and fruit? Where do they come from?

If you want to disabuse yourself of the notion that your house or flat is a calm and clean refuge from the chaos of the outside world, consult David Bodanis's *The Secret House*, a study of the natural world inside our houses. With the help of scary photographs, Bodanis shows us that for every cockroach we might see scampering across our kitchen floor, there are thousands of bed mites, tiny insects that subsist largely on a balanced diet of shedded human skin and hair.

Any time you slam a newspaper down on the dining room table or spray deodorant in the bathroom, you are traumatising thousands of creepy-crawlies. So it shouldn't be too surprising that the insects in our houses become interested in other types of food. Raw flour may not be too appetising to us, but compared to hair droppings, it becomes a reasonable alternative.

Many insects infest food before it is packaged, often in the form of eggs. According to Dr George W Rambo, of the National Pest Control Association, these insects are called 'stored product insects'. Everyone in the food industry expects a few insects and/or rodent hairs to infest many kinds of food.

Even if insects are not in the flour or fruit when you purchase it, they are attracted to the food once you bring it home. Many of the insects that infest flour, for example, are barely visible to the eye. It's easy for a bug less than 3 mm long to intrude into packaging, especially after it has been opened.

So it's a losing fight. Our advice is to worry about the ones you can see and try not to think about the others.

What happens to an **ant** that gets separated from its **colony?**

As we all learned in school, ants are social animals, but their organisation doesn't just provide them with friends – it furnishes them with the food and protection they need to survive in a hostile environment. All the experts we consulted indicated that an isolated worker ant, left to its own devices, would likely die a week or two before its normal three-week lifespan. And it would probably spend that foreshortened time wandering around, confused, looking for its colony.

Ants help each other trace the path between food sources and the colony by laying down chemical trails called pheromones. Our solitary ant might try following pheromone trails it encounters, hoping they will lead it back home.

Three dangers, in particular, imperil a lost ant. The first is a lack of food. Ants are natural foragers but are used to receiving cues from other ants about where to search for food. A single ant would not have the capacity to store enough food to survive for long. Furthermore, ants don't always eat substances in the form they are gathered. Naturalist Kathy Biel-Morgan provided us with the example of the leaf-cutter ant. The leaf-cutter ant finds plants and brings leaves back to the nest, where the material is ground up and used in the colony's fungus garden. The ants then eat the fruiting body of the fungus. Without the organisational assistance of the colony, a leaf does nothing to sate the appetite of a leaf-cutter ant.

The second danger is cold. Ants are ectotherms, animals that need heat but are unable to generate it themselves. When it is cold, ants in colonies will seek the protective covering of the nest. If left to its own devices, a deserted ant would probably try to find a rock or the crack of a footpath to use as cover, which may or may not be enough protection to keep it from freezing.

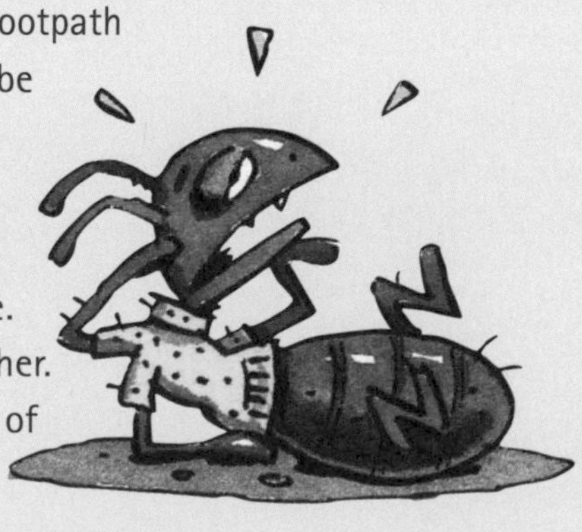

The third problem our lonesome ant would encounter is nasty creatures that think of the ant as their dinner fare. Collectively, ants help protect one another. Alone, an ant must fend off a variety of predators, including other ants.

Do butterflies (and other insects) sneeze or cough? If so, do they do so loud enough for humans to hear?

All of the entomologists we contacted were sure about this Imponderable. Butterflies and other insects don't sneeze or cough. It's particularly difficult for them to sneeze, as they don't possess true noses.

So then how do insects breathe? Leslie Saul-Gershenz, Insect Zoo Director at the San Francisco Zoo, explains:

> ‘Butterflies and other insects breathe through holes in the sides of their bodies called spiracles. Spiracles are provided with valve-like devices that keep out dust and water. Some insects, such as some flies, june beetles, lubber grasshoppers, and notably the Madagascar hissing cockroaches, make sounds for communication purposes by forcing air out through the spiracles. Hence they hiss.’

Karen Yoder, certification manager of the Entomological Society of America, concurs with Saul-Gershenz and adds that it isn't possible to hear insects breathing with the naked ear, either:

> ‘In my days of insect appreciation, I have never heard the expiration of air from an insect ... Certainly, it could be possible to hear the transpiration in insects with the aid of an amplifier, but not with the naked ear.’

But one needn't be wearing a stethoscope to hear the aforementioned hissing cockroach, better known to entomologists as *Gromphadorhina portentosa*. Our trusted informant, Randy Morgan, Head Keeper at Cincinnati's Insectarium, wrote an article for *Backyard Bugwatching*, a favourite magazine of our family's to pass around at barbecues, in which he chronicles the decibel-producing potential of these 5 to 8 cm cockroaches.

The Madagascar hissing cockroaches produce the hiss by contracting their abdomens and pushing the air out of constricted spiracles: the noise can be heard from several metres away. Whereas most cockroaches deter predators by running away, flying away or producing unpleasant secretions, not so the *Gromphadorhina portentosa*: 'Their secretive nature and ability to hiss seem to be their primary defence against enemies.' Morgan cites an example of a lemur, eager to dine on our poor cockroach. But the hiss convinces the lemur it might have a rattlesnake or other dangerous foe on its hands: 'In the leaves, a hissing cockroach continued feeding, unaware it had just narrowly escaped being eaten.' Even if the cockroach wasn't aware of its near demise, the lemur's flight wasn't a coincidence. The hiss is a voluntary reflex, generally used only when a cockroach is in danger from predators or competing for mates.

Where do butterflies go when it rains?

Butterflies don't just prefer sunny days. They need sunlight in order to regulate their body temperature. Whether it is raining or not, when the sun is obscured or the sun sets, butterflies fly for cover immediately.

Just as human beings might duck for cover underneath the canopy of a tree, butterflies seek the protection of natural coverings. According to Rudi Mattoni, Editor of the *Journal of Research on the Lepidoptera*, the favourite resting sites include the undersides of leaves or stems of bushes and on blades of grass.

Butterfly bodies are exceedingly delicate, so nature has provided them with other kinds of protection against the rain. When resting, the teardrop configuration of the butterfly prevents rain from pooling on the wings or body, and the surfaces of the butterfly's skin do not absorb water.

Richard Zack, Curator/Director of the James Entomological Collection at Washington State University, adds that many butterflies could not survive flying during a rainstorm. Not only does wind wreak havoc with their ability to fly, but the big raindrops themselves would pose a major risk.

Why do worms come out on the footpath after it rains?

What do you think the worms are coming out for? Their health? In fact, they are. Except for those that live as parasites, most worms live by burrowing little holes in the ground. When it rains, those little holes fill with water. If the worms didn't get out of the holes, they'd drown. Worms may be creepers, but they're not dummies.

Why do they congregate on the footpath after rain? Footpaths provide more solid support than dirt or grass during a rainstorm. If you investigated the grass adjacent to the footpath, you would find many worms trying to stay above water, wishing they had made it to the footpath.

Do fish sleep? If so, when do they sleep?

Our trusty *Webster's New World Dictionary* defines sleep as 'a natural, regularly recurring condition of rest for the body and mind, during which the *eyes are usually closed* and there is *little or no conscious thought or voluntary movement*'. Those strategically placed weasel words we have italicised make it hard for us to give you a yes or no answer to this mystery. So as much as we want to present you with a tidy solution to this Imponderable, we feel you deserve the hard truth.

Webster probably didn't have fish in mind when he wrote this definition of 'sleep'. First of all, except for elasmobranchs (fish with cartilaginous skeletons, such as sharks and rays), fish don't have eyelids. So they can't very well close them to sleep. No fish has opaque eyelids that block out vision, but some have a transparent membrane that protects their eyes from irritants.

Pelagic fish (who live in the open sea, as opposed to coasts), such as tuna, bluefish and marlins, never stop swimming. Even coastal fish, which catch a wink or two, do not fall asleep in the same way humans do. Gerry Carr, Director of Species Research for the International Game Fish Association, wrote to us about some of the ingenious ways that fish try to catch a few winks, even if 40 winks are an elusive dream:

> 'Some reef fishes simply become inactive and hover around like they're sleeping, but they are still acutely aware of danger approaching. Others, like some parrot fishes and wrasses, exude a mucous membrane at night that completely covers their body as though they've been placed in plastic bags. They wedge themselves into a crevice in the reef, bag themselves and remain there, semicomatose, through the night.
>
> Their eyes remain open, but a scuba diver can approach them and, if careful, even pick them up at night, as I have done. A sudden flurry of movement, though, will send them scurrying. They are not totally unaware of danger.'

In many ways, fish sleep the same way we plod through our everyday lives when we are awake. Our eyes are open but we choose, unconsciously, not to register in our brains most of the sensory data we see. If a crazed assassin burst into the room, we could rouse ourselves to attention, but if someone asked us to describe what fabulous tourist attraction we were watching, we couldn't say whether it was Stonehenge or the Blarney Stone.

If you accept that a fish's blanking out is sleeping, then the answer to the second part of the mystery is that fish sleep at night, presumably because of the darkness. Anyone with an aquarium can see that fish can float effortlessly while sleeping. They exude grace – which is more than we can say for how most humans look when they are sleeping.

Update

It turns out that some mammals are joining fish in the burning-the-candle-at-both-ends game. A team led by Jerome Siegel, head of the Siegel Lab at the Center for Sleep Research at the University of California, Los Angeles, reported in 2005 that newborn bottlenose dolphins and killer whales don't get any shuteye in their first month of life. Perhaps in exasperation, their mothers also forgo sleep during this period.

This finding astounded sleep specialists because the prevailing theory has been that REM sleep is necessary for brain development in mammals, and that hormones crucial for growth are released during sleep. While human babies sleep like, well, babies, and their mothers take every opportunity to catch some sleep, Siegel speculates that whales and dolphins might have developed this mechanism so that the babies can evade predators when they are most at risk. But wouldn't the same be true of any animal? Siegel proposes that 'in the water, there's no safe place to curl up'.

When older dolphins and whales do sleep, they usually float on the surface of the water or lie on the floor. But these newborns swim continuously and don't start sleeping as much as adults until they are four or five months old.

Unlike fish, dolphins have eyelids, so they can close their eyes when they sleep. But dolphins sleep with one eye closed. Sleep researchers have never found any proof that they experience REM sleep at all, and the best evidence is that only one hemisphere of the dolphin brain is experiencing the restfulness associated with sleep.

Just as some have suggested that fish might actually be sleeping (with their eyes open), perhaps whale and dolphin babies might be enjoying some form of sleep that we haven't identified yet. And just as fish seem to go into a trance when the water is dark, maybe these marine mammals indulge in some brief periods of sleep in the midst of swimming. Unlikely, but possible.

Why do you need to supply oxygen to a tropical tank when fish are quite capable of surviving without extra oxygen in the wild? Why do you see oxygen tanks more in saltwater aquariums than freshwater?

Robert Schmidt, of the North American Native Fishes Association, answers the first part of this Imponderable succinctly: 'You have to provide oxygen to any tank that has more fish (thus higher oxygen demand) than the plants and algae in that atmosphere can supply.'

Most natural bodies of water are replete with oxygen-producing plants – by comparison, the plant life in a home tank is like a sprig of parsley. Oceans tend to have a richer and more abundant plant life than freshwater environments, but the absence of sufficient flora is not the only reason why saltwater aquaria require oxygen tanks, as Dr Robert Rofen, of the Aquatic Research Institute, explains:

> Saltwater tanks need more aeration than freshwater aquaria to keep their inhabitants alive because the oxygen level is lower in salt water. With the added salt molecules present, there is less room around the H_2O molecules for O_2 molecules to be present. Salt water absorbs less O_2 than does fresh water.

Why do aquarium fish put pebbles from the bottom of the tank in their mouths and spit them out?

Humans should talk! We put odd things in our mouths as well: our fingernails, pens and pencils, and grape-flavoured bubble gum. But the question is about fish, not *homo sapiens*. Our aquatic experts offer three explanations:

1 You want to find a mate? Better have a nice pad! Biologist Glenda Kelley, of the International Game Fish Association, writes:

> One reason aquarium fishes may go to the bottom of a tank and pick up rocks in their mouths and spit them out is to choose or clean the spawning substratum before enticing a female to spawn there. In some fish, availability and selection of nest-building material is most important in reproductive behaviour. In the selection process, fish test the environment in various ways: mouthing potential nest material; settling on the bottom to feel it; or making preliminary digging or cleaning efforts.

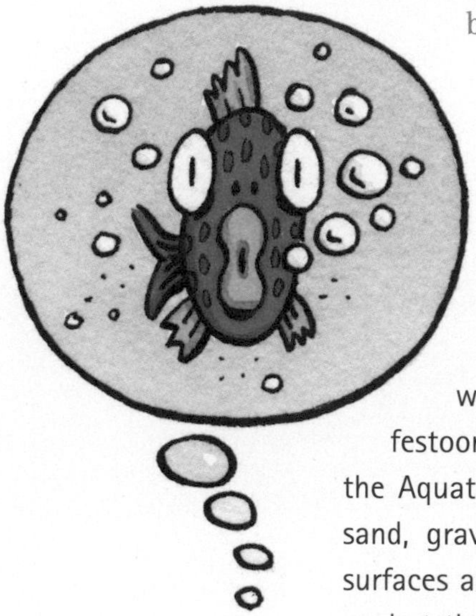

2 Yum. It's not that the fish doesn't appreciate that fish food you drop from on high, but variety is the spice of life. In the wild, with a rich and complicated plant life, pebbles can be festooned with all sorts of delicacies. According to Robert R Rofen, of the Aquatic Research Institute, many fish search for food 'by taking up sand, gravel and pebbles into their tongues to remove food on their surfaces and then spitting out what is inedible'. It might seem strange to us, but then we can imagine a fish writing a chapter about why humans put olives in their mouths and spit the pips out.

3 By all means necessary. Let's face it, fish aren't equipped with toothbrushes or dental floss. Doug Olander, of *Sport Fishing* magazine, told Imponderables that pebbles and gravel can be an impromptu substitute, a means to rid themselves of parasites that gather in their mouths.

Do fish urinate?

You don't see them swimming in your toilet, do you? Yes, of course, fish urinate.

But not all fish do it in the same way. Freshwater fish must rid themselves of the water that is constantly accumulating in their bodies through osmosis. According to Glenda Kelley, biologist for the International Game Fish Association, the kidneys of freshwater fish must produce copious amounts of dilute urine to prevent their tissues from becoming waterlogged. Compared to their freshwater counterparts, marine fish, who lose water through osmosis, produce little urine. For those readers who have asked us if fish drink water, the surprising answer is that saltwater fish do because they need to replenish the water lost through osmosis, as Kelley explains:

> This loss of water is compensated for largely by drinking large amounts of sea water, but the extra salt presents a problem. They rid themselves of this surplus by actively excreting salts, mainly through their gills.

Dr Robert R Rofen, of the Aquatic Research Institute, told *Imponderables* that fish are able to excrete liquids through their gills and skin as well, 'the counterpart to humans' sweating through their skin'.

Are lobsters ambidextrous?

Have you ever noticed, while digging into a lobster, that one claw is significantly larger than the other, as if one claw was pumping iron and taking steroids, while the other claw was used only for riffling the pages of library books? The large claw is called the 'crusher' and the smaller one the 'cutter' (terms that sound like the members of a new tag team in the World Wrestling Federation). The crusher has broader and bigger teeth but moves relatively slowly. The cutter has tiny, serrated teeth and moves swiftly.

The two claws do not start out distinctly different. Lobsters shed their shells more often than Cher has plastic surgery – they undergo three moults in the larval stage alone. When lobsters are first hatched, the two claws look identical, but with each successive stage in their development, the differences become more pronounced. It isn't until their fifth moult, and second postlarval moult, that the two claws are truly differentiated.

As you may have guessed, the crusher claw is important for defending against predators, and the cutter particularly useful in eating. Claws of lobsters are often torn off in accidents and in fights. Although there are some differences among species of lobsters, most lobsters will regenerate severed claws.

Most bizarre of all, if the remaining claw of an injured lobster is a cutter, many species with 'plastic dimorphism' will change the function of that claw from cutter to crusher, presumably because the crusher is more essential for survival. The next regenerated claw of that lobster is capable itself of shifting to the cutter function, so that the positions of the two claws are reversed.

According to Darryl Felder, Chairman of the University of Louisiana, Lafayette, Biology Department, lobsters are not always right- or left-'handed'. The crusher may be on the right or left side of a lobster.

The ultimate answer to this Imponderable depends upon how you define ambidextrous. Certainly, lobsters can use either cheliped (the scientific name for claw) with equal ease. Although their regenerative powers give lobsters a certain flexibility, the versatility of each claw is not as great as that of baseball players who can swing the bat equally well from both sides, or the pickpocket who can pilfer skilfully with either hand.

Do starfish have faces?

Starfish are not fish, and experts tend to get testy if you call them 'starfish', anyway – they are properly known as sea stars, and are classified as Echinodermata (spiny skinned), the same phylum of invertebrates as sea cucumbers and urchins. We tend to think of sea stars as unmoving lumps that lie on the ocean's floor, when they are actually voracious carnivores, and usually prowling for food.

It's hard to have a face when you don't even have a head. Unlike most animals that have a head, sea stars, like all echinoderms, are radially symmetrical with a top side and a bottom side, but no front or back. They feel comfortable moving in any direction, as well they should: they have five – or more – arms and absolutely no notion of forwards or backwards.

With the naked eye, it isn't easy to see the sensory organs of a sea star, but they have many of the skills of animals with heads. One thing they don't have is ears or a sense of hearing. And although they don't have eyes, they do have eyeholes on each arm that can sense light. Sea stars often lift an arm in order to uncover the eyespot, so they can perceive light or movement in the water. Most sea stars crave the dark, as they escape predators by taking refuge underneath or behind rocks where they cannot be seen.

Sea stars have a groove running along the bottom of each arm that contains hundreds of tiny 'tube feet'. These tube feet not only enable sea stars to move, but also are equipped with suction cups, which allow them to grip surfaces with some of the tube feet and propel themselves forward with the others. Each arm contains a single tube foot that is longer than the other feet and does not have a suction cup.

When a sea star moves, this special tube foot is able to sense chemicals in the water. Even if sea stars don't have noses, they do have a highly developed sense of smell, which comes in handy when they are seeking food – their 'vision' doesn't help them much to find prey.

No eyes. No nose. No ears. No heads. Do we come up blank? We are happy to announce that they do have mouths, usually located right in the centre of the bottom of the sea star.

We are not so happy to describe how they use these mouths to devour their prey. Bivalves, especially oysters, clams and mussels, are their favourite food source, but sea stars also feast on coral, fish and other animals that live near the floor of the sea. While it takes some skill and protective gear for us to pry open an oyster, sea stars have mastered their technique; they wrap their arms around the oyster and use their tube feet to pry apart the oyster shell. Once there is the slightest crack in the shell, the sea star extends its jellylike stomach out of its mouth (yes, its mouth) and inserts the stomach inside the shell of the oyster. The digestive juices of the stomach move into the crack of the shell while the inside-out stomach of the sea star digests its prey.

It can take 24 hours for a sea star to fully digest a feast of a single oyster, and all of this time the stomach is having an 'out of body' experience. Only when the food is fully digested does the sea star's stomach return to its mouth. If your eating habits were this appalling, you wouldn't show your face either.

Why do bats roost upside down? What prevents them from falling down?

Bats are a tad eccentric. They are the only mammals that can fly. At night, they flutter around, snarfing up assorted bugs for food, and during the day, most species of bats literally hang out: upside down.

The key ingredient in allowing bats to roost upside down is their specialised musculature. When we humans try to grip something with our hands, say, hanging on a horizontal bar, we clench our muscles, straining to keep not only our hands and wrists locked, but aggravating our shoulders and arms. It's almost the exact opposite for bats.

When a bat finds a suitable roosting site, it opens its claws and grabs with its talons; it doesn't clench its muscles, but rather relaxes them. The weight of the upper body actually keeps the talons locked, so it takes no more exertion for a bat to roost than for us to sit on a recliner chair. The lack of effort needed to stay roosting allows bats to enjoy a form of hibernation known as 'torpor'. During torpor, which bats can induce at will, their body temperature and blood pressure decrease, and they barely move. In very cold weather, bats can enter a full hibernation mode, roosting blissfully upside down the entire time.

How little effort does it take a bat to roost upside down? Dead bats are often found in typical roosting position, looking like they are just taking a snooze. Only when they want to take off from their roost do bats have to flex their muscles.

Other anatomical oddities also help bats roost upside down. Their necks are extremely flexible, so if they need to look behind them – no problem – they can turn their heads 180 degrees. The hind legs of bats are rotated so that their knees face backwards, which aids in roosting. Most bats don't have the ability to give birth upside down, though, so most species literally hang by their thumbs while delivering (as they do when urinating and defecating), which does take exertion.

So we know *how* bats roost upside down; now let's look at the *why*.

1 **Bats' legs are weak.** In exchange for the unique ability of bats to fly, Mother Nature saddled them with unusually weak legs, with light and slender bones. Light legs allow bats to fly faster, but lower their ability to stand, walk and support their own weight so that they could perch like birds.

2 **Roosting upside down improves bats' take-offs.** Although bats are efficient flying machines once aloft, their wings aren't strong enough to enable them to take off from the ground the way birds can. If bats are attacked by a predator, their roosting position allows them to escape quickly, even if they are in torpor, by simply dropping off their roosting spot. Some bat researchers believe that at one time in their evolution, bats might have been gliders rather than flyers, as their take-off pattern suits an animal unable to fly.

3 **Predators are foiled.** Bats' predators include owls, hawks, snakes, raccoons and, in many places, humans. Bats evade many of their predators simply by being active when their enemies are asleep. But roosting upside down allows bats the opportunity to find roosting sites unappealing to or unreachable by predators, such as the roofs of caves or the ceilings of attics and barns.

Why do monkeys in the zoo pick through their hair all the time? Why do they pick through one another's hair?

In the wild, primates pick at their own hair frequently but for short periods of time. Usually, they are trying to rid themselves of parasitic insects, insect webs or remnants of food.

Monkeys in captivity are much less likely to be riddled with parasites, but may be afflicted with another skin problem. Monkeys exude salt from the pores of their skin. The salt lands on loose bits of skin, and monkeys will often pick through their hair trying to shed the salty flakes.

A monkey, unlike a human, has no difficulty in scratching its back (or any other part of its body, for that matter). Most animal behaviourists assume that apes – be they gibbons or chimpanzees – search through one another's hair for purely social reasons. One psychologist, HH Reynolds, noted that chimpanzees are not altruistic or naturally cooperative: 'Grooming behaviour appears to be one of the most cooperative ventures in which chimpanzees engage.'

Perhaps mutual grooming in monkeys is akin to the human handshake, whose original purpose was to signal that a potential weapon, the outstretched hand, would not turn into a clenched fist.

Why do gorillas pound their chests?

Gorillas in the wild pound their chests for one fundamental reason: it scares the bejeezus out of other gorillas as much as it scares us.

The definitive study of chest-beating in gorillas was reported in GB Schaller's *Mountain Gorilla: Ecology and Behavior.* Schaller identifies a nine-step ritual of aggression in a fixed order: hooting; symbolic feeding; rising (the gorilla stands on two feet); throwing (usually throwing vegetation up in the air); chest-beating (usually two to 20 beatings, with open hands – sometimes accompanied by pounding of stomach or thighs, as well); leg kick (often, gorillas kick one leg in the air while chest-beating); running (usually sideways, first on two legs, then on all fours); slapping and tearing vegetation; and ground-thumping (a single thump with one or both palms usually culminates the ritual).

Only male silverback gorillas will exhibit all nine behaviours, but virtually any chest-beating will be accompanied by at least one of these other types of behaviour. Female gorillas have been observed chest-thumping in the wild too.

So when and why do they do it? Gorillas are most likely to pound their chests in the following situations:

1 According to Susan Lumpkin, Director of Communications of the Friends of the National Zoo, chest-beating occurs most often when 'a silverback (adult) male leading a group of females meets a potential rival for the affections of his females. Usually the rival is a lone silverback or, less often, another silverback with a female group'.
2 Dominant gorillas use chest-beating in order to establish dominance and status within a troop.
3 Chest-beating is a not too subtle way for gorillas to mark territory when challenged by another troop.
4 Location signal. In his book *Gorillas*, Colin Groves mentions that when one male chest-beats, he is likely to be answered. So one of the functions of chest-beating might be as simple as a way of keeping the group together to avoid contact with other, less friendly bands of animals.
5 Gorillas often perform the ritual when approached by people.
6 Excitement. In her book *Gorillas in the Mist*, Dian Fossey reports that chest-beating can simply be a signal for excitement or alarm.

Schaller also notes that gorillas will mimic the chest-beating displays of others and sometimes do it as play. Evidently, gorillas can tell when chest-beating is meant as a threat and when it is done for play. Indeed, at zoos we have observed a phenomenon described by Ed Hansen, President of the American Association of Zoo Keepers: '[Chest-beating] is a learned behaviour, so you will often see young animals clumsily displaying this behaviour in an attempt to imitate their elders.'

Actually, there is disagreement among experts about whether chest-beating is learned behaviour simply because gorillas raised in captivity exhibit chest-beating. Groves claims that the behaviour is innate and not copied, arguing that lone gorillas raised in captivity chest-beat.

Perhaps the most interesting response we received was from Francine Patterson, President and Research Director of the Gorilla Foundation. The foundation has received enormous attention for its Project Koko, what it calls 'the longest continuous interspecies communication project of its kind in the world'. Project Koko, launched in 1972, has been a long-range attempt to teach Koko American Sign Language. Although two other gorillas are involved, Koko has shown the most intellectual capability – she has a working vocabulary of more than 500 signs and has emitted more than 400 more. Koko understands approximately 2000 words and has a tested IQ of between 70 and 95 on human scales.

Yet even the 'intellectual' Koko and her two fellow gorilla-scholars chest-beat when playing both with each other and with their human caregivers. Patterson sent us a transcript of a charming exchange between Koko and her close friend, the late Barbara Chiller, one of the founders of the Gorilla Foundation:

BARBARA: Okay, can you tell me how gorillas talk?
(KOKO beats her chest)
BARBARA: What do gorillas say when they are happy?
KOKO: Gorilla hug. [expressed in sign language]
BARBARA: What do gorillas say to their babies?
(KOKO beats her chest).

Are lions really afraid of kitchen chairs?

Give us a bazooka, a long pole and 40 bodyguards, and we might consider going into the ring with a lion.

Come to think of it, we think we'll still pass on it. But how on earth did professional animal trainers choose such inappropriate tools as a whip and a kitchen chair? Why would a kitchen chair tame a lion? It doesn't even scare us!

At one time, animal trainers did use more forceful weapons against big cats. In his book *Here Comes the Circus*, author Peter Verney reports that the foremost trainer of the 1830s and 1840s, Isaac Van Amburgh, used heavy iron bars. Other trainers employed red-hot irons, goads and even water hoses to control unmanageable beasts.

As far as we could ascertain, the considerably calmer instrument of the kitchen chair was introduced by the most famous lion tamer of the twentieth century, Clyde Beatty, who trained lions from 1920 until the late 1960s (when, ironically, he died of a car accident). His successor at the Clyde Beatty Circus, David Hoover, has strong feelings about the psychology of lions. Hoover believes that each lion has a totally different set of fears and motivations. For example, one lion he trained had a perverse fear of bass horns, while another went crazy when the circus's peanut roaster was operating.

Hoover believes that the only way for a human to control a lion is to gain psychological dominance over the animal – what he calls a 'mental bluff'. He also feels it important that the lion believe it couldn't harm the trainer. When he sustained injuries in the ring, Hoover always finished the act 'because the animal is operating under the assumption that he can't hurt you. If you leave the cage after the animal has injured you, then the animal knows he's injured you. You can't handle that animal any more.'

Hoover favoured a blank cartridge gun over a whip. The purpose of the blanks was simply to disrupt the animal's concentration:

> They have a one-track mind. A blank cartridge goes off, and if you holler a command that the animal is familiar with, the animal will execute the command because he loses his original train of thought.

But what about the chair?

> The chair works the same way. The chair has four points of interest (the four legs). The animal is charging with the idea to tear the trainer apart. You put the chair up in his face. [When he sees the four chair legs] he loses his chain of thought, and he takes his wrath out on the chair and forgets he's after the trainer.

Ron Whitfield, lion tamer at Marine World Africa USA, told *Imponderables* that the chair is used more for theatrical reasons than for defence. If the instrument of the lion tamer is used as a tool of distraction rather than aggression, it makes sense to use flimsy props. Lions can be trained to bounce, swat at the chair – even to knock the chair out of the hands of the trainer. Ron assured us that if the lion wanted to attack, the chair would not offer any real protection.

Whitfield, who has trained lions for 22 years, has never used a chair. (He uses a stick and a crop whip.) The whip, he believes, is used as an extension of the hand of the trainer – to cue lions, who are lazy by nature. If they are sitting idly when they are supposed to be performing, a snap near them or a touch on their behinds will provide 'motivation' to perform. And the whip provides negative reinforcement. Like a child, the lion learns that certain behaviours will induce a sting on the behind and will alter its behaviour accordingly.

Even if lions have been performing in acts for years, they are still wild animals. Gary Priest, Animal Behaviour Specialist at the San Diego Zoo, says much of the behaviour of even a 'tamed' lion is instinctual and automatic. Like Hoover, Priest emphasises the necessity for trainers to demonstrate a lack of fear of the animal.

Without intervention of some kind, lions would revert to the appetitive cycle (crouching, eyes squinting, ears pinned back, lowering into a crouch and springing) characteristic of lions on the hunt.

If trainers run or show fear, Priest explains, lions will think of them as prey. But if you approach the lion before it snares you, the appetitive cycle is disrupted. In the wild, no prey *would* approach a lion, so the cat is not genetically encoded to respond to this aggressiveness. (Indeed, Priest told us that if you ever encounter a lion in the wild, especially one that is starting to crouch, do *not* run away. Instead, run *towards* the lion, yelling 'bugga bugga bugga' or some such profundity. Says Priest: 'This will probably save your life,' as the lion usually retreats when confronted.)

Priest thinks that the whip and chair are a good combination, with the noise from the whip a particularly good distraction and the chair allowing the trainer to approach the lion and still have some distance and (minimal) protection.

The one part of this Imponderable we would have loved to unravel is how and why Clyde Beatty thought of the idea of using a kitchen chair in the first place. Did he have a scare with a cat one day when the chair was the only object handy? Was he sitting on a chair when a lion attacked? Or did he just want an excuse to drag his favourite kitchen chair around the world with him?

How are animals different from people? Simple: when animals see food, they just eat it. We humans farm, process, package, name, refrigerate and cook our food; we decorate it, put it on pretty plates and talk endlessly about it. We even put on funny hats when we cook. Why? Here are some answers.

food and drink

What causes double-yolk eggs? Why do egg yolks sometimes have red spots on them?

Female chicks are born with a fully formed ovary containing several thousand tiny ova, which form in a cluster like grapes. A follicle-stimulating hormone in the bloodstream develops these ova, which will eventually become egg yolks. When the ova are ripe, the follicle ruptures and an ovum is released. Usually when a chicken ovulates, one yolk at a time is released and travels down the oviduct, where it will acquire a surrounding white membrane and shell.

Occasionally two yolks are released at the same time. Double-yolk eggs are no more planned than human twins. But some chickens are more likely to lay double-yolk eggs. Very young and very old chickens are most likely to lay double yolks; young ones because they don't have their laying cycles synchronised, and old ones because, generally speaking, the older the chicken, the larger the egg she will lay. And for some reason, larger eggs are most subject to double yolks.

If a chicken is startled during egg formation, small blood vessels in the wall may rupture, producing in the yolk blood spots – tiny flecks of blood. These eggs are perfectly safe to eat.

How does yeast make bread rise? Why do we need to knead most breads?

Yeast is a small plant in the fungus family (that's ascomycetous fungi of the genus *Saccharomyces*, to you botanical nuts), and as inert as baker's yeast might seem to you in that little packet, it is a living organism. Yeast manufacturers isolate one healthy, tiny cell, feed it nutrients and watch it multiply into tonnes of yeast. One gram of fresh yeast contains about ten billion living yeast cells, thus giving yeast the reputation as the rabbit of the plant world.

To serve the needs of bakers, manufacturers ferment the yeast to produce a more concentrated product. But the yeast isn't satisfied to idly sit by in the fermentation containers – it wants to eat. So yeast is fed molasses and continues to grow. A representative of Fleischmann's Yeast told *Imponderables* that under ideal conditions, a culture bottle of yeast holding about 200 g will grow to about 150 tonnes in five days, enough to make about 10 million loaves of bread.

After it has grown to bulbous size, the yeast is separated from the molasses and water, and centrifuged, washed and either formed into cakes or dried into the granulated yeast that most consumers buy. When the baker dissolves the yeast in water, it reactivates the fungus and reawakens the yeast's appetite as well.

Yeast loves to eat the sugar and flour in bread dough. As it combines with the sugar, fermentation takes place, converting the sugar into a combination of alcohol and carbon dioxide. The alcohol burns off in the oven, but small bubbles of carbon dioxide form in the bread and are trapped inside the dough. The carbon dioxide gas causes gluten, a natural protein fibre found in flour, to stretch and provide a structure for the rising dough without releasing the gas. When the dough doubles in size, the recommended amount, it is full of gas bubbles and therefore has a lighter consistency than breads baked without yeast.

By kneading the bread, the baker toughens the gluten protein structure in the dough, stretching the gluten sufficiently to withstand the pressure of the expanding carbon dioxide bubbles.

Why do soft breads get hard when they get stale while hard starches like crackers get softer when stale?

Bread turning stale is a perfect example of reversion to the mean. Bakery expert Simon Jackel told *Imponderables* that the typical soft bread contains 32 to 38 per cent moisture. If the bread is left unwrapped and exposed to the elements, it will become hard when it drops to about 14 per cent moisture.

Why do some hard-boiled egg yolks turn grey or green when soft-boiled eggs don't discolour?

The discolouring is caused by iron and sulphur compounds that accumulate when eggs are overcooked. Although grey egg yolks lack eye appeal, the iron and sulphur don't affect the taste or nutritional value of the eggs.

Probably the most common way of overcooking eggs is to leave them in hot water after cooking. Egg marketing bodies recommend either running cold water over cooked eggs or putting them in ice-water until completely cooled. This will not only avoid overcooking but also make the shells much easier to peel.

Why does the bread get stale and lose the moisture? Although food technologists don't fully understand all the causes, a process called 'retrogradation' occurs, in which internal changes take place in the starch structure. Although breads are formulated to have a softer crumb portion than crust area, during retrogradation some of the crumb moisture migrates to the crust, which results in the softening of the crust and a hardening of the crumb.

Tom Lehmann, Bakery Assistance Director at the American Institute of Baking, adds that as the bread retrogrades, a portion of the starch in the flour undergoes a gradual change, known as 'crystallisation', which results in a gradual firming of the bread. Some of the edible ingredients in the dough, such as enzymes and monoglycerides, act to slow up the rate of retrogradation, but the process is inevitable and will occur quickly if the bread is unwrapped and exposed to air.

Hard starches, such as crackers, are crisp because they are baked with an extremely low moisture level, usually 2 to 5 per cent. When they soften, their internal structure doesn't change like staling hard breads. As they are exposed to the ambient air, crackers absorb the air's moisture. According to Jackel, hard crackers will be perceived as soft once the moisture level reaches 9 per cent.

Why do rice cakes hold together?

Our correspondent, duly reading the ingredient list on his packet of rice cakes, notes that only rice and salt are listed. He rightfully wonders how rice cake makers manage to keep together what would seem to be fragile rice. Is there a secret binding ingredient in the mix?

We're sure the rice cake producers would say that the secret ingredient is love, but emotion has nothing to do with it. We contacted several rice cake producers and received the same explanation from all of them (a rarity in the Imponderables business) about how rice cakes are formed.

First, uncooked rice is soaked in water and then mixed with a little salt (and in some cases, with a bit of oil). This soaking is important because the moisture from the rice is going to help puff it up when it is heated in the grain-popping machine, as Quaker Foods and Beverages explains:

> A rice cake is formed when heat and pressure are added to the grain, causing it to expand abruptly. A portion of grain is set onto a round, metal pan – like a mini baking pan. As a hot

> cylinder presses down onto the pan, sizzling pressure is released. The heat is so intense that after only a few seconds, the grain makes a loud popping noise as it bursts. This process causes the grains to "pop" and interweave. There are no oils, additives or binding ingredients used during this process.

If the rice cake is flavoured, the seasonings are applied after the popping process, and doesn't affect the sticking together of the rice itself.

Rice cakes date back to 3000 BC in South-East Asia, and home cooks have never been privy to the specialised equipment that modern commercial rice cake makers enjoy. Home cooks in Asia make rice cakes by soaking glutinous rice overnight, steaming the rice until it is soft, grinding the heck out of it with a mortar and pestle, and then pounding the mashed rice with a mallet. Then they knead the rice like bread dough and cook it, resulting in a rice cake (or rice ball) with a smoother consistency than that of Western cakes.

Whether using the traditional methods or specialised metal moulds designed only for rice cake production, bakers seem to have no trouble getting rice cakes to hold together – now if only they could manage to produce some taste!

Why do two cereal flakes that are floating in milk tend to float towards each other once they get a couple of centimetres apart?

Our initial attempts to find the answer to this intriguing Imponderable met with total frustration, until Diane Dickey of Kellogg's took pity on us. Although she is in the communications department at the cereal giant, Dickey was carried away by the lure of quashing this Imponderable. As she wrote in *The Kellogg's News*:

> Our first instinct was to tell Feldman not to play with his food. However, because this question kept staring at us from the cereal bowl, we invited John Kepplinger from Product Research to accept the challenge of explaining why flakes do seem to attract each other in a bowl of milk.

Kepplinger then consulted with eight different Kellogg's experts, ranging from the divisions of Product Research, Food Research and Technical

Services. Kepplinger's summary of their conclusions was straightforward:

> The primary explanation for why two cereal flakes attract each other in milk is due to surface tension. Surface tension causes the milk to form a small valley around each flake. As the two flakes move closer together, these valleys meet to form a natural depression between the flakes, and they simply slide downhill towards each other.

But wanting to make sure that the answer was complete, Kepplinger contacted Philip A Sorenson, Vice-President of Advanced Technology Innovations, Inc. Sorenson called Dr Bob Park, Director of Public Affairs with the American Physical Society. In a letter, Sorenson summarised Park's findings:

> Using two leaves in a pond as our example, he [Park] said that the leaves essentially "take a random walk around the pond" until they get close enough to one another. Each leaf is pressing on the surface of the water; this weight deforms the surface tension of the water around the leaf, and the surface of the water "dips" if the leaves are close enough to one another, causing the leaves to effectively lean towards one another in this slight indentation.
>
> To illustrate this point, Dr Park said to picture stretched rubber, onto which two marbles are placed. Each marble presses the surface of the rubber downwards, causing the marbles to roll towards one another.

Another consultant that Sorenson contacted implied that the movement of the flakes might not be as random as Park suggested. So we consulted the physicists on the Usenet boards on the Internet, who proceeded to shower us with various other 'randomising elements' that can affect the movement of the two little flakes. Don Berkowitz, of Chesapeake College, mentioned that because both the average motion of the particles and surface tension are functions of temperature, the temperature of the milk would play a role. Others added that small air currents in the air, ripples from the spoon, sugar or other coatings on the cereal could all affect the movement of the flakes.

Physicist Stan Berry, of Nichols Research Corporation, reminded us that seemingly insignificant movements can alter the flakes' progress:

> ‘Bumping the table could work as well as hitting your spoon on the bowl. Also, the cereal flakes would automatically retain some inherent motion as they are dropped into the bowl. On a slippery surface (such as milk) it takes great care to ensure that two things start out at rest relative to each other.’

At the same time that we were weighing in with our cereal Imponderable, a similar question was embroiling the newsgroup: why do tea-leaves tend to congregate in the middle (and bottom) of a tea-cup? The consensus was that when stirred, tea-leaves group in the middle because of the lesser frictional force on the inside edge of the tea-leaves (slower currents) than on the outside edge of the leaves (where the currents are swifter).

Physicist Andrew De Weerd argued that surface tension might explain the bond between the flakes once they have joined, but that the initial attraction of cereal flakes might be explained by the same tendency to 'meet in the middle' as the tea-leaves. Noting that the pressures of stirring or pouring the milk will tend to drive the liquid either clockwise or counterclockwise, De Weerd writes:

> ‘I would assume that these currents are maintained for quite some time. Since the currents on the outside of the flake (bowl side) are greater, you would have a push towards the middle. I would also suspect that the flake turns slowly about its centre in the same angular direction as the milk in the bowl.’

Judging from the two contributions that follow, the United Kingdom seems to be the epicentre of cereal-attraction research. We received this report from Robert J Hill, of Krisalis Software, who wanted to test whether, if a cold bowl of milk was warmed slightly, convection would occur (i.e. heat rising from the edge of the bowl pushing the flakes together):

> ‘I have tried this experiment on a prerefrigerated bowl of milk taken straight from the fridge, to which I added two flakes. They were moving around but not towards each other a great deal, so I placed my hands around the bowl. Within a couple of minutes the flakes joined. Maybe they would have joined

without the heat from my hands, but I think we could be onto [a] major discovery.'

But we're afraid that we might have to award the 'discovery' prize to Ian Russell, of Interactive Science, a group that organises scientific exhibitions. He e-mailed us breathlessly, fresh from the thrill of revelation:

'I've just been down to the kitchen. No cornflakes available, but I can solemnly report that floating Rice Krispies like each other as well. And you're really going to enjoy this: bits of hydrophobic [i.e. incapable of uniting with or absorbing water or liquid] candle wax like each other as well. But they don't like hydrophilic [moisture-absorbent] Rice Krispies. They push each other apart. I suspect candle wax doesn't like cornflakes either.'

How do they keep all the raisins in cereal boxes from falling to the bottom?

The Rule of Popcorn Physics, which states that unpopped popcorn kernels fall to the bottom of the bowl, has saved many a tooth for generations. The explanation is easy enough to comprehend: unpopped kernels fall to the bottom both because their density is greater than expanded popcorn and because our handling of the corn creates crevices for the unpopped kernel to slide down.

Many inquisitive types have searched for corollaries to the Popcorn Physics rule. For example, the tenet of Slithery Sundaes posits that regardless of how much syrup or toppings one puts atop ice cream in a sundae, it will all fall to the bottom of the bowl anyway, collecting in a pool of glop.

So it was not without a feeling of reverence and awe that we approached the subject of raisins in cereal boxes, tiny dried grapes that seem to defy the usual laws of food gravity. Linda E Belisle, at US breakfast cereal maker General Mills, supplied the simple but elegant solution.

Raisins are added to boxes only after more than half of the cereal has already been packed. The cereal thus has a chance to settle and condense. During average shipping conditions, boxes get jostled a bit (the equivalent of our stirring the contents of a popcorn bowl while grabbing a fistful), so the raisins actually sift and become evenly distributed throughout the box.

Why do onions make us cry?

Let's look at it from the point of view of the onion. An onion is perfectly polite to us until we start hacking at it with a knife. Alas, the act of cutting enlivens a gas, propanethiol S-oxide, which works in tandem with the enzymes in the onion to unleash a passive sulphur compound found within the onion. The result: as you cut, the gas moves upwards and, combined with the water in your eyes, creates sulphuric acid.

Your eyes aren't happy, even if you are, and react in the only way they know how when irritated by a foreign substance – they start tearing. Rubbing your eyes with your hands is about the worst way to alleviate the problem, since your hands are likely full of the tear-inducing agent too.

We've heard all kinds of folk remedies for onion tears, ranging from rubbing the onion with lemon to wearing gloves as you cut to donning scuba diving masks while performing surgery. But we're of the old school: no pain, no gain.

The tendency of cereal to condense within the packet is responsible for the warning on most cereal packets that the contents are measured by weight rather than volume. Little did you know that this condensation was also responsible for the Law of Rising Raisins.

Why doesn't milk in the fridge ever taste as cold as the water or soft drinks in the fridge?

Actually, milk *does* get as cold as water or soft drinks. If you are having a particularly boring Saturday night, you might want to stick a thermometer into the liquids to prove this.

Milk at the same temperature as water or soft drinks just doesn't taste as cold to us because milk contains fat solids. We perceive solids as less cold than liquids. Taste experts refer to this phenomenon as 'mouth feel'.

If the milk/water/soft drink test wasn't exciting enough for you, run a test in your freezer compartment that will demonstrate the same principle. Put a container of premium high-fat ice cream in the freezer along with a container of low-fat or non-fat frozen yogurt. Consume them. We'll bet you two to one that the yogurt will taste colder than the ice cream.

For the sake of research, we recently performed this experiment with due rigour, and because we wanted to go out of our way to assure the accuracy of the experiment, we conducted the test on many different flavours of ice cream and yogurt. Oh, the sacrifices we make for our readers!

Why does milk obtain a skin when it is heated, while thicker liquids, like gravy, lose their skin when heated?

Proteins and starch react differently to heat. When heated, the protein in milk coagulates; the fat globules no longer can be suspended in water and, being lighter than water, float to the top.

Bruce Snow, a dairy consultant, told us that the fat globules 'adhere and form a surface skin when the liquid ceases to boil or simmer heavily'. But when gravy is heated, the starch, which has formed the skin in the first place, breaks down. Since starch is more soluble than protein, the result is that the ex-skin is reabsorbed into the rest of the gravy. The same process can be seen when soup is reheated after a skin has 'grown' in the fridge.

Why does warm milk serve as an effective sleep-inducer for many people?

Scientists haven't been able to verify it, but there is some evidence to support the idea that milk actually might induce sleep. Milk contains tryptophan, an amino acid, which is the precursor of a brain transmitter, serotonin, which we know has sedative qualities.

But does cow's milk contain enough tryptophan to induce sleepiness? This has yet to be proven. Representatives of the dairy industry, who might be the first to claim such a benefit for milk, are reluctant to do so and are openly sceptical about its sleep-inducing qualities.

Jean Naras, a media relations specialist at the American Dairy Association, although dubious about the sedative effects of milk, cited research that indicated it might take a dose as high as 2 litres to provide any sleep benefits. And with this quantity of milk intake, your bladder might argue with your brain about whether you really want to sleep through the night.

And does warm milk promote sleep any better than cold milk? It does if you believe it does, but none of the experts we consulted could provide a single logical reason why it should.

What is the liquid that forms on top of yogurt? Is it water or does it have nutrients? Should it be drained or stirred back into the yogurt?

That liquid is whey, the very stuff that Little Miss Muffet ate on a tuffet. When the bacteria that forms yogurt grows sufficiently, the milk coagulates. The proteins squeeze together and form curds, pushing out the watery whey.

Whey may be watery, but it isn't water. Whey contains sugar, minerals, some protein and lactose. Don't waste it. Mix it back in with the rest of the yogurt. You'll be a better person (nutritionally, anyway) for it.

What causes the holes in Swiss cheese?

The cheese industry prefers to call these openings 'eyes' rather than holes. The eyes are created by expanding gases that are released by a bacterium known as the 'eye former', introduced during the early stages of Swiss cheese production. The bacterium forms the holes, helps to ripen the cheese, and lends Swiss cheese its distinctive flavour.

So, the eyes are not there for cosmetic purposes. But, some 'Swiss' cheesemakers mechanically 'add' holes to already formed cheese produced without the eye-former bacterium. This shortcut is what robs some varieties of the mature flavour of genuine Swiss cheese.

Why does orange juice taste so awful after you've brushed your teeth?

Catherine Clay, of the State of Florida Department of Citrus, offers advice that is hard to refute:

> 'Most dentists suggest it is better to drink orange juice first, rinse the mouth with water, then brush the teeth, since we should brush after eating or drinking rather than before. Based on personal experience, I can tell you that drinking the orange juice prior to brushing seems to reduce the terrible taste problems considerably.'

Flawless advice, Catherine, but where's your sense of danger?

For those of you who have never walked on the wild side, you've probably experienced a lesser version of the 'toothpaste-orange juice syndrome'. Perhaps you've followed a heaping portion of sweet cake with lemonade and thought that someone forgot to put sugar in the lemonade.

The toothpaste-orange juice syndrome works in reverse too. We've always found that oranges taste particularly sweet after we've eaten some gherkins. These kinds of 'flavour synergies' can work for bad or good (oenologists would argue that a Bordeaux and a medium-rare steak work together to enhance the taste of each) but aren't the same phenomenon as an actual chemical reaction. Toothpaste contains a chemical base, such as baking soda, while orange juice and other citrus fruits contain citric acid. The experts we spoke to were not sure of whether there might be a chemical reaction that would affect the taste of orange juice so drastically.

Clay cited the mint flavourings of most toothpastes as an offender as well:

> Eating a peppermint, spearmint or other mint sweet, then drinking orange juice results in the same problem. Also, most toothpaste products are formulated to prolong the mint flavour to enhance the belief in long-lasting, fresh breath.

The most likely culprit in the particularly awful toothpaste-orange juice synergy, though, is an ingredient in all of the biggest brands of toothpaste: sodium lauryl sulfate, or SLS. You'll find SLS not only in toothpaste, but also in shampoo, shaving cream, soap and, ahem, concrete cleaners, engine degreasers and car wash detergents. What do all of these products have in common? The need for foam. SLS, a derivative of coconut oil, is a detergent foaming agent used to break down the surface tension of water and penetrate solids while generating prodigious amounts of foam.

Taste researcher Linda Bartoshuk, of the Yale University School of Medicine, notes that the active layer in the taste system is a phospholipid layer:

Why does butter get darker and harder in the fridge after it is opened?

Butter discolours for the same reason that apples or bananas turn dark – oxidation. And although butter doesn't have a peel to protect it from the ravages of air, it does have a wrapper surrounding it until it is first used. Only after the wrapper is eliminated or loosened does the butter darken.

Why does it get harder? The cold temperature in the refrigerator causes the moisture in the butter to evaporate. Many other foods, such as peanut butter, become less plastic when refrigerated because of evaporation of liquid.

> You know what happens to a layer of lipid when you add a detergent to it? Well, that's what happens to your taste system when you put detergent in your mouth, brushing teeth. So you brush teeth and the phenomenon is that your ability to taste sweet declines, and everything that should normally taste sweet, tastes as if a bitter taste has been added to it.

SLS will also affect your perception of salty foods. If you eat salty snacks such as potato crisps after brushing your teeth, the salt taste will be faint or missing, but any bitter taste will be magnified.

If toothpaste-orange juice syndrome is ruining your life, you can always look for a toothpaste in a health food store that doesn't contain SLS. Although we don't know of any country that bans the use of SLS in toothpaste, a search on the Internet indicates that some people are concerned about its harmful properties. Warnings abound that SLS can harm the skin, the eyes, hair and immune system.

Although SLS does help clean the teeth, there are many detergents that are as effective. But consumers believe that the more suds they can generate in anything from bar soap to shampoo to toothpaste, the more effective the cleaning will be. If that were true, we would all take daily bubble baths.

Why does 'smoke' escape from the bottle just after fizzy drinks are opened?

Who would better know the answer to this Imponderable than Lori A McManes, a senior consumer affairs specialist at Coca-Cola?

> The "smoke" seen escaping from a bottle of soft drink just after it is opened is condensed water vapour. Water vapour is present along with carbon dioxide in the bottle's head space, the space between the liquid soft drink and the bottle cap. When the bottle is opened, pressure inside the bottle is quickly released and these gases escape. This sudden release of pressure causes a rapid reduction in temperature in the area surrounding the opened bottle. This decrease in temperature, in turn, causes the water vapour that has escaped to condense, and gives it the wispy appearance of "smoke".

An old friend of *Imponderables*, Pepsi's Christine Jones, says that we see the same effect all the time in our everyday lives when we walk outside on a cold day and see our breaths creating 'smoke'.

How and why did 7UP get its name?

7UP (also known as Seven-Up) was the brainchild of an ex-advertising and merchandising executive, CL Grigg. In 1920, Grigg formed the Howdy Company in St Louis, Missouri, and found success with his first product, Howdy Orange drink.

Intent upon expanding his empire, Grigg spent several years testing 11 different formulas of lemon-flavoured soft drinks. In 1929, he introduced Seven-Up, then a caramel-coloured beverage.

So where did the '7' and 'UP' come from? Despite its identification as a lemon-lime drink, 7UP is actually a blend of seven natural flavours. According to Jim Ball, Vice-President of Corporate Communications for Dr Pepper/Seven-Up Companies, Inc., all of the early advertisements for the new drink described a product that was uplifting and featured a logo with a winged 7. Long before any caffeine scares, 7UP was promoted as a tonic for our physical and emotional ills:

- 'Seven-Up energizes – sets you up – dispels brain cobwebs and muscular fatigue.'
- 'Seven-Up is as pure as mountain snows ... '
- 'Fills the mouth [true, but then so does cough syrup] – thrills the taste buds – cools the blood – energizes the muscles – soothes the nerves – and makes your body alive – glad – happy.'

7UP's advertising has improved and changed markedly over the years, but its name has proved to be durably effective, even if customers don't have the slightest idea what 'Seven-Up' means. Grigg could have chosen much worse. Contemplate sophisticated adults sidling up to a bar and ordering a rum and Howdy Lemon-Lime drink.

Why do lobsters turn bright red when boiled?

Wouldn't you get flushed if you were dumped into a vat of boiling water? But seriously, before the lobster gets boiled, it has a dark purplish-bluish colour. But hidden in the exoskeleton of lobsters (and prawns) is a pigment called astaxanthin, in a class of compounds called carotenoids.

We spoke to Robert Rofen, of the Aquatic Research Institute, and Ray Bauer, of the Biology Department at the University of Louisiana at Lafayette, who explained that astaxanthin is connected to a protein. When you boil lobsters, though, the pigment separates from the protein and returns to its 'true colour', which is the bright red associated with hot flushes and hefty credit-card bills.

Why do chickens and turkeys, unlike other fowl, have white meat and dark meat?

Other birds that we eat, such as quail or duck, have all dark meat. Chickens and turkeys are among a small group of birds with white flesh on the breasts and wings. Birds have two types of muscle fibres: red and white. Red muscle fibres contain more myoglobin, a muscle protein with a red pigment. Muscles with a high amount of myoglobin are capable of much longer periods of work and stress than white fibres. Thus, you can guess which birds are likely to have light fibres by studying their feeding and migration patterns.

Most birds have to fly long distances to migrate or to find food, and they need the endurance that myoglobin provides. All birds that appear to have all white flesh actually have some red fibres, and with one exception, all birds that appear to be all dark have white fibres. But the hummingbird, which rarely stops flying, has pectoral muscles consisting entirely of red fibres because the pectoral muscles enable the wings to flap continuously.

The domestic chicken or turkey, on the other hand, lives the life of Riley. Even in their native habitat, according to Dr Phil Hudspeth, Vice-President of Quality and Research at Holly Farms, chickens are ground feeders and fly only when nesting. Ordinarily, chickens move around by walking or running, which is why only their legs and thighs are dark.

They fly so little that their wings and breasts don't need myoglobin. In fact, the lack of myoglobin in the wing and breast are an anatomical advantage. Janet

Hinshaw, of the Wilson Ornithological Society, explains why chicken and turkey musculature is perfectly appropriate:

> They spend most of their time walking. When danger threatens, they fly in a burst of speed for a short distance and then land. Thus they need flight muscles that deliver a lot of power quickly but for a short time.

Is the red colour in cooked beef simply blood? If so, why doesn't it discolour when exposed to oxygen?

Many people who don't like rare meat cite as the reason: 'I can't stand the sight of blood.' Actually they can't stand the sight of myoglobin. For this water-soluble protein is most responsible for the red colour we associate with meat.

For those of you who consider eating a rare steak the gastronomic equivalent of vampirism, you'd be surprised to learn what Dennis Buege, of the meat sciences department at the University of Wisconsin, told us: less than 20 per cent of the normal amount of blood found in living tissue remains in a piece of meat sold in a supermarket. Myoglobin functions much the same way as haemoglobin does in our bodies. Haemoglobin carries oxygen from our lungs to our bodies; myoglobin stores the oxygen the haemoglobin has brought to the tissues.

But myoglobin is also what's called a 'protein pigment'. It helps colour the meat. When meat is fresh cut and not exposed to oxygen, it has a purplish colour; once exposed to air (oxygenation), the muscle tissue quickly changes to red.

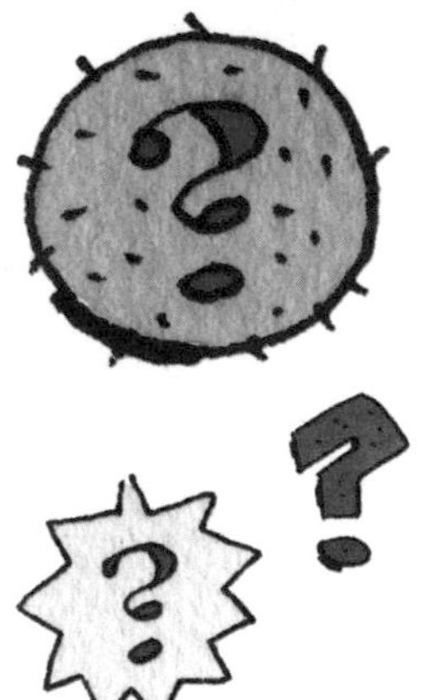

This red colour is what we associate with raw beef at the meat counter. Although it might seem that the clear film wrapping used to cover meat in supermarkets is designed to prevent oxygen from attacking the meat, Buege informed us that the opposite is the case. The film is designed to permit oxygen to pass through in order to maintain the red colour that consumers prefer. Oxygenation also explains why the inside of minced beef looks a different colour than its bright red exterior – for only the inside of the meat has been 'deprived' of oxygen and has retained its natural colouring.

Buege bemoans our aesthetic preference for 'red meat' because it accelerates the spoilage rate. If fresh meat were vacuum-packed, and did not go through the oxygenation process, we might be deprived of the chance to choose between fire-engine-red meats in refrigerated cases, but it would extend the shelf life of fresh meat from the current two to four days to an astonishing 10 to 14 days.

Why doesn't cooked meat discolour when confronted with ambient air? According to Janet Collins Williams, Vice-President of Scientific and Technical Affairs for the American Meat Institute, the colour change caused by oxygenation is reversible in the muscle:

> as long as there remains adequate stored energy in the muscle for the pigment conversion. However, once the energy is depleted, and/or once the protein portion of the pigment is heated (when the muscle is cooked), the colour is "set" ... Depending upon the degree of heating of the tissue (degree of doneness in the meat), the protein is actually denatured, and the original colour(s) is destroyed. Therefore, the meat does not change colour or discolour when exposed to air – it is stable.

What's the difference between virgin olive oil and extra virgin olive oil?

We promised ourselves that we wouldn't make any jokes about virgins being hard to find and extra-virgins being impossible to find, so we won't. We will keep a totally straight face while answering this important culinary Imponderable.

We may have trouble negotiating arms reductions, but on one issue the nations of the world agree; thus, the International Olive and Olive Oil Agreement of 1986. This agreement defines the terms 'virgin olive oil' and 'extra virgin olive oil'.

Any olive oil that wants to call itself virgin must be obtained from the fruit of the olive tree solely by mechanical or other physical means rather than by a heating process. The oil cannot be refined or diluted, but may be washed, decanted and filtered.

The lowest grade of virgin olive oil is semi-fine virgin olive oil, which is sold in stores as 'virgin'. This oil must be judged to have a good flavour and no more than 3 g of free oleic acid per 100 g of oil. The next highest grade, fine virgin olive oil, cannot exceed 1.5 g of oleic acid per 100 g and must have excellent taste. Extra virgin olive oil must have 'absolutely perfect flavour' and maximum acidity of 1 g per 100 g. According to José Luis Perez Sanchez, Commercial Counsellor of the Embassy of Spain, extra virgin olives are often used with different kinds of natural flavours and are quite expensive, which any trip to the local gourmet deli will affirm.

As with many other food items, the prize commodity (extra virgin olive oil) is the one that achieves quality by omission. By being free of extraneous flavours or high acidity, the 'special' olive oil is the one that manages what wouldn't seem like too difficult a task: to taste like olives.

What happens to olives after the oil is removed?

Extracting olive oil from olives is a little trickier than juicing a grape or an orange. Olives don't contain as much moisture content as grapes and possess nasty, hard pips.

The first important step in making olive oil, after separating the olives from dirt, leaves and other contaminants, is pushing them through a mill or grinder, which turns them into a fine paste. Usually, the olive pips are left in before processing; they don't have much effect on flavour and contribute little to the volume of oil – but 'destoning' olives adds another step, and expense, to the process.

After the olives are mashed into paste form, the paste is mixed ('malaxation') for about half an hour, which allows larger bubbles of oil to coalesce. The next stage is crucial – extracting the oil from the water in the paste, usually accomplished by one of two types of machine: a press or a centrifuge.

Although the valuable oil has been extracted, and the olives have lost all of their original texture, olive oil producers don't discard the waste product, which is called 'pomace'. Paul Vossen, a University of California farm advisor, told *Imponderables* about the fate of the pomace:

> ‘The pomace can be used for compost, or if the pit fragments are removed and it is somewhat dried, it can be fed to livestock. In Europe, North Africa and the Middle East, the pomace is placed into solvent tanks and the remaining small amount of oil is removed; the solvent-extracted oil is refined and sold as pomace oil. The spent pomace is usually burned to generate heat and dry the pomace before it is solvent-extracted.’

The pomace olive oil is controversial in the trade. As we discussed above, virgin and extra virgin olive oil are prized not only for their low acidity and fine taste, but also for the lack of processing used to extract them. Purveyors of fine olive oils tend to look down on solvent-extracted pomace oil, especially because pomace can legally be labelled 'olive oil'. Betty Pustarfi, owner of Strictly Olive Oil in Pebble Beach, California, refers to pomace olive oil as industry-denigrated oil because it is used to:

> mix itself with the real stuff so it can be sold to consumers as premium, or most frequently, sold or used to be blended with the real stuff for use in the food service or production industry. Pomace olive oil is a lubricant, not a condiment, though it has most of the health values of the real stuff and is an accepted carrier for the real stuff as long as it is so labelled.

Why does pasta create foam when boiling?

Pasta is made from durum wheat, a particularly hard wheat. More precisely, pasta is created from durum wheat semolina, fine particles derived from the much coarser durum. The extraction of the semolina is largely responsible for the foaming of pasta when cooking, as Farook Taufiq, Vice-President of Quality Assurance at the US pasta maker Prince Company, explains:

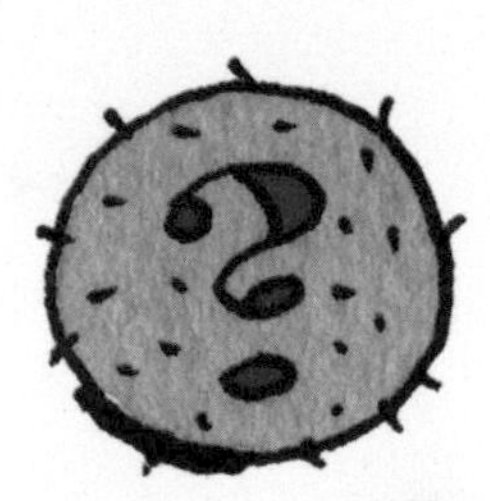

> Durum wheat semolina consists of carbohydrates (starches) and protein. In the process of grinding wheat to extract semolina, some starch links are broken. When pasta is put in boiling water, these broken starch links swell up, taking in tiny air bubbles, along with water.
>
> These air bubbles come to the surface of the boiling water and appear as foam. So the foam is a combination of starch molecules, water and air.

Why does grease turn white when it cools?

You finish frying some chicken. You reach for the old coffee tin you use to discard hot oil. You open the lid and the congealed grease inside is thick, not thin, and not the yellowish-gold colour of the frying oil you put in before, but whitish, the colour of glazed cake icing. Why is the fat more transparent when it is an oil than when it is grease?

When the oil cools, it changes its physical state, just as transparent water changes into more opaque ice when it freezes. Bill DeBuvitz, a longtime *Imponderables* reader and, more to the point, Associate Professor of Physics at Middlesex County College in New Jersey, explains:

> When the grease cools, it changes from a liquid to a solid. Because of its molecular structure, it cannot quite form a crystalline structure. Instead, it forms "amorphous regions" and "partial crystals". These irregular areas scatter white light and make the grease appear cloudy.
>
> If grease were to solidify into a pure crystal, it would be much clearer, maybe like glass. Incidentally, paraffins like candle wax behave just like grease: they are clear in the liquid form and cloudy in the solid form.

Why does pepper make us sneeze?

Other hot, spicy foods make us wince, make us gasp for air and make us pour huge quantities of cold liquids down our throats. But why does only pepper make us sneeze?

The essential oils found in pepper are the culprit, according to Polly Murphy, Manager of Consumer Affairs for spice maker McCormick and Company. These oils, which can be extracted from the berries of the pepper plant, are used by food manufacturers to flavour sausages, sauces, salad dressings, processed meats and many other foods.

But eating meat seasoned with pepper doesn't make you sneeze. The major culprit is piperine, a chemical found in black and white pepper. Thomas F Burns, Executive Vice-President of the American Spice Trade Association, explains:

> Piperine provides the pleasant biting sensation that accompanies the aroma to the mouth when it is tasted. Since piperine bites the tongue, it obviously also bites the delicate membranes of the nose.

Other chillis also contain chemicals that 'bite' much like piperine. Our table pepper, though, tends to be ground finely. When particles of, say, black pepper, are drawn into the nose, our body has the good sense to try to expel the particles, just as it would try to expel any other dust particles.

Burns suggests, in the spirit of the James Bond entreaty that martinis should be 'shaken, not stirred': 'Pepper should be smelled, not sniffed. Its delicate aroma is one of its great attributes and can only be appreciated when inhaled slowly.'

Why is saffron ridiculously expensive?

The saffron threads used to colour and flavour many dishes, especially in Middle Eastern and Asian cooking, are the golden orange stigmata of the autumn crocus, a plant of the iris family. Autumn crocuses aren't rare. So why is saffron so dear?

There are two reasons. The crocus flowers must be picked by hand to extract the saffron threads. As many as 500,000 flowers (1.5 million stigmata) are needed to collect just 500 g of saffron.

The flowers are picked immediately after they blossom, and the stigmata are cut with fingernails and then dried by the sun or by fire. During this drying process, the saffron loses about 80 per cent of its weight.

Saffron could be cultivated in the West and still is grown in parts of the Mediterranean, but where could affluent countries find labour inexpensive enough to produce saffron as cheaply as the 'ridiculously expensive' price we pay today?

Why do baked goods straight from the oven often taste (sickeningly) richer than they do after they have cooled?

When you ponder this Imponderable for a while, you realise there are only two approaches to the answer: one, the baked item really is different straight from the oven than it is 10 or 20 minutes later, or two, that for some reason, the taster perceives the same item differently depending upon when it is consumed. It turns out there are some experts who subscribe to each explanation.

Bakery expert Simon S Jackel assures us that items really do change in structure after being cooled because of a process called 'starch retrogradation'. In raw flour, starch exists in a coiled, closed structure. When flour is baked into bread or cakes, the starch uncoils and opens up when exposed to the water in the dough and the high temperature of the oven.

When the product comes out of the oven, it starts to cool down, and the starch begins to revert or 'retrograde' to a partially coiled structure. Most importantly for our purposes, when the starch retrogrades, it absorbs some of the flavours and locks them up in the coiled starch so that the taste buds cannot process them. In other words, less flavour is available to the consumer as the product cools. Jackel states that retrogradation continues until the product is stale.

Two other baking experts lay the 'blame' on our noses. Joe Andrews, Publicity Coordinator for Pillsbury Brands, explains:

> ‘A great deal of taste perception is determined not only by the taste buds, but also by the olfactory senses ... When a food is hot, it releases many volatiles that the nose may perceive as sweet. Thus a cake may seem sweeter when it is warm than when it is cold. The volatiles are perceived by the nose, both by sniffing through the nostrils and by the aromatics released in the mouth that make their way to the nose via a hole in the back of the mouth, the nasopharynx. We say we "taste" these, but in actuality we are smelling them.’

Andrews believes that the 'richness' our correspondent complains about may actually be sweetness.

Tom Lehmann, of the American Institute of Baking, also emphasises the importance of volatiles in taste perception. Many aromatics, including spices, are simply too powerful when hot. Lehmann blames egg whites as particular culprits in making hot baked goods smell vile and taste awful. Angel food cake, a dessert with a high concentration of egg whites, is particularly horrible hot, Lehmann says, because egg whites contain volatiles that are released in heat and have to cool completely in order to avoid producing an unpleasant smell.

Of course, there is nothing mutually exclusive about the retrogradation and volatiles theories. Unlike arguments about creationism versus evolution, the theories can coexist peacefully and respectfully. After all, bakers are engaged in an important and soul-lifting pursuit; it's hard to get bitter and angry when your life revolves around a task as noble as trying to concoct the perfect doughnut.

Why does a loud bang or opening and closing the oven door sometimes make soufflés and cakes fall in the oven?

Tom Lehmann, of the American Institute of Baking, told *Imponderables* that while a cake is being baked, the mixture rises to a point slightly higher than its fully baked height. The baking powder in the batter produces gas that causes the leavening effect. 'At a time when the batter is at its maximum height, but has not "set" due to starch gelatinisation and protein coagulation, the batter is very unstable.' The cake is at its most fragile and delicate because, according to bakery expert Simon S Jackel, 'the air cells holding the entrapped gases are very thin and weak'.

Not all cakes will crash if confronted with a loud noise. But most will fall during this vulnerable time during the cooking process, and soufflés are always in danger. Joe Andrews, Publicity Coordinator for Pillsbury Brands, explains:

> 'The basic structure of a soufflé is developed by egg proteins, which are whipped into a foam and then set by baking. When whipping of the egg whites occurs, large pockets of air are trapped by the albumen, and, in the process, this protein is partially denatured. The denaturation (or setting) continues (along with the expansion of the air bubbles) when the proteins are heated in the oven. If the oven is opened while this expansion is taking place, the air pressure change and temperature change can cause the whole structure to collapse.'

The most common bang, of course, is the opening and closing of the oven door. Anyone near a loudspeaker at a rock concert knows that sound vibrations can be felt; a soufflé or cake can be pummelled by a nearby noise. Although cakes are usually hardier than soufflés, Andrews indicates the same problems that afflict soufflés also make cakes fall, especially if the primary source of leavening for the cake is beaten egg whites (e.g. angel food or whisked sponge cakes). Layer cakes contain more flour and the structure is formed as much by starch gelatinisation as egg denaturation, so they would not be as susceptible to falling when the door is opened – unless the door is opened too early in the baking process (during the first 20 minutes), before the cake structure has set.

Only when the internal temperature of the cake reaches a range of 70 to 80°C is the cake out of the woods, because, as Jackel puts it, 'the liquid batter is now converted to a solid cake structure'.

Why do doughnuts have holes?

The exact origins of doughnuts and their holes are shrouded in mystery and are a topic of such controversy that we have twice been caught in the middle of heated arguments among professional bakers on radio chat shows. So let us make one thing perfectly clear: we offer no conclusive proof here, only consensus opinion.

Some form of fried cake has existed in almost every culture. 'Prehistoric doughnuts' – petrified fried cakes with hole – have been found among the artefacts of a Native American tribe. The Dutch settlers, though, are usually credited with popularising fried cakes (without holes) in the United States, which they called 'oily cakes' or *olykoeks*. Washington Irving, writing about colonial New York, described 'a dish of balls of sweetened dough fried in hog's fat, and called dough nuts or oly koeks'.

Fried cakes became so popular that shops sprouted up that specialised in serving them with fresh-brewed coffee. In 1673, the first store-bought fried cakes were made available by Anna Joralemon in New York. Mrs Joralemon weighed 100 kg and was known affectionately as 'the Big Doughnut'.

The gentleman usually credited with the 'invention' of the doughnut hole was an unlikely candidate for the job – a sea captain named Hanson Gregory. Supposedly, Captain Gregory was at the helm of his ship, eating a fried cake one night, when stormy weather arose. Gregory, needing both hands to steer the ship, spontaneously rammed the cake over one of the spokes of the steering wheel. Impressed with his creation, Gregory ordered the ship's cook to make fried cakes with holes from then on.

Many other legends surround the creation of the doughnut hole. Plymouth, Massachusetts, advances the notion that the first doughnut hole was created when, in the seventeenth century, a drunken Native American brave shot an arrow through a kitchen window, punching out a piece of dough from the centre of a cake just about to be fried. Pretty lame, Plymouth.

Regardless of the origin of the holes in doughnuts, we have learned that bakers disagree about its role in the making of a quality doughnut. Certainly, good doughnuts can be made without holes.

Tom Lehmann, of the American Institute of Baking, told us that yeast-raised doughnuts can be made quite easily without the hole and points to the bismarck, or jam-filled doughnut, as a perfect example. Lehmann adds, though, that if bismarcks were fried on the surface, the same way as conventional yeast-raised doughnuts, the holeless dough would tend to overexpand, turning into a ball shape. That is why most bakers prefer submersion frying, which results in a more uniform and symmetrical finished product.

'Cake' doughnuts, which are chemically leavened, can also be made without holes, but many experts believe that they lose their desired consistency without them. Glenn Bacheller, Director of Product Marketing for the US doughnut chain Dunkin' Donuts, explains why the hole is important:

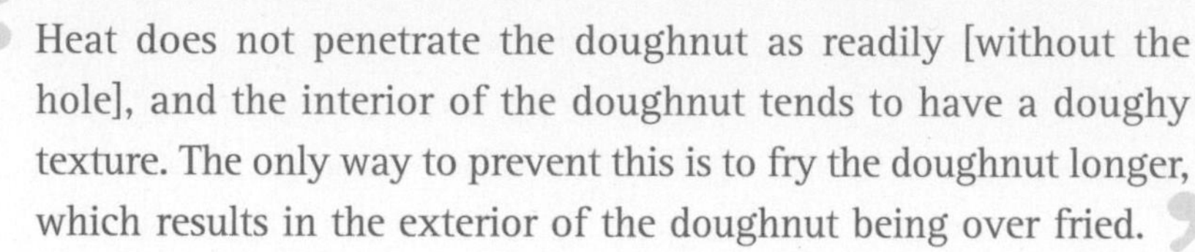

> Heat does not penetrate the doughnut as readily [without the hole], and the interior of the doughnut tends to have a doughy texture. The only way to prevent this is to fry the doughnut longer, which results in the exterior of the doughnut being over fried.

Why do ketchup bottles have necks so narrow that a spoon won't fit inside?

Heinz has had a stranglehold on the ketchup business in the Western world for more than a century, so the story of ketchup bottle necks is pretty much the story of Heinz Ketchup bottle necks. Ironically, although Heinz ads now boast about the difficulty of pouring their rather thick ketchup, it wasn't always so.

When Heinz Ketchup was first introduced in 1876, it was considerably thinner in consistency. It came in an octagonal bottle with a narrow neck intended to help impede the flow of the product. Prior to the Heinz bottle, most condiments were sold in crocks and sharply ridged bottles that were uncomfortable to hold.

Over the last 130 years, the basic design of the Heinz Ketchup bottle has changed little. The 1914 bottle looks much like today's. Heinz was aware that as their ketchup recipe changed and yielded a thicker product, it poured less easily through their thin-necked bottle. But they also knew that consumers preferred the thick consistency and rejected attempts to dramatically alter the by-now-familiar container.

Heinz's solution to the problem was the marketing of a 12-ounce (350 ml) wide-mouthed bottle, introduced in the 1960s. Gary D Smith, in the communications department of Heinz USA, told *Imponderables* that the wide-mouthed bottle, more than capable of welcoming a spoon, is the 'least popular member of the Heinz Ketchup family'. He added, though, that 'its discontinuance would raise much fervour from its small band of loyal consumers who enjoy being able to spoon on' their ketchup.

In 1983, Heinz unveiled plastic squeeze bottles, which not only solved the pourability problem but also solved the breakability problem. The plastic bottles, while available in sizes up to 1.2 kg, still have a relatively thin neck.

Until 1888, Heinz bottles were sealed with a cork. The neckband at the top of the bottle was initially designed to keep a foil cap snug against its cork and sealing wax. Although it was rendered obsolete by the introduction of screw-on caps, the neckband was retained as a signature of Heinz Ketchup.

Why do bananas, unlike other fruit, grow upwards?

If you knew about the tumultuous birth process of the banana, perhaps you would be more charitable the next time you encounter some bruised specimens when you go shopping.

The banana is actually a giant herb in the same biological family as lilies, orchids and palms. It is the largest plant on earth without a woody stem – a banana stalk is 93 per cent water – and is consequently extremely fragile. Although it can reach a full height of 5 to 10 m in one year, even moderate winds can blow down a plant.

The fruit stem or bunch originates at ground level. At this stage, the bunch consists of all of the fruit enclosed in leaf bracts. The individual fruit 'fingers' (the technical name for a single banana) are pointed upwards. As the bunch or bud is pushing its way through the mass of lightly packed leaf sheaths known as the pseudostem, the fruit fingers remain pointed upwards until they emerge at the top of the plant.

The bananas exert tremendous pressure on the pseudostem. Before the fruits expand, the leaves enclosing them roll around on themselves inside the trunk. After the fruit emerges from the leaves, the fingers point downwards, but only because the bud surrounding them has changed direction.

Once the entire bunch of bananas is mature, fully emerged from its sheath, and pointing downwards, the individual leaf bracts enclosing the hands (the female flower cluster) fall away, exposing the fruit. At this point, the individual flowers grow rapidly, filling out. Their increased weight bends the main stalk so that the individual fruits on the hand start to turn upwards in about seven to 10 days.

Dr Pedro Sole, of Chiquita Brands, points out that, in the past, 'primitive bananas grew upwards, like the seeds of most grasses forming a spike'. So is there a logical reason for the banana's tortuous up-and-down birthing process now?

Jack D DeMent, of the Dole Fresh Fruit Company, sees the answer in the behaviour of the traditional non-commercial banana plant:

> A flower is found on the tip of each individual fruit. This flower is removed during [commercial] packing but is present during fruit development. As the hands turn up, the flower is better exposed to insects and nectar-eating birds and bats. Their feeding would normally aid in fertilisation of the fruit. Today's commercial banana is sterile and rarely – almost never – produces a viable seed.

DeMent theorises that the commercial banana's tendency to grow upwards is a holdover from its ancestors that needed to point upwards for their very survival.

Presumably, natural selection will simplify the growth process of the banana over the next few hundred thousand years or so.

Why do apples and pears discolour so quickly when they are peeled?

Our theory about this Imponderable is simple: we have had it drummed into our heads by teachers, parents and nutritionists that the peels of fruits are the 'best' part, full of vitamins and fibre. The spotting is nature's way of forcing the point – who is going to peel an apple when one ends up with leopard-skin flesh?

Why aren't cashews ever sold in their shells?

Cashews aren't sold in their shells because they don't have a shell. Don't all nuts have shells? Yes. Then what gives? We would never be pedantic, but we must insist that a cashew is a seed, not a nut. It is the seed of a pear-shaped fruit, the cashew apple, which is itself edible. The cashew seed hangs at the lower end of the fruit, vulnerable and exposed. Cashews grow not on trees, but on tropical shrubs. A hard or leathery shell is what differentiates a nut from a seed. Kernels with thin, soft shells, such as pumpkins and sunflowers, are properly called seeds.

But pomologists (who study fruits) insist on a more technical explanation. The discolouration in fruits, including peaches, apricots and bananas, as well as apples and pears, is caused by oxidation. The catalyst for the oxidation is an enzyme, polyphenol oxidase.

According to John B Williams, of California Apple Products, Inc., polyphenol oxidase occurs naturally in all sugar-producing fruits in varying amounts: 'The amount of this enzyme will determine how quickly the browning occurs. The peel of most fruits will not allow oxygen to penetrate in sufficient quantities to act as a catalyst for the enzyme.' Banana peels are more porous than apple or pear skins, allowing oxygen to penetrate into the fruit while the skin is still in place. The sturdier apple peel is unlikely to discolour unless it is bruised or cut open.

Why aren't macadamia nuts sold in their shells?

Macadamia nuts do have shells. But selling them in their shells would present a serious marketing problem. Only Superman could eat them. According to the Mauna Loa Macadamia Nut Corporation, the largest producer of macadamias in the world, 'It takes 300-pounds-per-square-inch [about 2000 kPa] of pressure to break the shell.'

After macadamias are harvested, the husks are removed, and then the nuts are dried and cured to reduce their moisture. The drying process helps separate the kernel from the shell; without this separation, it would be impossible to apply the pressure necessary to shatter the shell without pulverising the contents. The nuts then pass through counter-rotating steel rollers spaced to break the shell without shattering the nutmeat.

How do they grow seedless grapes when all fruits grow from seed?

Seedless grapes are not really seedless at all. It's just that the seeds are impossible to detect when you eat them. You can see the seeds in a seedless grape if you split one in half, though. There they are: white, soft seedlings that are never going to get stuck in your teeth.

Those tiny seedlets are actually embryonic seeds that have been engineered not to grow. This can be done by fertilising the vine with pollen from an incompatible species; after a while the vine realises it's in a mismatch and gives up on the seed, but the fruit keeps on growing. Alternatively, the plant can be treated with a hormone that mimics fertilisation, so rendering the seed redundant and stunting its growth. Once an (almost) seedless grape variety has been produced, it's easy to propagate it endlessly from cuttings: seeds never need be part of the process again.

Why is peanut butter sticky?

Sometimes life is not simple. Peanuts are not nuts (they are legumes). Peanut butter isn't butter (there are no milk products in peanut butter). Peanuts aren't sticky (but peanut butter is).

It's not like we would use peanut butter in lieu of Super Glue, but we wonder what happens to the 850 whole shelled peanuts that go into one 500 ml jar of peanut butter to up their stickiness quotient. You've probably seen peanut butter ground from fresh salted peanuts in health food stores. No other ingredients are added, and yet the end result is as sticky as the best-selling commercial brands, which may contain small quantities of sugar or stabilisers (usually vegetable oil-based, to prevent the natural oil in the peanuts from separating). Although we thought that perhaps added oils were responsible for the stickiness of peanut butter, all of our sources agreed that the answer lies elsewhere.

What exactly is stickiness? When we think of a sticky substance, we tend to think of glue or masking tape, something that adheres to other stuff. But in its simplest terms, when a substance's molecules bond together in some way, we call it sticky. The stronger the bond, the stickier it is. Although peanut butter has some adhesive qualities, its adhesive qualities are not strong enough to tempt us to try securing a box of books with it.

But there's another form of stickiness – viscosity. A viscous fluid resists flowing and resists changing form when subjected to an outside force. We usually equate fluids with liquids, but thick substances such as peanut butter can be considered a fluid and possess a viscosity. Water has low viscosity, flows quickly and smoothly and can be stirred with a spoon with virtually no resistance.

High-viscosity fluids, such as tar and motor oil, do not move so efficiently, and peanut butter, as you might suspect, isn't likely to flow down a drain easily. Try stirring peanut butter (as fans of 'natural' peanut butter are likely to do to mix the oil that rises to the top with the rest of the 'butter') – it will strengthen your wrist.

On a plate or in our mouths, we tend to perceive high-viscosity foods as sticky, but not in the same way as the jelly babies that have clung to our teeth or the burned eggs that have stuck to an untreated frying pan. When we spread peanut butter with a knife, some of it sticks to the utensil, partly from adhesion, but mostly because adjacent molecules in the peanut butter stick together because of the food's high viscosity. The peanut butter resists flowing – it wants to stay in the same shape it was in.

Of the two main reasons why peanut butter is stickier than peanuts, both have to do with the higher viscosity of peanut butter. The first culprit is the size of the nut particles used in peanut butter. We corresponded with Harmeet S Guraya, a research food technologist at the Agricultural Research Service, a branch of the US Department of Agriculture. Guraya, whose specialty is analysing the textures and flavours of food, wrote:

> When you eat peanuts, when the particles are bigger during initial rupture or break-up of peanut, it is easy to chew. When you masticate the peanut and make it into a fine paste, then it gets sticky in your mouth.
>
> Commercial machines that make peanut butter grind the peanuts to different particle sizes, which is why you have different [levels of] stickiness [and thus spreadability] in different brands.

Although it may seem counterintuitive, the smaller the particle size, the more viscous the final product will be. This explains why peanuts get harder and harder to chew as you eat them – you are making peanut butter in your mouth!

The second reason why peanut butter is stickier than peanuts is that the grinding of the peanuts changes the molecular structure of the legume, releasing more viscous components. Sara J Risch, PhD, a food scientist and consultant to the Institute of Food Technologists, told *Imponderables*:

> In whole peanuts, the components such as the proteins and carbohydrates are enclosed in cells and held together. When the peanuts are ground, all of the cells are broken down and these materials released. This yields a material that is very viscous and thus sticky to the touch. Some of the stickiness

> [of the final product] could also be due to the proteins and carbohydrates. It is not from the oil.

Guraya emphasises that viscosity is not the same thing as stickiness, and that:

> the sensory perception of stickiness could be due to a variety of reasons for different foods. When I gave you the reasons for stickiness of peanut butter, it pertains only to peanut butter, although the definition of stickiness stays the same.

Although a few other factors, such as the type of stabilisers and the inclusion of high-moisture peanuts, can increase the viscosity quotient of peanut butter, the grinding process itself explains the perception of stickiness.

What causes green-tinged crisps?

Potatoes are supposed to grow underground, but occasionally one becomes ambitious and sticks its head out. Nature punishes the potato by giving it a nasty sunburn.

But why do potatoes turn green rather than red? No, it's not out of envy. The green colour is from chlorophyll, the natural consequence of a growing plant being exposed to light. According to Beverly Holmes, a public relations representative of Frito-Lay, crisp producers try to eliminate the green ones:

> We store our potatoes in dark rooms and have "pickers" on our production lines who attempt to eliminate [green] crisps as they move along on the conveyer belts because of their undesirable appearance. Nevertheless, a few green crisps can make their way through the production process.

Is it harmful to eat a green-tinged crisp? Not at all. Chlorophyll contains no artificial ingredients, and chlorophyll stains are harmless.

Why are crisps curved?

Potato crisps themselves, let alone their shape, were a fortuitous accident. The popular snack food was invented in 1853 by George Crum, a Native American, who was a cook at Moon Lake Lodge, an exclusive resort in Saratoga Springs, New York. A guest complained that the fried potatoes that Crum had cooked were too thick (in many accounts, this guest is said to be Commodore Cornelius Vanderbilt, the railroad magnate), and in retaliation for what he considered to be a supercilious request, the chef sliced potatoes paper thin and fried them.

The practical joke backfired. Vanderbilt, or whoever Crum's intended 'victim' was, loved what soon became known as 'Saratoga Chips', and the new dish became a staple at the resort. Other restaurants in the eastern United States borrowed the idea, but crisps were not produced for home use until William Tappenden of Cleveland, Ohio, started the first crisp factory in a converted barn in Cleveland.

The shape of Crum's and Tappenden's chips was the result of slicing the potatoes in the most efficient way possible. Marsha McNeil Sherman, Technical Director of the US Snack Food Association, told *Imponderables* that from the very beginning of the product until today, all the technology involved in washing, peeling, slicing, frying and packaging potato chips has revolved around avoiding waste by gearing equipment to take advantage of the natural, rounded shape of the potato:

> ‘The more uniform in size and shape the potato is, the less trimming is required to achieve crisps that are similar in size and shape, and that result in a greater yield of finished product. Round or oblong-shaped potatoes that are about 2.5 inches [about 6 cm] in diameter are ideal for crisp production.’

If the shape of the finished crisp is dictated by nature, so is the curl at the edges of crisps. Potatoes are composed of approximately 25 per cent solids (mostly starches and sugars) and 75 per cent water; but that ratio is not uniform throughout, as Sherman explains:

> ‘Generally, more of the solids' content is concentrated near the surface layers of the potato from the peel to the centre of the potato. Frying is a drying process, which means that potatoes with a high water content require more time and energy to cook

than potatoes with a high solids content. Potato crisps are cooked to a moisture content of about 1.5 per cent. The area of the slice with less moisture will fry faster than the area with more moisture. Therefore, the edges of the slice will fry faster than the middle and will curl. ’

What’s the difference between popcorn and other corn? Can any kind of corn be popped?

There are five different types of corn: dent, flint, pod, sweet and popcorn. Popcorn is the only variety that will pop consistently. Gregg Hoffman, of American Popcorn, told *Imponderables* that other corn might pop on occasion but with little regularity.

The key to popcorn’s popping ability is, amazingly, water. Each popcorn kernel contains water, which most popcorn processors try to maintain at about a 13.5 per cent level.

The water is stored in a small circle of soft starch in each kernel. Surrounding the soft starch is a hard enamel-like starch. When the kernel is heated for popping, the water inside heats and begins to expand. The function of the hard starch is to resist the water as long as possible.

When the water expands with such pressure that the hard starch gives way, the water bursts out, causing the kernel to explode. The soft starch pops out, and the kernel turns inside out. The water, converted into steam, is released (fogging the glasses of four-eyed popcorn makers), and the corn pops.

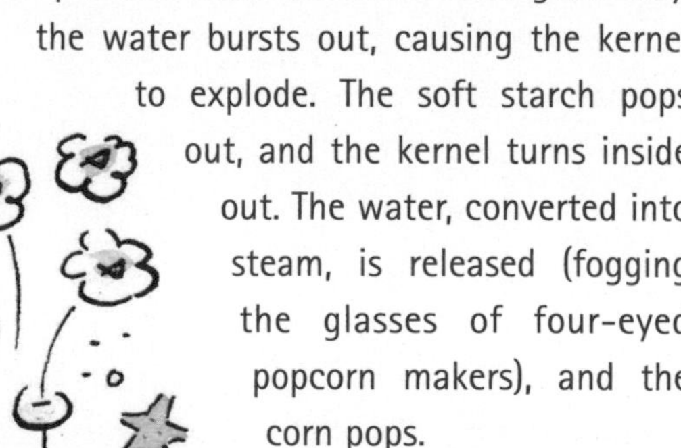

The other four varieties of corn are able to store water effectively. But their outer starch isn’t hard enough to withstand the water pressure of the expanding kernel, and so nothing pops.

How in the world were marshmallows invented?

We don't think it will shock you to discover that marshmallows are not a natural substance. No, marshmallows don't grow on trees, vines or underground.

But they weren't invented out of whole cloth, either. For there is a mallow plant, which, not coincidentally, tends to grow on marshes. The first people that we know to have eaten the mallow plant were the ancient Egyptians, long before the reign of Cleopatra. They dried and pulverised the plant and considered it a delicacy.

But marshmallows as we know them weren't possible until someone came up with the idea of combining the mallow plant with sugar, and it was almost certainly an accident. Sugar's first use was as a way of making medicines more palatable, but a recurring problem was the tendency of sugar to crystallise. In India, they solved the problem by using gum arabic, but some countries did not have access to this form of gum. When boiled in hot water, the ground roots of the mallow plant turned out to be an effective gum. Combined with sugar, the first marshmallow was born.

The French were the first to turn marshmallows into a confection for the masses. Kraft Foods supplied a report researched by the Marshmallow Research Foundation (there is a foundation or association for just about anything):

> 'The marshmallow in its present fluffy form originated in France and was known as *Pâté de Guimauve*. As made in the early nineteenth century, it contained the extract of the marshmallow root, dried and reduced to a powder. A light cream in colour, the genuine marshmallow base contained starch, sugar, pectin, asparagine and a substance allied to lecithin ... However, because marshmallow root reputedly possessed medicinal properties, it was early abandoned by confectioners as a necessary marshmallow ingredient.'

Mallow trees were naturalised in the salt marshes of the United States not long after they were introduced in Europe. At first, mallow root was used, but it was later abandoned in order to save money, and replaced by a combination of gum arabic and egg white.

Today, you can buy big marshmallows, little marshmallows, chocolate marshmallows and coconut marshmallows. But you can't find a marshmallow with mallow in it. We are left in the strange situation of eating a product that is named after an ingredient that is no longer in it.

How do they **print** the 'M&M' on M&M's chocolate **sweets?**

We contacted the consumer affairs division of Mars Incorporated, and although they were as helpful and friendly as could be, mere flattery, bribery and appeals to humanitarian instincts were not sufficient to pry away a definitive answer.

Despite wild theories to the contrary, the 'M&M' is printed on each sweet by machine, but the process is proprietary. The 'M&M' insignia separates the Mars product from present and future knock-offs, so the company is understandably sensitive about guarding its technological secrets. Mars did reveal that the process is similar to offset printing, from which one could infer that the stamper does not strike the sugar coating of the sweet directly. Many pill manufacturers print their logos with a similar offset technique.

What does **M&M** stand for?

Two names – Mars and Murrie, the head honchos at M&M Candies in the early 1940s.

How did chocolate Easter bunnies come about?

No doubt, the chocolate bunny was introduced to make more money for the confectionary industry. Purveyors of non-essential gift items (flowers, greeting cards, chocolates) are always looking for new reasons to compel customers to buy their products. If one were inclined towards conspiracy theories, one could look on everything from Mother's Day to Secretary's Week as nothing but blatant attempts to pry a few pounds from hapless citizens.

Chocolate bunnies date back to the 1850s in Germany. Along with bunnies, chocolatiers sold chocolate eggs and chickens. Switzerland, France and other European chocolate producers followed soon after.

Most of the chocolate companies we contacted felt that the bunnies symbolised renewal and rejuvenation, and were intended to symbolise the 'Rites of Spring', not strictly Easter.

At present, chocolate eggs and bunnies help bridge the 'chocolate gap' that befalls the confectionary industry between St Valentine's Day and Mother's Day.

Why doesn't sugar spoil or get mouldy?

Virtually all living organisms can digest sugar easily. So why isn't sugar prone to the same infestation as flour or other kitchen staples?

Because sugar has an extremely low moisture content – usually about 0.02 per cent – it dehydrates microorganisms that might cause mould. As John A Kolberg, Vice-President of Operations at the Spreckels sugar division of Amstar Corporation, explains it, 'Water molecules diffuse or migrate out of the microorganism at a faster rate than they diffuse into it. Thus, eventually the microorganism dies due to a lack of moisture within it.' Sugar's low moisture level also impedes chemical changes that could cause spoilage.

All bets are off, however, if sugar is dissolved in water. The more dilute the sugar solution, the more likely yeasts and moulds will thrive in it. Even exposure to high humidity for a few days will allow sugar to absorb enough moisture to promote spoilage and mould.

Storing sugar in an airtight container will retard the absorption of moisture even in humid conditions. If stored in an atmosphere unaffected by swings in temperature and humidity, sugar retains its 0.02 per cent moisture level and has an unlimited shelf life.

Why does granulated sugar tend to clump together?

It isn't the heat, it's the humidity. Sugar is hygroscopic, meaning that it is capable of absorbing moisture from the air and changing its form as a result of the absorption. When sugar is subjected to 30 per cent or higher relative humidity, the moisture dissolves a thin film of sugar on the surface of the sugar crystal. Each of these crystals turns into a sugar solution, linked to one another by a 'liquid bridge'.

According to Jerry Hageney, of the Amstar Corporation, when the relative humidity decreases:

> ‘the sugar solution gives up its moisture, causing the sugar to become a crystal again. The crystals joined by the liquid bridge become as one crystal. Thus, hundreds of thousands of crystals become linked together to form a rather solid lump.’

Although we can't see the moist film on sugar exposed to high humidity, it won't pour quite as smoothly as sugar that has never been exposed to moisture. But when it dries up again, the liquid bridge is a strong one. Bruce Foster, of Sugar Industry Technologists, told us that the technology used to make sugar cubes utilises this natural phenomenon.

To make sugar cubes, water is added to sugar in a cube-shaped mould. After the sugar forms into cubes, it is dried out, and – *voilà!* – you have a chemical-free way to keep sugar stuck together.

What makes bubblegum blow better bubbles than standard chewing gum?

All chewing gums consist of gum base, some form of sugar (or sorbitol in sugarless gums), softeners and flavouring. The key to producing good bubbles is the proper gum base. As a representative of Amurol Products Company, a US bubblegum maker, put it, 'Gum base is the part that puts the "chew" in chewing gum and the "bubble" into bubblegum.' Until recently, the gum base consisted mostly of tree resin; now, most manufacturers use polyvinyl acetate, a synthetic resin.

In order to produce a substantial bubble, the gum must be strong enough to withstand the pressure of the tongue and the formation of an air pocket but also flexible enough to stretch evenly as it expands. The secret ingredient in bubblegum is a class of ingredients called 'plasticisers', a synthetic gum base that stretches farther than plain resin. Plasticisers guarantee sufficient elasticity to ensure that little kids can pop bubbles big enough to plaster pink goo all over their chins and eyes simultaneously.

Why are non-sweet wines called 'dry'?

'Sweet' makes sense. Sweet wines do in fact have more sugar in them than dry ones. The main purpose of the sugar is to combat the acidity of the tannic and other acids found in wine. Consumers may disagree sharply about how much sugar they prefer in wines, but can't we all agree that 'dry' wine is just as wet as sweet wine?

Surprisingly, few of our wine experts could make any sense of 'dry' either, but two theories emerged. Wine expert W Ray Hyde argues that the terminology stems from both the sensory experience of tasting and more than a little marketing savvy:

> Sugar stimulates the saliva glands and leaves the mouth wet. Acids, on the other hand, have an astringent quality that leaves the mouth feeling dry. Winemakers know that the consumer prefers a "sweet" wine to a "wet" wine and a "dry" wine to an "acidic" wine.

But Irving Smith Kogan, of the Champagne News and Information Bureau, wrote to *Imponderables* about an intriguing linguistic theory:

> ... the explanation is in the French language. "*Sec*" is a synonym of lean, and means *peu charnu* (without flesh), without softness or mellowness. This image appears in the English expression "bone-dry". "*Sec*" also means neat, as in undiluted, pure, bare, raw ("*brut*" in French), i.e. unsweetened.
>
> The issue of "dry" versus "sweet" is not the same for champagne as for still wines. In the case of champagne, the wine was

originally labelled "*doux*", which is the French word for sweet. But in the mid-nineteenth century a champagne-maker named Louise Pommery decided to make a less-sweet blend and called it "*demi-sec*" (half-dry), which is still quite sweet but less so than the *doux*. Since her day, champagnes have been blended progressively dryer (i.e. less and less sweet). So, today we have a range of champagnes in ascending order of dryness: demi-sec, sec, extra-dry, brut and extra-brut. ’

Kogan adds that the above etymology of 'dry' does not apply to still wines, for which 'dry' simply means not sweet.

How do they get white wine from black grapes?

Most people are surprised when they learn that white wine is often made from black grapes. How can this be? First of all, black grapes aren't exactly black. Although some black grapes are bluish-black, many are really deep red. But this merely begs the question and adds a new one: how do they get white wine out of deep-red grapes?

The answer is simple, and you can demonstrate it to yourself. Go into your fridge and pull out the darkest grape you find. Or if you are so inclined, run without delay to your friendly greengrocer and purchase a few of his or her darkest grapes. Place a grape between your thumb and forefinger. Crush it. Look at the liquid that comes out. Pretty puny stuff, huh?

Almost any grape juice will be a white or yellowish colour. The only reason your red wine is so deep and vivid is that the colour is derived not from the juice of the grape but from the fruit's fermented skin. Without the skin, a white wine can be made from just about any colour grape.

Why is there aluminium foil on the neck of champagne bottles?

According to Irving Smith Kogan, of the Champagne News and Information Bureau, the aluminium foil is there to cover up the less than attractive wiring that helps keep the cork under pressure (the French word for the wire is *muselet*, which means 'muzzle').

Before the days of aluminium foil, lead was used to cover the wire muzzle. Kogan adds that triangular 'weep holes' were added to rid the lead of condensation. Even now, some champagne makers add triangular or diamond-shaped holes to the foil for decorative purposes and as a nod to tradition.

The muzzle was a late-nineteenth-century addition to champagne making. Before then, corks were hammered into place and secured by hand-tied twine.

We had heard a rumour that the foil was there to obscure the occasional bottle of champagne that had a short fill. But Kogan assured us that in this high-tech age, the possibility of a short fill is highly unlikely. Champagne is given its dosage injection at the same table where cork is injected. There isn't enough time for the champagne to bubble away.

Why are there so many different types of wine glasses? Would champagne really taste worse if drunk out of a burgundy glass?

We have always been a tad suspicious about the pretensions of wine connoisseurs, and we, too, have wondered whether the 'flute' glass for champagne truly enhances its taste. We were shocked when we found out that Riedel, the Austrian specialist in glassware for wines, now sells 23 different glass types – each is designed to be used with one particular variety of wine.

To help answer this Imponderable, we contacted Pat McKelvey, librarian of the Wine Institute in San Francisco, California. She told us that appropriate glassware meets three criteria:

1 It is thin and clear, to best show off the beauty of the wine.
2 Its shape is best suited to enhance and accentuate the natural bouquet of the wine.
3 Perhaps most importantly, the shape of the rim should direct the wine onto the appropriate portion of the tongue.

Our tongues are full of taste buds – four distinctive types. The buds at the tip of the tongue are most sensitive to sweetness; the buds at the edges are most sensitive to salt (which is why we put salt on the edges of tequila glasses); the buds at the sides of the tongue are most sensitive to acidity; and the buds at the back of the tongue are most sensitive to bitterness. Until recently, most glassmaking technology has focused on designing the appropriate shape and size of the bowl of the glass. The deep, narrow champagne flute was designed to conserve and accentuate the bubbles; the wide burgundy glass, tapered at the top, attempted to catch and release the fruity aroma, while letting in as little ambient air as possible that might dissipate the wine's character.

But even if the bouquet were enhanced by the shape of the glass, it meant little if the wine didn't taste better; this is why the emphasis, increasingly, is on 'rim technology'. In a young burgundy, for example, the high acid level can sometimes overcome the desired fruity taste. The solution was to flare the rim so that the wine hit the tip of the tongue, which detects the sweetness of the grapes.

Some wines tend to become unbalanced, with the acid/fruit quotient at one extreme or the other. This is one reason why wine lovers swirl the filled glass. A cabernet sauvignon glass is wide, so that swirling will blend the flavours more easily. The mouth of the glass is narrow, so that when you drink from it, the liquid hits the middle of the tongue. The proper cabernet sauvignon glass is designed to hit all four types of taste buds each time you take a swallow.

Riedel has changed the shape of the classic German riesling glasses. Riesling used to be sweeter, so glasses were designed to direct the wine to the sides of the mouth, where the buds would detect acids more acutely. But now that vintners have made German rieslings more dry by introducing more acids into the wine, Riedel's glass has an out-turned rim, in order to guide the wine directly to the tip of the tongue, where the wine's sweetness will be perceived first.

Riedel conducts blind taste testings, in which the same wine is poured into many different glass configurations. If the 'right' glass is not preferred, then Riedel knows it's time to go back to the drawing board.

Why do beer steins have lids?

When we first started researching this Imponderable, we posed the mystery to the partisans of rec.beer, the Internet newsgroup devoted to the love of lager. Soon we were offered all sorts of plausible theories. These are the four we liked the most. Which do you think makes the most sense?

1 The lids keep the beer from overflowing. As Tim Harper put it: 'A good hearty pour down the middle,

as you know, often results in suds runneth over. A quick capping, however, would keep all the nectar in the stein, to settle back down without a drop being wasted.'

2 It keeps insects out of the beer. Bernie Adalem wrote: 'Without a lid, you'd be picking flies off the top of the rich, creamy, foamy head of your favourite beer. Drinking a full glass on a hot day outdoors in the country will attract all manner of flying vermin that are drawn by the sweet malt aromas of a fine beer.'

3 The lid helps keep the beer cool.

4 The lid keeps the beer fresher longer, and helps retain its head.

Believe it or not, the correct answer is number two. Although all the theories *might* have helped explain why lids were put on steins, the precipitating event was a law passed in Germany in the late nineteenth century that mandated that manufacturers put lids on all steins. Fred Kossen, a collector of steins, wrote to *Imponderables*:

> I asked the same question when I first got into stein collecting more than 20 years ago. I found out that it was because of lack of sanitary conditions of the time and the common belief that insects, predominately flies, caused disease. After Europe experienced the plague, many steps were taken to minimise the spread of diseases.
>
> Germany had many drinking establishments, a good portion of them outdoors, especially during the Oktoberfest in Munich. Therefore, Germany passed a law prohibiting stein-makers from producing them without lids.

Another cyberspace beer expert, John Lock ('The Beer Info Source' at www.beerinfo.com), notes that people often enjoyed their beer outdoors in gardens, under the shade of a nearby tree. Unfortunately, Murphy's Law seemed to dictate that various flora and fauna floated straight into the suds. Lids thus proved to be effective in eliminating problems with plant, as well as insect, infestation.

The German law mandating lids caught stein-makers unprepared. Most were not equipped to make their own lids. Even the most renowned stein-maker, Villeroy & Boch of Mettlach, Germany, realised that stoneware was their specialty and chose local pewterers to furnish their lids. Villeroy & Boch and most stein manufacturers offered consumers a choice of lids at many different price ranges. But even the humblest of lids did a fine job of keeping thirsty flies at bay.

Why do some tequila bottles have a worm on the bottom?

Because worms aren't good swimmers?

Those worms are a marketing concept designed to demonstrate that you've bought the real stuff. In order to research this topic with the rigorousness it deserves, we recently undertook a worm-hunting expedition to our local liquor store but found no tequila bottles with worms. We had heard about the worm-filled tequila bottles for years but had never found one ourselves.

So we beseeched one of our favourite wine and spirit authorities, W Ray Hyde, to help us. As usual, he knew the answer immediately. We couldn't find worms in tequila bottles because they are included only in bottles of mescal, as he explains:

> 'Tequila and mescal are related beverages. Both are distinctive products of Mexico. While mescal is any distillate from the fermented juice of any variety of the plant *Agave Tequiliana Weber* (also known as maguey), tequila is distilled from the fermented juice of only one variety of this plant and only in one restricted area of Mexico. Therefore, all tequila is [technically] mescal but not all mescal is tequila.
>
> The worm is placed in bottles of mescal as an assurance that the beverage is genuine since the worm used lives only in the *Agave Tequiliana Weber* plant.'

The worm is found only in the agave cactus in Oaxaca province. Natives of Oaxaca consider the worm a delicacy and believe that the agave possesses aphrodisiac powers. Although actual worms were once the rule, most are now replicas, made of plastic or rubber.

How did the toque become the traditional chef's hat? Does it serve any functional purpose?

Most men, in their daily lives, wear neither rags nor haute couture. We don a pair of trousers and a shirt – maybe a jacket or suit and tie if the occasion warrants it. But in the kitchen, headgear has always been schizophrenic. Cooks wear either ugly but functional hairnets or *toques blanches* ('white caps'), smart-looking caps with long tops. Isn't there a middle ground? Why can't a chef wear a baseball cap or a beret? Can there possibly be a logical function for the shape of toques?

As early as the Roman and Greek empires, master chefs were rewarded for their achievements by receiving special headwear. For the ancients, laurel-studded caps were the honour. In France up until the seventeenth century, chefs were awarded different coloured caps depending upon their rank. Apprentices wore ordinary skullcaps. During the early eighteenth century, Talleyrand's chef required his entire staff to don the toque blanche for sanitary reasons. The toque blanche was designed not only to keep the chef's hair from entering food but to register any stains upon the white background.

But this original cap was flat. The high hat gradually gained popularity not as a fashion statement, not to hide Mohawk hairdos, but to provide some ventilation for the head, as chefs frequently work under extremely hot conditions.

Viennese chef Antonin Careme, not willing to leave well enough alone, decided that the toque blanche needed still more oomph. He put a piece of round cardboard inside his toque to give the cap a stiffer, more dashing appearance. The cardboard has been replaced today by starch.

The toque blanche is no more functional than a hairnet, and almost as silly looking. But any hat bestowed upon someone as an honour is likely to be worn proudly by the recipient, regardless of how funny it looks.

cust

and

prac

Why are there 21 guns in a military salute? Why do auctioneers talk so quickly? Why is Friday the 13th considered so unlucky? Why did pirates love parrots? Sometimes there are wonderful stories behind the rituals of life. And sometimes traditions take hold for no good reason at all.

customs and practices

How was the order of our alphabet determined? Is there any particular reason why A comes before B or that Z is the last letter of the alphabet?

This is another Imponderable without a tidy answer, and it is necessary to delve into some pretty unpleasant subjects, like ancient history, in order to give it a good crack. We must also admit that this is the condensed version of this story – we aren't even going to bother examining the noteworthy Etruscans, for example. But in order to explain why our alphabet is in the order it is, we have to explore at least five different cultures.

The Egyptians

Thousands of years before the birth of Christ the Egyptians were busily writing. This was the civilisation that worked out it might be easier to write on papyrus, with a reed pen, than to carve on stone. Although the Egyptians never created a proper alphabet, their hieroglyphics evolved considerably during the height of their ancient civilisation. At one point, they used over 400 different hieroglyphs, but their written language became more and more streamlined as it went through five distinct stages.

1. Hieroglyphs as pictures of things. A hieroglyph of a horse meant horse. This necessitated a separate hieroglyph for every word and promulgated a written language based on things rather than abstract concepts.
2. Idea pictures. A picture of a leg not only could mean leg, but also ideas associated with legs, such as run or fast.
3. Sound pictures. One symbol was now used to describe a sound that existed in words of the spoken language rather than as a graphic depiction of the word signified.
4. Syllable pictures. One symbol represented a syllable of a word. One hieroglyph was now able to appear in many unrelated words that happened to have one syllable in common.
5. Letter sounds. One symbol took the place of one letter in a word. With the use of letter sounds, syllable and sound pictures were rendered obsolete, since letter sounds were so much more flexible, even if more hieroglyphs were needed to create a word. At first there were hundreds of letter sounds, but the Egyptians eliminated many redundancies by combining them. Eventually, they reduced the number of letter sounds to twenty-five.

An alphabet is a fixed system of written signs, each of which, in theory, stands for one spoken sound. In an efficient alphabet, all the spoken words of a language should be able to be expressed by rearranging these letters. At the point when the Egyptians developed letter sounds, they were close to inventing an alphabet as we know it. Even though their letter sounds gave them the means to write *horse* by sounding out the phonics of the word rather than illustrating its meaning, the Egyptians clung to the first three types of hieroglyphs, never able to figure out why the best way to express *horse* wasn't to draw a picture of a horse.

The Ugarits

Although the Phoenicians are widely hailed as the inventors of the alphabet, it is now conceded that the first ABCs were in the city of Ugarit, in north-west Syria. A German scholar, Hans Bauer, found tablets that have Ugaritic letters displayed opposite a column of known Babylonian syllabic signs, proving that the Ugarits consciously ordered their alphabet. It is unclear whether this tablet was used as an instructional primer.

Although the phonetics of the Ugaritic alphabet were identical to the Phoenician symbols, the actual script was different from the later Phoenician alphabet and from the earlier Egyptian and Semitic languages.

The Phoenicians

The Phoenician alphabet was probably developed around the same time as the Ugarits', but the Phoenicians were much more important in the history of language, for they spread their alphabet throughout much of the world. The Phoenicians weren't aesthetic types. They were traders and needed an alphabet not for literature or history (they didn't leave behind any books) but for business – to track inventories, to standardise accounting procedures and other such mercenary tasks. By 1000 BC, the Phoenicians were carrying their alphabet with them to most of the major ports of the Mediterranean.

The Phoenicians completely dropped the picture signs of hieroglyphics and kept only the symbols that signified sound. The Phoenician's word *aleph* meant 'ox', and the letter *a* was made to look like an ox's head. The ox, the most important farm animal of the time, was the basis for the first letter of most European and Semitic languages, including, later, English.

The Greeks later adapted the Phoenician language to their needs. They took 16 characters from the Phoenicians, all consonants. It was up to the Phoenician reader to decide where the vowels belonged in a given word. A headline of a Phoenician critic's review of this book, for example, might have read like this:

'MPNDRBLS, PRTTY GD BK'

Every spoken language has vowels and consonants, but a remarkable number of ancient written languages did not include vowels in their alphabet. Technically, a consonant, according to *Webster's New World Dictionary*, is a sound produced 'by stopping and releasing the air stream (e.g. p, t, k, b, d, g) or stopping it at one point while it escapes at another (m, n, l, r) or forcing it through a loosely closed or very narrow passage (f, v, s, z)'. Consonants are formed by the vocal chords with the assistance of the tongue, teeth or lips. A vowel, on the other hand, is formed simply by the motion of the vocal chords, with no obstruction by the other speech organs. The lack of vowels in the Phoenician alphabet is about all that keeps it from being a modern language.

The Greeks

The ancient Greeks were scavengers, taking their favourite elements from the Semitic and Phoenician languages, and synthesising their own. Around the ninth century BC, the Greeks added five vowels to what were essentially the Phoenician consonants, and these are the five vowels that English speakers can recognise, not only because the names of each vowel start with the five letters that are our vowels, but also because the names of all but the 'o' vowel have become household words themselves: alpha, epsilon, upsilon, iota and omikron. Alpha became the first letter in the Greek language.

Sharp-eyed readers might ask how, if the Phoenicians didn't have vowels, their *aleph* metamorphosed into the Greeks' *alpha*. Actually, the *alpha* was taken from the Hebrew language rather than Phoenician, and its similarity to Phoenician is because aleph also means 'ox' in Hebrew. The first letters of the Hebrew alphabet are *aleph, beth, gemel* and *dalth,* which mean 'ox', 'house', 'camel' and 'door', respectively. The Greek equivalents are *alpha, beta, gamma* and *delta.*

The driving element in adaptation of written languages is whether the old language can express the sounds already verbally expressed in the adoptive country. The Greeks needed letters to express vowel sounds that already existed in their spoken language. The Phoenician alphabet did not have them, and although the Hebrew language did have vowel sounds, they were used erratically and sporadically. But the Hebrews did have some consonants that used sounds the Greeks did not have. This was the case with the first letter of the alphabet.

In Hebrew, the aleph was a soft breathy sound that had no phonic equivalent in the Greek language. The Greeks took such 'useless' consonants from the Hebrews and converted them to vowels in the Greek languages. Thus, the Greek vowels were Hebrew in origin and the consonants Phoenician.

By adding a few consonants of their own, the Greeks ended up with a 24-letter alphabet. They had no equivalent of our *c* or *v*, and some of their letters stood for sounds different from their modern equivalents. Their *p*, for example, sounded like our *r*. Still, their alphabetical order is roughly the same as ours today, with several notable exceptions, including the fact that their *z* was the sixth, rather than the last, letter of their alphabet.

The Romans

The Etruscans, who used the Greek alphabet, once ruled the Romans. Before their masters' decline, the Romans adopted the Greek alphabet and then began to make changes. The Romans established the current alphabetical order used by English-speaking countries, but their alphabet contained only 23 letters. *J*, *u* and *w* were introduced well after the birth of Christ.

The letter *j* was originally used as a variant of the vowel *i*. Until the seventeenth century, Caesar's name would have been spelled Iulius. The *w* was expressed in Anglo-Saxon by the notation *uu* or *u* until about 900 AD. The *u* itself was used as a variant of the letter *v*. It wasn't until the eighteenth century that the letter *u* was used exclusively as a vowel.

Why did the Romans rearrange the order of the Greek alphabet? There were various reasons for the changes, perhaps none as interesting as why *z* got dumped at the end of the alphabet. At first, the Romans dropped the Greeks' sixth letter altogether, figuring it was unnecessary. When Rome conquered Greece in the first century BC, the Romans decided they needed the letter back again, primarily in order to transliterate Greek words into Latin. By this time, however, the Romans had formalised their alphabet, and the *z*, having lost its rightful place in line, got sent to the back of the bus. Other Romance languages haven't seen the need to reassert *z*'s original position.

Clearly, the placement of letters in the alphabet was essentially an arbitrary one. It would make more sense, probably, to have all of the vowels lumped together separately at the beginning or end of the order: learning alphabetical order doesn't matter much in helping to master English. Would we read or spell any less effectively if we learned the alphabet in reverse order? Yet the Ugarit tablets indicate that the alphabet was taught in alphabetical order, and linguists have found in most cultures that lists of alphabets invariably were written in the same order, despite the fact that, unlike numerical order, the order of letters has no intrinsic meaning.

It is the utter serendipity of our alphabetical order that makes the explanation to this Imponderable so disarming. Would anyone guess that *a* comes before *b* because, for an ancient Semitic culture, 'ox' came before 'house'?

Why do many Irish surnames have 'O'' at the beginning of them?

We almost didn't research this Imponderable because we assumed the 'O'' was a variation of the abbreviation of 'of' (as in 'five o'clock'). Wouldn't it make sense that James O'Hara would be a descendant (i.e. 'of') his father named O'Hara?

Close, but not quite. 'O'' does mean 'descendant' in dialect, but the Irish use it more specifically to mean 'grandson of'. This usage, according to the Irish American Foundation's John Whooley, came into use after the time of St Patrick (presumably, in the fifth or sixth century).

Of course, most Irish names are Anglicisations of Gaelic names. Shirley Starke, of the Mensa Irish special-interest group, told *Imponderables* that the original Gaelic 'O' was not followed by an apostrophe but had an accent mark above it (Ó). Thus, O'Hara in Gaelic was expressed as 'Ó Leadhra' (grandson of a man named Eadhra).

Why didn't they honour the father rather than the grandfather? Sometimes they did, for Mc (Irish) or Mac (Scottish) meant 'son of'.

Our guess is that more than a few readers might wonder how half the Irish population was described by 'O', for daughters and granddaughters carried surnames that connote that they were of the opposite sex. We can only respond: feminism wasn't an accident. As in most cultures, women were identified, essentially, as appendages of men.

Tom Horan, Executive Director of the American Irish Historical Association, told us that a few prefixes were developed especially for females. In Gaelic, 'Ne' preceded surnames to indicate 'daughter of' (e.g. Mary Ne Flannery) and 'Béan' meant wife of (e.g. Béan O Reilly was the Gaelic equivalent of Mrs O'Reilly). But these usages never made their way to the lands of English speakers, where, until recently, virtually all women adopted the names of their fathers or husbands for life.

What does the 'D' in D-Day stand for?

On 6 June 1944, 156,000 Allied soldiers headed to the shores of France (most famously, in Normandy), as part of Operation Overlord, the code name for the entire Allied invasion of north-west Europe. Not all of the soldiers landed on the beaches on June 6, but that day became known as D-Day, the beginning of the pivotal Battle of Normandy.

In an unscientific sampling of friends and acquaintances, we received all kinds of guesses about what the 'D' might represent. Some of the guesses included: Decision, Disembarkation, Debarkation, Doomsday, Deliverance and most commonly, Dunno. We contacted the D-Day Museum in Portsmouth, and a representative wrote to *Imponderables* that the museum's own web site's explanation was as good as any:

> When a military operation is being planned, its actual date and time is not always known exactly. The term "D-Day" was therefore used to mean the date on which operations would begin, whenever that was to be. The day before D-Day was known as "D–1", while the day after D-Day was "D+1", and so on. This meant that if the projected date of an operation changed, all the dates in the plan did not also need to be changed. This actually happened in the case of the Normandy landings. D-Day in Normandy was originally intended to be on 5 June 1944, but at the last minute bad weather delayed it until the following day. The armed forces also used the expression "H-Hour" for the time during the day at which operations were to begin.

Both the US and British military have the same designations for 'D' and 'H' in military planning. We haven't been able to find its first use in England, but in the United States it dates back at least to World War I. According to the US Army Center of Military History:

> The earliest use of these terms by the US Army that the Center of Military History has been able to find was during World War I. In Field Order Number 9, First Army, American Expeditionary Forces, dated 7 September 1918: "The First Army will attack at H-hour on D-day with the object of forcing the evacuation of the St Mihiel Salient."

Why is X used as the symbol of the unknown in algebra?

We can give most of the credit for the X-factor to René 'I think, therefore I am' Descartes, the famed philosopher-mathematician-scientist who was literally and figuratively a Renaissance man.

No symbols were used in algebraic equations until the sixteenth century. For example, the general solutions to the cubic equation by Cardan and Tartaglia in the sixteenth century were all done without any symbols, just words.

David Joyce, maths historian and Associate Professor of Mathematics and Computer Science at Clark University, reports:

> In the sixteenth century, symbols for plus and minus appeared. In Italy, the letters *p* and *m* were used, but in Germany + and –. Eventually, the German symbols became universal. Also, letters began to be used for quantities, both known and unknown.
>
> François Vieta [a French mathematician who predates Descartes by half a century] was the greatest populariser of letters for quantities.

Descartes's greatest contribution to maths was the development of analytic geometry, which allowed geometric shapes and concepts to be expressed with equations. Descartes also invented the system of using *X* (horizontal) and *Y* (vertical) axes when drawing the graphs on paper (presumably, *Z* was reserved for the third dimension).

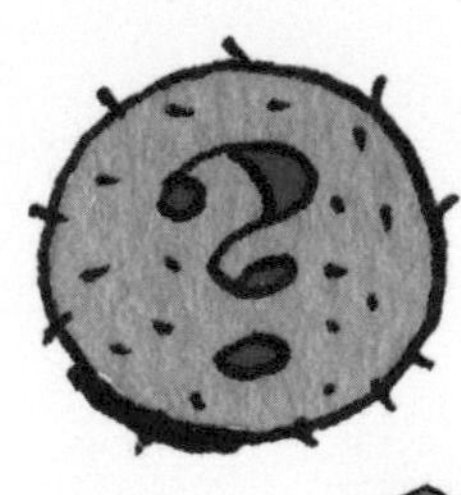

But he used *X* differently in algebraic equations, as Joyce elucidates:

> In the seventeenth century, Descartes used a different rule to distinguish between known and unknown quantities. He used letters from the beginning of the alphabet for known quantities, and letters from the end of the alphabet for unknown ones. That's the general rule that caught on, but even today it is not a hard-and-fast rule.

But if he chose a letter at the end of the alphabet, why did Descartes choose *X* instead of the last letter, *Z*? No one knows for sure. It could be because Descartes was used to working with *X* on his horizontal axis of graphs. Or it might be that the *Z* could be confused with the numeral '2'. Lynn D Yarbrough, head of the consulting firm Mathematical and Computational Sciences, offers an intriguing theory: 'He chose *X* because it's simple to draw on a blackboard or in the sand. It's the same reason that illiterate people use *X* to represent their name.'

Actually, in the Middle Ages, even the most educated aristocrats signed important papers with an *X*, as we will explain in the next Imponderable. The legibility and ease of writing were probably what led Descartes to decide that *X* should mark the spot.

Why does an X stand for a kiss?

Those *XXX*s we affix to Valentine's Day cards and love letters, with or without their companion *OOO*s, began not as symbols of affection, but as substitutes for signatures in the Middle Ages, when the vast majority of citizens were illiterate.

But the *X* was also used by well-educated people, who were quite capable of signing their names, and was found on even the most formal and important documents – wills, contracts, deeds and proclamations. Even kings and queens signed with the *X* as a symbol of good faith – an oath that the contents of a document were true. In some cultures, an *X* became a binding oath – without it, a contract or agreement was considered invalid and not legally binding.

It was not an accident that the *X* was chosen as the substitute for a signature, and, contrary to popular belief, it did not gain acceptance because of its simplicity for the illiterate.

The acceptance of the *X* had everything to do with Christian symbolism. The *X* was the sign of St Andrew, one of the 12 apostles: signing the *X* implied a guarantee to live up to one's promises in that saint's name.

The *X* also had intimate associations with Christ himself. The *X* was regarded as a visual representation of the Cross of the Calvary and the Crucifixion, and *X*, as well as an English letter, is the first letter of the Greek word for Christ, Christos. (The Greek letter, of course, is *chi*.)

How did this legal and religious symbol metamorphose into a romantic one? To further guarantee the sincerity of intentions, people in the Middle Ages solemnly kissed their signatures. This kiss became known as the 'kiss of truth', and because the kiss finalised and bound many agreements, it spawned another saying that many think had romantic origins – 'sealed with a kiss'.

Over the years, as notaries public, literacy and lie detectors lessened the need for the mark, the *X* lost its sacred connotations.

It reached its peak in popularity in the early and mid-twentieth century. During the Second World War, the British and American military were so alarmed by its constant use that they forbade their soldiers from putting *XXX*s in their letters home, fearing that spies might insert cryptic codes into these humble marks, which once stood for truth.

Who decides where the boundary line is between oceans? If you're on the ocean, how do you know where that line is?

Much to our shock, there really is a 'who'. The International Hydrographic Organization (IHO) is composed of about 70 member countries, exclusively nations that border an ocean (eat your heart out, Switzerland!). Part of their charter is to assure the greatest possible uniformity in nautical charts and documents, including determining the official, standardised ocean boundaries.

All of the oceans of the world are connected to one another – you could theoretically row from the Indian Ocean to the Arctic Ocean (but, boy, would your arms be tired!). No one would dispute the borders of the oceans that hit a landmass, but what about the 71 per cent of the earth that is covered by sea?

The IHO issues a publication, *Limits of Oceans and Seas*, that sets out exactly where these water borders are located, but it is used more by researchers than sailors. Michel Huet, chief engineer at the International Hydrographic Bureau, the central office of the IHO, wrote to *Imponderables* and quoted *Limits of Oceans and Seas*:

> The limits proposed ... have been drawn up solely for the convenience of National Hydrographic Offices when compiling their Sailing Directions, Notices to Mariners, etc., so as to ensure that all such publications headed with the name of an ocean or sea will deal with the same area, and they are not to be regarded as representing the result of full geographic study; the bathymetric [depth measurements of the ocean floor] results of various oceanographic expeditions have, however, been taken into consideration so far as possible, and it is therefore hoped that these delimitations will also prove acceptable to oceanographers. These limits have no political significance

> whatsoever. Therefore, the boundaries are established by common usage and technical considerations as agreed to by the Member States of the IHO.'

Essentially, a committee of maritime nations determines the borders and titles for the oceans.

How would the IHO decide on the border between the Atlantic and Pacific? A somewhat arbitrary line was agreed upon that extends from Cape Horn, on the southern tip of South America, across the Drake Passage to Antarctica. A specific longitude was chosen, so the border goes exactly north–south from the cape to Antarctica.

Of course, there are no YOU ARE LEAVING THE PACIFIC OCEAN, WELCOME TO THE ATLANTIC OCEAN signs posted along the longitude. But a sailor with decent navigational equipment could determine which ocean he was in – likewise with the boundaries between other oceans.

Unlike the United Nations, most of the time the IHO does not become embroiled in political disputes, presumably because the precise location of the oceans' borders has no commercial or military implications. Disputes are not unheard of, though. For example, South Korea and Japan tussled about the designation of the sea that divides their countries. Traditionally, the body of water has been called the Sea of Japan, but South Korea wanted it changed to 'East Sea'.

Perhaps we were dozing during some of the year 2000 hoopla, but much to our surprise, the IHO was involved with a rather important event in that year – the debut of a new ocean. The southernmost parts of the Pacific, Atlantic and Indian oceans (including all the water surrounding Antarctica), up to 60 degrees south, were dubbed the 'Southern Ocean'. The name was approved by a majority of the IHO and went into effect in 1999, with Australia among the dissenters. Why wasn't this a bigger deal than the new millennium?

How do you tell directions at the North and South poles?

By definition, every time you gave directions to someone at the South Pole, you would start with 'Head north'.

In practical terms, though, the distances aren't great at the science stations, and it's not like there are suburbs where you can get lost. But scientists do have a solution to this problem, as Nathan Tift, a meteorologist who worked at the Amundsen-Scott South Pole Station, explains:

> If someone does talk about things being north or south here, they are most likely referring to what we call "grid directions", as in grid north and grid south. In the grid system, north is along the prime meridian, or 0 degrees longitude, pointing towards Greenwich, England, south would be 180 degrees longitude, east is 90 degrees, and west is 270 degrees. It's actually quite simple. Meteorologists like myself always describe wind directions using the grid system. It wouldn't mean much to report that the wind at the South Pole always comes from the north!

How do they tell time at the North and South Poles if all time zones converge there?

Imagine that you are a zoologist stationed at the South Pole. You are studying the night-time migration patterns of emperor penguins, which involves long periods observing the creatures. But you realise that while you watch them waddle, you are in danger of missing a very special episode of *Survivor* unless you set the video recorder for the right time. What's a scientist to do?

Well, maybe that scenario doesn't occur too often, but those vertical line markings on globes do reflect the reality. All the time zones do meet at the two poles, and many *Imponderables* readers wonder how the denizens of the South Pole (and the much fewer and usually shorter-term residents of the North Pole) handle the problem.

We assumed that the scientists arbitrarily settled on Greenwich Mean Time (the same time zone where London is situated), as GMT is used as the worldwide standard for setting time. But we found out that the GMT is no more! It is now called UTC (or Coordinated Universal Time – and, yes, we know that the letter order is mixed up). The UTC is often used at the North Pole as the time standard, and sometimes at the South Pole.

We veered towards the humanities in school partly because the sciences are cut and dried. If there is always a correct answer, then teachers could always determine that we came up with the wrong answer. Science students were subjected to a rigour that we were not.

But when it comes to time zones, the scientists at the poles are downright loosey-goosey: they use whatever time zone they want! We spoke to Charles Early, an engineering information specialist at the Goddard Space Flight Center in Greenbelt, Maryland, who told us that most scientists pick the time zone that is most convenient for their collaborators.

For example, most of the flights to Antarctica depart from New Zealand, so the most popular time at the South Pole is New Zealand time. The United States' Palmer Station, located on the Antarctic Peninsula, sets its time according to its most common debarkation site, Punta Arenas, Chile, which happens to share a time zone with Eastern Standard Time in the United States. The Russian station, Volstok, is coordinated with Moscow time, presumably to ease time-conversion hassles for people back in Mother Russia.

We researched this subject earlier to answer a question from a child who asked what time Santa Claus left the North Pole in order to drop off all his presents around the world. Based on our lack of goodies lately, we think Santa has been oversleeping, and now we know that time-zone confusion is no excuse.

Why do some places, such as Newfoundland, Australia, India and parts of the Arab world, have half-time zones? Why do some large countries have only one time zone?

As we write this, it is 6.40 pm in Pittsburgh, Pennsylvania, and three hours earlier, 3.40 pm, in Reno, Nevada, about 3800 km west. While we're toiling away, people in Shanghai, China, are just waking up. It is 7.40 am in Shanghai on the East Coast of China, but it is also 7.40 am in the city of Uramqi, located 3800 km to the west of Shanghai. People in Sydney are already at work – it's 10.40 am, but Perth residents are still commuting at 8.40 am. How about the people in central Australia? For those in north-central Australia, such as residents of Darwin, it's 9.10 am (Australian Central Standard Time). South of them, in Adelaide, it's 10.10 am (Australian Central Daylight Savings Time).

If you are catching our drift, you might have already come to the conclusion that time zones are not uniformly applied throughout the world. When such large countries as China and India have only one time zone each, and places like Australia, India, Iran and Newfoundland feature half-time zones, then something besides scientific considerations has affected the way people tell time.

The notion of uniform timekeeping throughout the world is a surprisingly recent phenomenon – until the late nineteenth century, towns would set their own standards. If there was a big clock in the central square, an official would try to calibrate noon to when the sun was directly overhead, and hope to be reasonably accurate. No one seemed to be highly perturbed by this haphazard arrangement until railways demanded a more precise way of timetabling routes, especially in the United States and Canada. It was a trifle difficult to print train timetables when a 10-minute trip could send passengers to their destination earlier than when they had left! Ruth Shirey, of the National Council for Geographic Education, wrote to *Imponderables*:

> ‘Before railways allowed us to travel fast enough that time zones were standardised so that trains could be scheduled, communities all over the world went by local sun time. In many parts of the world, people still use local time.’

The inventor of our time zone system was a Canadian railway engineer, Sandford Fleming. His notion was elegant in its simplicity: if the earth takes 24 hours to rotate, and there are 360 degrees of longitude, why not create 24 time zones of 15 degrees of longitude each?

In 1884, US President Chester Arthur convened a Prime Meridian Conference in Washington, DC, to standardise the concept Fleming had developed just six years before. And although not quite unanimous (San Domingo voted against, and Brazil and France abstained), 22 other nations voted for naming Greenwich, England, as the location of the Prime Meridian.

But there has never been total compliance with Fleming's scheme. China, for instance, should have five time zones, but it has one (in the western part of China, the sun is often overhead at 3 pm). India has only one time zone (in Fleming's scheme, it should have two), and that one is a half-time zone.

According to Shirey, by far the most common reason for half-time zones (or 'offset time zones') is to shift key cities closer to their actual sun time. For example, all of Newfoundland is half an hour ahead of Atlantic Standard Time, the zone used by the other Atlantic provinces in Canada. Newfoundland lies on the eastern edge of its geographically correct time zone, so it chose an offset time zone to better reflect its actual sun time. Newfoundland's offset time zone is so popular that when the government tried to change to Atlantic Standard Time to conform to Labrador and the other Atlantic provinces, the public outcry prevented it from happening.

The offset time zone in central Australia has a different story. Thomas H Rich, a curator at the Museum of Victoria in Melbourne, took an interest in this Imponderable and unearthed proceedings from the South Australian Parliament in 1898 that showcased the debate in Adelaide about whether to reject the Fleming system that it had adopted in 1894. The reason for the opposition in Adelaide had nothing to do with the sun and much to do with dollars:

> 'Commercial men who received cable advices from Great Britain were put to great disadvantage under the present system as compared with businessmen in the other colonies ... commercial cablegrams are generally delivered in the morning, and in consequence of the present arbitrary law by which the Adelaide time is made one hour later than that of Melbourne and Sydney, South Australian merchants are placed at a great disadvantage, their competitors having one hour to act on the cablegrams before the local commercial men are in receipt of theirs ...'

The original reason for the offset is long past, but reversals of offset time zones are rare – all politics is local.

Meanwhile, anomalies exist all over the globe. Nepal, just to the west of Bangladesh, has a 15-minute offset. All of Russia is one hour off, sort of – it is on permanent daylight savings time. But our favourite brouhaha is the controversy about Daylight Savings Time (DST) in the United States. Until 2005, Indiana had a byzantine structure, in which most of the counties in the Eastern time zone refused to switch over to DST, but there were renegades who did, along with a few 'traitors' from the Central time zone as well. Indiana's localities gave timetable makers a nightmare.

Arizona is the last of the original 48 states not to endorse Daylight Savings Time, but even here there is an exception. The Navajo Nation in Arizona observes Daylight Savings Time, but the Hopi Nation, which lives within the Navajo Reservation, does not.

If we can conclude anything about this topic, it is that although astronomy might have inspired our attempts at measurement, in practice politics, business considerations and human psychology dictate how we tell time.

How did they designate years before the birth of Christ? And how did they designate years in non-Christian civilisations?

Reader Tim Goral writes:

> We live in 2009 AD or *anno Domini* (the year of our Lord); the time period of human history that supposedly began with the birth of Jesus Christ. The historical references before that are all "BC" (or sometimes "BCE"), so my question is: how did the people that lived, say, 2500 years ago, mark the years? I understand that we count backwards, as it were, from 2 BC to 150 BC to 400 BC, etc., but the people that lived in that time couldn't have used that same method. They couldn't have known they were doing a countdown to one. What did they do? For example, how did Aristotle keep track of years?

In his essay, 'Countdown to the Beginning of Time-Keeping', Colgate University Professor Robert Garland summarised this question succinctly: 'Every ancient society had its own idiosyncratic system for reckoning the years.' We'll put it equally succinctly and less compassionately: 'What a mess!'

Since we couldn't contact ancient timekeepers (a good past-life channeller is hard to find), this is a rare Imponderable for which we were forced to rely on books. We can't possibly cover all the schemes to mark time that were used, so if you desire in-depth discussions of the issue, we'll mention some of our favourite sources at the end of this answer.

Our calendar is a gift from the ancient Romans, but because early reckonings were based on incorrect assessments of the lunar cycles, our system has changed many times over the millennia. 'AD' is short for *Anno Domini Nostri Iesu Christi* ('in the year of our Lord Jesus Christ'); the years before that are designated 'BC' (before Christ). Obviously, the notion of fixing a calendar around Jesus did not occur immediately on his birth. Religious scholars wrestled with how to fix the calendar for many centuries.

In the early third century AD, Palestinian Christian historian Sextus Julius Africanus attempted to fix the date of creation (he put it at what we would call 4499 BC, but he had not yet thought of the BC/AD calendar designation). In the sixth century, Pope John I asked a Russian monk, Dionysius Exiguus, to fix the dates of Easter, which had been celebrated on varying dates. Exiguus, working from erroneous assumptions and performing errors in calculation, was the person who not only set up our BC/AD system, but helped cement December 25 as Christmas Day (for a brief examination of all of the monk's mistakes see www.westarinstitute.org/Periodicals/4R_Articles/Dionysius/dionysius.html). Two centuries later, Bede, an English monk later known as Saint Bede the Venerable, popularised Exiguus's notions. Christians were attempting to codify the dates of the major religious holidays, partly to compete with Roman and Greek gods and the Jewish holidays, but also to make the case for a historical Jesus.

Although the world's dating schemes are all over the map (pun intended), most can be attributed to one of three strategies:

1 **Historical Dating.** Christian calendars were derived from the calendars created by the Roman Empire. The early Romans counted the years from the supposed founding of Rome (ab urbe condita), which they calculated as what we would call 753 BC. The ancient Greeks attempted to establish a common dating system in the third century BC, by assigning dates based on the sequence of the Olympiads, which some Greek historians dated back as far as 776 BC.

2 **Regnal Dating.** If you were the monarch, you had artistic control over the calendar in most parts of the world. In the ancient Babylonian, Roman and Egyptian empires, for example, the first year of a king's rule was called year one. When a new emperor took the throne – bang! – up popped a new year one. Although Chinese historians kept impeccable records of the reign of emperors, dating back to what we would call the eighth century BC, they similarly reset to year one at the beginning of each new reign. In ancient times, the Japanese sometimes used the same regnal scheme, but other times dated back to the reign of the first emperor, Jimmu, in 660 BC.

3 **Religious Dating.** Not surprisingly, Christians were not the only religious group to base their numbering systems on pivotal religious events. Muslims used hegira, when Mohammed fled from Mecca to Medina in 622 AD to escape religious persecution, to mark the starting point of their calendar. In Cambodia and Thailand, years were numbered from the date of Buddha's death. Hindus start their calendar from the birth of Brahma.

Looking over the various numbering schemes, you can't help but notice how parochial most calendar making was in the ancient world. Even scholars who were trying to determine dates based on astronomical events often ended up having to bow to political or religious pressure. And modern society is not immune to these outside forces – Japan still uses a dating system based on the emperors' reigns. The current era, marking Emperor Akihito's reign, is called Heisei.

Why does a thumbs-up gesture mean 'okay'?

Any Roman gladiator movie worth its salt includes the obligatory Colosseum combat scene wherein the sated, corpulent sovereign seals the fate of a beaten warrior by giving the thumbs-down signal. The crowd, with their thumbs, advise the king; in films, at least, death was the rule, though people may have been prejudiced by the foreboding music on the soundtrack.

Most people assume that the modern-day thumbs-up signal originated from this Roman affirmative meaning. Not so. In his book *Gestures*, Desmond Morris explains that the Romans signified their approval of a beaten warrior not by signalling thumbs up but by covering their thumbs. When the crowd wanted the victorious gladiator to finish off the loser, they extended their thumbs, which Morris theorises mimicked the act of stabbing the beaten man.

If Rome was the birthplace of the thumbs-up signal, we would expect the gesture to be popular there today, and yet Italy (followed by Greece) was found to be the country in Europe where this meaning is least signified. In many parts of southern Italy and Greece, the thumbs-up gesture is a sexual insult rather than a sign of approval. It is likely that the thumbs-up gesture started somewhere else.

If the early Roman derivation has been debunked, why do we use a thumbs-up signal to indicate 'okay'? The historical evidence, as with most gestures, is murky and contradictory. Morris and other authorities believe the predominant reason is that Western culture tends to associate upward movements with positive, optimistic feelings and downward movements with negative, pessimistic emotions. Obviously, any finger pointed upwards is heaven-bound. In the 1970s, the gesture of a forefinger extended upwards became a symbol of fundamentalist Christians. The solitary forefinger not only indicated 'one God' and 'one way', but where God resided and where the good Christian could some day reside.

The thumb might have been selected as the raised digit because it is the most easily isolated finger. Try raising your finger and withdrawing your other fingers, and you'll realise why the thumb was a more natural choice.

For more information about this subject, one of the best online sources can be found at http://webexhibits.org/calendars/index.html. Some of the books we consulted include *Anno Domini: The Origins of the Christian Era* by George Declercq, *Countdown to the Beginning of Time-Keeping* by Robert Garland and, maybe best of all, the *Encyclopaedia Britannica* section on 'calendar'.

Why do newspaper columns give differing dates for the sun signs of the zodiac?

Although even many of the diehard practitioners don't profess to know why astrology 'works', this doesn't keep them from being rigorous about how they work. Astrologers are faced with the same dilemma as calendar makers. The year and the zodiac are divided into 12 months/signs and 365 divided by 12 simply will not yield an even number.

But the signs of the zodiac are based on the movement of the sun, a heavenly body that is much more logical in its movements than the human calendar. Astrologer Debbi Kempton-Smith told us that the moment of the vernal equinox varies from year to year, so that the birth sign of a baby born at the exact same moment will one time be an Aquarius and another year be a Pisces.

When a newspaper column identifies the date parameters for a given sign, it means that babies born on this day in this year fall within that sun sign. To indicate a typical yearly fluctuation, Debra Burrell, of the New York School of Astrology, shared the precise moment the sun enters the sign of Pisces in three consecutive years (based on Eastern Standard Time in North America):

1989: the Sun enters Pisces on February 18, 4.21 pm, EST.
1990: the Sun enters Pisces on February 18, 10.15 pm, EST.
1991: the Sun enters Pisces on February 19, 3.59 am, EST.

Why are the number 13 and Friday the thirteenth considered unlucky?

Although these are two of the most frequently posed mysteries by readers, we've resisted answering them for a couple of reasons. When in doubt, we try not to use mysteries that can be answered only by other books. But since we can't travel back in time or channel the long-deceased to answer this Imponderable, we are stuck with written sources.

Most of the books we have consulted leave us frustrated. There are literally scores of books about superstitions, and just about all of them address the fear of the number thirteen. Most of them contend that the fear of 13 stems from the Last Supper, where Judas was the thirteenth guest to sit at the table.

The other most common theory is that the superstition predates Christianity and is based on an ancient Norse legend in which Baldur, the god of light, is killed by the evil Loki. In a story quite reminiscent of the Last Supper, 12 gods are dining in Valhalla when they are 'crashed' by the evil Loki. Baldur is killed soon afterwards, because of the plotting of Loki.

Most books about superstitions assume that Friday is particularly reviled because it was the day of the Crucifixion. In other variations, it is the day that Adam ate the apple.

But there are problems with all of these theories, and we thought the arguments were too shaky to include in an *Imponderables* book. Then one day, while visiting one of our favourite bookshops – The Tattered Cover in Denver, Colorado – a book with the title of *13* caught our attention. Written by Nathaniel Lachenmeyer, *13* is a fascinating cultural history of 'the world's most notorious superstition'. In the book, Lachenmeyer articulates our misgivings about prior explanations, and, through meticulous research, offers informed opinions about the origins of triskaidekaphobia (the fear of thirteen).

Lachenmeyer swats away most of the conventional wisdom. Yes, there is a Norse legend of Baldur, but there were actually 13 gods, not 12, when Loki appeared on the scene, so 14 should be the unlucky number. Yes, there were 12 'regular' seats for the gods at Valhalla, but there was a 'high-seat' for the supreme Odin, and there is no mention of 13 (or 14, for that matter) in the legend itself. There isn't even any evidence that this supposed ancient superstition predated Christianity. Lachenmeyer says that the first recorded source of the Baldur myth is in the *Prose Edda*, written in the fifteenth century, 'two centuries after the conversion of Iceland to Christianity'.

And there are just as many holes in the Last Supper theory. Nowhere in the accounts of the betrayal of Christ is the number 13 mentioned, while 12 is mentioned several times. Lachenmeyer also argues that the 12 Apostles and Jesus had many meals together (so why weren't the others unlucky?) and that it is 'inconceivable that the New Testament's authors would have wittingly embraced the blasphemy of implying that a group that included Jesus Christ – the son of God, the saviour of man – was unlucky'.

On the contrary, Lachenmeyer contends that 13 had positive connotations for Christians, 'precisely *because* of its association with Christ and his 12 disciples. To the Christian, 13 represented the benevolent 13 of Christ and his disciples in general, not the fateful 13 of the Last Supper'. Lachenmeyer lists many examples of prominent Christian theologians, such as St Augustine, invoking the number 13 positively.

Another problem with tracing the roots of triskaidekaphobia is that there is no written record of a fear of 13 before the second half of the seventeenth century, in England, when the notion developed that it was unsafe if 13 people sat at a table (often expressed as the fear that one of the 13 would die within a year). Lachenmeyer attributes the fright to the Great Plague of 1665, and the genuine panic caused by London losing nearly 15 per cent of its citizens to the epidemic.

The European fear of 13 sitting at a table crested in the nineteenth century, when triskaidekaphobia mutated into a general fear of thirteen.

Considering the separate superstitions about Friday and 13, it's surprising that there is no recorded evidence of any special fear of Friday the thirteenth until the twentieth century. Lachenmeyer traces the fear of Friday in the United States to the New Testament and the Crucifixion, although he notes that Friday was also the traditional day for executions in the United States.

But what spawned the growth of the new fear? There is no smoking gun answer to this question. Newspapers started taking note when Good Friday landed on the thirteenth day of the month in the early twentieth century, an indication that the superstition was gaining currency by the first decade of the last century.

But one huge event occurred in 1907. Thomas W Lawson published a novel called *Friday, the Thirteenth*. As Lachenmeyer writes:

> It was this novel that redefined the coincidence of unlucky Friday and the 13th as one superstition, and launched Friday the 13th in the popular imagination. Lawson kept the superstition front and centre from the opening sentence ... to its dramatic conclusion ... With a plot that hinged on a speculator's attempt to manipulate the market on Friday the 13th, *Friday, the Thirteenth* was as successful as it was awful.

And Lawson's success did not end with a print bestseller. In 1916, a feature length silent film version of *Friday, the Thirteenth* was released, furthering the superstition's grip. In 1980, the frightening character Jason Voorhees carried on the tradition of trying to scare the dickens out of us with the first of the *Friday the Thirteenth* films.

So we buy the notion that a combination of the Last Supper, Good Friday and Thomas Lawson is responsible for triskaidekaphobia, but it's important to remember a point that Lachenmeyer makes in *13*, perhaps the main reason we were reluctant to tackle this Imponderable until we read his book. Most of the books about superstitions were cavalier about ascribing the fear of 13 to one particular cause, and discussed the superstition as if it had not been mutated by different times and cultures:

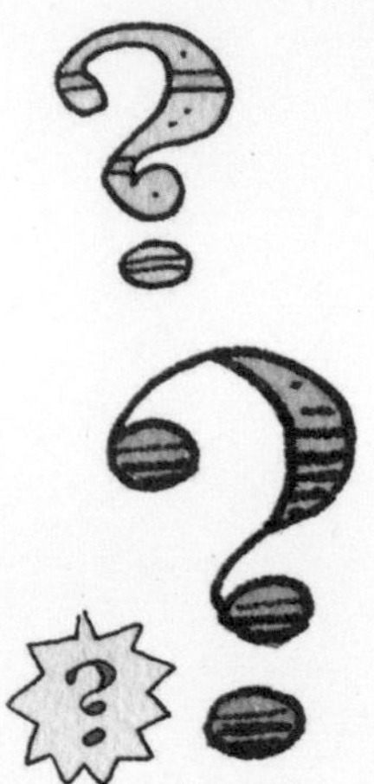

> 'However, continuity of belief needs to be proved, not assumed. This is all the more critical in the case of number superstitions because numerology has been so widely practised in so many cultures throughout history that it is difficult to find a number between 1 and 24 that has not been considered unlucky by more than one culture.'

Exactly. You have to be methodical and analytical to untangle the messiness of irrational thinking.

Do the police really make chalk outlines of murder victims at the scene of the crime? Why do they use chalk?

As soon as law enforcement officials descend upon a murder scene, a police photographer takes pictures of the corpse, making certain that the deceased's position is established by the photographs. The medical examiner usually wants to have the body as soon as possible after the murder; the sooner an autopsy is conducted, the more valuable the information the police are likely to obtain.

Right before the body is removed, the police do indeed make an outline of the position of the victim. More often than not the body is outlined in chalk, including a notation of whether the body was found in a prone or supine posture.

A police investigation of a murder can take a long time, too long to maintain the murder site as it appeared after the murder. Forensic specialists cannot rely on photographs alone. Often, the exact position of the victim can be of vital importance in an investigation. By making an outline, the police can return to the murder scene and take measurements that might quash or corroborate a new theory on the case. Outline drawings may also be used in the courtroom to explain wound locations, bullet trajectories and blood trails.

Herbert H Buzbee, of the International Association of Coroners and Medical Examiners, told *Imponderables* that chalk is not always used to make outlines. Stickum paper or string are often used on carpets, for example, where chalk might be obscured by the fabric. Carl Harbaugh, of the International Chiefs of Police, says that many departments once experimented with spray paint to make outlines, but found that paint traces were occasionally found on the victim, confusing the forensic analysis.

The ideal outline ingredient would be one that would show up, stay put and do no permanent damage to any surface. Unfortunately, no such ingredient exists. Chalk gets high marks for leaving no permanent markings, but is not easily visible on many surfaces. Tape and string (which has to be fastened with tape) have a tendency to mysteriously twist out of shape, especially if they get wet.

None of these flaws in the markers would matter if murder victims were considerate enough to die in sites convenient to the police. Harbaugh says that on a street or highway any kind of outline will do. But what good is a chalk outline on a bed covered with linens and blankets?

Why are there so many different police forces in Britain? Why is there not just one national force, as in France, Russia and many other countries around the world?

The British bobby is famed throughout the world. But not everyone is aware that the term does not apply to all British policemen. Strictly speaking, a bobby is a member of just one particular force, the Metropolitan Police, which is responsible for Greater London. This was the first professional police force in Britain; it was established by Sir Robert Peel in 1829, and it was financed out of the rates paid by Londoners themselves. Other cities and counties followed London's example, and founded their own independent police forces. According to Roger Appleby, curator of the City of London Police Museum, the financial background is the key to understanding the organisation of the British police.

> The essential thing is that all the funding was done locally, in response to local problems. In Robert Peel's time, parliament passed a series of Police Acts. These enabled city and county authorities to set up their own forces. Most localities had a police service in place by the 1860s. But all the new police forces were paid for by those local authorities; there was no central political control.

So from the start, English coppers were recruited from their local communities to work in their local communities. They never 'belonged' to the government of the day, and this was seen as an essential characteristic of the force. 'State police' had been invented by Napoleon, and so were associated in English minds with the worst kind of continental dictatorship. The very word 'police' was for decades viewed with suspicion because it was French in origin: in Victorian English law enforcement, officers were generally known by the good old-fashioned Middle-English word 'constable' (and often still are). The top man or woman in most forces is to this day a 'chief constable' rather than a 'chief of police'.

The British police officer's aversion to direct government control has never entirely gone away. There is a residual fear – going right back to those earliest days – that a national police force, maintained and controlled by Parliament, could be used to impose a ruling party's political will, rather than to uphold the rule of law. This spectre raised its head during the miners' strikes of the 1980s, when Margaret Thatcher, prime minister at the time, bussed policemen from all over the country to confront the strikers. Many individual police officers deeply resented being deployed in this way, in the role of political shock troops as they saw it.

Another reason that policemen support the present locally based arrangements is that many forces now have proud local traditions going back almost two centuries – or even longer, as Roger Appleby points out.

> The City of London Police, who I work for, was established in 1839 – but you could say policing in the City goes back to Roman times. Even then, there were officers of the law, dealing with drunkenness, murder, theft, public order – all the

things we still do now. The City Police is still responsible for the "Square Mile", the area inside the walls of old Roman London, and is quite separate from London's Metropolitan Police (though we came within a whisker of amalgamation with the Met in the last big reorganisation at the beginning of the 1970s). As with every police force in Britain, our uniform is distinctive: the City of London cap band is a red-and-white check; every other force wears a black-and-white one. You can tell a City copper from a Metropolitan officer by the design of the helmet: ours has a different crest, and a coxcomb ridge running down the back. It is based on the helmet of the Prussian Royal Guard. ’

In Britain there is still talk of creating a single, national police force – or at least of amalgamating smaller forces such as the City of London with bigger neighbours, such as the Metropolitan Police. Most police officers don't like the idea – although a national police force is not necessarily a worrisome thing. Many thoroughly democratic nations – including France, Sweden, the Netherlands and New Zealand – have one main police organisation for the entire country, and do very well with it. But locally based police forces are also popular worldwide, nowhere more so than in the USA, where there are almost 18,000 separate police forces large and small, where every county has its sheriff (another good Middle-English word), and where some police forces consist of a sole officer, single-handedly upholding the rule of law.

Why do military personnel salute one another?

Every Western military organisation we know of has some form of hand salute. In every culture, it seems the inferior initiates the salute and is obligated to look directly into the face of the superior.

The origins of the hand salute are murky. In ancient Europe, where not only military officers but also freemen were allowed to carry arms, the custom for men about to encounter one another was to lift their right hand to indicate they had no intention of using their sword. Many of our friendly gestures, such as tipping hats, waving and handshaking, probably originated as ways of proving that one's hand was not reaching for a sword or a convenient rock.

By the time of the Roman Empire, salutes were a part of formal procedure among the military. Soldiers saluted by placing their right hands up to about shoulder height with the palm out. The hand never touched the head or headgear during the salute.

In medieval times, when knights wore steel armour that covered their bodies from head to toe, two men often encountered each other on horseback. To display friendship, two knights supposedly would raise their visors, exposing their faces and identities to view. Because they held their reins in their left hands, they saluted with their right (sword) hands, an upwards motion not unlike the salute of today.

In 1796, the British Admiral, the Earl of St Vincent, commanded that all British officers must henceforth take off their hats when receiving an order from a superior 'and not to touch them with an air of negligence'. Although the British navy made salutes compulsory, it didn't codify the precise nature of the salute. In many cases, inferiors simply 'uncovered' (doffed their caps).

Even if the motivations of ancient saluters were to signal friendly intentions, the gesture over the years has been transformed into a ritual signifying respect, even demanding subjection, and a tool to enforce discipline.

Why are military medals worn on the left?

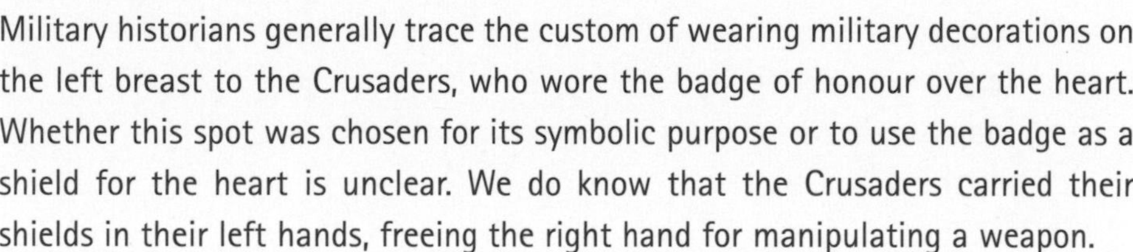

Military historians generally trace the custom of wearing military decorations on the left breast to the Crusaders, who wore the badge of honour over the heart. Whether this spot was chosen for its symbolic purpose or to use the badge as a shield for the heart is unclear. We do know that the Crusaders carried their shields in their left hands, freeing the right hand for manipulating a weapon.

Military decorations are a relatively recent phenomenon and were originally worn at the neck or from a sash. According to SG Yasnitsky, of the Orders and Medals Society of America, the practice changed in the first decades of the nineteenth century. During the Napoleonic campaigns, many awards were given to and by the different governments that participated in these wars. More and more orders were created for the lower classes, as well as medals given to all classes of the military and civil participants, with the proviso that they were to be worn 'from the buttonhole'.

Many fighting alliances between countries were forged during the Napoleonic period, and decorations were exchanged frequently. Medal inflation was rampant.

A good soldier could expect to be decorated not only by his own country but also by an ally or two as well. Buttonholes were bursting. Only tailors were happy. What could be done about this crisis? As Yasnitsky told us:

> Common sense prevailed. No one wanted to hide his gorgeous accumulation of gold and enamelled awards, so several methods were tried out. Some had their jewellers make smaller copies of these medals, so that they would all fit into one prescribed space on their uniforms. Others – and this became the more popular method – would display their own country's decoration from the buttonhole, but mount the other awards so that they extended in a line from that buttonhole, from left to right.

Why do all the armed forces start marching with the left foot? Is there a practical reason? Is this custom the same all over the world?

We can only answer the third question with any confidence. As far as we can ascertain, soldiers all over the world step off on the left foot.

We contacted many of our trusty military sources about why the practice spread. They collectively shrugged their shoulders.

Imponderables has been besieged by questions about the origins of left/right customs (e.g. why many countries drive on the right side of the road, why the hot water tap is on the left, why military medals are worn on the left) and found that usually the practices stem from a technical advantage.

What possible advantage could there be in starting a march with the left foot? We received a fascinating speculation on the subject by Robert S Robe, Jr, President of the Scipio Society of Naval and Military History, which may not be definitive but is certainly more sensible and interesting than anything else we've heard about the subject:

> When warfare was institutionalised in pre-biblical times so that trained armies could fight one another on a battlefield, the evolution of infantry tactics in close formation required regimented marching in order to effectively move bodies of heavy and light infantry into contact with an enemy.

> I am hypothesising that some long-forgotten martinet discovered by accident or otherwise that a soldier advancing at close quarters into an enemy sword or spear line could, by stepping off on his foot in unison with his fellows, maintain better balance and sword contact to his front, assuming always that the thrusting or cutting weapon was wielded from the right hand and the shield from the left. The shield would also protect the left leg forward in close-quarter fighting. ’

Robe's explanation echoes the usual explanation of why we mount horses from the left. The horse itself couldn't care less from what side its rider mounts it. But in ancient times, when riders wore swords slung along the left side of the body (so that the swords could be unsheathed by the right hand), riders found it much easier to retain their groin if they mounted on the left.

Why are there 21 guns in a 21-gun salute?

The original intention of gun salutes was probably to assure the royalty or nation being honoured that they were physically secure – that the weapons that were meant to pay tribute could also be used to kill. Before any recorded history of formal gun salutes, many cultures were known to discharge ordnance indiscriminately at festivals and holidays. Some good old-fashioned noise, be it fireworks in China or cheering at football games, has always been an accompaniment to joyous rituals.

Twenty-one-gun salutes have existed since at least the sixteenth century (the final scene from *Hamlet* mentions one), but the number of guns fired evolved gradually and inconsistently from country to country. The English were the first to codify the practice. According to a study conducted in 1890 by CH Davis, a commander and chief intelligence officer in the US Navy, the earliest English regulation, formulated in 1688, prescribed that the birthdays and coronations of royalty should be solemnised 'by the Fleet, Squadrons and every single ship of war, by the discharge of such number of their great guns', but allowed that the number of guns used should be decided upon by the chief officer. By 1730, the British Naval Regulations were amended so that the number of guns discharged was still at the discretion of the chief officer, but was not to exceed 21 for each ship.

The notion of 21 as the highest gun salute undoubtedly stems from this royal origin. Salutes were always in odd numbers in the British military, with lower-ranking officers receiving, say, a five-gun salute and each increasing rank offered two more guns. The 1730 regulation was probably a response to rampant inflation in gun salutes; the navy wanted to assure that no one received more guns than the royalty. In 1808, 21 guns was mandated as the only proper salute for royalty.

Why were duels always fought at dawn? Or is this depiction in fiction and films not true?

Not true, we're afraid. Historians assured *Imponderables* that duels were fought at any time of the day, but dawn was definitely the preferred time.

It doesn't make much sense to us. We might be convinced to get up at dawn to go fishing. But if we knew we had an approximately 50-50 chance of dying on a particular day, we'd at least want a decent night's sleep and time for a doughnut or two before we fought.

Historian CF 'Charley' Eckhardt speculates on this strange predilection of duellists to fight to the death at inconvenient hours:

> Just at sunrise, if the list [the technical term for a duelling ground] was oriented north–south, neither man got the sun-to-the-back advantage. Also, either the local law was still abed or, if there was a regular police force in the area, the day watch and night watch were changing shifts. Fighting at dawn minimised the likelihood of interference by the law.

Why did pirates make prisoners or enemies 'walk the plank' instead of just throwing them overboard?

Try as we might, we couldn't find any pirates to talk to us, on or off the record. Instead, we had to rely on a librarian and historian, Toby Gibson (who has made a lifelong study of pirates, and maintains an entire web site devoted to pirate lore at http://blindkat.hegewisch.net/pirates/pirates.html), and on more than 20 books about pirates. Pirates have always captured the imagination of writers, both nonfiction and storytellers, and it has become difficult to separate the myths about pirates from serious documentation.

The reader who posed this Imponderable rightly wondered why pirates would bother with the elaborate ritual of forcing a victim to walk on a wooden plank with eyes blindfolded and hands behind his back, when it would have been far easier simply to throw the poor fellow overboard. Either way, the victim would end up as shark food.

The stories about walking the plank usually refer to the 'Golden Age' of piracy, from approximately 1690 to 1720, when such legendary pirates as Blackbeard, William Kidd and Stede Bonnet terrorised the oceans. But accounts of piracy have been documented as long as there have been ships, and include tales of skulduggery in the Mediterranean in ancient Greek and Roman times.

We are lucky that many contemporaneous accounts of piracy written in the seventeenth and eighteenth centuries still exist. Many purport to be first-hand reports, but unfortunately, exaggerated and outright fabricated adventure stories often masqueraded as nonfiction in those days, so much of the information therein must be taken with more than a few grains of salt. Several pirates were tried and executed for their crimes, however, so court records do exist, including minutes of the proceedings for many of them.

The bottom line: there is little, if any, proof that walking the plank existed. Three other forms of punishment are clearly documented:

1. **Flogging.** Miscreants were beaten with the dreaded cat-o'-nine-tails.
2. **Marooning.** Offenders of the worst variety (murderers, rapists, despised captains) were given the clothes on their backs (and sometimes were even stripped of those), a bottle of water, a pistol, a bottle of powder and a handful of shot, and were abandoned on an inhospitable island. They were never left on a romantic island with abundant vegetation, as depicted in Robert Louis Stevenson's *Treasure Island*. Marooning was a nonviolent but nevertheless torturous death sentence.
3. **Throwing overboard.** This form of punishment, while not common, has been amply documented.

Some historians maintain that walking the plank did exist. In his book, *The Age of Piracy*, Robert Carse claims:

> The story about prisoners being forced to walk the plank is almost complete fiction. Examination of the record gives only a single

example. Men were thrown in over the side, though, and strung up from the yards for musket practice, pistolled point-blank.

Carse's 'single example' is a reference to Major Stede Bonnet, a soldier rather than a seaman, who in the early eighteenth century forsook a comfortable life as a gentleman in the West Indies to become a pirate. Carse writes:

> Bonnet died with two distinctions as a pirate. He was the first man ever in recorded history to have bought a ship with his own funds and then to have gone forth deliberately on a piratical venture. He was also, by the record, the only captain of his kind to make his victims walk the plank.

Perhaps the most famous real-life pirate was Blackbeard, whose real name was Edward Teach. In his 1935 book, *Sinbad's Book of Pirates*, author AE Dingle claims that Teach tortured the skipper of a captured ship:

> Blackbeard laid a plank across the brig's open hatch, dragged the skipper towards it, and promised him that if he could walk across it blindfolded he would be set free and his brig given back to him. He was even permitted to walk across the plank with his eyes unbound, and he performed this part of the task with agility. He was much astonished to land safely on the other side of the deck, unhindered, and submitted to the blindfolding with a little laugh of returning confidence.
>
> But the pirates turned him about, shoving him here and there while the bandage was being tied, a dozen of them vowing that it was not well fastened, shifting him about until when at last he was set with his feet on the plank he never noticed that it now projected out through the gangway and over the sea instead of across the hatch.

The victim's wife, angry at her husband for surrendering to Blackbeard so easily, protested and was sent below into the cabin: 'There she saw her husband tumble past her open window from the end of the plank.'

Neither of these two stories is substantiated in any way, and the second, at least in the manner of expression, 'feels' like fiction.

Most of our sources discounted the reality of walking the plank. In his 1951 book, *The Great Days of Piracy in the West Indies*, George Woodbury argues that pirates' ferociousness has been greatly exaggerated. Pirates made most of their money from holding wealthy shipowners hostage. There was every reason to keep such valuable booty alive. On the other hand, 'Those of poorer estate were usually invited to jump overboard, encouraged and finally coerced, to do so.'

In general, though, pirates did not injure, let alone kill their captives unless the victims provided physical resistance. In fact, it was common for pirates to recruit their prisoners, often offering them equal rights, although some were forced into indentured servitude. Even if violence was a by-product of their work, Woodbury describes pirates as less than bloodthirsty:

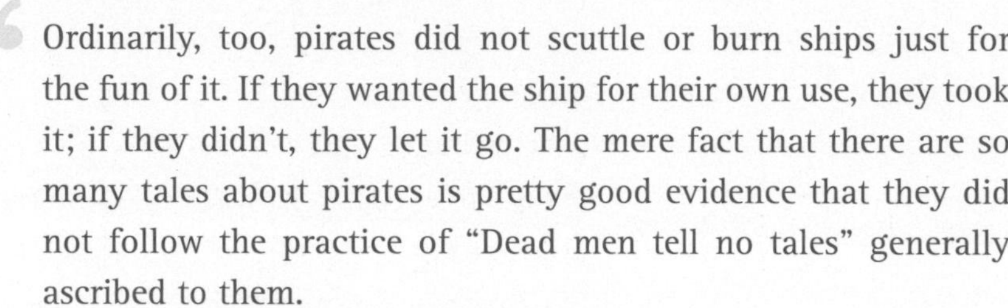

> Ordinarily, too, pirates did not scuttle or burn ships just for the fun of it. If they wanted the ship for their own use, they took it; if they didn't, they let it go. The mere fact that there are so many tales about pirates is pretty good evidence that they did not follow the practice of "Dead men tell no tales" generally ascribed to them.

> Only one atrocious practice, marooning, seems to be really characteristic of piracy. Marooning was a form of punishment usually meted out to backsliders from their own numbers.

Even stronger in his 'defence' of pirates and the denial of the reality of walking the plank is perhaps the most prestigious historian to write extensively about pirates, Patrick Pringle. In his 1953 book, *Jolly Roger, The Story of the Great Age of Piracy*, Pringle notes:

> I have ransacked official records, reports of trials and much other documentary evidence without being able to discover a single case of walking the plank. I do not mean merely that I have not found an authenticated case. In all the documentary literature on pirates I could not find even an accusation or suggestion that the practice was ever used. The very expression seems to have been invented many years after the Age of Piracy.

Pringle argues that it was to the advantage of pirates to have potential victims fear them. And seamen of merchant ships had little reason to resist – who would want to risk their lives to protect the merchandise of the ship's owner?

And although Bonnet is the one famous pirate often 'credited' with having prisoners walk the plank, Pringle discounts the contention:

> Bonnet's career is even more fully documented than Blackbeard's, for a full report of his trial has been preserved. The evidence against him was considerable, yet not one of the witnesses accused him of ill-treatment of prisoners. It seems as if this is another myth.

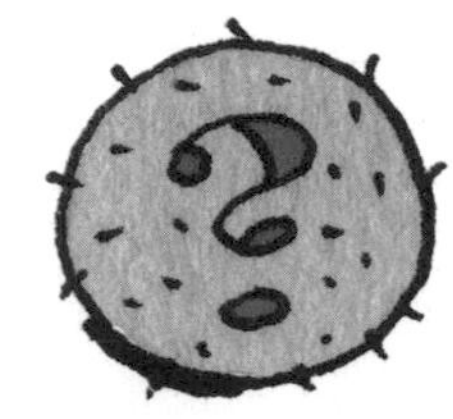

So, then, how did these myths begin? They began with early 'classics' of pirate literature, such as *Bucaniers of America* (1679) and *A General History of the Robberies and Murders of the Most Notorious Pyrates* (1724), which contained facts mixed in with hyperbole. The latter book, written by 'Captain Charles Johnson', is widely suspected to have been the work of Daniel Defoe, author of *Robinson Crusoe*.

Pirate stories remained popular in the nineteenth century. Several of the most popular, Stevenson's *Treasure Island* and Gilbert and Sullivan's *Pirates of Penzance*, had no mention of walking the plank.

But Howard Pyle, a popular author and illustrator who worked in the last half of the nineteenth century into the beginning of the twentieth, used pirates as one of his most common subjects. And one of Pyle's most popular pictures depicted a man walking the plank, along with this commentary by the artist:

> With Blackbeard, we have a real, ranting, raging, roaring pirate who really did bury treasure, who made more than one captain walk the plank and who committed more private murders than he could number on the fingers of both hands.

Probably totally untrue, but even people in the nineteenth century needed a good scare now and then.

When we first asked Toby Gibson about walking the plank, he answered, 'There's little doubt that pirates threw people overboard, especially enemies. We also know that Hollywood has turned walking the plank into a pirate tradition.'

Perhaps no Hollywood rendition is more famous than in *Peter Pan*, in which the nefarious Captain Hook forces Wendy to walk the plank. Luckily for Wendy, Peter

Pan just happens to be hiding under the plank, eager and able to snatch her and fly away, with Hook none the wiser.

Even if pirates were not the brutes they have been commonly depicted to be, they are without a lobbying organisation to better their image.

Why did pirates love parrots?

Our image of the colourful parrot astride the peg-legged, patch-eyed pirate might come from cartoons and comic strips, but the inspiration was surely Robert Louis Stevenson's *Treasure Island*, published in 1883. The beloved pet of cook Long John Silver, the parrot squawks 'Pieces of eight!' with annoying regularity and becomes the 'watchbird' for the pirates after the miscreants take over the treasure hunters' fort on the island.

Stevenson admitted that he borrowed the idea of the parrot from Daniel Defoe's *Robinson Crusoe*. After being stranded on the island, Crusoe knocks a young parrot out of a tree. He teaches the bird to speak its own name ('Poll'), 'the first word I ever heard spoken in the island by any mouth but my own'.

But did pirates really carry parrots on their ships in real life? The evidence suggests yes. Kenneth J Kinkor, Director of Project Research at the Expedition Whydah Sea-Lab and Learning Center in Provincetown, Massachusetts, told *Imponderables*, 'Many pirates kept parrots and other animals, as many sailors did.' Kinkor says that parrots were most common among the Central American pirates who spent some time ashore, logging in places not under direct control of Spain, such as Belize, that possessed large parrot populations.

David Cordingly, former curator of the National Maritime Museum in Greenwich, England, wrote in his book, *Under the Black Flag*:

> ‘It was common for seamen who travelled in the tropics to bring back birds and animals as souvenirs of their travels. Parrots were particularly popular because they were colourful, they could be taught to speak, and they were easier to look after on board ship than monkeys and other wild animals.’

Call us cynical, but pirates never struck us as the most sentimental of men. Perhaps some parrots were kept on board as pets or mascots, but might there have been other, less humanitarian considerations? In the most often cited contemporaneous account of the pirate world, Captain William Dampier's *A Voyage Around the World*, written in 1697, Dampier claims that his band of privateers (pirates who are authorised by a country to commandeer ships sailing other states' flags) ate parrots along with other birds, while cruising off Venezuela.

No pirate would get fat from eating parrots, so our bet is that the primary purpose of carrying parrots was financial. In his research on pirates, David Cordingly found government records from Elizabethan times indicating that pirates gave parrots to well-placed employees of government officials, presumably as bribes.

But other people were willing to put down hard cash to buy parrots. Dampier discusses his shipmates buying 'an abundance' of cockatoos and parakeets, presumably to sell or trade. Pirates had a ready venue to sell their booty, for there were established bird markets in London and Paris in the eighteenth century, and exotic birds from the New World presumably were attractive purchases for the wealthy and status-seeking. Indeed, Cissie Fairchild wrote an entire book, *Elephant Slaves and Pampered Parrots: Exotic Animals in Eighteenth-Century Paris*, about the bustling trade in exotic animals (the Sunday bird market still exists on the Île de la Cité in Paris).

Pirates might have admired the colours of parrots, been amused by their mimicking ability and have been satiated by their succulence. But love? Only money could buy a pirate's love.

Why did pirates wear earrings?

A famous painting by Howard Pyle depicts the notorious Captain Kidd, clearly wearing an earring. And film pirates usually don them too. Did they wear them in real life? Evidently so. Our resident pirate expert, Toby Gibson, writes:

> While I'm sure Hollywood was trying to make leading men such as Errol Flynn and Douglas Fairbanks, Sr, look suave and exotic, real pirates were piercing their ears for a more practical purpose. It was believed that piercing the ears with such precious metals as silver and gold improved one's eyesight. This was the main reason pirates performed such a ritual. It must also be noted that most other seafaring men also indulged in this practice.

While for years this was considered an old wives' tale, today the art of acupuncture lends some credence to the practice of ear piercing. The earlobe is an acupuncture point for several eye ailments. It is quite possible that the practice of ear piercing may have been brought to the West from the Oriental trade routes.'

We decided to speak to some acupuncturists, to determine whether practitioners, then and now, believe in a relationship between piercing the ear and improved vision. When we asked Dr Steve Given, an acupuncturist who also teaches the art at Emperor's College in Santa Monica, California, he gave us a shock. We asked him about the ear–eye connection, and before we could broach the subject, he brought up pirates: 'There are reports of people enjoying vision improvements after having their ears pierced. In fact, when I studied acupuncture, the subject of pirates piercing their ears just for this reason was discussed.'

Given doesn't dispute that pirates pierced their ears for this reason. He discussed how the ear is often used in acupuncture as a focus point for eye problems in general, and vision problems, in particular. A point on the ear, called the 'eye point' or 'vision point' corresponds to the area on an earlobe where piercing might take place. But he doubts that any lasting vision improvement could be attained from piercing:

'If they did get a benefit by puncturing the master sensorial [the eye point] in a fortuitous manner, it certainly wouldn't be a lasting thing. Once the ear is pierced, scar tissue forms around the hole. This will block any further beneficial effects.'

Given's arguments were corroborated by two other acupuncturists we consulted. Timothy Chen, of the Acupuncture Clinic of Pasadena, California, told *Imponderables* that he has found nearsightedness and conjunctivitis to be conditions helped by acupuncture on the ear, but doubted whether piercing could help general vision on a long-term basis. Dr Michael Apelian, of the Acupuncture Therapy Center in Santa Monica, California, has heard of cases of vision being harmed and helped by ear piercing:

'I've heard it go both ways. I've also heard because you're damaging that area by

> piercing, it can inhibit vision. I think that most of the more ancient beliefs (and Chinese literature) felt that it would stimulate vision rather than hinder it.'

We asked Dr Apelian if he treated people on the ear for vision problems. 'Sure,' he told us. 'However, I think that other body points, especially on the face and feet, are stronger.'

Maybe pirates pierced their faces and feet too. But it would he hard to find rings underneath the bushy beards and salty footwear.

In films and television dramas, what is the purpose of boiling water when babies are delivered at home?

Considering the urgency with which characters in films bark orders to boil water as soon as it becomes evident a woman is going to give birth at home, we assumed there was a better reason for the command than to brew up some tea. But we've never seen the boiled water actually being used on-screen.

Most of the medical authorities we contacted echoed the sentiments of Dr Steven P Shelov, Professor of Paediatrics at the Montefiore Medical Center:

> 'This is an attempt to make as sterile an environment as possible, though clearly it is far short of inducing any sterility whatsoever. There might be some ability with hotter water to allow for a cleaner, more efficient cleansing of the baby and of the mother postpartum.'

Obviously, it can't hurt to sterilise equipment that comes in contact with the mother or baby, such as scissors, cord clamps, white shoelaces (used in lieu of cord clamps), syringes and tongs (used to lift the other sterile items), or even more importantly, to sterilise other household implements commandeered to act as sterilised medical equipment.

But boiling water isn't confined to emergency deliveries. Midwives have been boiling water for years for planned home deliveries. Most attempt to boil sterile equipment for 30 minutes and then place instruments in a covered dish (syringes are usually wrapped in a sterile cloth).

Dr William Berman, of the Society for Pediatric Research, indicated that it couldn't hurt to sterilise water for washrags used to cleanse mother and baby, whether they are washcloths or ripped-up bed sheets. Actually, it could hurt – if they forget to let the boiled water cool down.

Why is the colour blue associated with baby boys? Why is pink associated with baby girls?

The association of colours with babies undoubtedly started as an attempt to identify the gender of that one group of humans to whom the cliché 'they all look alike' often applies.

But why blue for boys? In ancient times, it was believed that evil spirits lingered over nurseries and that certain colours possessed the capability to combat evil. Blue was considered the most powerful colour, possibly because of its association with the sky and, thus, heavenly spirits. Since boys were then considered the most valuable natural resource to parents, blue clothing was a cheap form of insurance.

Evil spirits apparently couldn't be bothered with pestering baby girls. Not only were girls not dressed in blue, but they had no colour to call their own until centuries later. Our association of pink with girls stems from European legend, which professed that baby girls were born inside of pink roses.

European legend also holds that baby boys are born in blue cabbage patches.

Why does the groom carry the bride over the threshold?

With the price of housing being what it is today, we think it might be more appropriate to have the estate agent carry both the bride and groom over the threshold of their new home.

This superstitious countercharm dates back to the Romans, who believed that spirits resided at a home's entrance. Stephanie de Lys, in her book *A Treasury of American Superstitions*, writes that the Romans believed good and evil spirits slugged it out at the threshold. They also believed that if one walked into the house with the left foot first, evil would triumph; if the right foot came first, the good spirits would predominate. So why don't the bride and groom simply take care to put their right foot forward when entering their new abode?

Those Romans were just a tad sexist, as de Lys explains:

> The groom, knowing that a woman in a highly emotional state is very apt to be careless, took no chances and picked her up in his arms and carried her into the house.

Why do auctioneers talk funny? And why do they often speak unintelligibly?

Auctioneering dates back to Anglo-Saxon times, when all sorts of merchandise and commodities were sold in open markets. Bernard Hart, executive secretary of the National Auto Auction Association, wrote to *Imponderables*:

> The reason for the talk by auctioneers is that before the advent of public-address systems, especially the portable type, an auctioneer had not only to be in good voice but to talk in a method that was pleasing rather than irritating to the ears of his audience of prospective buyers.

The auctioneer's technique has not changed much since its origins, as Peter Lukasiak, Executive Director of the National Auto Auction Association, explains:

> A typical auctioneer describes the products offered for sale; chants to find the lowest (or floor) price for the items being sold; acknowledges each bid received; and attempts to move bidders to the highest bid level possible. This results in a rolling, sonorous tone that actually builds competition among bidders and secures the highest market price for sale goods and the seller.

Although the 'chant' might sound funny to the uninitiated, it's an essential element in the strategy of the auctioneer. The auctioneer usually must try to sell as much merchandise as possible in the shortest amount of time (not only so that more goods can be sold but also so that buyers uninterested in the particular item on sale won't leave the premises before they have had a chance to bid on later items). As Joseph Keefhaver, Executive Vice-President of the National Auctioneers Association, put it:

> Rhythm is as important as speed in developing an effective chant. Auctioneers will adjust their speed, depending on the bidding experience level of their crowd, and the numbers of a good chant will be readily understood.

Lukasiak indicates that some auctioneers have personal preferences for slow or fast paces, but conditions often dictate the chant speed. A wholesale tobacco buyer does not want a leisurely pace at an auction, and an auctioneer trying to sell a multimillion-dollar Monet at Sotheby's had better not carry off the bidding at a breakneck pace, as Keefhaver amplifies:

> The purpose of an auction is to sell items at a rapid and steady pace. Unlike other types of sales, an auction is a one-time event where all the customers are present at the same time. Thus, the auctioneer is responsible for selling all the items within a few hours, and his or her use of the chant helps keep the items moving. Since auctioneers have a limited amount of time to sell many items, they need to move at a rapid pace.
>
> At an average household estate auction, the auctioneer's chant uses speed and rhythm to sell an average of 60 items per hour. Certain types of auctions go even faster; wholesale automobile auctioneers frequently sell 125 to 175 cars per hour and tobacco auctioneers may sell 500 to 600 lots per hour.

Obviously, it is far more difficult for the uninitiated to understand what is going on at a tobacco auction. Many auctioneers pepper their chants with regional speech patterns or terms understood only by the cognoscenti within the field.

Okay. We've established that the form of the auctioneer's chant makes some sense, but why can't you understand them? When we've gone to auctions, a typical chant might sound to bidders something like this: 'Hey, budda budda budda 25, hey wonka wonka wonka 30, got 25, 30, budda budda, 25, 30, hey 30, budda budda budda, do I have a 30? Budda budda.'

Of course, that's not what the auctioneer is actually saying. More likely, he or she is using 'real words'. Joseph Keefhaver provides a classic, basic chant: 'One-dollar bid, now two, now two, will you give me two? Two-dollar bid, now three, now three, will you give me three?'

The culprits in misunderstanding the chants – in the previous example the 'buddas' and 'wonkas' are called 'filler words' (or simply, 'filler') by auctioneers. The purpose of filler is to give bidders a chance to think about bidding while keeping the momentum of the chant (and with luck, a frenzy of interest in the item) alive. Bernard Hart told *Imponderables* that a good auctioneer develops several different filler words and alternates them throughout an auction, to avoid the monotony of 'budda budda budda':

> In one of the auction schools where I worked, they trained the students to base their fillers on words that would encourage an increase in the bids such as "make", "bid" and "go". For example, "I have 25, will you make it 30?" ... Only a few are able to handle that many words. It can be shortened in several ways such as "25 go 30", "25 bid 30" and so on.

We were shocked when every single one of the auctioneers we consulted insisted that the bidder should be able to understand every single word of the auctioneer, even the fillers. The comments of J McBride, Director of Information at the Livestock Marketing Association, were typical:

> Actually, if you can't understand what an auctioneer is saying, he or she is not doing their job, and we should know, because we sponsor the granddaddy of all auctioneer contests, the World Livestock Auctioneer Championship.
>
> I direct your attention to the judging criteria for the contest. Under the section "Advancing to World Finals", you can see that "clarity of chant" is a major judging criterion. [Indeed, it is the first criterion mentioned – others include "voice quality", "bid-catching ability" and "conduct of the sale".]
>
> It may take a while for you as an auction observer to "pick up" on the auctioneer's particular chant. And the auctioneer may sometimes use patter or fill words that are not crystal clear. But to sell, you have to be understood – that's true whether you're auctioning off cattle or fine crystal, farmland or Rembrandts.

Why are most dinner plates round?

With the research help of Harry Frost, Director of the Dyson-Perrins Museum in Worcester, Doris Nixon, Director of Educational Services for the National Bridal Service, sent a fascinating letter tracing the history of plates. Here are some of the highlights:

> ‘It has been generally assumed that pottery was preceded by basket-making. Most baskets were round, for ease in weaving. Prehistoric man, or rather woman, strengthened basketwork bowls by smearing the outside with clay. The idea of pottery may have started when such a basket was accidentally burnt. Fired clay pieces with basketwork imprints dating from 15,000 to 10,000 BC have been found in Gambles Cave in Kenya.
>
> The other most common freehand method of modelling pottery was coiling, the building up of vessels by long coils. With this method, forming round shapes is the most natural construction method.
>
> Casting involving liquid clay was used in ancient Palestine, but this method has only been used in Europe since 1730 AD. To make a plate in a shape other than round involves casting, which is more expensive than other methods used.
>
> The introduction of the potter's wheel, probably humankind's oldest machine, marked the beginning of the mechanisation of pottery. The earliest known use of the potter's wheel was in the Mesopotamian town of Worka, 5000 BC. Potters also used wheels during the Indus Valley civilisation, 3250–3000 BC, as did the Mayan people for making ceramic toys for their children. By Old Testament times, 2000 BC, the potter's wheel was in common use in Southern Palestine. In fact, one of the gates of Jerusalem was called the "Gate of Potsherds" (broken pots).
>
> So, going back in history as far as 5000 BC, plates were round, as they were made by the potter's wheel.’

Some cultures also used wooden plates, and fashioned them from found trees. If trees were square, they probably would have fashioned square dinner plates.

Even today, round plates have distinct advantages for the manufacturers. According to Judy Stern of Noritake, 'Other shapes can be made, but oval and square pieces, for example, must be cast in a mould. This process is much more expensive, more labour-intensive and takes more time.'

Round plates also tend to be more durable than other shapes. Helen Grayson, of the American Restaurant China Council, told *Imponderables* that rectangular plates, with sharp edges, are more likely to chip or break off.

In the 1930s and 1940s, square plates were in vogue briefly, but then went out of style. Ever since, other non-round shapes have been far more popular in Europe than in North America, but china manufacturers keep trying to spring other shapes on a public perfectly satisfied with round plates: fish plates in the shape of fish; oval plates for steaks; and octagonal plates for aesthetes.

But we seem to always come around to Doris Nixon's point of view: 'If you can't improve history, don't attempt to change it! The fact of the matter is, round plates will continue to be.'

Why did the Chinese first use chopsticks?

The conventional wisdom on this subject is that the Chinese consider it the chef's duty to carve meat or slice vegetables into bite-sized morsels. Chopsticks were then invented to serve as efficient tools to pick up morsels of food and rice. But there is much evidence to suggest that their use was originally motivated not by aesthetics but by practical considerations.

Why do dinner knives have rounded edges?

Since the purpose of a knife is to cut, why do dinner knives have rounded edges, necessitating 'steak knives' to accomplish serious comestible surgery? Actually, knives, ancient eating utensils, did have sharpened points until the seventeenth century, when the renowned Cardinal Richelieu changed all that. Richelieu, a finicky and fastidious eater, objected to a house guest who used the point of his knife as a toothpick. The next day, Richelieu ordered his steward to round the ends of all the cardinal's knives. Richelieu's style of cutlery spread throughout France and most of the Western world. By the nineteenth century, most decent people had a difficult time spearing their peas with their knives.

Chopsticks were introduced sometime during the Chou Dynasty, probably a century or so before the birth of Christ. Until the Chou Dynasty, stir-frying did not exist. But China faced a serious fuel (i.e. wood) shortage. Forests were cut down to clear land for agriculture to feed a burgeoning population.

Stir-frying developed as the most efficient method to use the least amount of wood as fuel for the shortest period of time. Because the food was cut before stir-frying, the meat and vegetables cooked much faster than by other methods.

During the Chou Dynasty, few people owned tables (a luxury, especially with the wood shortage), so a utensil was needed that would allow diners to eat with one hand only – the other hand was needed to hold the bowl of rice. Because most Chinese dishes have sauces, chopsticks enabled users to scoop up food without getting it all over their fingers. And now chopsticks allow non-Asians the opportunity to propel food all over the tablecloths of Chinese restaurants.

And why did the Chinese decide to use chopsticks in the middle of this supposed wood shortage? Only some of the chopsticks were made of wood. More were made of ivory and bone.

Why is 'par avion' used to designate 'airmail' even in English-speaking countries? Is French the international language of mail?

We knew it was the language of love, but little did we know that French was the parlance of post offices. Michael F Spates, manager of delivery for the United States Postal System, explains why:

> 'Virtually every country in the world is a member of the Universal Postal Union [UPU, based in Bern, Switzerland], which governs and sets the terms for mailing between countries. The language of the UPU is French and the term "par avion", which dates back to before the Second World War, is the chosen designation for airmail.'

What do all the chime signals on airlines mean? Are they uniform from airline to airline?

We might not be white-knuckle fliers anymore, but let's put it this way: we're closer to a pale pink than a full-bodied red. So we're not too happy when we find ourselves sitting next to fearful fliers.

Why is our fate in life always to be seated alongside a middle-aged passenger taking his or her first flight? Invariably, our rowmates quake when they hear the landing gear go up. And more than one has reacted to the chime signals as if they were a death knell; one skittish woman knocked our Diet Coke off our tray when she heard the chimes. She assumed that the three-chime signal must signify that our flight was doomed. Actually, all that happened of consequence was that our pristine white shirt soon resembled the coat of a Dalmatian.

But we always have been curious about the meaning of these chime codes, so we contacted the three largest airlines in the United States – American, United and Delta – to ask if they would decode the mystery. We were surprised at how forthcoming they were. Nevertheless, for the first time in the history of *Imponderables*, we are going to withhold some of the information our sources willingly provided, for two reasons.

First, airline chime signals vary not only from airline to airline but from plane to plane within companies, and today's signals are subject to change in the future. Second, every airline does have a code to signify a true emergency, and the airlines aren't particularly excited about the idea of passengers decoding such a signal before the cockpit crew has communicated with flight attendants. Airlines are justifiably concerned about readers confusing emergency signals with innocuous ones and confusing one company's codes with another's. We agree.

Michael Lauria, an experienced United Airlines pilot, told *Imponderables* that he has never had to activate an emergency chime signal. He is much more likely to sound one chime, to indicate that the cockpit wishes to speak to the first-class cabin attendant or (two chimes) to the coach flight attendants. Even if Lauria's passengers are enduring particularly nasty turbulence, chances are that the cry for help from the cockpit, expressed by the chimes, is more likely to be for a coffee or a juice than for draconian safety measures.

The number of chimes is not the only way of differentiating signals. Some United planes emit different tone frequencies: a lower-tone chime is heard for a passenger call than for a crew call, and a 'bing bong' indicates a call from one flight attendant to another.

American Airlines uses different chime configurations to inform attendants when they should prepare for landing, remain seated with seat belts fastened and call the cockpit crew. Although American does have a designated emergency signal, like other airlines it is rarely used.

Delta Air Lines features an array of different chime signals, which specify events during a flight. For example, when the 'fasten seat belt' signs are turned off, a double high-low chime marks the event. These chimes also tell the flight attendants what elevation the plane has attained.

On most Delta planes, each phone station has a select tone, so that on a widebody plane, the flight attendant can recognise who is calling, and the flight crew can call any one or all of the flight attendant stations at one time. Alison Johnson, manager of aircraft interiors for Delta, told *Imponderables* that during an emergency, it is important for the flight crew to be able to speak to flight attendants without causing panic among passengers. Obviously, if the entire staff is briefed, a game plan can be established before informing passengers about a potential problem.

Why do we kiss under the mistletoe?

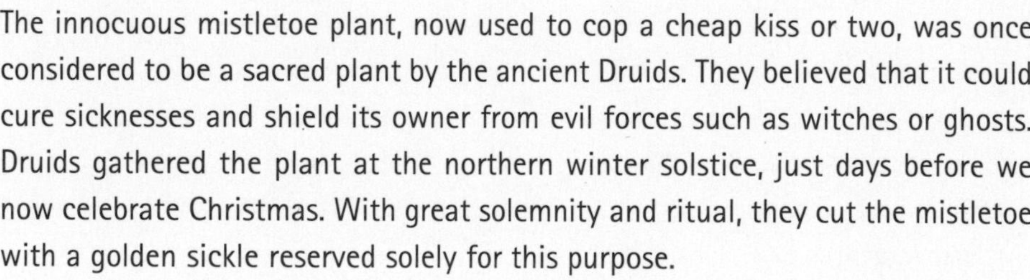

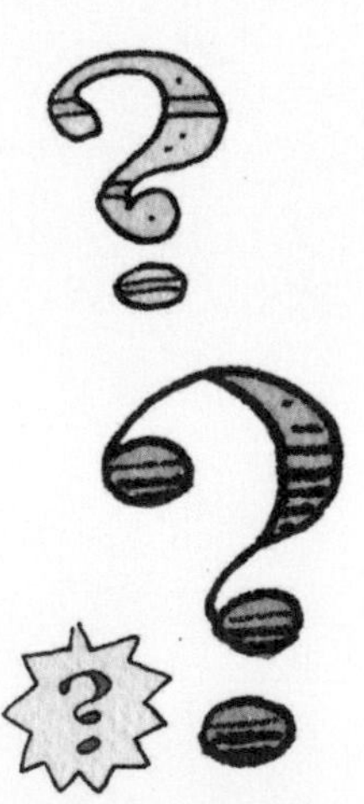

The innocuous mistletoe plant, now used to cop a cheap kiss or two, was once considered to be a sacred plant by the ancient Druids. They believed that it could cure sicknesses and shield its owner from evil forces such as witches or ghosts. Druids gathered the plant at the northern winter solstice, just days before we now celebrate Christmas. With great solemnity and ritual, they cut the mistletoe with a golden sickle reserved solely for this purpose.

The plant was so sacred that the Druids never allowed it to touch the ground, which probably explains why we still hang mistletoe over our doorways. The Druids believed that by placing it over their doorways, they could not only protect the health and safety of all who passed through but also promote romance and fertility. If a boy kissed a girl under the mistletoe and gave her one of the plant's white berries, the ritual meant they would get married within the year.

Ironically, although mistletoe is now associated with Christmas, the Christians in Celtic regions, ashamed of their pagan antecedents, did everything possible to dissociate themselves from the belief in the power of mistletoe. But the practice took hold. And although a kiss under the mistletoe no longer promises marriage, at least we've retained the fun part of the ritual.

Why is Easter observed on such wildly different dates?

We don't know the exact day when Jesus was born, but at least we know when to expect to see Christmas on our calendar every year. Easter's date varies so much because the timing of Easter is based on the lunar calendar.

Early Christians celebrated Easter on the same date as the Jewish Passover, but Christians, wanting to distance themselves from Jewish practices, changed the time of observance at the Council of Nicaea in 325 AD. Like legislators everywhere, the council was prone to pass some pretty complicated laws: Easter was henceforth to be celebrated on the first Sunday after the first full moon on or after the northern spring equinox (March 21).

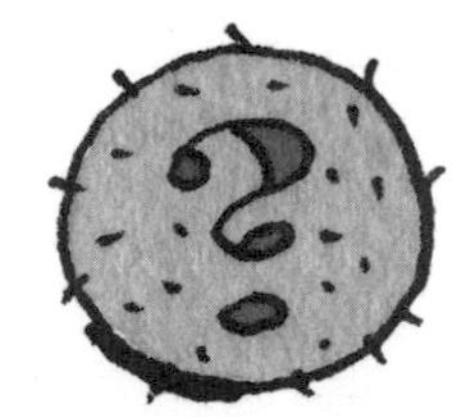

Long before the resurrection of Jesus was celebrated, virtually every Western society celebrated the rebirth of nature in the spring. Ironically, one of the holiest Christian holidays is named after a pagan goddess. The name 'Easter' derives from the Anglo-Saxon goddess Eostre, who governed the vernal equinox.

Why is the holiday called 'Good' Friday when it commemorates the crucifixion of Jesus?

This Imponderable was posed by a Sunday school teacher who has always wondered about the strange name of this sombre day. Could, he wondered, have the 'Good' been ironic?

One expert, Erroll F Rhodes, an assistant director at the American Bible Society, indicates that such an interpretation is possible. But he, like all of the other sources we contacted, was more inclined to see the 'Good' as a demonstration of Christian faith:

> 'One settles on the rhetorical level by calling it an example of irony. Another [rationale] is based on a recognition that humanity was redeemed through the supreme sacrifice of Christ on the cross. Superficially, this may be described as a paradox, but theologians have traditionally called it a mystery, recognising that without Good Friday there can be no Easter – a profound truth of experience that (in the words of Mark Twain) is stranger than fiction.'

It might be difficult for non-Christians to comprehend how believers could not see the anniversary of their Saviour's death as a day to be mourned rather than celebrated. But from the religious perspective, many 'tragedies' are perceived through the prism of later redemption. As Marie Anne Mayeskie, of Loyola Marymount University's department of theology, eloquently puts it:

> Good Friday is called "Good" because it is the day on which Christians celebrate the accomplishment of salvation by Christ. It is, in Christian liturgical celebration particularly, not essentially a sad, though certainly a solemn event, which is viewed from the perspective of the Resurrection. The Christian tradition understands the work of Christ to have transformed the human realities of death, and even sin.

Why do Scotsmen wear kilts? And why didn't men in surrounding areas wear kilts?

Entire books have been written about the history of the kilt, so the first part of this question is hardly imponderable. Our reader's focus is on why this strange garment was a mainstay in the Highlands of Scotland and elsewhere.

How did *Xmas* come to stand for *Christmas*?

The use of the colloquial 'Xmas' has often been singled out as an example of how the holiday has been commercialised and robbed of its religious content. The *X* in Xmas is actually the descendant of the Greek equivalent of Ch, as in 'Christos', which means 'Christ'. The letter *X* has stood for Christ since at least 1100 AD, and the term 'Xmas' was first cited in 1551. Word expert Eric Partridge points out that the scholarly abbreviation for 'Christianity' is 'Xianity'.

So many people dislike 'Xmas' for its supposed crassness that its use is now virtually confined to commercial literature and banners. *The New York Times Manual of Style and Usage*, for example, offers this simple recommendation for 'Xmas': 'Never use.'

Although we are most likely today to see a Scot in a kilt, inside or outside Scotland, only in a parade or on a formal occasion, its initial popularity was based on practical rather than ceremonial or aesthetic considerations. Although the contemporary kilt resembles a skirt, early kilts covered not only the waist to knee region of the body but also the upper torso. Essentially, the earliest kilts were huge blankets, which were wrapped around the body several times and draped over the shoulder. This one garment served as blanket, sleeping bag, cloak and trousers.

The geography of the Highlands of Scotland was no doubt responsible for the kilt's longevity. The Highlands are mountainous and damp, with many streams and rivers. Anyone traversing the countryside in long trousers and shoes would quickly be wearing wet long trousers and wet shoes. The kilt saved the wearer from continually rolling up his trousers. By rearranging the kilt, he could shield himself from the cold and wind. Perhaps most importantly, shepherds could leave their home base for months at a time wearing one garment and no 'extra' clothes.

As kilts were constructed out of elements easily obtainable in the Highlands (wool from the omnipresent sheep and the plaid prints from native vegetable dyes), even the poorest of Highlanders could afford one. And the poor wore the kilt the most. According to Steward MacBreachan, a Scottish historian, performer and demonstrator of Highland games and ancient Scottish culture, the kilt was of special importance to those who had to spend most or all of the day outdoors. More affluent Highlanders could switch from kilts to trousers once they returned home from a day's work.

We had a long talk with Philip Smith, PhD, one of 13 fellows of the Scottish Tartan Society worldwide and an author of several books about Scotland. He informed us that kilts, or their equivalents, were worn in many parts of Europe in the ancient world. The Scottish kilt is not too different from the garb of the ancient Romans and the Portuguese.

Smith feels that the widespread use of the horse in other countries eventually led to the abandonment of kiltlike clothing. For rather obvious anatomical reasons, kilts and horseriding are, let us say, an uncomfortable fit for men.

After an unsuccessful Jacobean uprising in 1745, the English Prohibition Act of 1746 (more commonly known as the 'Dress Act') banned the wearing of both the kilt and any tartan material by anyone except the Highlands regiment. Ironically, the prohibition is probably responsible for our current association of Scotsmen with kilts. Scotsmen kept their kilts during the ban and wore them surreptitiously at closed gatherings. Along with the tartan, which identifies the clan of the wearer, the kilt became a symbol of Scottish pride.

As Scotsmen needed the blanketlike garment less and less for practical reasons in the nineteenth and twentieth centuries, the kilt, if anything, gained in significance as a way for Scotland to carve its psychic independence from England. As proof, we need only point to the wearing of kilts in ceremonial occasions by Scotsmen from the south, who never wore them in the eighteenth century.

Why are the Netherlands also called Holland and the Low Countries? Why are its people called Dutch?

Our pet theory was that the official name of the country was 'the Netherlands', but that 'Holland' was used to make it easier for mapmakers to fit the name within the confined borders. Actually, the official name of the country is Nederland, the name native inhabitants call it – 'Netherlands' is simply the closest English equivalent.

The word 'nether' means below the earth's surface. The low and marshy lands near the mouth of the estuary of the Rhine River are responsible for the name, 'the Low Countries'. The German name 'Niederlande' and the French name 'les Pays-Bas' are exact translations.

By why 'Holland'? Holland was the name of a province, not the whole country. In the sixteenth, seventeenth and eighteenth centuries, it was by far the most important province commercially, and Hollanders displayed more devotion to their province than to the nation as a whole. Holland eventually became so dominant that, much in the same way that the Soviet Union was mislabelled 'Russia', Holland came to represent all of the Netherlands.

Further confusing the issue is the term 'Dutch', used to describe the citizens of the Netherlands. 'Dutch' is actually older than 'the Netherlands'. Until the sixteenth century, inhabitants of the Netherlands called themselves Diets (which means 'the people'). This word, pronounced 'deets', was corrupted in English as 'Dutch'. The British continued to use the medieval name long after Netherlanders stopped using it themselves.

Netherlanders have to deal with confusion not only about the name of their country, but about the name of their capital. Amsterdam is the official capital, but the seat of government is at The Hague. The official name of The Hague is 's-Gravenhage, 'the count's hedge', except nobody calls the city 's-Gravenhage, preferring the colloquial Den Haag (the hedge). For such a small country, the Netherlands has its share of identity problems.

Why are all gondolas black?

This Imponderable was thrown at us on Jim Eason's KGO chat show in San Francisco. We were totally stumped, but many callers offered their theories, most having to do with the advantage of black in absorbing the sun. We were sceptical since not too many boats we have ever seen were painted black. We considered flying to Venice to check out this Imponderable personally, but we stumbled upon the answer before we had obtained our tickets.

The origins of these boats are obscure; no one can find the derivation of the word 'gondola'. Gondolas have probably existed since the eleventh century and were probably painted many different colours. But in 1562, a sumptuary law was passed in Venice mandating that all gondolas be painted black. Many sumptuary laws were primarily attempts to avoid extravagant or unnecessary expenditure. But during this period, the Catholic church encouraged the passage of laws that banned ostentation for its own sake, particularly in clothing and decoration.

Still, the Italian flash has always shone through in the gondola. For, in contrast to its sombre colour, the gondola sports a gleaming ferro that decorates the upcurving prow of the boat. Nobody knows whether the seven metal prongs on the prow ever had a symbolic meaning or if they were purely ornamental, but the steel ferro has always undermined the intention of the sumptuary law.

Why is Oktoberfest celebrated in September?

Oktoberfest always struck us as little more than an excuse to drink a lot of beer. But even if it is far from a sacred observance, can't it at least be held during the month for which it is named?

If we go back, though, and trace the roots of the first Oktoberfest, celebrated in Munich in 1810, we find that, wonder of wonders, the festivities did begin in October – October 17, to be exact. The first festival commemorated not the worship of beer but the marriage of Crown Prince Ludwig of Bavaria (later King Ludwig I) to Princess Therese von Sachsen-Hildburghausen. The prince invited the citizens of Munich to attend, and an enormous party was held on the fields in front of the city gates. The event turned into a full-day party capped by a horserace witnessed by 40,000 spectators.

The event was such a success that the horserace was repeated the next year, and the festival took on a life of its own. In 1811, an agricultural show was added, along with booths and exhibits. Slowly, amusements (originally a carousel and swings) were added. But the most popular diversion proved to be the beer stands.

On the twenty-fifth anniversary of the wedding, the festival was especially large and elaborate, and drew visitors from far and wide. But perhaps the key event in cementing the enduring popularity of the event occurred in 1896, when big beer tents replaced the more modest stands, and local breweries started sponsoring them.

Today the Munich Oktoberfest is the largest folk festival in the world, with an estimated seven million visitors per year, who consume about five million litres of beer. More than 3000 separate Oktoberfests are held around the world, with Cincinnati, Ohio's, being the largest outside of Munich.

So what accounted for the movement of Oktoberfest? According to Don Heinrich Tolzmann, of the Society for German-American Studies, the answer lay in the inclement weather in October. Since the celebration was always held out in the Theresienwiese ('Theresa's fields', named in honour of the princess-bride), the organisers didn't want cold, damp weather to dampen the spirits of the revellers. In order to continue to honour the original purpose of Oktoberfest, the festival was moved back exactly one month, to the seventeenth of September, although, as Tolzmann points out, in practice Oktoberfests outside Munich can take place as early as late August and as late, as, well, October.

Where is Old Zealand?

The first thing we did after reading this Imponderable was to laugh for an extended period of time. Then we had a brilliant idea. We looked up 'Zealand' in the dictionary. We found the following: 'largest island of Denmark, between Jutland and Sweden'.

We remembered that the first European to land on New Zealand was Abel Tasman, a Dutchman. Now we know that all of the famous explorers blundered upon their discoveries, but this was too much. Did Tasman actually name his island after the wrong country? Was he a traitor?

Not quite. Tasman worked for the powerful Dutch East India Company, which wanted to find new trading partners willing to part with gold or silver in exchange for Dutch cloth and iron (now you know why the Dutch East India Company was successful).

Dutch explorers had already come upon Australia, which they called 'New Holland'. But they didn't realise that it was an island; the company thought that New Holland might extend south to where Antarctica is located. Abel Tasman didn't find the long continent he expected, but he and his crew were the first Europeans to discover several islands. The first was what Tasman named Van Diemen's Land (after his Governor-General) – its name was later changed to Tasmania, for obvious reasons.

Sailing east from Van Diemen's, Tasman bumped into a big land mass that, much to his consternation, was occupied by Maori tribesmen who didn't appreciate European intruders. The Maoris paddled up to the strange boats in their canoes, shouting and sounding combat trumpets. The Dutch thought they were being met by a welcoming committee and blew their trumpets back! Eventually, the Dutch did get the message when tribesmen killed several of Tasman's men and made it impossible for the crew to explore the land.

Tasman's diaries record that he named his discovery 'Staten Landt'. Tasman theorised that this island was actually only a small part of a great continent stretching all the way from the South Pacific to the foot of South America. So he named his discovery after Staten, the land off the southern tip of Argentina.

The very next year, another Dutchman discovered that Staten was an island and not part of South America, so Staten Landt no longer was a suitable name for Tasman's discovery. The Dutch renamed the island 'Zeeland' ('sea land'), not after the Danish island but after a province of the same name back in Holland.

Why does the Japanese flag sometimes have red beams radiating from the sun?

A flag is an icon, imbued with emotions, dreams and fears that extend far beyond its cloth and dyes. You can tell quite a bit about a country by its attitudes towards its flag. Case in point: Japan.

You may be familiar with the Japanese flag, the *Hinomaru* ('sun disc'), which some trace back to the time of the Emperor Monbu in the early eighth century. According to Dan Scheeler, librarian at the Sasakawa Peace Foundation USA Library in Washington, DC: 'Legend has it that a priest named Nichiren presented a sun flag to the Shogun at the time of the Mongol Invasions [launched by Kublai Khan] in the late thirteenth century.'

During the fifteenth and sixteenth centuries, when various clans and military figures were vying for control of Japan, *Hinomaru* were displayed as military insignia (sometimes with different colour schemes to designate particular factions, but the red sun on white background was most common).

For almost 300 years, Japan isolated itself from the West, but in 1853, the militias of two feudal lords fought and killed some sailors from the Royal Navy. One of the clans, the Satsumas, fought under the *Hinomaru*, and the English mistakenly assumed that this was their national flag. In order to avoid being mistaken for foreign vessels, the Shogun agreed that it might be advisable for Japanese vessels to all carry the same flag, as Richard Allen Jones, of the Japan Information Center of the US Consulate General of Japan, explains:

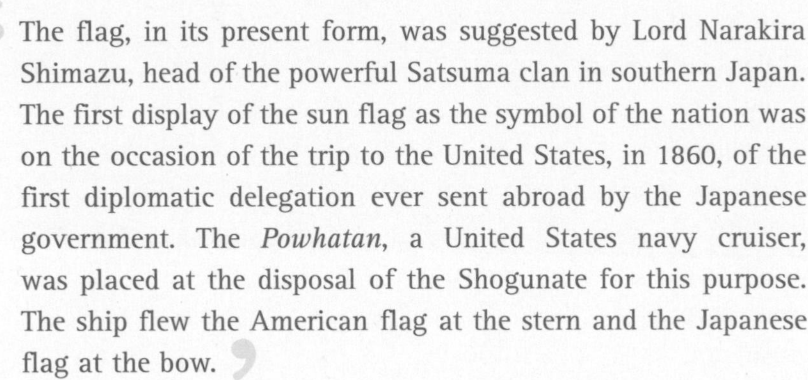

> 'The flag, in its present form, was suggested by Lord Narakira Shimazu, head of the powerful Satsuma clan in southern Japan. The first display of the sun flag as the symbol of the nation was on the occasion of the trip to the United States, in 1860, of the first diplomatic delegation ever sent abroad by the Japanese government. The *Powhatan*, a United States navy cruiser, was placed at the disposal of the Shogunate for this purpose. The ship flew the American flag at the stern and the Japanese flag at the bow.'

None of this activity likely had the slightest effect on the average Japanese person. But things were about to change. In 1868, the Tokugawa Shogunate was stripped of power, and the Emperor Meiji assumed power. In January 1870, the Prime Minister proclaimed that all ships must fly the *Hinomaru*, and mandated the dimensions of the flag, which still remain the same today.

According to Jones, the first time the *Hinomaru* was flown at a national ceremony was in 1872, at the opening by Emperor Meiji of Japan's first railway. For more than 100 years after the beginning of the Meiji era, Japanese citizens might fly the flag on important holidays, yet the *Hinomaru* did not possess great iconic value, possibly because it wasn't officially the national flag of Japan.

Soon after Meiji's reign, a special flag for the Imperial Navy was introduced. Beginning in 1889, naval vessels flew a sun disc flag with 16 rays extending to its borders. Masahiko Noro, Executive Director of the Japan Foundation in New York, wrote to *Imponderables*: 'This flag was used by the Japanese military, particularly the Japanese navy, from the Meiji era until the end of World War II. The Japanese have not used this flag to represent their country since 1945.'

The naval flag, then, is not another version of a national flag. Indeed, there really was no official national flag to be a variation of! So this Imponderable was based on an understandable misconception. We mistakenly assume that the 'ray' flag is a variation of the national flag, when it is not related.

Many of us are familiar with the 'ray' flag because so many depictions of the Japanese flag we have seen come from war films, specifically ones set during the Second World War, where the naval flag is (realistically) depicted as the military ensign of the Japanese warriors.

Even more confusing, the Treaty of San Francisco, which settled the conclusion of the Second World War, mandated that Japan eliminate its armed forces, so there wasn't much need for the naval flag after 1945. But in 1952, Japan started to build up 'self-defence' forces, which looked suspiciously like a navy to most foreigners. In 1954, the Japanese Maritime Self-Defence Forces reclaimed the naval ensign as its own, and it still flies today.

Ironically, while the military flag's re-emergence stirred little passion in the West, the Japanese exhibited deep ambivalence about the *Hinomaru*. To leftists, intellectuals and union members, in particular, the flag represented a period (1931-45) of xenophobia and unjustified military aggression. Even those without such strong political feelings tended not to be preoccupied with displaying the flag – even government buildings often did not fly the sun disc.

It was not until 1999 that the *Hinomaru* was officially proclaimed the national flag of Japan, and even then, only a particularly sad incident prompted the change. In Hiroshima, a high school principal was unsuccessfully attempting to use the *Hinomaru* and a patriotic song, the 'Kimigayo', in the school's commencement ceremony. Teachers objected not just to the flag, but also the song, which they thought glorified the imperial system that was responsible for abhorrent military practices during the war. The lyrics do give credence to the grievance: 'May the reign of the emperor continue for a thousand, nay, eight thousand generations and for the eternity that it takes for small pebbles to grow into a great rock and become covered with moss.'

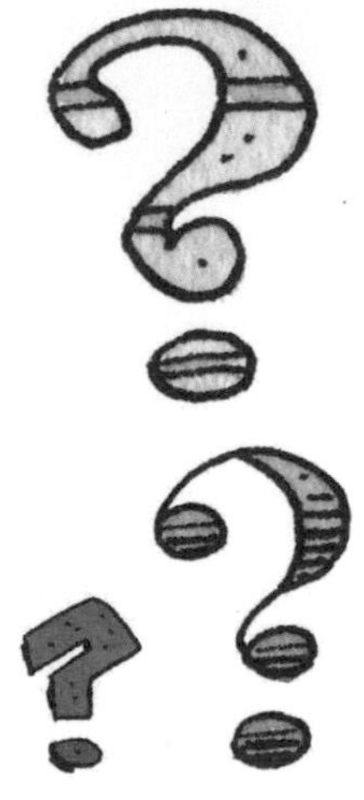

The principal, caught between a school board that wanted the flag to be flown and the song to be played at commencement and a faculty that was balking, committed suicide the day before the graduation. Within days, the government pushed for legalising the *Hinomaru* as the official national flag (and the 'Kimigayo' as the national anthem) of Japan, and within six months accomplished the task.

The controversy over the resurrection of the sun disc flag proves that it had become an icon in Japanese culture. Even for those who disagreed with making the *Hinomaru* the official flag, the symbol became worth fighting for.

Why do we fly flags at half-mast to honour the dead?

Although we now mourn dignitaries by flying the flag at half-mast on dry land, all of our sources agree that the custom has British naval origins. Prior to half-masting, ships would sometimes fly a black flag to honour a death. No doubt the old custom had at least two disadvantages: it necessitated bringing two sets of flags, one of which was unlikely to be used; and it failed in its primary purpose of signalling to others – a ship in the distance was much more likely to recognise a flag sailing at half-mast than to discern the colour of a flag.

Although there are reports of flags at half-mast as early as the fourteenth century, the first recorded instance of half-masting occurred in 1612. An Inuit killed Englishman William Hall, who was searching for the North-West Passage (in what we now call Canada), and the Royal Navy lowered its flags at sea to honour him.

By the mid-seventeenth century, the Royal Navy had adopted the custom more formally, and its fleet flew its flags at half-mast annually to honour the death of King Charles I. Later, a commanding officer's death would lead to flying a ship's flag at half-mast, but eventually any crew member's passing would prompt a tribute.

Why honour the dead by lowering the flag? In his 1938 book *Sea Flags*, British Commander Hillary P Mead speculates that the origins of half-masting date back to a deliberate attempt to make the boat as slovenly as possible, the opposite of shipshape:

> ‘Untidiness and slovenliness of appearance were supposed to be the signs of grief, and this writer refers to biblical customs (amongst which may be mentioned sackcloth and ashes), and to the fact that in the Merchant Service ropes are left trailing and yards are scandalised in furtherance of this principle. This idea of slovenliness, at any rate in modern times, has no counterpart on land.’

Another theory speculates that in the seventeenth century, regimental flags were placed on the ground when the Royal Family or foreign heads of states were saluted; merchant ships dipped their ensigns to warships. As Mead puts it: 'It naturally follows that national flags should be lowered as a salute to the departed, and remain lowered for a length of time proportionate to the importance of the deceased person.'

As more countries mimicked the British custom, half-masting became common on land throughout the world. But not everywhere. The Flag Research Center, based in Winchester, Massachusetts, mentions one exception in its *Flag Bulletin*:

> Because the religious inscription appearing on the national flag of Saudi Arabia is considered holy, the etiquette of that country forbids the flag being flown at half-staff, vertically or upside down. Other forms of mourning have been used for national flags, including the addition of a black stripe at the fly end, a border of black on the three free edges, and the placement of black streamers on the pole above the flag.

Why do most people wear wristwatches on their left hand?

At first, we thought: this is obvious. Most people are right-handed and use the right arm more often than the left. Therefore, they are more likely to damage the watch while wearing it on their dominant hand.

We spoke to several experts about the subject, including horologist Henry Fried, Bulova's Pat Campbell and Lowell Drutman of Timex. They concurred with our theory but added a couple of their own. 'Have you ever seen a right-handed person trying to buckle up a leather strap on his right wrist?' asked Drutman. 'They aren't very successful.' Try it. He's right.

But all three also offered another theory that helps explain why many left-handers wear their watches on their left hands too. Ever since the days of the pocket watch, the stem (the round part you wind) has been placed adjacent to the '3' (on the right-hand side of the watch). This location makes it awkward to wind the clock with the left hand, whether you are left-handed, right-handed or ambidextrous. Whether generations of windless watches will change wrist preferences is a matter for sociologists of the future to keep tabs on.

Henry Fried reports that no watchmaker has ever tried to market a 'left-hander's' watch, although an occasional iconoclastic designer has placed the stem on the '9' side.

Why do priests wear black?

Imponderables readers are asserting their spiritual side. At least you seem to be curious about superficial questions about Catholic priests and the clothes they wear, and that's good enough for us.

Most readers assume that every vestment was adopted for its symbolic meaning, but in reality many of the clothes priests wear reflect the everyday dress of non-religious people nearly two millennia ago.

As John Dollison, author of the whimsical but solidly researched book *Pope-Pourri*, put it:

> Because they believed the second coming of Christ was imminent, [early Christians] didn't bother to formalise many aspects of their new religion. Clerical dress was no exception – nobody gave any thought to what priests should wear during Mass; they just wore the same clothes that laypeople did ...
>
> Fashions changed over time, but the priests didn't. They stuck with the same clothes they had always worn ... until their garments became so different from what everyone else was wearing that they were associated exclusively with religious life.

Not until the sixth century did the Church start to codify the dress of priests and mandate that special garb be worn outside of the sanctuary. Even if most Catholics have no idea of the reasons for the uniforms, Dr Brian Butler of the US Catholic Historical Society feels: 'The Church wants priests to be recognised easily by the laity. This is in the interest of both parties.' You're unlikely to see priests in pastels soon.

Some priests began wearing black vestments in the early days of Christianity, as Father Kevin Vaillancourt of the Society of Traditional Roman Catholics explains:

> The practice of priests' wearing black originated in Rome centuries ago. Since the priesthood involves a renunciation of pleasures that the laity can practise, black was worn as a symbol of death – death to these desires, and death to slavish attachment to the fashions of the world. They were to concentrate solely on the service to God and others.

But by no means was there uniformity among priests in their garb until much later. Professor Marie Anne Mayeski, of the theology department of Loyola Marymount University in Los Angeles, points out that no specific colour was required until after the Council of Trent (1545–63), and that a response to the Reformation might have been partly responsible for the codification of clerical garb: 'Perhaps Catholic and Anglican clerics did not want to appear less sober and upright than their Puritan challengers.'

There are exceptions to the generalisation that priests wear black vestments. Higher-ranking priests put a little colour in their garb. Cardinals' cassocks feature scarlet buttons, trim and inside hems; bishops and other higher officials don amaranth; and chaplains to the pope wear purple trim. During liturgical ceremonies, the cardinals wear all-scarlet cassocks, bishops wear purple, while parish priests wear black, although there are even exceptions here – a few dioceses, especially in warm-weather areas such as South America, Asia and Africa, allow priests to wear white cassocks, with trim indicating their rank.

Since priests wear black, why does the pope wear white?

Blame it on Pius V, who assumed the papacy from 1566 until his death in 1572. For centuries before that, popes wore red. Why the change? Reverend Monsignor Dr Alan F Detscher, Executive Director of the Secretariat for the Liturgy, explains:

> Religious men who became bishops wore a cassock in the same colour as the habit worn by their religious community. Pius V, being a [member of the] Dominican order, continued the practice

of using the colour of his religious habit, even after he was elected pope. The practice of the pope wearing white continued on after his papacy. On some occasions, the pope will wear a red cape over his white cassock. This is a reminder that the more ancient papal colour was not white, but red. ’

Like other religious traditions, what might have started as a personal predilection became codified to the point where now there are elaborate agreements about colour codes. For example, when the Queen of England visits the Vatican, she wears black, as she is technically representing the Protestant Anglican church. But when the pope visits her at Buckingham Palace, she can wear chartreuse if that's what she fancies.

Why does the pope wear a white skullcap, and when did this custom begin? How does he keep it fastened? And why at other times does he wear a double-pointed hat?

We have our old friend Pope Pius V to 'blame' for the pope wearing white, but he did not originate the use of the skullcap, properly called a zucchetto. Its use goes back to at least the thirteenth century. The zucchetto resembles the Jewish skullcap, the yarmulke, but its original purpose was quite different.

In the Middle Ages, when Catholic priests embraced celibacy, a ring of hair was removed from the top of their head, the tonsure. Churches and monasteries of this era weren't renowned for their creature comforts – the purpose of the zucchetto was to cover the 'bald spot' in order for these often elderly men to retain heat in cold, draughty conditions. A cap that was sometimes used by clerics in the same era, the *camauro*, covered the ears and the whole back of the head, and was even more effective in staving off the cold. The tonsure was eliminated after the Second Vatican Council, but the headgear has lived on.

At no point has the zucchetto been worn exclusively by the pope, but since a proclamation by Pope Paul VI in 1968, only members of the hierarchy are required to wear the skullcap. You can tell the rank of a cleric without a scorecard – the colour of the zucchetto is a tip-off.

Only the pope may wear white, with the exception of orders whose habits are white, such as the Norbertines and Dominicans.

Why are graves six feet deep and who determined they should be that deep?

Graves haven't always been that deep. Richard Santore, Executive Director of the Associated Funeral Directors International, told *Imponderables* that during the time of the Black Death in Europe, bodies were not buried properly or as deep as they are today. These slovenly practices resulted in rather unpleasant side effects. As soil around the bodies eroded, body parts became exposed, which explains the origins of the slang term 'boneyard' for a cemetery. Beside the grossness content, decomposing flesh on the surface of the earth did nothing to help the continent's health problems.

England, according to Santore, was the first to mandate that graves be 6 feet (about 2 m) deep, with the idea that husband and wife could be buried atop each other, leaving a safe cushion of 2 feet of soil above the buried body, 'the assumption being that if each casket was 2 feet high, you would allow 2 feet for the husband, 2 feet for the wife, and 2 feet of soil above the last burial'. At last, there were no bones in the boneyard to be found.

The six-foot-under rule also puts coffins out of reach of most predators and the frost line in colder climes. Of course, caskets could be buried even deeper, but that would be unlikely to be popular with gravediggers, as Dan Flory, President of the Cincinnati College of Mortuary Science, explains: 'Six feet is a reasonable distance for the gravedigger [to shovel] and is usually not deep enough to get into water or rock trouble.'

Once again, Pope Pius V claimed the white colour in honour of his Dominican order. Cardinals wear red zucchettos. Patriarchs, archbishops and bishops sport a violet-like amaranth red zucchetto, and the 'lower' deacons and priests wear black, although few priests wear zucchettos anymore.

How do clerics fasten the zucchetto on their heads? Evidently with some difficulty. According to Reverend Monsignor Dr Alan F Detscher, 'The zucchetto is not fastened on, but merely is set on the back of the head.'

The mitre, the double-pointed hat that the pope wears during ceremonial proceedings, is even older than the zucchetto – dating back to the tenth century – and can be worn by bishops and cardinals, as well as the pope. The hat features two cone-shaped peaks, divided by a piece of material that can fold together.

The mitre has undergone so many transformations in form that it is hardly recognisable as the original, simple cone-shaped hat that was worn by laypeople in Rome. At one point in the twelfth century the mitre was shaped with the two points on the end, with a 'valley' in between. But as John Dollison, author of *Pope-Pourri* notes, this created a problem: 'The points reminded people so much of the devil that they became known as horns ... so the popes rotated their hats 90 degrees. They've worn them that way ever since.'

Why does the pope change his name upon assuming his office?

The tradition of name changes for Church officials dates back to the beginnings of the Christian movement. In the Book of Matthew, Jesus appoints his disciple Peter to be the first head of the Church. Yet Peter's birth name was Simon.

According to Lorraine D'Antonio, the retired business manager of the Religious Research Association:

> 'Their names were changed to signify the change in roles, attitudes and way of life. When the pope assumes his role as head of the Church, it is assumed that he will change his life as his name is changed when he dedicates his total being to the service of the Church. Quite often, when a person dedicates his or her life to the service of God (during ordination, confirmation, etc.), the person assumes a new name, as he or she assumes a new role and commitment.'

The first pope who we know changed his name was John II, in 533 AD. Presumably, his given name, Mercurio, a variation of the pagan god Mercury, was deemed unsuitable for the head of the Church. So Mercurio paid tribute to John I by adopting his name.

No other pope changed his name until Octavian chose John XII for his papal name in 955. A few decades later, Peter Canepanova adopted John XIV. Brian Butler, President of the US Catholic Historical Society, told *Imponderables* that John XIV was the first of several popes with the given name of Peter to start a tradition – no pontiff has ever taken the name of the Church's first pope.

Butler notes that the last pope to keep his baptismal name was Marcellus II, born Marcello Cervini, who served in the year 1555.

Why is the colour purple associated with royalty?

Although pagans once believed that purple dye was the creation of Satan, we actually have the Phoenicians to thank for the association of purple with royalty. Somehow, and we always wonder how anyone ever stumbles upon this sort of stuff, an anonymous Phoenician discovered that the spiny shell of the murex sea snail yielded a purple substance perfectly suited as a dye base. Phoenicians, the greatest traders and businessmen of the ancient world, soon developed purple cloth as one of their most lucrative trading commodities.

Since purple cloth was more expensive than other hues, only aristocrats could afford to wear it. But the Romans codified the practice, turning the colour of clothing into a status symbol. Only the royal family itself could wear all-purple garments. Lesser aristocrats wore togas with purple stripes or borders to designate their rank – the more purple on the clothing, the higher the status.

The original 'royal purple' was a different colour than what we call purple today. It was a dark wine-red, with more red than blue. Many written accounts liken the colour to blood. Indeed, the Phoenician dye was prized because it symbolised the unity, strength and bonding of blood ties, and the continuity of royal families based on bloodlines.

The association of purple with royalty crossed many cultures and centuries. Greek legend explained royal purple as the colour of Athena's goatskin dyed red. Kings in Babylonia wore a 'lanbussu' robe

Why do nurses wear white? Why do surgeons wear blue or green when operating?

Florence Nightingale always wore a white uniform. White, of course, is a symbol of purity, and, in the case of a nurse, an appropriate and practical one – white quickly shows any dirtiness.

Surgeons also wore white until 1914, when a surgeon decided that red blood against a white uniform was rather repulsive and needlessly graphic. The spinach green colour he chose to replace it helped neutralise the bright red.

At the end of World War II, the lighting was changed in operating rooms, and most surgeons switched to a colour called 'misty green'. Since about 1960, most surgeons have used a colour called 'seal blue', which contains a lot of grey. Why this latest switch? According to Bernard Lepper, of the Career Apparel Institute of New York City, seal blue shows up better on the TV monitors used to demonstrate surgical techniques to medical students.

of the same colour. Mark's Gospel says that Jesus' robe was purple (although Matthew describes it as scarlet).

In many churches, purple became the liturgical colour during Lent, except for Good Friday. Consistently, in the succeeding centuries, the colour purple was always identified with blood, as late as the time of Shakespeare, for the Bard himself referred to the 'purpled hands' of Caesar's assassins, 'stained with the most noble blood of all the world'.

Curiously, marketing research indicates that today purple is one of the least popular colours, which helps explain why it is so seldom used in packaging. Is the current aversion to purple stirred by a rejection of the patrician origins of the colour, its close approximation to the colour of blood or a rejection of our contemporary purple royalty, Prince?

Why do hospital gowns tie at the back?

It's bad enough being laid up in the hospital. Why do patients have to undergo the indignity of having their backsides exposed to all? This is a fashion statement that even sick people don't want to make. We realise that hospital gowns aren't the top priority of hospital administrators, that items like nursing staff, research budgets and surgical care justifiably occupy much of their time. But while hospitals pursue the impossible dream of serving edible food, the eradication of the back-tied gown is possible right now.

The original justification for the back closure of hospital gowns was that this configuration enabled health care workers to change the gowns of the bedridden without disturbing the patients. If the gown tied in the front, the patients would have to be picked up (or lift themselves up) to remove the garment.

Perhaps it is growing concern for 'patient modesty' (buzz words in the 'patient apparel' industry), or perhaps it is jockeying for competitive advantage among hospitals, especially private hospitals, but many health care administrators are starting to recognise the existence of alternatives to the back-tied gown. Scott Hlavaty, Director of Patient/Surgical Product Management of uniform giant Angelica, told *Imponderables* that ties on the sides provide a maximum of patient modesty while requiring no more patient inconvenience to remove.

Angelica and other companies manufacture gowns that minimise patient exposure and inconvenience when procedures are performed. Hlavaty explains:

> ‘There are specialised gowns with “IV sleeves” that allow the gown to be removed by unsnapping the sleeves so that the IV tubes do not have to be removed from the patient in order to change a gown. Also, with the advent of pacemakers and heart monitors, “telemetry pockets” have been placed in the centre of gowns. These pockets have openings in the back to allow for the pass through of the monitoring device so that these do not have to be disconnected either.’

Some nurses we spoke to said that gowns with back closures make it more convenient to give shots (in the backside, of course). But many patients prefer to wear their own pyjamas, and nurses always manage to administer the shot.

Even if a patient were so incapacitated that a back closure was deemed best, many improvements have been made in hospital gowns to prevent patients from exposing themselves to roommates and passersby. Back-closure gowns wouldn't be such a problem if the closures were made secure. Gowns are now available with metal or plastic grippers, as well as Velcro. And just as important, gowns are available with a 'full overlap back', which provides enough material to overlap more like a bathrobe than a traditional hospital gown.

Of course, these improvements in gown design cost a little more, but it's money well spent. After all, how can you encourage post-surgical patients to take a stroll around the hospital corridors when they're more concerned about being the objects of peeping Toms than they are about aches and pains?

Why are there two title pages in most books?

Open almost any book, including this one, and you will find that the first printed matter is likely to be the title of the book printed simply on the right-hand side. Turn the page, and you are likely to find the 'official' title page, with the name of the author included, and the name of the publisher, or its imprint, at the foot of the page. What is the purpose of that first title page? Why start a book with such a drab opening when the title information and more is provided by the elaborate and larger sized 'real' title page?

The name of the first title page is the half-title. Most of the time, it doesn't serve any purpose. But it once did.

In the early days of publishing, before mass distribution, scribes hand-printed books and there was no such thing as a title page. Books were produced by commission, so customers, usually noblemen, already knew the title and contents of the book they were buying. Books then were bound immediately upon completion and were thus protected from fingerprints and dirt.

When books began to be printed rather than handwritten, booksellers were usually the publishers as well. Printers sent bundles of hand-tied finished copies to bookstores to be bound, leaving naked pages exposed to the elements. The top page of the book was most often damaged, just as the front pages of newspapers today sometimes get pulverised or soiled. In anticipation of the problem, printers started leaving the first page of each manuscript blank. The binder would then eliminate this page when the book was ready to be bound.

The only problem with leaving the top page blank was that it hid the identity of the book. When potential customers looked at books (which were usually custom bound to the specifications of the retail buyer), they turned over the blank page to see what the title was, again exposing the first page of the book to abuse.

To solve this ridiculous problem, printers started identifying the title of the book on the front page in a style resembling our current half-title. Although this page was still intended to be cut before the book was bound, the same problem reoccurred – once the title page became a popular feature, customers wanted it in pristine shape; there was now a need for a sheet of paper to protect the title page, but also to identify the contents of the book. Thus the half-title was born. The reason it is so simple compared to the full-title page is that it was originally not even supposed to remain in the finished book. To indicate the less than noble origins of the half-title, it is called the *schmutztitel*, or 'dirt title', in Germany.

When printers began binding books immediately upon their completion, there was no longer a real function for the half-title. The hard cover now protected the title page. The title page as we know it today, with the title, author and publisher's name, became commonplace by the sixteenth century. The original purpose of the half-title was probably forgotten, but it became and remains a traditional feature of most books.

Publishers, like most business people today, are cost-conscious, and more books of late have been produced without half-titles. Many publishers bind books only in increments of eight or 16 finished pages. Many romance-novel series, for example, are always exactly the same number of pages. If a manuscript runs 250 words over the desired length, the book would have to be, not one page, but eight or 16 pages longer than desired, thus substantially increasing the cost to the publisher. The type size could be reduced to make the extra words fit, but most likely those words will be cut. The only alternative is to fiddle around with what publishers call the oddments, all the stuff in the book that is not contained in the chapters. One of the most dispensable oddments is the half-title, a feature that cover art and book jacket titles have long rendered obsolete.

What is the difference between an introduction, a foreword and a preface of a book?

These three terms have become virtually interchangeable. One can encounter all or none of these three features in any given book, and all or none of them might be written by the author. Traditionally, however, there has been a distinction between the introduction and the other two elements. While a preface or foreword usually tells the reader what to expect, the introduction typically starts the process of orienting the reader to the subject matter itself.

In a preface or foreword, an author might explain what burst of inspiration ignited the masterpiece you are reading. He might talk about how this book should totally change your life and about how, although his book will make you a perfect person, he is not legally or morally responsible for that transformation. He will also wittily acknowledge all of the little people whom he trampled upon in order to purvey his deathless prose.

In the introduction, the author dips into the actual subject matter, supplementing what is in the book and ensuring that the reader adopts the properly respectful attitude towards his material.

Although most publishers observe the above distinction, they have varying policies about just how interchangeable the foreword and preface are. Some publishers arbitrarily title remarks by the author as the foreword and those by editors or outside endorsers as the preface. Nowhere has *Imponderables* found any legitimate distinction between the contents of a foreword and a preface.

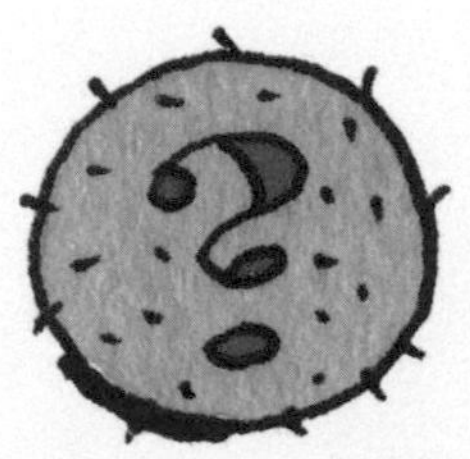

Publishers do concur on the order in which these three elements should be placed in a book. Copy-editing guides usually recommend that the preface is placed after the table of contents (and after the list of illustrations, if there is one). If there are two prefaces, the editor's preface is placed before the author's. The foreword comes next. The introduction can be part of the text; if not, it comes after the foreword.

Why were do-re-mi-fa-so-la-ti-do chosen to represent the notes of the musical scale?

If it were not for some modifications made in the seventeenth century, the hit song from *The Sound of Music* would have been 'Ut-Re-Mi', for our current octave was a modification of a hexachord scale called the 'solfeggio system'. Invented by Guido d'Arezzo, an Italian Benedictine monk who lived in the early eleventh century and composed chants, the mnemonic to remember the scale was borrowed from the first syllables of each line of an existing hymn to St John:

Ut queant laxis
Resonare fibris
Mi gestorum
Famuli polluti
Solve polluti
Labii reatum

When the octave replaced d'Arezzo's six-note scale, a seventh note was needed, so the last line of the hymn was appropriated:

Sancte Iohannes

Do was later substituted for *ut* because it is more euphonious, and *ti* was substituted for *si* because it is easier to sing. (Try it!)

Why don't male ballet dancers dance 'on pointe'?

Why do only ballerinas have the thrill of torturing their toes when dancing? This masochistic tradition dates back nearly 200 years. According to Margot Lehman, past President of the American Dance Guild, the first known print of a dancer on pointe is from 1821.

But the groundbreaking moment came a decade later. Elsa Posey, President and Director of Posey School of Dance, explains:

> Pointe shoes and pointe technique ... began in the 1830s. The first full-length ballet danced *en pointe* was *La Sylphide* of 1832, starring Marie Taglioni, whose father is sometimes credited with inventing the stiffening of the ballet shoe to enable her to appear to be floating or flying with lightness and delicacy.

Soon, Taglioni and her pink satin slippers became the dance personification of womanhood. Rebecca Hutton, Executive Director of the US National Dance Association, told *Imponderables* that choreographers prized on pointe dancing because it made ballerinas taller and yet more ethereal. Indeed, the toes of ballerinas became the weapon to launch what we now call the 'Romantic Era', as Margot Lehman amplifies:

> The Romantic ballet, a reflection of the Romantic Era's concern with the ethereal and the exotic, had as a main theme the escape from the real world into the world of the supernatural – a world of ghosts, spirits and sprites unconstrained by gravity. Lightness and grace were seen and developed as the essential female qualities. Toe dancing became one of the most important tools of the Romantic ballet to help dancers create the illusion of weightlessness.

Giselle, A Midsummer Night's Dream, Coppélia, The Nutcracker, Firebird, Swan Lake and *Sleeping Beauty* are but a few of the ballets with featured female roles danced on pointe.

There is absolutely no anatomical distinction between the sexes that would make females better able to dance on pointe. If you look hard enough, you can find men on their toes. Lehman suggests many anomalies:

> ‘The British choreographer Frederick Ashton choreographed for on-pointe male dancers in a feature film about the world of Beatrix Potter. His dancers were from the Royal Ballet and wore toe shoes in their roles as dancing mice and other delightful creatures. The all-male American Trocadero Ballet does tongue-in-cheek versions of *Swan Lake* and other ballet classics on pointe and in tutus. And the male dancers of the Republic of Georgia dance on the tips of their boots while performing athletic ethnic and folk material ...’

Posey adds that often the parts of the stepsisters in *Cinderella* and Bottom in *A Midsummer Night's Dream* are played by males on pointe.

All the experts we consulted indicated that it is not uncommon for men to participate in the ‘pointe’ segment of class, whether to strengthen their feet, stretch their arches, discover the change of balance entailed in order to become better partners for their ballerinas, or even as Rebecca Hutton reports Mikhail Baryshnikov does, just to have fun.

But these exceptions prove the rule. Dancing on pointe is associated not only with females but with femininity itself. While fewer contemporary than Romantic ballets require ballerinas to dance on pointe, there is also a trend among modern choreographers to emphasise male dancers' strength and athleticism. Daintiness is out.

The ethereality of dancing on pointe is achieved only through intense training and specialised equipment. The toe shoe, according to Lehman:

> ‘is a satin slipper with a thin, stiff leather sole and a hardened box at the tip which encases the toes. The dancers often pad the inside of this toe box with lamb's wool for comfort and extra protection. The point of contact with the floor is this tip – about the size of a silver dollar [about 25 mm across] – which must carry the body's entire weight.’

The tip of the shoe is hardened by the gluing together of layers of material. The box covers the dancers' toes tightly, so that, in effect, as Posey puts it, 'the body weight is transferred through the structure of the foot as a single unit'.

If there is anything we learned from researching this Imponderable, it's 'Don't try this at home.' Elsa Posey, who has researched and written about dance education for the young, warns that the shoes alone can't provide sufficient protection for fledgling ballerinas:

> A contraction of the muscles of the feet, ankles, legs and torso enables the dancers to "push" themselves upwards without injury to their feet. No one should attempt to dance on pointe without years of practice.

Most juvenile ballerinas should not even attempt dancing on pointe until they are 12 or their feet have stopped growing. It's ironic that the very technique that conveys femininity and weightlessness requires brute strength. In this case, traditional sexual stereotypes have made life much easier for men.

mach

and

dev

We explore the often surprising world of manufacturing with profound questions, such as why are there 88 keys on a piano? Whatever happened to A- and B-sized batteries? Why are portholes round? And were Roman chariots really as flimsy as the ones we see in the movies?

machines and devices

Why do petrol gauges in cars take forever to go from registering full to half-full, and then drop to empty at the speed of light?

On a long car trip, we will do anything to fight boredom. The roadway equivalent of reading cereal boxes at breakfast is obsessing about odometers and fuel gauges.

Nothing is more dispiriting after a fill-up at the petrol station than travelling 100 km and watching the petrol gauge stand still. Although part of us longs to believe that our car is registering phenomenal fuel efficiency, the other part of us wants the gauge to move to prove to ourselves that we are actually making decent time and have not, through some kind of *Twilight Zone* alternate reality, actually been riding on a treadmill for the last hour. Our petrol gauge becomes the arbiter of our progress. Even when the needle starts to move, and the gauge registers three-quarters full, we sometimes feel as if we have been travelling for days.

How nice it would be to have a gauge move steadily down towards empty. Just as we are about to give in to despair, though, after the gauge hits half-full, the needle starts darting towards empty as if it had just discovered the principle of gravity. Whereas it seemed that we had to pass time zones before the needle would move at all, suddenly we are afraid that we are going to run out of petrol.

There must be a better way. Why don't gauges actually register what proportion of the tank is filled with petrol? The carmakers and gauge manufacturers are well aware that a half-full reading on a petrol gauge is really closer to one-third full, and they have reasons for preserving this inaccuracy.

The gauge relies upon a sensor in the tank to relay the fuel level. The sensor consists of a float and linkage connected to a variable resistor. The resistance value fluctuates as the float moves up and down.

If a petrol tank is filled to capacity, the liquid is filled higher than the float has the physical ability to rise. When the float is at the top of its stroke, the gauge will always register as full, even though the tank can hold more petrol. The gauge will register full until this 'extra' petrol is consumed and the float starts its descent in the tank. At the other end of the float's stroke, the gauge will register as empty when the float can no longer move further downwards, even though liquid is present below the float.

We asked Anthony H Siegel, of Ametek's US Gauge Division, why sensors aren't developed that can measure the actual status of petrol more accurately. We learned, much as we expected, that more precise measurements could easily be produced, but the carmakers are using the current technology for our own good:

> Vehicle makers are very concerned that their customers do not run out of fuel before the gauge reads empty. That could lead to stranded, unhappy motorists, so they compensate in the design of the float/gauge system. Their choice of tolerances and calibration procedures guarantees that slight variations during the manufacturing of these components will always produce a combination of parts which falls on the safe side. The gauge is thus designed to read empty when there is still fuel left.

Tens of millions of motorists have suspected there is fuel left even when the gauge says empty, but few have been brave enough to test the hypothesis.

Why does inflating tyres to the proper pressure help fuel efficiency?

Do you remember, as a child, how hard it was to ride a bicycle with a flat or seriously soft tyre? It was harder than trying to pedal a Stairmaster for an hour now, wasn't it?

When you drive a car, the same principle applies. The mission of tyres is to soften the bumps and bruises you would otherwise experience while negotiating roadways, but a tyre that bends too much, whether from underinflation or overloading, is going to take a lot of extra energy to push. Tyre pressure can actually affect how much petrol your car burns, retired Firestone executive KL Campbell explains:

> About 80 per cent of the energy in the fuel you buy is used up within your car engine. Of the 20 per cent that is available to move the car, a small percentage goes into friction losses in the various rotating and moving parts outside the engine. Most of the available energy goes into overcoming wind resistance and in rotating the tyres, or in climbing grades.
>
> In order for tyres to perform their function of softening the ride of the vehicle, they must deflect under the

load of the vehicle and the irregularities encountered on the road. When they deflect, there is internal movement throughout the tyre that absorbs energy. The greater the deflection, the more energy the tyre consumes as it is rolling.

Tyre deflection is increased either by putting more load on the tyres (filling up your trunk ... or piling a few passengers in the rear seat) or by reducing the pressure in the tyres. ’

When you inflate the tyres to the proper pressure, you reduce the rolling resistance. In other words, as Jean Bailey, of General Tire, puts it, 'It requires much more force or energy to rotate a tyre that is underinflated than it does to rotate a tyre that is inflated to the proper pressure.'

Campbell estimates that by decreasing a typical radial tyre pressure of 32 psi (pounds per square inch) to 24 psi, a car travelling at 90 km/h would increase fuel consumption by about 2 per cent.

One of the reasons why modern radial tyres perform much better than their bias-ply predecessors is that radials distribute the deflection around most of the tyre, whereas bias plies concentrated the deflection near the road surface. Unfortunately, the by-product of this technological improvement is that it is difficult to see with the naked eye when a radial is underinflated. A pressure gauge is a necessity.

Don't think that you can get even better mileage if you overinflate your tyres. Once you get above 35 psi, a diminishing effect occurs. Not only do you not increase fuel efficiency, but you will be rewarded with a harsh and potentially wild ride.

How does a petrol pump 'know' when to shut off when the fuel tank is full?

A sensing device, located a couple of centimetres from the end of the nozzle, does nothing while petrol is flowing into the tank, but is tripped as soon as fuel backs up into the nozzle. The sensing device tells the nozzle to shut off. Because of the location of the sensing device and the relatively deep position of the nozzle, a petrol tank is never totally filled unless the customer or attendant 'tops off' the tank. Topping off tanks is illegal in most places and is a dangerous practice anywhere.

What causes the clicking sound inside a car when you put your indicator on? Why don't some indicators make that clicking noise?

The mechanics of the indicator are simple. Frederick Heiler, Public Relations Manager for Mercedes-Benz of North America, explains the technology:

> The electrical current to make turn signals blink usually comes from a relay – a small box enclosing an electromagnetic switch. Whenever the electromagnet is energised, it mechanically pulls together a pair of contacts, sending a pulse of current to the signal lights and, at the same time, making a clicking sound.

Why do some cars not have clicking indicators? It's all up to the manufacturer. Most carmakers choose to make the clicking noise loud and obvious just in case the driver leaves the indicator on unintentionally.

What's the big deal if the turn signal is left on too long? If a pedestrian is thinking of crossing the road and sees an oncoming car signalling to make a turn, the pedestrian is lulled into a false sense of security. Oncoming cars and pedestrians often make their decisions about when to proceed based on indicators, and a little gratuitous clicking is a small price to pay for added safety.

What exactly are we smelling when we enjoy the 'new-car smell'?

You didn't think that only one ingredient could provide such a symphony of smells, did you? No. Carmakers endeavour to provide the proper blend of constituents that will provide you with the utmost in olfactory satisfaction.

CR Cheney, of Chrysler Motors, provided us with the most comprehensive explanation and the most poignant appreciation:

> The smell we all enjoy inside a new vehicle (that "new-car smell") is a combination of aromas generated by fresh primer and paint, and the plastic materials used on instrument panels, around the windows and on door trim panels. Plus, there are odours given off by carpeting, new fabrics, leather and vinyl

used for soft trim and upholstery. Rubber, adhesives and sealers also play a part in creating this unique smell that never lasts as long as we would like and seems nearly impossible to duplicate. ’

Update

When we wrote about the new-car smell, little did we know that only a few years later, Cadillac, a division of General Motors, would be working on a way to assure that every car had a pleasing, uniform smell. Armed with the results of chemistry labs and focus group research, GM's Cadillac division launched Nuance, an aroma designed to appeal to consumers on the fence about whether to spring the extra money for its luxury brand.

In a 2003 *New York Times* story about how carmakers were engaging all the senses of consumers, GM's James T Embach remarks: 'You pay the extra money for leather, you don't want to smell like lighter fluid. You want it to smell like a Gucci bag.' The trend is accelerating, with Porsche now introducing its own proprietary scent.

Meanwhile, the US car manufacturers' biggest rival has been concerned not so much with adding smells as it is with eliminating the ones already there. Recent research indicates that 'volatile organic compounds', the chemicals that leach from the plastics and vinyl found in cars, may be a serious health hazard, at least in the first six months or so of the car's use. The big five Japanese carmakers vow to reduce these emissions, even if the end result is a no-car smell.

Why do wagon wheels in cowboy films appear to be spinning backwards?

Motion-picture film is really a series of still pictures run at the rate of 24 frames per second. When a wagon being photographed moves slowly, the shutter speed of the camera is capturing tiny movements of its wheel at a rate of 24 times per second – and the result is a disorienting strobe effect. As long as the movement of the wheel does not synchronise with the shutter speed of the camera, the movement of the wheel on film will be deceptive. This effect is identical to disco strobe lights, where dancers will appear to be jerking frenetically or listlessly pacing through sludge, depending on the speed of the strobe.

EJ Blasko, of the Motion Picture and Audiovisual Products Division of Eastman Kodak, explains how the strobe effect works in films:

> As the wheels travel at a slower rate they will appear to go backwards, but as the wheel goes faster it will then become synchronised with the film rate of the camera and appear to stay in one spot, and then again at a certain speed the wheel will appear to have its spokes travelling forwards, but not at the same rate of speed as the vehicle.

This strobe effect is often seen without need of film. Watch a roulette wheel or fan slow down, and you will see the rotation appear to reverse.

Were Roman chariots as wobbly and flimsy as depicted in movies? If so, how could they be used effectively in wartime?

If the defence of Rome was dependent upon the stability of its chariots, no wonder the mighty empire fell. The Romans may have been decadent, but they weren't dumb: the chariot was far from a potent weapon of war.

Chariots were created almost 2000 years before the Roman Empire and were suitable only for flat terrain. Earlier, ancient armies used them only because horses were not bred large and strong enough to withstand the weight of an armoured soldier with weapons. The Roman legions rode on horseback and reserved chariots for ceremonies and games such as the infamous Roman circus. According to military historian Art Ferrill, author of *The Origins of War*, 'Caesar's troops were amazed by the British use of them. For all practical purposes, chariots were last used in ancient Near Eastern warfare by the Assyrians.'

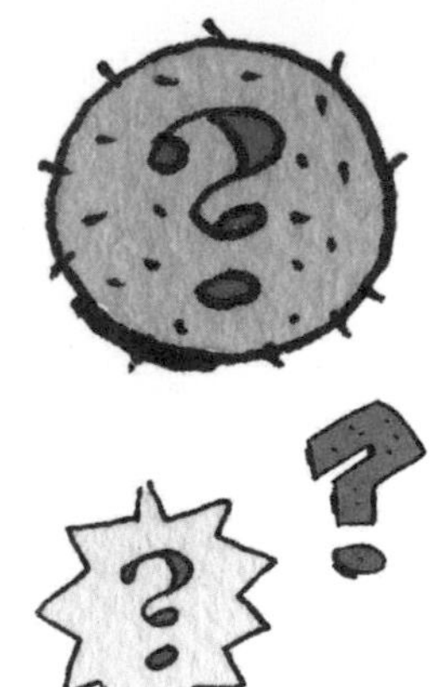

What were the problems with using chariots for transportation? Let us count the ways. Carol Thomas, Professor of History at the University of Washington, acknowledging research by JG Landels in *Engineering in the Ancient World*, which addressed these issues directly, wrote to us:

> The wheels of chariots probably were not flimsy. They were either spoked (in one of a couple possible arrangements) or solid. They may well have been wobbly, though, because any of the

> three or four possible arrangements for attaching the wooden wheels to the wooden axles of the vehicles led to grooves being worn on the bearing surfaces, which give the components more freedom of play.
>
> According to Landels, there's no evidence of any swivelling mechanism in two- or four-wheeling vehicles, which would have allowed a chariot to corner with all wheels turning. Thus a driver had to skid at least one wheel around a corner, which also would have added to wear on the wheel-axle joints, reduced efficiency of the use of the animal-derived motive power, and also reduced stability of the vehicle. ’

Lest you think that these fits and starts would be handled with the finesse of a Lexus, think again. Stanley Burstein, Professor of History at California State University and former President of the Association of Ancient Historians, wrote:

> ‘ My guess, for what it is worth, is that chariots were every bit as unstable as they appear, since they had no suspension systems and would react violently to any surface unevenness. They would also have been hard to control because ancient Western horse harnessing techniques were extremely inefficient. ’

Abandoned as a war vehicle, the Romans adopted chariot racing as the ancient equivalent of a car race: the danger was half the fun.

Why do men's bicycles have a crossbar?

We're sure you'll be overjoyed to learn that everyone we talked to agreed on the paramount issue: that crossbar at the top of the frame makes men's bikes far sturdier than women's. After centuries of experimentation, manufacturers have found that the best strength-to-weight ratio is maintained by building frames in the shape of diamonds or triangles. Without the crossbar, or as it is now called, the 'top tube', part of the ideal diamond structure is missing.

A man's bicycle has its top tube parallel to the ground; on a lady's bicycle, the top tube intersects the seat tube several centimetres above the crank axle. Why is the women's top tube lower than the men's?

The tradition is there for no other reason than to protect the dignity and reputations of women riding a bicycle while wearing a skirt or dress. Now that most women bicyclists wear pants or fancy bicycle tights, the original purpose for the crossbar is moot, although Joe Skrivan, a product development engineer for bicycle manufacturer Huffy, points out an additional bonus of the lower top tube: it allows for easy mounting and dismounting.

Skrivan notes that the design difference creates few complaints from women. Casual women bicyclists don't necessarily need the rigidity of the higher crossbar. Serious female bicyclists buy frames with exactly the same design as men's.

Why do the back wheels of bicycles click when you are coasting or back-pedalling?

Has there ever been a child with a bicycle who has not pondered this Imponderable? We got the scoop from Dennis Patterson, Director of Import Purchasing of the Murray Ohio Manufacturing Company:

> The rear sprocket cluster utilises a ratchet mechanism that engages during forward pedalling but allows the rear wheel to rotate independently of the sprocket mechanism. When one ceases to pedal, the wheel overrides the ratchet and the clicking noise is the ratchets falling off the engagement ramp of the hub. The ramp is designed to lock engagement if pedalled forward. The ratchet mechanism rides up the reverse slope and falls off the top of the ramp when you are coasting or back-pedalling.

Why do bicycle tyres go flat when the bike isn't used for long periods of time?

When spring beckons, we go looking for our trusty, rusty bicycle, which we haven't used since autumn. More often than not, we find two flat tyres. Why?

1 Air escapes from the valve stem. Although a valve stem cover will help reduce the outflow, nothing can prevent leakage

completely. As KL Campbell, of Firestone Tire & Rubber Company, explained, 'No materials are completely impervious to migration of gases (such as air) through them when there is a pressure differential between the inside and the outside. The bigger the pressure differential, the faster the migration.' The typical car tyre will lose from half a pound to one pound of air pressure per month, even when in regular use.

2 Inner tubes of bicycles are more porous than car tyres. No inner tube can be made totally airtight. Butyl rubber, the best type of material for reducing leaks in inner tubes, is the most impermeable rubber-like substance available (car tyres are made with a butyl inner liner). Less expensive, non-butyl rubber inner tubes tend to leak even more.

3 The actual volume of air in a bicycle tyre is quite small. There might be about half a litre of air at 60 psi in a typical bicycle tyre, compared to 20 l of air at 35 psi in a car tyre. A small loss of air volume in a bicycle tyre thus affects the bike tyre much more than it would affect the car tyre.

4 Bike tyres typically require about twice the air pressure of car tyres, making it much harder for them to maintain high air pressure.

5 Tyre pressure lowers as the temperature goes down. This demonstrates Amonton's law, which postulates that for a body of ideal gas at constant temperature, the volume is inversely proportional to the pressure.

6 Bikes contain more structural hazards to tyres than cars do. To quote Huffy Corporation's Manager of Marketing Research, Robert J Fink, 'A bike wheel provides 36 opportunities to cause 'pinholes' via the spokes and nipples. Car wheels do not (usually) have spokes.'

7 Leaks in car tyres are much less noticeable than bicycle leaks. With a naked eye or even a good kick or squeeze, we could never detect the usual one pound per month loss of air pressure. Why not? The sheer bulk of the car tyre itself, primarily, for car tyres consist of many ply layers (actually, layers of rubberised fabric surrounded by a belt topped off with tread rubber). A bicycle tyre is usually one layer of tread with an inner tube. The heavier bead of the car tyre, along with its solid rims, lack of spokes and much lower air pressure all conspire to make the contrast between a level of 30 psi and a level of 35 psi visually and tactilely indistinguishable.

Bike makers have tried to reduce leakage problems by introducing plastic tyres, which, though less porous, yield a stiff, shock-laden ride. Porous rubber is likely to be with us for a long, long time.

Why do aeroplanes, though they travel at hundreds of miles per hour, seem to move so slowly across the sky?

The human eye is easily fooled. This is one of the core facts of the science of visual perception, and it's the bread and butter of magicians and illusionists everywhere. We humans are programmed by evolution to make the obvious assumption about everything that enters our field of vision, because that obvious assumption is usually the safest. So if we see a fast-moving object out of the corner of an eye, we flinch or jump – that is, we prepare ourselves to run away or fight – until we realise that what we caught a glimpse of turns out to be only a plastic bag caught in the wind.

When it comes to aeroplanes in the sky, our brains make a number of assumptions that create the impression that the aeroplane is creeping at a snail's pace – but in this instance there is no logical cue to tell us that we are wrong. First, we tend to assume that a passing plane is reasonably nearby – not bird-in-flight nearby, but a mile away, say, or maybe two. In fact, a plane cruising overhead at 35,000 feet is nearly seven miles away from an observer on the ground. This error of perception is crucial, because if you don't know how far away an object is, then you cannot judge how fast it is moving. It follows that if you underestimate how far away an object is, then it will appear to be moving more slowly than it is.

It does not help that aeroplanes come in many sizes. A small aircraft three miles high will look exactly the same size as one that is twice the size and six miles away. And there are no visual markers in the sky to give the eye a clue as to size or distance. More confusingly still, the brain tends both to 'shrink' any small object seen against a large, plain background (such as the heavens), and to magnify objects when they are seen in the company of smaller items. So, for example, a rubber ball alone in a middle of a lawn looks like a smaller object than the same ball on a table with a selection of marbles. When it comes to aircraft, you'd think that anybody with a passing interest in aircraft ought to be able to tell a small jet from a large airliner at any distance. But this is harder than you might think. During the Second World War, the authorities found that trained RAF spotters often mistook high-flying German bombers for low-flying fighters, and vice versa.

A misplaced estimate of distance goes a long way on its own to explaining the slow progress of an aeroplane across the sky. But this perceptual error is amplified by a second false assumption that has to do with the the sky itself.

People imagine that the vault of the heavens is far smaller than it is. There is no hard-and-fast way of putting a figure on the breadth of the sky – it depends on how much architectural clutter there is on the horizon, and on what part of the sky you are looking at. But most people would be surprised to learn that in a normal urban environment an upward glance from left to right might encompass about 25 to 30 miles of clear blue firmament.

So our distant aeroplane, travelling at the usual speed of about 400 miles an hour, might take four minutes or so to pass out of sight from the moment it first came into view. Four minutes is quite long enough for an idle watcher of the skies, sitting in his back yard reading the newspaper, to glance up a couple of times and think: 'Is that plane still there?'.

Why are there more windows than rows in commercial airliners? Why aren't the windows aligned with the rows of seats?

When we first posed this Imponderable to Ken Giesbers, a Boeing employee, he wrote:

> I understand this one on a personal level. On one of the few occasions that I flew as a child, I had the good fortune of getting a window seat, but the misfortune of sitting in one that lined up with solid fuselage between two windows. Other passengers could look directly out their own window, but not me. I would crane my neck to see ahead or behind, but the view was less than satisfying. Why would designers arrange the windows in this way?

From the aeroplane maker's point of view, the goal is clearly, as a Boeing representative wrote *Imponderables*, to 'provide as many windows as they reasonably can, without compromising the integrity of a cabin that must safely withstand thousands of cycles of pressurisation and depressurisation'.

But the agenda of the airlines is a little different. Give passengers higher 'seat pitch' (the distance between rows of seats) and you have more contented passengers. Reduce the seat pitch and you increase revenue if you can sell more seats on that flight.

As we write this, soaring fuel prices are squeezing the airlines' costs, so there isn't much incentive to offer more legroom. Their loads (percentage of available seats sold) are high; if they reduce the number of seats available on a flight, there is a good chance they have lost potential revenue on that flight. And passengers who are concerned with legroom might pay for more lucrative seats in business or first class. On the other hand, the more you squish your passengers, the more likely you are to lose your customer to another airline that offers higher seat pitch. Web sites such as SeatGuru.com pinpoint the exact pitch dimensions of each aircraft on many of the biggest airlines, heating up the 'pitch war'.

A few centimetres of legroom can have huge consequences. Tens of millions of dollars can be involved in such decisions. Cabin seats can be moved forwards or backwards on rails fairly easily, but the real costs involved are not just for equipment and the labour involved in reconfiguring the planes, but in the downtime while they are reconfigured. As you might guess, the sight lines of window passengers aren't uppermost in the minds of the airlines. If you happen to have a clear shot at the window from your seat, consider it nothing more than serendipity.

Why do pilots turn off the interior lights before taking off?

'If you're talking about the lights going out for any period of time,' replied one pilot, 'that's when the crew is having a party in the cockpit.'

Thanks, we didn't need that.

There are actually two moments when the lights are killed in the cabin. The first is merely a flicker. John Payton, an airline electrician, explains:

> While the aircraft is at the boarding gate, it is hooked up to an auxiliary power unit, which provides power for lighting and ventilation. When the engines are running, the crew switch over to power generated by the engines and disconnect this auxiliary unit.

But if you are referring to the practice of main cabin lights being extinguished during take-off, it has nothing to do with safety or technical problems. The flight attendants turn out the lights. United Airlines captain Mike Lauria claims that the lights-out custom is motivated by passengers' desire to better see the lights outside the plane on take-off.

Is there any logic to the numbers assigned to Boeing jets? What happened to the Boeing 717?

The first Boeing aeroplane was, appropriately enough, assigned the number 1 in the late 1910s. From then on, Boeing has grouped its product lines in series.

The first series, numbers 1–102, featured mostly biplanes. The first pressurised airplane, the Boeing 307 Stratoliner, was part of the 300 series that also included the Boeing 314 Clipper seaplane. Many military planes were included in the 200 and 400 series (the B-17 bomber was also known as the 299; B-47 and B-52 jet bombers were part of the 400 series). Boeing reserved the entire 500 series for industrial products, such as gas turbine engines. GAPA and Bomarc missiles were grouped in the 600 series.

When the prototype for the 707 jet was being designed, it was given a working number of 367-80. The intent was to disguise the jet as if it were just an update of the Boeing Stratocruiser. When the plane was ready to be unveiled, the 700 series was created in its honour.

Why was the first plane named the '707' instead of the '700'? According to Boeing, the name was picked:

> ‘simply because it was catchy. Since then, Boeing has built on that base of publicity and continued the naming sequence.
>
> The numbers are assigned in the order the aeroplane was designed, not by the number of engines or even dates of introduction. Hence the 727, which came before the 737, has three engines while the 737 has only two. The 767 was introduced into passenger service in late 1982, while the 757 came on the air transport scene in early 1983.’

So what happened to the Boeing 717? Perhaps because the company didn't realise that their 7-7 series would become a staple of the international aviation scene, Boeing assigned the 717 number to another jet – the KC-135, an aerial refueller produced for the US Air Force.

To forestall any future questions on this subject – yes, 800- and 900-model series already exist and have been assigned to such esoterica as lunar orbiters and hydrofoil boats.

Update

Since we first answered this question, Boeing has become a beehive of 7-7 activity, and a stalwart *Imponderables* reader and Boeing employee, Ken Giesbers, makes sure we're regularly updated. While the 707, 727 and 757 are currently out of production, the Boeing 777 has proved popular, particularly among international carriers; in 2005 the 777-200LR Worldliner set a record for the longest nonstop flight ever by a commercial airplane (from Hong Kong, flying east, to Heathrow Airport).

Next on tap is the 787 Dreamliner, formerly known as the less mellifluous Boeing 7E7. In its continuing game of cat and mouse with the European consortium's Airbus, the Dreamliner is Boeing's attempt to launch the most efficient jumbo jet in the sky.

But the big news from the *Imponderables* front is that the Boeing 717 came back, at least for a while. After Boeing merged with McDonnell Douglas in 1996, one of the planes it acquired from MD was the 100-seat MD-95, which Boeing re-branded as the 717. While the slightly bigger 737 has been the best-selling jet in history, the 717 wasn't competitive, and Boeing discontinued production of new 717s in 2006. You can't keep track of Boeing's sevens without a scorecard.

What causes the 'pop-pop' noise of helicopters?

Much to our surprise, 'pop' is the term actually used by pilots to describe the distinctive noises generated by helicopters. Entire books have been written about the racket initiated by choppers, but John Shaw, Technical Director of the American Helicopter Society, explains the common threads that all 'pops' share:

> The "pop-pop" noise is created by the whirling rotor blades as they sweep through the air above the helicopter. It may be

helpful to think of the air "swept" by the rotor blades as forming a large, thin "disk". "Pop-pop" sounds occur when some spot on this disk is "ready" to create a sharp disturbance in the air (which we hear as noise, like a balloon popping in the distance) when a blade passes through that spot. The noise is a sequence of "pops" because the individual blades pass one after the other – "pop-pop-pop" – through the noise-generating spot. ’

The generic name for this type of noise is 'blade slap', and three discrete types of blade slap have been identified:

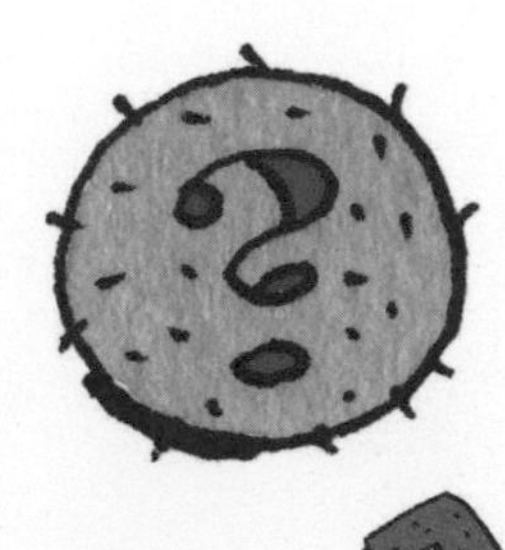

1 Ernie Stephens, President of Werewolf Aviation ('Driving "Egg Beaters" is what we do best!'), told us that as the rotor blades spin, each one leaves a wake of turbulent air behind it: 'The following blade then advances and 'slaps' into its wake, causing a 'pop' sound. This phenomenon is called blade-wake interaction and is similar to the hull of a boat hitting a wave.'

2 The second noise is duller than the first, perhaps more accurately described as 'thud-thud' than 'pop-pop'. John Shaw describes it:

‘ Each rotor blade, as it moves along, pushes the air away in front of it. This causes pressure waves to radiate ahead. We hear the pressure waves as sound. The faster the blade moves through the air, the more intense the pressure waves become. The time of fastest motion is when the blade, once per revolution, reaches the area where it is sweeping "forward" in the direction of flight. The blade passes through the "spot" very quickly so the most intense pressure waves occur in a burst. ’

3 At certain times, a helicopter can cause a mini sonic boom. Shaw explains:

‘ When the helicopter is flying very fast, the forward speed of the helicopter and the speed of a forward-sweeping blade combine to approach the speed of sound. The pressure waves ahead of the rapidly moving blade cannot move fast enough to get away from the blade. The waves build up and combine to form a shock wave – a small version of the shock wave ahead of a supersonic airplane. The airplane forms a shock wave constantly, but the helicopter forms its shock wave only briefly as each blade sweeps forward through the spot where its speed is nearly supersonic. As each shock wave forms and collapses, we hear a "pop". The resulting "pop-pop-pop" noise is most noticeable when the helicopter is approaching the listener.

Ernie Stephens says that this phenomenon creates the most 'pop-like' sound of the three and was frequently heard in households during the Vietnam War via US HUH-1 Huey helicopters. According to Stephens:

> The rotor blades on this particular aircraft turn so fast they compress the air while advancing through it. Newer helicopter rotor systems are more efficient and spin at speeds slow enough to eliminate most of this noise.

Is there any particular reason why boats and planes have red lights on the left side and green lights on the right?

The origins of this practice are obscure. Wayne Young, of the Marine Board of the US National Research Council, suggests that side lights might be a descendant of the system originally used for hand buoys. As far back as 1889, the International Marine Conference agreed on a uniform colouring system, subsequently changed by a League of Nations subcommittee in 1936 to the current Uniform System of black buoys with green or white lights on the starboard side and red buoys with red or white lights on the port side.

In practice, the colour scheme of side lights makes right-of-way decisions a snap for pilots or navigators, using colour associations we have all known since childhood. B Scott Coe, of *Sail* magazine, explains the 'stop and go' theory:

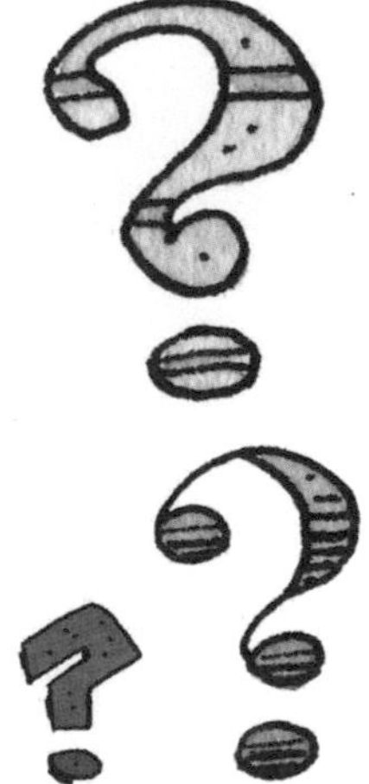

> Picture a four-way intersection. The boat to your right has the right of way. Looking at him, you see his left, or port side, which shows a red light. This means you stop, he goes. Presumably he sees your green (starboard) light and will go. If you look at the boat on the left of you at the crossing, you see his green light. This means you go and he stops. Presumably, that boat is seeing your red (port) light and will stop. An old sailing ditty goes: "If to starboard red appear, 'tis your duty to keep clear."

Side lights also enable airplanes and ships to pass each other in the dark. Rexford B Sherman, Director of Research and Information Services at the American Association of Port Authorities, wrote *Imponderables* that he believes:

> The explanation lies with navigational "rules of the road" that require ships or aircraft to pass each other on the right side. Thus the position of the lights vis-a-vis an approaching vessel or airplane would indicate whether your craft is properly positioned in relation to the other.
>
> Of course, air traffic controllers endeavour to prevent planes from passing each other too closely. Still, the side lights, which can be seen from a surprisingly long range, enable a plane to detect the presence and flight direction of nearby aircraft.

Why are portholes round?

Windows have two main jobs: to let in light and fresh air. This doesn't seem too much to ask of a sheet of glass surrounded by a base frame, but ships pose a few extra little problems. Obviously, portholes on ships need to contend with water (windows that don't seal properly aren't too popular on ships, especially windows that are underwater at times). But a more pernicious danger is the movement of the boat itself.

When most ships were made out of wood, portholes were usually rectangular. But once steel construction came into vogue, sharp corners morphed into arcs. Wood may not be as hard as steel, but it has one feature that makes it more porthole-friendly: wood absorbs the stresses of the rocking of boats on the sea far better than metal. When steel hulls came into vogue in the late nineteenth century, sailors discovered quickly that stress fractures were endemic to rectangular portholes, starting at the corners. Round portholes, on the other hand, distribute the stress evenly, and naval architects figured out the spherical solution quickly.

Rectangular portholes are far from extinct, however. Some wooden ships still have them. And cruise liners often sport large rectangular windows on decks. But the more violent the weather a boat encounters, the rougher the seas it navigates, and the farther down in the boat it resides, the more likely the porthole is to be cornerless.

Why are the windows in airline passenger cabins oval?

May we exert executive privilege and pose this Imponderable, which occurred to us after researching the previous Imponderable about portholes? Surely, aeroplane windows are subject to extreme pressures in the air.

Ken Giesbers, our mole at Boeing, confirmed it:

> 'Rounded holes in the thin fuselage are structurally more sound, and much less prone to stress fractures. Stress fractures in a pressurised cabin can lead to explosive decompression and outright structural failure.'

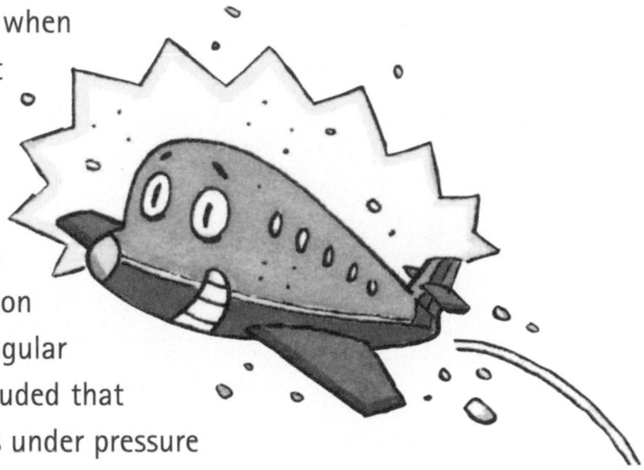

The seriousness of the issue was highlighted when the first commercial jet, the De Havilland Comet of Britain, was plagued with three crashes shortly after its introduction in 1952. Much to their shock, thorough investigations revealed that the main culprit in all three crashes was likely metal fatigue. And most of the deterioration started at the corners of the Comet's large, rectangular windows. The US Attorney General's report concluded that 'up to 70 per cent of the aircraft's ultimate stress under pressure was concentrated on the corners of the aircraft's window'.

The Comet was then redesigned with a stronger fuselage and round windows.

If round windows are best, why do Boeing and Airbus provide us with oval ones? According to Giesbers, they just aim to please:

> 'Having round windows would necessarily mean more solid material in the gap between windows. By elongating the windows vertically, aircraft designers can provide more viewing area (more surface area devoted to windows) and also better accommodate passengers of differing heights.
>
> Boeing is very proud of the large [48 cm x 26 cm] windows its new 787 will have. The windows can be larger because the 787 will use more composite materials than before. Boeing makes no bones about the reason [for the big windows]: a better experience for the passengers.'

Do submarines have anchors?

They certainly do. Submarines need anchors for the same reason that other ships do. Any time a submarine needs to maintain its position on the surface but doesn't happen to be near a pier or another vessel, the anchor is used. Anchors aren't needed while submarines are submerged, but subs have to resurface sometime, so anchors come in handy.

One of our favourite correspondents, George Flower, who happens to be in the US Navy, wrote to us: 'A submarine on the surface is a very unstable platform, as any sub sailor will be willing to tell you.'

We were under the misapprehension that an anchor would help stabilise a submarine, but Captain GL Graveson, Jr, Public Affairs Director of the Naval Submarine League, disabused us of the notion. Captain Graveson told *Imponderables* that in a rough sea with the anchor down, the ship will tend to position itself perpendicular to the wind; to this extent, an anchor might help cut turbulence on the surface.

But Graveson claims that submarines aren't noticeably more unstable on the surface than other ships. He says the worst instability on a submarine is usually experienced in the process of diving or resurfacing; as the centres of gravity and buoyancy change, so do the complexions of some of the queasier sailors.

How do they assemble tall cranes without using another crane?

George O Headrick, Director of Public Relations and Administrative Services at the US Construction Industry Manufacturers Association, was kind enough to direct us to several manufacturers of cranes. While they were uniformly generous in sharing their knowledge of how cranes are erected, they tended to provide us not with more than we wanted to know but a great deal more than we were capable of understanding.

So we are indebted for the following explanation to the former Secretary-Treasurer of the Construction Writers Association, EE Halmos, Jr, who is now the head of Information Research Group, an editorial consulting group in Poolesville, Maryland:

> ‘The tall cranes, which often carry booms (known to the trade as sticks) of 120 feet [about 35 m] or more, are assembled on the ground, at the construction site. If you'll notice, most of the tall booms are built as steel latticework structures and are thus comparatively lightweight. Usually, the machine arrives on the scene on its own, carrying only the base stub of the boom.
>
> The sections for the full length of the boom usually arrive separately, via trailer-truck. At the site, the stub of the boom is lowered to a horizontal position, and the sections of the finished boom laid out on the ground, attached together (much like a child's Meccano set), then mounted on the stub, and raised into position by cables attached to the crane body.’

Likewise, extensions can be added by laying the boom on the ground.

The use of these conventional rigs has been steadily declining, however, in favour of the 'tower crane'. These are the cranes that sit in the middle of a site and can be raised after they have been erected. The centre column on which the control cab and the moving 'head' sit is built up to three or four storeys. As the building rises around the crane, added height is built onto the centre column, and the whole top assembly is 'jumped' upwards.

Halmos reports that tower cranes have largely eliminated the need for elevators (known as skips) and the lifting of loads from the ground by mobile cranes. 'The tower crane operator can see what he's picking up, and can spot the load almost anywhere on the job, without a lot of elaborate signalling.'

Why do some escalator handrails run at a different speed from the steps alongside them?

The drive wheel that powers the steps in an escalator is attached to a wheel that runs the handrails. Because the steps and the handrails run in a continuous loop, the descending halves of the stairs and handrails act as a counterweight to their respective ascending halves. The handrails, then, are totally friction-driven rather than motor-driven.

If the escalator is properly maintained, the handrail should move at the same speed as the steps. The handrails are meant to provide a stabilising force for the passenger and are thus designed to move synchronously for safety reasons. Handrails that move slower than the accompanying steps are actually dangerous, for they give a passenger the impression that his feet are being swept in front of him. Richard Heistchel, of Schindler Elevator Company, informed *Imponderables* that handrails were once set to move slightly faster than the steps because it was believed that passengers forced to lean forward were less likely to fall down.

Why don't traffic signal light bulbs ever seem to burn out? Can we buy them?

To answer the second part of the Imponderable first: certainly, you can buy the same bulbs that light our traffic signals. But you probably wouldn't want to.

Yes, the bulbs found in traffic lights do last much longer than standard household bulbs. The traffic light bulbs are rated at 8000 hours, compared to the standard 1000 hours. Incandescent lights can be manufactured to last any length of time. However, the longer life a bulb has, the less efficiently it burns. According to General Electric's J Robert Moody:

> 'The incandescent light is like a candle. If you burn it dimly, the candle will last a long time. If you burn the candle on both ends, you get a lot of light but short life. The traffic signal light must use 100 watts to get 1000 lumens [units of light]. To obtain the same 1000 lumens a household lamp needs only 60 watts. At an electric rate of, say, 10p/kWh, the electric cost for 100 watts is £10 per 1000 hours.
>
> For the 60 watts the electric cost would be £6 per 1000 hours. Thus, the consumer would save £4 per 1000 burning hours [or 40 per cent] by using a household light bulb rather than a traffic signal light bulb.'

Traffic signal bulbs are also specially constructed and are filled with krypton gas rather than the less expensive argon gas used in standard bulbs.

Local governments obviously feel the added expense of the special bulbs is more than offset by the cost of labour for replacing burned-out bulbs and the fewer dangerous situations created by malfunctioning traffic signals.

We're as lazy as the next man, but even we think it is worth changing bulbs to save nearly 50 per cent on our lighting costs.

What are you hearing when you shake a light bulb?

Would you believe the ocean? We didn't think so.

Actually, what you are hearing depends upon whether you are shaking a functional or a burned-out bulb. If you are shaking a newish, functioning bulb, chances are you are hearing the delightful sound of loose tungsten particles left over in the bulb's glass envelope during its manufacturing process.

According to Peter Wulff, editor of *Home Lighting & Accessories*, these loose particles don't affect the bulb's operation or lifespan. Wulff adds that although the tungsten particles aren't left in the bulb deliberately, at one time manufacturers of high-wattage tungsten halogen bulbs did leave such residue: 'Occasionally, it was recommended that after use and after the bulb cooled, the bulb should be turned upside down and then shaken to allow the loose particles to clean the inside of the glass.'

But today if you hear something jangling around, chances are that you are shaking a burned-out bulb. In fact, this is the way most consumers determine whether a bulb is 'dead'. Richard H Dowhan, GTE Products' Manager of Public Affairs, told *Imponderables* that in this case you are hearing particles of a broken filament, 'the most common type of bulb failure'. Barring the rare case of loose tungsten particles inside the bulb, Dowhan says, 'you should hear nothing when you shake a light bulb that is still capable of lighting'.

Why do fluorescent lights make a plinking noise when you turn them on?

We went to Peter Wulff again for our answer. Older fluorescent fixtures used a 'preheat system', which featured a bimetallic starter (the small, round silver

Why are traffic signals **red, yellow** and **green,** and why is the red light on top, green light on the bottom and yellow light in between?

Traffic signals actually predate the existence of the automobile. One was installed in London, outside Parliament, in 1868. This signal had two semaphore arms, like a railroad signal, that acted as a physical impediment to oncoming traffic.

The device was designed to control the flow of pedestrians, and some feature was needed to make it functional at night. The easiest solution was to adapt the system used for railway signals – red and green gas lamps would signify when one could proceed (green) or had to stop (red). This prototype wasn't a rousing success – it blew up shortly after its introduction, killing a policeman.

A lively controversy has developed over where the first modern traffic signal designed to control automobile traffic was in use. Although the US cities of Salt Lake City, Utah, and St Paul, Minnesota, lay claim to the crown, the green-red signal installed on Euclid Avenue in Cleveland, Ohio, in 1914 is generally credited with being the first.

Although the traffic signal's colours might have been arbitrarily lifted from the railway's, there is an important safety reason for the consistency of the configuration today. As recently as the 1950s, many traffic signals, especially in busy urban intersections, were displayed horizontally rather than vertically. The current vertical design with red on top was adopted in order to aid colourblind individuals who might be confused by different layouts. According to Eugene W Robbins, President of the Texas Good Roads/Transportation Association, the red in traffic signals has some orange in it and the green has some blue to make it even easier for the colourblind to distinguish them.

piece). Wulff told us that inside the starter is a bimetallic switch, which 'pings' when energised. Newer fluorescent systems, such as the 'preheat' or 'rapid start', are rendering the 'ping' a relic of our nostalgic past.

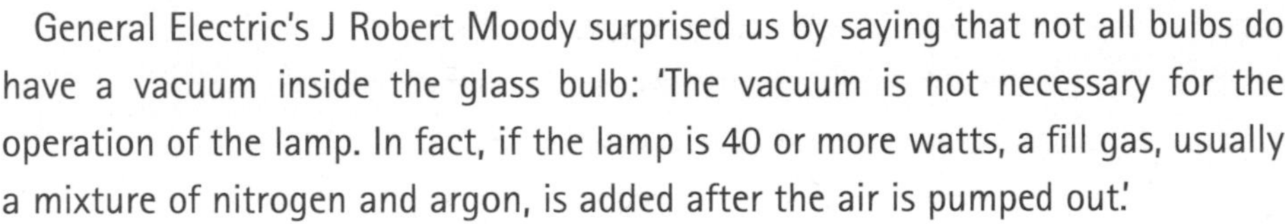

How do they keep air out of light bulbs when they are manufactured? Is a vacuum important for a bulb to function?

As we learned in fire prevention class, oxygen is fire's best friend. If oxygen were inside a light bulb while it operated, the filament would melt as soon as electricity was applied. So at the last stage of manufacture, the air is pumped from the incandescent bulb through a glass exhaust tube that is part of the filament support assembly. Richard Dowhan, of GTE Products, told *Imponderables* that the exhaust tube is shortened and sealed so that air cannot re-enter and so that the screw base can be installed. Any air that remains is removed with a chemical called a 'getter'.

General Electric's J Robert Moody surprised us by saying that not all bulbs do have a vacuum inside the glass bulb: 'The vacuum is not necessary for the operation of the lamp. In fact, if the lamp is 40 or more watts, a fill gas, usually a mixture of nitrogen and argon, is added after the air is pumped out.'

Inert gases allow the filament to operate efficiently at higher temperatures, and simultaneously lessen the rate at which the tiny pieces of tungsten evaporate from the filament, yielding a longer bulb life.

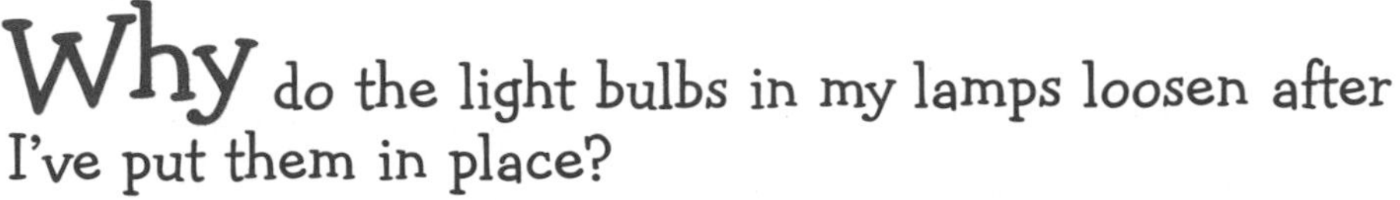

Why do the light bulbs in my lamps loosen after I've put them in place?

An unscientific poll conducted by the Imponderables Research Board indicates that creeping bulb loosening is a problem for many, although a majority of respondents never faced the problem. Is some sadist running around loosening the bulbs of selected victims?

Perhaps, but a natural explanation is more likely. The greatest culprit in loosening light bulbs is vibration. Friction keeps the socket threads of a light bulb tightly fitted into the base threads of a fixture. J Robert Moody, of General

Electric, informed *Imponderables* that 'vibration weakens the friction force, allowing the light bulb to back out of the socket on its own. If the vibration is intense, like on a car or an aeroplane, then a bayonet base must be used in place of the screw-threaded base.'

Perhaps that incessant bass drone emanating from the heavy-metal fan upstairs caused your problem. The only solution might be the purchase of a bayonet base for your lamp or a bayonet to use on your upstairs neighbour.

Why do power lines hum?

In an attempt not to make your eyes glaze over, we won't begin this answer with a treatise on alternating current versus direct current.

Instead, we will attempt to make your eyes glaze over in the next few paragraphs (electrical engineers may skip to the fifth paragraph). Simply put, in direct current (DC), the electrons continuously flow through a circuit in one direction. For example, if you use a dry-cell battery in a torch, the electrons flow from the negative end of the battery, through a wire to the bulb, and then through another wire to the positive end of the battery. At every point of the operation, the flow of electrons is in the same direction.

In alternating current (AC), the electrons flow in one direction and then switch directions. This alternation occurs several times a second. AC current is usually produced by a generator that converts mechanical energy (from a spinning coil) into electrical energy. By spinning a wire coil in a magnetic field, electric current is generated in the wire coil.

In order to understand what generates the hum, it's also necessary to understand that alternating current doesn't just change from maximum strength in one direction to maximum strength in the other direction. As the coil spins, the strength ebbs and flows. Once the current is going in one direction, it continues to spin in the same direction but loses some force. A quarter of the way through the cycle, the current stops flowing completely. But with the coil continuing to spin, the current starts flowing again, weakly, but this time in the opposite direction. It builds up until maximum force is reached at the halfway point in the revolution of the coil. The current wanes again until it reaches zero force at the three-quarter point, when it begins to flow again in the original direction.

Now that we are all electrical engineers, we can better understand that the steady humming sound we are hearing is actually a physical vibration in the power wire because some of the force driving the electrons is transferred to the wire itself. Depending upon the type of wire and how rigidly the wire is strung between poles, the wire vibrates, and the hum we hear is that sound. If the current has been standardised at a frequency of 60 cycles per second, the hum turns out to be a low-pitched drone, close to the musical note A, three octaves below middle C.

The sound isn't unbearably loud. David Murray, power service engineer for the Nashville Electric Service, told *Imponderables* that this type of physical wire vibration produces 'very faint' hums that 'would be hard to hear with the human ear'. The size of the power lines is a factor in the volume of the noise. Martin Gitten, of Con Edison in New York, tells us that the larger the power lines, the more likely they are to generate audible hums.

Allen Bradley, Manager of Power-Use Engineering at Nashville Electric Service, notes an additional reason why the hum is so soft:

> ‘Large AC power lines are not one big piece of wire surrounded by insulation. Rather, inside the insulation is a bundled set of stranded conductors [wires]. That's because AC tends to flow around the perimeter of the wires, not so much in the interior of wires. So, to increase the surface area of the wires, we generally use several smaller wires together rather than one large wire.’

DC current has a more uniform flow throughout the wire, so one big wire is just as effective in transmitting power as the bundle of wires used in AC power. Because the AC cables are stranded together, one wire interferes with the others while each is 'trying' to vibrate. They don't all vibrate at the same time, so as one cable tries to vibrate, the other wires near it are impeding the vibration. DC power lines, with a single bigger wire, generate louder hums than AC lines, if not the cacophony of heavy metal group AC/DC.

Speaking of cacophony, there is another sound that Bradley claims is far more common than the steady hum – a crackling sound that has scared us on occasion:

> ‘The sound that I usually hear near power lines is not so much a hum, but rather a crackly noise. This is due to an undesirable phenomenon known as the corona effect. It happens as air near the power lines becomes ionised in the vicinity of the power

> poles. The insulators on high-voltage lines (at the poles) sometimes break down a bit and a bit of current leaks onto the poles. The current is attracted to metal surfaces, especially the pointed protrusions on the poles. This ionises the air around those points, producing a faint glow near the conductors. As the air particles become ionised, a crackly sound is created. ’

Any strong electrical current will produce a magnetic field in the vicinity of the current. With AC current, the magnetic field oscillates (contracts and expands) along with the current. Ionised atoms have either gained or lost electrons and are more common in stormy or humid weather. Indeed, Frank Young, Senior Vice-President of Enertech Consultants, notes that the crackling sound is most often heard after rainstorms that have caused a partial corona effect.

Lest you think that electrical engineering is dryly scientific, we must alert you to the wacky good times that must be had at engineers' conventions. For both Gitten and Murray had exactly the same initial response when asked why power lines hum: 'The reason they hum is because they don't know the words.'

Why are typewriter keys in their current configuration?

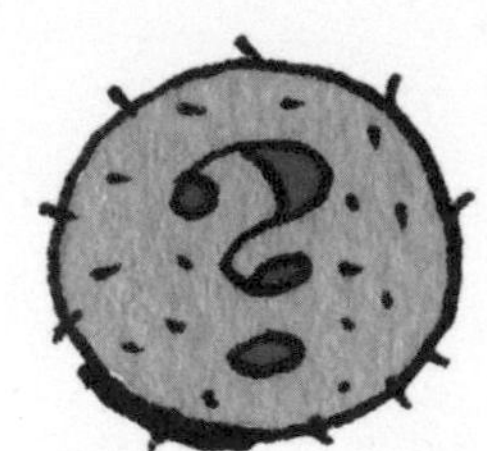

The early developers of typewriters were obsessed with similarities between their keyboards and piano keyboards. Most typewriters therefore had eight to 10 rows, since separate keys were needed for capital letters before the invention of the shift key. Most of these pioneer keyboards were arranged in strictly alphabetical order.

Christopher Latham Sholes, the US inventor responsible for the first production typewriter in 1873, found that the alphabetical arrangement of keys led to jamming when the typewriter bars of fast typists were on the upstrike. Sholes consulted his brother, a teacher, who developed the idea that the bars of letters used frequently in combination should come from opposite directions.

The brothers Sholes created the 'QWERTY' keyboard we have today. The real purpose of this configuration was to avoid key jamming. At the time Sholes introduced the QWERTY keyboard, even the most proficient typists used two fingers – it was thought impossible to learn how to touch-type, even though the letters were arranged in alphabetical order!

Sholes, aware of consumer resistance towards new configurations of previously standardised products, sold his customers on the 'scientific arrangement' of his new keyboard. He claimed that the QWERTY keyboard required the least possible movements of the hands while typing. The exact opposite was the truth. Sholes' QWERTY arrangement necessitates a finger trek of great movement around the keyboard to form the most basic English words. Yet Sholes' misleading advertising is still believed by most typists.

With the advent of sophisticated typewriters, word processors and computers that work without traditional bars, the need for the QWERTY configuration is gone. Many theorists have proposed more efficient letter arrangements, and the Dvorak keyboard has gained rabid adherents, but the question remains whether a century of QWERTY keyboard use can be overcome by such a mild force as logic.

What's the purpose of the 'SysRq' key on most computer keyboards?

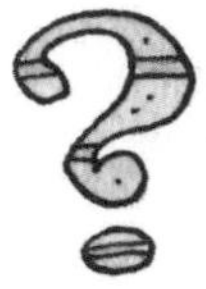

The 'SysRq' key, short for 'System Request', is one of those features added by computer geeks to let us average users know that we are but mere interlopers in their world. The good news is that pressing the SysRq key (sometimes labelled 'Sys Req') by mistake is unlikely to do any damage to your computer session. The bad news is that pressing the SysRq key is unlikely to do anything at all.

On most PC keyboards, the SysRq key shares a key with the Print Screen command, which has the virtue of actually doing something (creating screen shots of what you see on your monitor), but usually only if preceded by pressing Ctrl+Alt. In other words, if you are typing and mistakenly hit the Print Screen/ SysRq key, nothing seems to happen (in some systems, hitting Print Screen will make a copy of the screen on your clipboard).

At one time, IBM had great hopes for the now obscure SysRq key. It appeared as a function key on the keyboards used to control IBM's popular 3270 terminals (designed to interact with IBM's mainframe computers). SysRq allowed users to directly communicate with the underlying operating system to, say, switch sessions on the host server. Circumstantial evidence indicates that IBM had the same role in mind for the key for personal computers, as SysRq did not appear on the 83-key PC/XT keyboard but became the 84th key on the AT keyboard (designed to work with Intel's then-snazzy 286 processor) in 1984. But most programs never took any advantage of the opportunity to develop this 'attention' key.

SysRq is making a bit of a comeback, though, as the free and open-source operating system, Linux, offers users a 'magic SysRq key'. Once this feature is enabled, by pressing Alt+SysRq, users can communicate directly with the underlying operating system. Once invoked, the magic SysRq key can do things like reboot the system when it is unresponsive to the usual methods or dump current memory to your console, helpful when debugging.

Although keyboards now sport 20 more keys than they did when the AT keyboard was king, most popular programs seem to utilise fewer function keys than ever (when's the last time you used the 'Scroll Lock' key?).

Why are computer circuit boards green?

Before we get deluged with mail – we know! Yes, you can find circuit boards in almost as many colours as Crayola has crayons, including red, gold, pink, yellow, brown and black. Tracy Elbert, Product Manager for PCBexpress, wrote *Imponderables* that her company used to manufacture rainbow-coloured boards, with 'a drizzle of all the colours spiralled around randomly'. But dark-green boards have become the default colour. Why?

On one level, the answer is easy. The green colour on most circuit boards, not just on computers, but on everything from pinball machines to television sets, comes from the 'solder mask'. The solder mask, found on both the top and bottom of a PCB (printed circuit board), can be applied as a dry film, printed in a silk screen-like process, or, now most commonly, applied in a liquid form.

The purpose of the solder mask is not to look pretty but to cover and insulate the parts of the circuit that don't require soldering. All kinds of bad stuff can result if solder strays from its intended destination – shorts being the most serious consequence, as Mike Lopez, of PCB manufacturer Prototron Circuits, explains:

> 'The green colour actually is an epoxy-based material that acts as a solder resist. When components are loaded onto a board, the solder mask resists the solder from jumping over to another hole or pad location, which would cause a short in the circuit. Now the assembly process becomes easier knowing that if you load all the components from one side and run it along with a conveyor belt and flowing solder beneath it, all of the leads that

> come through the holes will wick up perfectly and keep the solder to the metal only and not form a big solder mess.

We also know there is a certain amount of inertia with the colours of things. If circuit boards have always been green, why rock the boat? The manufacturers don't have much incentive to change, unless customers seek new colours. Elbert points out that there is clean-up and waste involved in her plant switching back and forth between different colours – the dark-green default is fine with her.

We know that the oldest circuit boards were not green. Bob Dietzel, who spent 29 years at Bell Labs doing integrated circuit research and development, told *Imponderables* that before commercially applied coatings were available, Bell Labs made its own boards, which were translucent white:

> These boards were soldered by hand in those days so no mask was needed. We had a shop full of "wiremen" who placed the components on the boards and soldered them.
>
> The earliest circuit boards were masked by hand with a tar-like substance and etched by hand in an acid solution. This soon was replaced with masks made with rub-on masking and etched with ferric chloride solution.

Tom Wagner, an audiovisual technician and web designer from Malaspina, British Columbia, wrote about the rainbow of colours found on early boards:

> The colour of the board shows the composition of it, hence the use of it. Original and older boards were Bakelite composition, and were brown. Phenolic [boards were] ... tan. Most "non-filled" fibreglass boards used in computers are green. Filled fibreglass is blue. Teflon is white.

But why was the solder mask green in the first place? One theory, advanced in 2000 on IPC's TechNet E-Mail Forum by David Albin, of Coates Circuit Products, is that the solder mask manufacturers used the materials at hand, in this case a 'copper phthalocyanine pigment, which at the time of the first boards was the only heat-stable organic colour [available]'.

Others 'blame' the military for our dark-green solder mask. Mike Lopez writes: 'I've heard that PCBs were starting to develop colours back in World War II days and green was the colour of choice for the military.'

Another poster on the TechNet board sides with the armed forces theory:

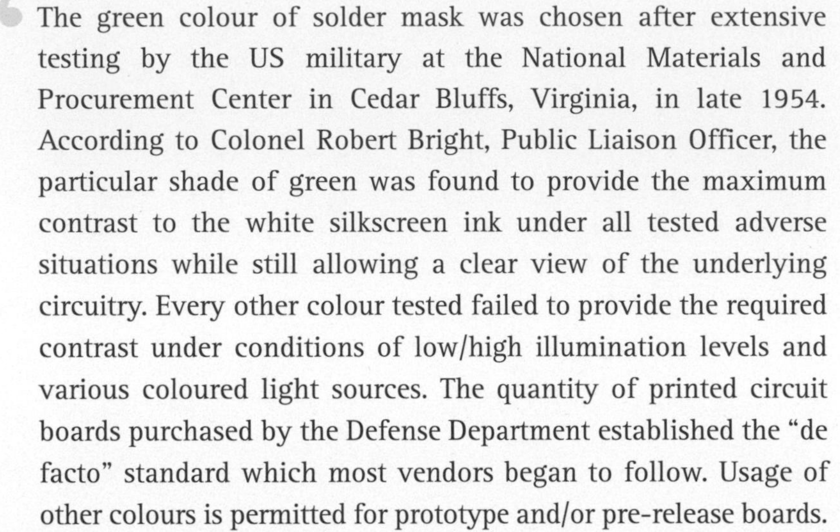

> The green colour of solder mask was chosen after extensive testing by the US military at the National Materials and Procurement Center in Cedar Bluffs, Virginia, in late 1954. According to Colonel Robert Bright, Public Liaison Officer, the particular shade of green was found to provide the maximum contrast to the white silkscreen ink under all tested adverse situations while still allowing a clear view of the underlying circuitry. Every other colour tested failed to provide the required contrast under conditions of low/high illumination levels and various coloured light sources. The quantity of printed circuit boards purchased by the Defense Department established the "de facto" standard which most vendors began to follow. Usage of other colours is permitted for prototype and/or pre-release boards.

Regardless of whether or not the military mandated dark-green, some argue that green is the colour easiest on the eye, especially for long periods, while providing sufficient contrast for board assemblers and inspectors who were supervising their work. Even the manufacturers of PCBs have a selfish reason to prefer green, as Tracy Elbert explains: 'The liquid solder mask we use is like an epoxy, which needs to be cured to harden. Green is the easiest colour for the UV light to accept, making the process easy for us.'

Most big PCB manufacturers offer designer colours, sometimes at premium prices. But it will take more than a passing fad to make anything other than dark-green the 'new black' in the solder mask business.

Why is the telephone touch-tone keypad arranged differently from the calculator keypad?

Conspiracy theories abound, but the explanation for this Imponderable reinforces one of the great tenets of Imponderability: when in doubt, almost any man-made phenomenon can be explained by tradition, inertia or both.

A theory we have often heard is that the phone company intentionally reversed the calculator configuration so that people who were already fast at operating calculators would slow down enough to allow the signals of the phone to register. It's a clever theory, but it isn't true. Even today, fast punchers can render a touch-tone phone worthless.

Both the touch-tone keypad and the all-transistor calculator were made available to the general public in the early 1960s. Calculators were arranged from the beginning so that the lowest digits were on the bottom. Telephone keypads put the 1-2-3 on the top row. Both configurations descended directly from earlier prototypes.

Before 1964, calculators were either mechanical or electronic devices with heavy tubes. The keypads on the first calculators actually resembled old cash registers, with the left row of keys numbering 9 on top down to 0 at the bottom. The next row to the right had 90 on top and 10 on the bottom, the next row to the right 900 on top, 100 on the bottom, and so on. All of the early calculators were 10 rows high, and most were nine rows wide. From the beginning, handheld calculators placed 7-8-9 on the top row, from left to right.

Before the touch-tone phone, of course, rotary dials were the rule. There is no doubt that the touch-tone keypad was designed to mimic the rotary dial, with the 1 on top and the 7-8-9 on the bottom. According to Bob Ford of AT&T's Bell Laboratories, a second reason was that some phone-company research concluded that this configuration helped eliminate dialling errors.

Ford related the story, which may or may not be apocryphal, that when AT&T contemplated the design of their keypad, they called several calculator companies, hoping they would share the research that led them to the opposite configuration. Much to their chagrin, AT&T discovered that the calculator companies had conducted no research at all. From our contacts with Sharp and Texas Instruments, two pioneers in the calculator field, it seems that this story could easily be true.

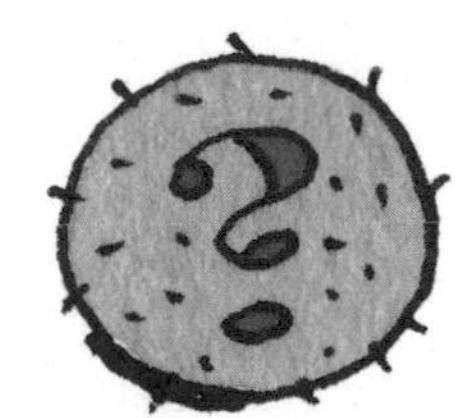

Why do most staplers have a setting to bend staples outward?

Stapler manufacturers are asked about this mystery often enough that Swingline put an answer on the FAQ (frequently asked questions) section of its web site:

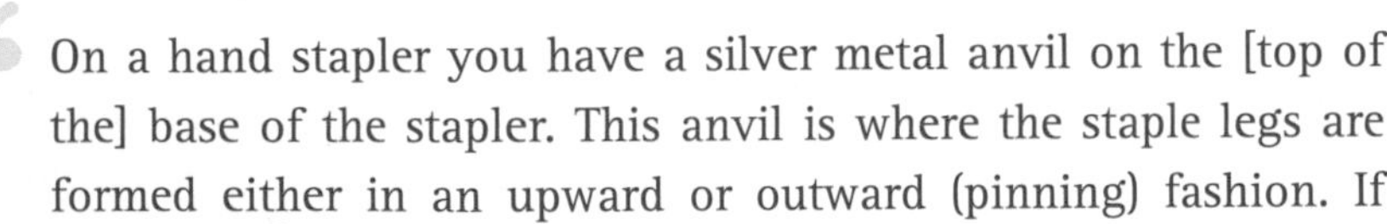

> On a hand stapler you have a silver metal anvil on the [top of the] base of the stapler. This anvil is where the staple legs are formed either in an upward or outward (pinning) fashion. If

your staples are forming outward, this means that the anvil has been turned. To resolve, push the button under your anvil upward. This will raise the anvil, now rotate the anvil. This will change the position of the forming slots.'

Staplers were invented in the late nineteenth century but were too expensive and labour intensive (early staplers could hold a grand total of one staple) to be widely available. Before the proliferation of staples in the early twentieth century, papers were fastened together by pins, the origin of the pinning term for outwardly oriented staples. Because pins were not clinched, it was relatively easy to remove them without damaging the documents they were fastening. And that's still the primary advantage of the pinning feature today – Lori Andrade, at staple manufacturer Stanley Bostitch, said that drycleaners are fond of pinned staples for their short-term stapling jobs, precisely because it is easier for customers to detach the staples from boxes or bags. Pinning isn't as reliable a fastener as the clinched staple, but it does make it easier to add new documents to already gathered papers.

Why are you unlikely to have used the pinning orientation for your stapler? In our experience, the minuses outweigh the pluses for any job. Not only do pinned staples not fasten well, but the 'legs' of the staple stick out, and can catch on other objects, such as your hands! If you are worried about damaging documents with the standard staple, consider some other obscure alternatives – such as paper clips or a folder.

How do they keep staples in their packages clumped together?

Ah, the irony. Although their product is used as a fastener, staple manufacturers must turn to a competitor to fasten the staples together. Those clumps of staples, more properly called 'strips', are kept together by glue.

Staples are made of wire. A machine called a 'wire winder' wraps the wire around a spool. According to Lori Andrade, of Stanley Bostitch, the cement is applied while the wire is wrapped around the spool. Then the flat wire is rolled off the spool, is cut into strips and is pressed into that lovable staple shape.

Why do telephone cords spontaneously get twisted up? What can you do about this dreaded affliction?

Spontaneously twist themselves up, you say? You mean you sit on your sofa innocently watching television and suddenly the telephone cord starts winding like a snake?

After considerable research into the matter, we must conclude that telephone cords do not twist up spontaneously. *You've* been turning around the headset. We're not accusing you of doing this intentionally, mind you. As far as we know, twisting a headset is not even a misdemeanour in any country or locality. But don't try to blame your indiscretions on the laws of nature. Cords don't cause twisted cords – people do.

Now that we've chastised you, we'll offer the obvious, simple yet elegant solution. Remove the plug that connects the headset to the body of the phone. Hold the cord by the plug side and let the headset fall down (without hitting the floor, please). The cord will 'spontaneously' untwist.

Why is a watch called a 'watch'?

Do you have to watch a watch any more than you have to watch a clock? The trusty dictionary tells us that the word 'watch' has the same Old English roots as the words 'wake' and 'awaken'. Were the first watches alarm clocks? Probably not. Some word historians have speculated that the word 'watch' derives from an Old English word meaning 'to keep vigil' and that the naming of the timepiece had to do with the fact that they were carried by night watchmen.

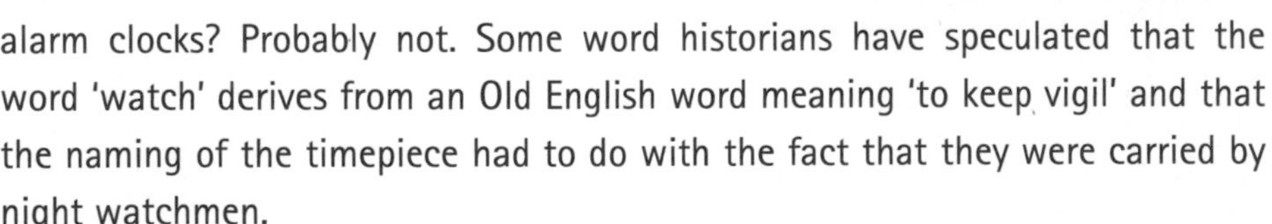

Perhaps the most fascinating, if unverifiable, source was provided by Stuart Berg Flexner in his book *Listening to America*. When watches were introduced, clocks had no hour or minute hands. Rather, clocks struck on the hour – a totally auditory signal (indeed, 'clock' derives from the Latin word *cloca*, meaning 'bell'). But watches sported minute and hour hands, so people had to literally 'watch' their watches to find out the time.

Why is four usually noted as IIII rather than IV on clocks and watches with Roman numerals?

Watch and clock makers are given great latitude in designating numbers. Some use Arabic numbers, most use Roman numerals, and a few use no numbers at all.

But have you noticed that while the number nine is usually designated as IX, four is almost universally IIII? We contacted some of the biggest makers of watches, and even they couldn't pinpoint the derivation of this custom. But they sent us to horologist Henry Fried, who swatted away this Imponderable like a fly.

When mechanical clocks were first invented, in the fourteenth century, they were displayed in public places, usually on cathedrals. The faces themselves were only ornamental at first, for the early models had no hour or minute hand but merely gonged once for every hour of the day.

Clocks were thus of special value to the common, almost universally illiterate, people. Most peasants, even in Italy, could not read Roman numerals or subtract. They made calculations and told time by counting on their fingers. Four slash marks were easier for them to contend with than IV, taking one away from five.

Many early clocks displayed 24 hours rather than twelve. While some German clocks in the fifteenth and sixteenth centuries used Roman numerals to denote am and Arabic numbers for pm, all-day clocks remained especially troublesome for the illiterate. So some clock designers always displayed all numbers ending with four or nine with slash marks rather than IV or IX.

Why do clockmakers use Roman numerals today? Primarily because a bit of antiquity pleases consumers. Dependable clocks and watches can be produced for less than they could decades ago, so manufacturers need design elements to convince consumers to spend more. The touch of class Roman numerals connote is their biggest selling point. The delicious irony, of course, is that this touch of class stems from a system designed for peasants.

How did people wake up before alarm clocks were invented? How did they make specific appointments before clocks were invented?

Imagine an average man during the Dark Ages, let's say in the ninth century. After a hard day's work, he decides to meet a friend for a drink. Was there an awkward pause after, 'Okay, why don't I meet you at my place at ... '? Or he got a new job as an apprentice carpenter. His boss says, 'Be here right on the dot of ... '. How did he know when to show up?

Although the Egyptians and Chinese used water clocks much earlier, the mechanical clock was not invented (in Italy) until the mid-fourteenth century. Presumably, before clocks, most people reckoned the time by following the progress of the sun. On clear days, following the shadows on trees or on 'noon marks' etched on buildings would indicate the approximate time.

Before then, people were forced to rely on natural events to wake them up. Although approximately 90 per cent of the European population lived in rural settings, even most town dwellers had animals, such as chickens, that made it abundantly clear when the sun had risen.

And it's not as though medieval peasants had much leisure time, as Martin Swetsky, President of the Electrical Horology Society, explains: 'Life was casual, yet demanding. The workman or farmer was awakened by the rising sun, performed his day's duties until the sun set, and thus ended his day to retire until the next morning.'

Presumably, just as most of us don't need an alarm to wake up every morning, people in those days had the same 'biological clock', the same circadian rhythms, that we do today.

Even centuries after the invention of the mechanical clock, most people couldn't afford them. In early America, roosters, the sun, servants, the town crier, church bells and factory whistles were all more likely to wake up the average person than an alarm clock. In his fascinating book *Revolution in Time*, David S Landes speculates that these signals were likely to have been irregular:

> '... dictated by nature, weather and the varying requirements of agriculture, conforming not to schedule but to opportunity and circumstances. They were not so much a sign of punctuality as a substitute for it.
>
> The pattern of work in the cities was a little different. There, too, the craftsman awoke with the dawn and the animals, and worked as long as natural light or oil lamps permitted. In the typical household workshop, one person, usually the newest apprentice, would "sleep on one ear", wake before the others, start the fire, get the water, then get the others up; and the same person would usually shut things down at night. Productivity, in the sense of output per unit of time, was unknown. The great virtue was busyness – unremitting diligence in one's tasks.'

When tower clocks were installed in villages, they often provided a wake-up service. But in the Middle Ages, clocks reflected the casual approach to time: the earliest mechanical clocks had neither minute nor hour hands; their bells rang on the hour, occasionally on the quarter hour.

The Chinese were the first to experiment with timepieces devoted to waking up their owners. Milton Stevens, Executive Director of the American Watchmakers-Clockmakers Institute, provided *Imponderables* with a glimpse of some of the primitive alarm clocks:

> The Chinese are credited with using the first rope clocks. The clock consisted of a rope saturated with an oil to support combustion. Through experimentation, they learned the length of rope that burned in an hour. With this knowledge, they tied a knot at the proper length for each hour. To awaken at a given time, the rope was tied to the toe. Thus, when the proper time to awaken arrived, the individual felt the heat on the toe and had little trouble waking up.
>
> With the candle clock, by experimentation it was learned how far down a candle would burn in one hour. Hours, then, were marked on the candle at the appropriate locations. To make this serve as an alarm, the candle was mounted in a large metal dish. A small hook with a small bell was inserted into a location on the candle, which indicated the time to be awakened. When the candle burned to that point, the bell fell into the metal dish, which made a noise – with luck, enough to arouse the sleeper.

The demand for more precise alarm clocks came, not as one might expect, from the world of commerce, but from religion. Muslims traditionally prayed five times a day, and Jews three times a day, but early Christians had no set schedule. The emergence of monasticism, a full-time vocation, established the need for routines. And these monks, devoted to the service of God, were methodical in organising their prayer schedule. Although different orders varied, many monasteries divided the day into six segments, mandating prayer six times a day. This demanding schedule included night-time vigils, which required the monks to be awakened after they had gone to sleep. Before alarm clocks, one person was often designated to stay up while other monks slept; the 'waker' had the unenviable task of rousing the others for prayer.

The mechanical alarm clocks created by the monks were more akin to today's eggtimers than the devices on today's bedside tables, as Martin Swetsky explains:

> 'The first alarm clocks were primitive devices, without hands or dials. They were mechanical contrivances intended to ring bells at the desired time, with this accomplished by a peg placed in a hole nearest the hour and a linkage system connected to this mechanism that provided the bell-ringing service.'

Subsequent clocks were set to strike at the six (later seven) canonical hours, with varying numbers of bells indicating which prayer service was to begin.

And how did people, before the advent of clocks, make that hot date or crucial job interview on time? Most likely, they played it safe, arriving for appointments long before they needed to. If courtiers needed to be at the palace for a predawn ceremony, they arrived at midnight and waited for the drums to beat and the gate to open, rather than risk oversleeping. Time, as we know it, belonged to the wealthy, and peasants were forced to play by their betters' new rules. And just as most appointments today are set for round numbers (few make reservations at restaurants for 7.38 pm), many times were set to coincide with natural events ('Meet you when the sun sets!').

Eventually, many towns had clocks on the towers of their tallest buildings, giving more people access to precise times. But this access was a double-edged sword, allowing the wealthy to rigidify, and in some cases increase, the already taxing workloads of peasants and craftsmen. Later, the proliferation of clocks and watches (which were invented in the early sixteenth century) helped fuel the efficiency and regimentation of the Industrial Revolution.

Why do clocks run 'clockwise'?

In horseracing and most forms of skating, we are accustomed to seeing movement in a counterclockwise direction. Is there any particular reason why clocks run 'clockwise'? Henry Fried, one of the foremost horologists in the United States, gives a simple explanation for this Imponderable.

Before the advent of clocks, we used sundials. In the Northern Hemisphere, the shadows rotated in the direction we now call 'clockwise'. The clock hands were built to mimic the natural movements of the sun. If clocks had been invented in the Southern Hemisphere, Fried speculates, 'clockwise' would be the opposite direction.

Why do divers spit into their scuba masks before entering the water?

When we conjure up images of the underworld of Jacques Cousteau, we tend to linger on the splendors of the iridescent colours of tropical fish, the subtle beauty of the coral reefs, the fierce determination of sharks and the vastness of the oceans. But upon closer inspection, we noted that whenever he went diving, Jacques Cousteau could be seen spitting into his mask and rubbing the spittle around the inside of the lens. Yuck!

The pre-dive ritual is one of the few socially sanctioned rationalisations for spitting, for this is expectoration with a cause: spitting helps prevent mask lenses from fogging up. Even casual divers are aware of the problem of lenses fogging up on them in the water, and no one prefers to dive into murky waters.

What causes the fog? During a dive, the air inside the mask becomes more and more humid (full of water vapour). In very close quarters, you are continually breathing, expelling water vapour, plus you are perspiring. Inside the mask, the water vapour turns into liquid water (condensation), leading to fogging.

Why condensation? The air in the mask can become oversaturated with water vapour. Also, the inside of the mask gets cooler as you continue to dive. The lens of a mask is cooler than the air inside the mask because the outside of the lens comes in constant contact with the water, which is considerably colder than the temperature of your breath (unless you are diving in a spa). Cooler air has a lower relative humidity than warmer air, so condensation occurs.

If the air inside the mask is saturated with water, it must find something to condense onto. As air hits the lens, it condenses onto the lens itself, forming microscopic 'sweat beads', which are tiny droplets of water. These droplets refract light in all directions, making the lens appear opaque: instant fog.

Most of the diving experts we spoke to indicated that dirty lenses exacerbate the problem. Small specks of dirt lend tempting spots for water to condense onto. Even irregularities in the glass are effective sites for condensation.

So how does spitting help (after all, you're adding more water to the inside of the lens)? Water molecules are 'dipoles', molecules with a small positive charge on one end and a small negative charge on the other end. They tend to want to condense onto a charged particle or attach themselves onto large molecules (which may also be charged). As a result, you have clusters of microdroplets that are spread out. These microdroplets refract light in unpredictable directions.

When you spit on the mask, you coat the inside of the lens with many diffuse charges. This increases the number of nucleating sites exponentially, so that the water condenses in a uniform manner. Instead of the sweat beads that normally form, you've created a smooth 'sheet' of water. Once this 'sheet' is formed, when new water molecules get added to the lens, they join the continuous sheet rather than clustering up at one site; as a result, the forces of gravity cause the water to run off the mask in a sheet, Because the water that remains adhered to the lens is a continuous sheet itself, it doesn't refract light in all directions – we can see through it. This 'sheeting action' is the same process used in dishwasher detergents designed to remove water spots. It doesn't clean the glasses any more than other products, but it coats the glasses and disperses the charged molecules so that imperfections don't cluster at one site.

Alas, spitting is not a cure-all. Jay Stone, a scuba-diving instructor who works at Blue Cheer Dive Shop in Santa Monica, California, told *Imponderables*:

> Many divers do spit into their masks, and rub the spit around before diving. This prevents the mask from fogging, at least for a while. However the mask will still tend to fog up eventually.
>
> When it does fog, you can clear it out underwater. You must remove the mask, let the seawater slosh around the mask, and maybe wipe the lens. Then put the mask back on. You clear the water out of the mask by blowing in air.

Why do the agitators in washing machines go back and forth rather than spin 360 degrees?

To loosen dirt from soiled laundry, the clothes must move in the machine. If the agitator spun continuously, centrifugal force would actually make the clothes stick in one spot. So the back and forth movement of most top-loading washing machine agitators actually moves the clothes more.

> However, this tends to work for only about 15 minutes. Then the mask will tend to fog up again.

Is there an alternative anitfogging method? Divers have been experimenting for aeons. Black indicates that toothpaste, liquid soap, chewing tobacco(!) and even kelp have all been used. But all pose problems. The abrasiveness in toothpaste that helps clean your teeth can also scratch the dive mask. Dishwashing detergent works well but can irritate your eyes. Kelp isn't always readily available. And your doctor would not approve of your using tobacco.

So two better alternatives have surfaced. The most popular are commercial antifogging products. We spoke to Bob Heck, Product Manager at McNett Corporation, which produces Sea Drops, the industry's leading no-fog product. A diver simply squeezes two drops onto a dry lens. Although the instructions specify that you rub the product on both the inside and outside of the lens, Jay Stone indicated that rubbing the product on the inside only seems to work just as well.

In February 1996 *Scuba Diving* magazine published an article, 'Spit or Squirt', written by John Francis, that compared various methods of antifogging mask lenses. Francis concluded that the commercial products do a better and longer-lasting job than saliva, and one of the two highest-rated products was 500 psi Mask Defog. The creator of the product, Brad Ogle, told us that because it comes in the form of a thick gel, it can be applied underwater and will stick to the lens.

The second alternative to spitting is to buy no-fog lenses. We spoke to Don Patten, Manager of Technical Services at Scuba Pro, which manufactures and distributes scuba and diving gear and accessories. Scuba Pro sells no-fog lenses, and Patten claims that they work well:

> The lenses are tempered glass, but they are treated with special antifog coating. The coating is applied to the masks with a polycarbonate adhesive. The coating causes the condensed water to disperse evenly around the lens. To activate the mask before a dive, all you do is submerge the mask in water.

Some divers seem almost to relish the challenge of sticking with normal lenses and fighting the good fight against fog. We asked some divers for their opinions about spitting on the mask, and the responses ranged from the antagonistic:

> There are definitely downsides to spitting in a mask. One, it is simply *gross* and *nasty*. Two, it is potentially dangerous. There

is at least one case of a Herpes infection resulting in partial blindness caused by transferring the virus from a cold sore in the mouth, via spit, into the eyes. There is nothing wrong with using one of the commercial defog agents on the market today.'

... to the zealous: 'I started diving last summer. At first, I used commercial antifoggers, but I kept losing the little bottles. By the end of the season, I was a confirmed spitter. It works really well!'

How do 3-D films and 3-D glasses work?

Three-dimension (3-D) films are a variation of the stereovision systems that we see used in tourist trinkets and children's toys. These devices present two different views a few centimetres apart from the viewpoint of the human eye. The left image is presented only to the left eye and the right image is sent directly to the right eye.

But the technology for a 3-D film is more complicated, because the filmmaker must invent some way to keep the left eye from seeing what only the right eye is supposed to view, even though both images are being projected on the screen simultaneously. The history of the technology was reviewed for us by David Gibson, of the Photo Equipment Museum of Eastman Kodak Company:

'The first system was invented in the 1890s, and the images are called anaglyphs. The left-eye image was projected with a red-coloured filter over the projector lens and a blue-green filter [was put] over the lens of the projector for the right-eye image. Glasses with the same colour filters were used in viewing the images – the red filter for the left eye transmitted the light from the left-image projector and blocked the light from the right-image projector. This system has also been used to print such things as stereo comic books and has been used experimentally with stereo images broadcast on colour television.'

The only problem with this technology is that it works best with monochrome images. The red and blue-green tints of the glasses add unwanted and unsubtle colouration to a colour 3-D film.

The solution, Gibson generously admitted, came from rival Polaroid, which developed, appropriately enough, a polarisation method specifically for 3-D films. The Polaroid technology beams 'the angle of polarisation for one eye at right angles to that for the other eye, so that one image is transmitted while the other eye is blocked. This is the system used for the 3-D films made in the 1950s.'

Why are there no A- or B-sized batteries?

Because they are obsolete. A- and B-sized batteries once existed as component cells within much larger zinc carbon battery packs. The A cells supplied the low-voltage supply for the filaments in the vacuum tubes used to supply power to early radios and crank telephones.

Of course, the descendants of the old A- and B-sized batteries are still with us. As electronic devices have become smaller, so have the batteries that power them. As might be expected, the A cell came first, then B, C, and D cells. The batteries were lettered in ascending order of size. James Donahue, Jr, of Duracell, Inc., says that as cells smaller than the original A cells were developed, they were designated as AA and then AAA cells. Donahue reports that there is even a AAAA battery.

So the old A- and B-sized batteries are no longer in production. It's no use having a battery larger than the device it powers.

Why are 9-volt batteries rectangular?

Most of the best-selling battery configurations (e.g. AA, AAA, C, D) are 1.5 volts. Nine-volt batteries, formerly known as 'transistor batteries', contain six 1.5-volt batteries. The 1.5 cells within the casing are cylindrical.

If you stacked six cylinders in the most economical shape, wouldn't a rectangle be the most natural choice? Just try putting six cylinders into a square or cylindrical casing without wasting space.

Dan Halaburda, Marketing Manager for Panasonic, told us that the shape of 9-volt batteries goes back to when they were used to power communication devices in which space was at a premium. Today, the most common application for 9-volt batteries is in smoke detectors.

Do batteries wear out faster if you turn up the volume of a radio?

Absolutely.

The Battery Applications Manager of Eveready Battery Company, Inc., BG Merritt, told us about some research that proved the point conclusively:

> We recently tested a major manufacturer dual cassette "boom box" powered by six D-sized cells. From lowest setting to highest setting on the volume control, the power necessary to drive the "box" increased three times. This power increase directly translates into one-third battery life at full volume when compared with zero volume. This power increase is necessary to drive the speakers.

Don French, Chief Engineer of Radio Shack, confirmed Eveready's findings. He estimated that a shirt-pocket portable radio would use at least '200 per cent more battery charge at the loudest volume setting than at the softest'. French pointed out that even tiny radios have audio amplifiers that must be powered. A home stereo might require 50 watts and a shirt-pocket radio 200 milliwatts, but the principle is the same – the more power required, the more juice required.

Why do car batteries have to be so heavy? Why can't they be miniaturised?

Of course, most consumers would prefer car batteries to be AA-size. If a car stalled, a driver could just reach into the glove box and pull out a little battery that had been recharged at home. Car manufacturers also want to downsize batteries. Any heavy material, whether it is the steel in the body of a car or the engine and cylinders, interferes with achieving better fuel efficiency.

Battery manufacturers have responded. In some cases batteries are half the size they were 20 years ago. But alas, don't look forward to AA-sized car batteries in the foreseeable future. As Stephen Bomer, of the Automotive Battery Charger Manufacturers, wrote to *Imponderables*, high-density lead plates are a major component of a battery: 'No substitute for lead has been found that can do the job or generate the voltage required.'

H Dale Millay, a staff research engineer for Shell Oil, told *Imponderables* that the greater the surface area of lead in the battery, the easier it is to generate power. Millay claims that we have already paid the price for downsizing batteries: although modern batteries are good at cold starts, they have low reserve capacities. Translation: they don't last as long as they might under strain.

We received our most emphatic endorsement of the heavy battery from John J Surrette, Vice-President of Rolls Battery Engineering:

> 'The thinner you make the plates in a battery, the lesser the material inside ... The heavier the material, the more rugged the batteries are and the longer they will last. When you use thinner plates ... this lessens the amount of ampere hour capacity. When heavier material is used, like we do in marine and industrial applications, it results in considerably longer life and less exposure [to the elements], which reduces the chance of plates buckling in hard service or the active material shedding from the positive grids ... Miniaturised batteries would probably be preferable but would stand little or no abuse or neglect.'

Rolls' marketing strategy is to emphasise the heaviness of its battery. It boasts a marine battery with 3.2 mm-thick positive plates (in contrast, some car batteries have plates as thin as 1.4 mm, which Surrette believes is too fragile to withstand abuse or neglect).

Why do website addresses have to start with 'www'?

There is not now, and never has been, any reason why a web address has to begin with 'www'. The address of the first ever website didn't have the 'three-dub': its address was http://nxoc01.cern.ch. That site existed on the computer of

Why do whips make a cracking sound when snapped?

Whips can attain a speed of more than 1000 km/h when snapped, breaking the sound barrier. What you are hearing is a mini sonic boom.

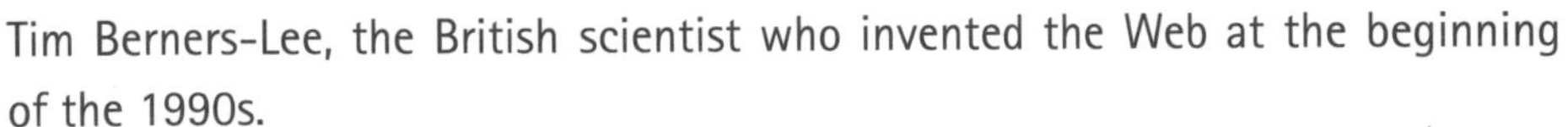

Tim Berners-Lee, the British scientist who invented the Web at the beginning of the 1990s.

It should be said that the World Wide Web is not the same thing as the Internet. The Internet has been around since the 1960s, and is a global network of computers, all of them linked by cables and phone lines. The World Wide Web, on the other hand, is a way of using that physical network to share data in the form of words and pictures on computer screens. The Net is machines; the Web is information.

Berners-Lee considered calling his world-changing invention the 'Information Mesh' (which he decided sounded too much like 'mess') or the 'Mine of Information' (but the double-meaning of the word 'mine', he thought, made it sound like he was claiming to 'own' the Web). 'World Wide Web' was his best idea. The universal use of the three Ws in Web addresses came about later as a mere convention; it was a prior indication of the genre, so to speak, of the data to be found at that location. Increasingly, Web designers are doing away with it – not least because, at nine-syllables, 'www' is the longest three-letter acronym in English, and so is a tiresome thing to have to say out loud.

Why do eyes sometimes come out red in photos? Why is this particularly true of cats' and dogs' eyes?

Have you ever seen 'red-eye' in a professional's photographs? Of course not, because they know that paying customers want a portrait of the topography of their faces, not an intrusive journey into the blood vessels of their eyes.

Yes, the red you see is blood, and you get more red than you ever wanted to see because your flash is too close to the camera lens. Ralph E Venk, President of the Photographic Society of America, says that the light from the flash 'enters the lens of the eye directly and is then reflected off the back surface of the eyeball, the retina, and bounces back to the camera'. The problem of red-eye is compounded because flashes are used in dark environments and the human eye automatically opens wider in the dark.

A few simple tips should banish red-eye from your lives:

1 Try using a separate flash that can be held further away from the lens axis than a built-in flash. An extra 8 cm should do. Thomas J Dufficy, of the National Association of Photographic Manufacturers, says that when camera makers noticed the problem with red-eye when flash cubes were first introduced, they offered flash cube extenders, 8 cm-high posts that increased the angle between the camera lens axis and the flash cube.

2 When taking photographs in the dark, don't have subjects look straight into the camera. Notice that in group shots, the red-eye victim is always the one looking straight into the lens. Your subjects will also enjoy the photographic process more too, since an oblique angle lessens the chances of them being temporarily blinded by flashes.

3 A modest suggestion: try not to take photographs when it is pitch black. Even without red-eye, they never seem to come out well anyway. Leave the cave photographs to the professionals.

And why do cats and dogs seem to be especially prone to contracting red-eye in photographs? Both cats and dogs have larger and more open pupils than humans, which allow the flash to penetrate into their innocent retinas.

Why is film 8, 16, 35 and 70 mm wide?

Eight is half of 16, 35 is half of 70, but 16 isn't half of 35 – is there any logic to how film widths were derived?

Leica solved the problem of how to make a big picture out of a small negative by using cine film in still cameras. At about the same time that George Eastman introduced his first camera, Thomas Edison and his assistant, WLK Dickson, were developing a motion picture camera.

The film for the first Kodak camera in 1888 used a paper base and a strippable gelatin emulsion. After processing, the emulsion had to be transferred to hardened gelatin 'skins' so that the negatives could be printed. One year later, Eastman introduced transparent film base, which eliminated the need for 'skins'.

The film for the first Kodak camera was 70 mm wide. Kodak has been manufacturing 70 mm film continuously since 1888.

Edison was excited about Eastman's transparent base, and he obtained this 70 mm film. Edison wanted to use narrower film for his camera and tried using one-quarter and one-third of Kodak's width. Edison and Dickson finally settled on one-half of Kodak's 70 mm width. The Eastman Kodak Company informed *Imponderables* that right from the start, Europeans referred to Edison's film as 35 mm, whereas it was often called 'Edison standard' film in the United States.

The smaller sizes of film were introduced later, as a Kodak historian related:

> Sixteen millimetre was derived from tests that began before 1916, when it was determined that a picture 1/6 the size of the standard cine frame would produce a satisfactory image. To this image size of 10 x 7.5 mm, edges of 3 mm were added for the perforations. This also divided evenly into the width of the film base, so that 70 sixteen-millimetre "cuts" could be made across the width of the film coating. Eight millimetre is obviously derived by splitting 16 mm film.

There have been other film widths marketed that have not proven so enduring. Kodak tried splitting 35 mm film with one row of perforations, and in a different format, 35 mm film was split into 16 mm, 21 mm and 22 mm for the Edison Home Kinetescope.

Although 8 and 16 might not be even divisors of 70, all three of the other standard film widths were developed in direct response to Eastman Kodak's 70 mm camera introduction of 1888.

Why doesn't the countdown leader on films count all the way to one?

The countdown leader, though less and less used in this digital age, is, of course, there to help the projectionist time when a film is going to start. Each number is timed to appear precisely one second after the other. The projectionist usually uses the number two as the cue to allow the projector light to hit the screen and begin the show. What would be number one is simply the start of the picture.

Wouldn't it work just as well to have zero represent the beginning of the film, so that frustrated audiences could have the satisfaction of counting down from 10 to one? Of course it would. But as in most areas, tradition and inertia rule.

Why is the piping under kitchen sinks so circuitous? Why is it S-shaped? Why not just have one straight vertical pipe?

Believe us, this is not a plot by the plumbing industry to sell you more piping. You want those curves.

The piping under sinks (and under toilets, for that matter) is called a 'P' trap. The curvy pipe dips down below the horizontal pipe so that a water seal is formed in the bend, assuring that water, and not air, fills the area below the horizontal pipe.

Why would you want to create a deliberate water blockage? Because the water blocks sewer and other foul smells from drifting up the pipe and into the room.

And on occasion, the 'P' trap blocks certain items from going downstream. Gary Felsinger, a marketing manager at Kohler Co., explains: 'In some cases, the "P" trap also saves valuable rings from falling into the sewer when accidentally dropped down the drain.'

Why does water drawn from the tap often seem cloudy at first? And why does hot water tend to have more 'clouds'?

The cloudiness that you see in just-drawn-from-the-tap water is nothing more than air bubbles. Many of these bubbles are created as the water hits the metal aerator just as it is about to be released out of the tap. Even more bubbles are created as you pour 'new' water into a container that already holds water. The just-poured water creates turbulence in the container as the onrushing tap water 'churns up' the existing water in the container; the inevitable sloshing and intermixing traps more air bubbles in the water.

The cloudiness disappears quickly because the bubbles, less dense than the water, rise to the surface and burst, while other bubbles dissolve lower down in the water before they reach the top. Warm air can hold more water vapour than cold air. But hot water cannot hold as much air vapour as cold water. Cold water dissolves trapped air bubbles faster than warm water does, so hot-water cloudiness not only might be more pronounced but also tends to linger longer.

Because cold water tends to dissolve more gases, cold water tends to taste better than hot water, which is why most recipes and coffee maker instructions urge you to use cold water when preparing foods.

When I open a hot-water tap, why does the sound of the running water change as it gets hot?

The whistling sound you hear occurs with cold water too, but is more common with hot water. Whistling occurs when there is a restriction of water flow in the pipes.

According to Tom Higham, Executive Director of the International Association of Plumbing and Mechanical Officials, the source of the noise depends on the construction of the plumbing: 'If the piping is copper, the cause is usually attributed to undersized piping. If the pipe is galvanised steel, noise is usually caused by a build-up of lime, which reduces the area for the flow of the water.'

Water flow is restricted more often with hot water, as Richard Church, President of the Plumbing Manufacturers Institute, explains it, because of 'additional air in the hot water formed when the molecules expand during the heating process.'

The crackling noise you hear in the water heater is caused by lime accumulations in its tank. As the water heater expands and contracts, depending on the temperature, the lime breaks off and falls to the bottom of the tank. The water pipes simply transmit and amplify the glorious sound.

How do they put the hole in the needle of a syringe?

Needles are used to poke patients. But are needles poked to create the holes through which the vaccine is pumped into our veins? The answer is a resounding no. As Jim Dickinson, President of K-Tube Corporation, wrote to us:

> 'I have been involved with making the stainless steel tubing used for hypodermic needles for the past 34 years, and the question about how the hole is put in this tube has been asked many times. The secret about the hole is that we don't put it in after, but before!'

How? The answer comes from Michael DiBiasi, a senior mechanical engineer at medical supply giant Becton-Dickinson, who declares, 'I am the guy who, among other things, puts the hole in the needle.'

"The stainless steel "needle" part of the syringe is more commonly referred to as the "cannula", and the "hole" that has aroused your curiosity is called the "lumen". Cannulae are produced from large rolls of stainless steel strip stock. Depending upon the size requirements of the finished product, which is dictated by its intended use, the strip stock could be about as wide and as thick as a piece of Wrigley's chewing gum, and may range down to about the width and thickness of one of the cutting blades in a disposable, twin-bladed razor.

The steel strip is drawn through a series of dies that gradually form the strip into a continuous tube. As the tube closes, the seam is welded shut and the finished tubing is rolled up onto a take-up reel. In this manner, the entire roll of flat steel is converted into a continuous roll of tubing. At this point, the tubing may be anywhere from about the diameter of a common wooden pencil, to about the diameter of an ink pen refill tube.

Next, the tubing is drawn through a series of tiny doughnut-shaped dies that further reduce its diameter while stretching the material, which thins the cross-section of the tubing wall. Depending upon the desired target thinness of the cannula, and the physical properties required of the finished product, this process may or may not be accomplished using heat. In general, cannula tubing that is to be used for injecting liquids into the body may be produced with an outside diameter of about 0.33 mm, with a wall thickness of about 0.08 mm. Thus, the lumen may be as small as 0.16 mm.

When all of the reduction processes are complete, the tubing is fed onto another take-up reel for transportation to one of several machines which cut the cannula stock into specific lengths for the next operation – point grinding [the point of the needle is chiselled or filed until the point is at its proper degree of sharpness]."

As the stainless steel tube is pulled and lengthened by the dies, the dies create a bright, mirror-like finish on the outside of the needle. The seam where the cylinder was welded together when the sheet metal was rolled into a tube all but disappears during this stretching and polishing process.

Even with changes in the production of needles, the holes prevail, as Jim Dickinson explains:

> The most recent technology uses a laser to weld a very thin stainless steel jacket around the hole, where in older processes electric welding required a thicker jacket. Once the hole has been jacketed, we then make it smaller and smaller by squeezing the jacket down around it.
>
> When we squeeze the hole it elongates, but try as we can, we have never been able to squeeze it completely out of the jacket. In other words, we have never been able to close the hole.

Why is the French horn designed for left-handers?

We hope that this Imponderable wasn't submitted by left-handers who learned the instrument because they were inspired by the idea that an instrument was finally designed specifically for them. If so, they are in for a rude awakening.

If we have learned anything in our years toiling in the minefields of Imponderability, it is that *nothing* is designed for left-handers except products created exclusively for lefties that cost twice as much as right- (in both senses of the word) handed products.

In case the premise of the Imponderable is confusing, the French horn is the brass wind instrument with a coiled tube – it looks a little like a brass circle with plumbing in the middle and a flaring bell connected to it. The player sticks his or her right hand into the bell itself and hits the three valves with the left hand. So the question before the house is: why isn't the process reversed, with the difficult fingering done by the right hand?

You've probably worked it out already. The original instrument had no valves. Dr Kristin Thelander, Professor of Music at the University of Iowa School of Music and a member of the International Horn Society, elaborates:

> In the period 1750–1840, horns had no valves, so the playing technique was entirely different from our modern technique. The instruments were built with interchangeable crooks, which placed the horn in the appropriate key for the music being

played, and pitches lying outside of the natural harmonic series were obtained by varying degrees of hand stopping in the bell of the horn. It was the right hand which did this manipulation in the bell of the horn, probably because the majority of people are right-handed. [Another theory is that earlier hunting horns were designed to be blown while on horseback. The rider would hold the instrument with the left hand and hold the reins with the right hand.]

Even when the valves were added to the instrument, a lot of hand technique was still used, so the valves were added to the left-hand side. ’

On the modern French horn, this hand technique is no longer necessary. But so many generations grew up with the old configuration that the hand position remains the same. Inertia triumphs again, even though it would make sense for right-handers to use their right hands on the valves. But fair is fair: lefties have had to contend with all the other right-dominant instruments for centuries.

Most of our sources took us to task for calling the instrument the 'French horn'. In a rare case of our language actually getting simpler, the International Horn Society voted in 1971 to change the name from 'French horn' to 'horn'.

Why? Because the creators of the instrument never referred to it as the 'French horn', any more than French diners order 'French' dressing on their salads or 'French' fries with their steak. As we mentioned earlier, the horn was the direct descendant of the hunting horn, which was very popular in France during the sixteenth and seventeenth centuries. The English started referring to it as the 'French horn' as early as the late seventeenth century, and the name stuck.

Why do many guitar players leave a long bit of string hanging off in the air at the tuning end of the guitar?

Guitar strings are considerably longer than needed, largely to compensate for the varying lengths of different instruments. Rock stars hire roadies to take care of mundane activities such as clipping off excess string with wire cutters before the guitarist needs to play. Less successful professionals and home players usually cut the strings themselves, usually with wire clippers.

What is the difference between men's and women's razors?

Our examination of this issue, conducted with the naked eye, reveals that the main difference between men's and women's razors, at least the disposable type, is their pigment. Women's razors are usually pink; men's razors are found in more macho colours, like royal blue and yellow.

But the naked eye can deceive. Chats with representatives at Bic, Schick and Wilkinson indicate that there are at least three significant differences:

1 The most important difference to the consumer is the 'shave angle' of the two. A man's razor has a greater angle on the blade, what the razor industry calls 'aggressive exposure', for two reasons. Men's beards are tougher than women's leg or underarm hair, and require more effort to be cut, and, at least as important, women complain much more than men about nicks and cuts, the inevitable consequence of the aggressive exposure of the men's blades. Women don't particularly like putting hosiery over red splotches, while men seem perfectly content walking around their offices in the morning with their faces resembling pepperoni pizzas.

2 Most women's razors have a greater arc in the head of the razor, so that they can see the skin on the leg more easily as they shave.

3 Women don't shave as frequently as men, especially in the winter, when most wear pants and long-sleeved blouses. Schick offers a 'Personal Touch' razor line for women that features guard bars that contain combs, so that longer hair is set up at the proper angle for shaving.

As far as we can ascertain, all the major manufacturers use the same metallurgy in men's and women's razors.

After listing the design features that his company incorporates to differentiate men's and women's razors, Fred Wexler, Director of Research at Schick, offered a rueful parting observation: despite all of their design efforts, Schick's research reveals that a big majority of women use razors designed for men.

Why?

Still, the picture of the guitar soloist with face contorted behind a mass of labyrinthine string ends (the tuning end of the guitar is known as the 'headstock') is enough of a cliché to lead us to the inevitable 'Why?' We received a charming letter from Mark W Blythe, a guitar technician at Fender Musical Instruments. Blythe offered the five theories below. We've supplemented his quotes with our correspondence with guitarists on both the Internet guitarists' Usenet group (rec.music.guitars) and Prodigy's music/musicians' board:

1 'The roadie did not have time to clip the excess string off the machine before the guitarist needed the instrument.'

2 'The roadie [or guitarist] lost his wire clippers.'

3 'Some musicians are just lazy.' Guitarist Joshua Bardwell says that if you can't find a wire cutter, then the safest way to cut the wire is to do the 'bend-back-and-forth-'til-it-breaks method', the ritual by which most of us break paper clips.

4 'The excess string is used in emergency string repair situations. You can take the string off and retie the ball end to the end of the string. The extra amount of string is then used to compensate for the amount of string that was lost when it was broken.'

Amateur guitarist Rich Beerman not only saves himself from 'emergencies' but saves money by using this method. When he breaks a string, he unlocks it from the tremolo, throws out the part of the string connected to the tremolo, and then takes the part attached to the tuner on the headstock and pulls it towards the tremolo. 'Once the end of the string is back at the tremolo, you lock it back in place.'

5 'Some musicians are eccentric and believe the removal of the extra string will result in lost tone.'

Paul Bagley, who performs in several bands, wrote to us:

> ' I used to leave my strings at full length until a pro musician friend convinced me to run a simple test. After the strings are installed and at proper pitch, there was no difference in tone between the cut and uncut strings. Since then I've cut them off pretty close to the tuning machine. '

Echoing this sentiment is guitarist Stephen Teter, who points out one disadvantage of extra-long strings: 'If you are recording, the hanging strings can be picked up slapping against each other, bleeding into the recording (usually in a "silent" spot).'

Our cyberspace sources added three more possible explanations for the case of the dangling string:

6 Sometimes the 'extra' string actually is a string. British musician Jonathan Egre points out that some guitarists place string around the headstock in order to be able to hang the guitar on a peg in the wall, and, in the case of some thrifty types, as a substitute for a proper guitarstrap.

7 The Ouch Theory. Player Steve Cowell writes: 'The guitarist may be tired of poking the ends of fingers on short cut-off wires – you bleed like a stuck pig.'

8 The Cool Theory. Guitarist Tim Shelfer agrees: 'There's a lot of prestige in loose wire on your headstock, for only who knows why.'

Rick Nedderman knows why:

> I think it's some sort of artistic statement or trade secret that we uninitiated, uncool dweebs just haven't been made privy to. If you've seen photos of players with a tangle of excess strings at the headstock, it's obvious from the intense facial expression (you know the one: eyes closed, eyebrows lifted way up) that it makes one a much more creative player. After all, untangling your left hand (or right) from that mess after you just played the most awesome open E power chord of your entire life takes a lot of creative thinking.

Why do pianos have 88 keys?

Our pianos have a peculiar configuration, with 52 white keys and 36 black keys, ranging from A, three-and-a-half octaves below middle C, to C, four octaves above middle C. Why not 64 or 128 keys?

Before there were pianos, there were pipe organs. In medieval times, some pipe organs included only a few keys, which were so hard to depress that players had to don leather gloves to do the job.

According to piano historian and registered piano technician Stephen H Brady, medieval instruments originally included only the white keys of the modern keyboard, with the raised black keys added gradually: 'The first fully chromatic keyboards [including all the white and black keys] are believed to have appeared in the fourteenth century.'

Clavichords and harpsichords were the vogue in the fifteenth and sixteenth centuries, but they kept changing in size and configuration – none had more than four octaves' range. Octave inflation continued along, as the ever more popular harpsichord went up as high as a five-octave range in the eighteenth century.

In 1709, Bartolomeo Cristofori, a Florentine harpsichord builder, invented the pianoforte, an instrument that trumped the harpsichord by its ability to play soft (*piano*) or loud (*forte*) depending upon the force applied on the keys by the player. Brady notes that the first pianos looked very much like the harpsichord but:

> 'were fitted with an ingenious escapement mechanism that allowed the tones to be produced by tiny hammers hitting the strings (the mechanism attached the hammers to the keys), rather than by quills plucking the strings as was the case in the harpsichord.'

Others soon created pianos, but there was little uniformity in the number of keys or even in the size of the piano itself.

Michael Moore, of Steinway & Sons, theorises that it was a combination of artistic expression and capitalism that gave rise to the 88-key piano. Great composers such as Mozart were demanding instruments capable of expressing the range of the music they were creating. Other composers piggybacked on the expanded range provided by the bigger, 'modern' pianos. Piano makers knew they would have a competitive advantage if they could manufacture bigger and better instruments for ambitious composers, and great changes were in store between 1790 and 1890, as Stephen Brady explains:

> 'By the end of the eighteenth century, towards the end of Mozart's career and near the beginning of Beethoven's, piano keyboards had reached six full octaves, and a keyboard compass of six and a half octaves was not uncommon in early-nineteenth-century grands. For much of the middle to late nineteenth century, seven full octaves (from lowest A to highest A) was the norm. A few builders in the mid-nineteenth century experimented with the seven and a quarter octave keyboard, which is in common use today, but it did not become the de facto standard until about the 1890s.'

Steinway's grand pianos had 85 or fewer keys until the mid-1880s, but Steinway then took the plunge to the 88 we see today, and other manufacturers rushed to meet the specifications of their rival. But why stop there? Why not a nice, round one hundred? Michael Moore explains:

> 'Expansion into still greater numbers of keys was restrained by practical considerations. There is a limit to the number of tones that a string can be made to reproduce, especially on the bass end, where low notes can rattle, as well as a limit to the tones that the ear can hear, especially on the treble end. There is a type of piano, a Boesendorfer Concert Grand, which has 94 different keys [and a full eight-octave range, with all six of the extra keys added to the bass end], but by and large our 88 keys represent the extent to which pianos can be made to faithfully reproduce tones that our ears can hear.'

Even if more keys would gain the slightest advantage in tones, there is also the consideration of size and weight. The Boesendorfer is almost 3 m in length, exceeded only by the 3.1 m Fazioli Concert Grand. Only a handful of compositions ever require these extra keys, not enough reason to motivate Boesendorfer to add the keys in the first place. According to Brady, 'The Boesendorfer company says the extra strings are really there to add sympathetic resonance and richness to the regular notes of the piano's range.'

Scotland Yard is in England. Dog food stinks even though dogs have a sensitive sense of smell. Shampoo lathers up much better if you wash your hair a second time. Most teddy bears look miserable. Sometimes you wonder how the people responsible for such madness keep their jobs. We'll explain.

everyday stuff

Why do bath towels smell bad after a few days when they are presumably touching only clean skin?

Most towels are made of 100 per cent cotton. While you have eliminated most of the germs and dirt from your skin after a shower, the process of rubbing a towel against the body rubs off dead skin that sticks to the moist towel. Towels become an ideal nesting place for the mildew endemic to humid bathrooms.

Most people flip a fan on or open the windows when showering but then turn off the fan or close the windows when they dry themselves. Jean Lang, Director of Marketing at towel behemoth Fieldcrest Cannon, says it is much more important to promote circulation after the shower. Without dispersing the moisture, the bathroom becomes like a terrarium. The same type of mildew that afflicts plastic shower curtains attacks towels, especially if the towels have never dried completely from their last use.

We remember our windowless school changing room with little nostalgia. The lack of ventilation led to mildew and smelly towels. We would have gladly endured the smell of rubbish over the odious aroma of schoolmates' moist towels.

Why do many towels have one smooth side and one textured side?

Some towels are two-faced. The 'smooth' side is sheared – the terry loops are extricated by a machine that has cutting blades similar to an old-fashioned push lawnmower. According to WG Hamlett, Vice-President of Research and Quality Control at Fieldcrest Cannon, the smooth side is sheared purely for aesthetic reasons: many consumers like to put the smooth side out on the towel rail, displaying a velour or crushed velvet-like look and feel.

Towels with special designs display them on the sheared side, so that the motifs will stand out more obviously in relief, according to Tim Jackson, Manager of Bath Marketing at Fieldcrest Cannon. Putting the designs on the unsheared side (also known as the 'terry' or 'loop' side) would be akin to setting a design on a shag rug or the fur of a wolfhound.

But lurking on the other side is the workhorse. It might not have the glamour and pretty looks of the sheared side, but the unsheared 'loop side' is more absorbent. Most consumers of two-faced towels relegate the shaggy side to the background while the sheared side hogs the glory on the towel rail.

Alas, the Plain Jane seems to have won the battle over the two-faced towel. Hamlett reports that while sheared towels used to be more popular, 93 to 97 per cent of most towels now manufactured have terry loops on both sides.

Why do ceiling fans get dusty?

You'd think that the constantly turning blades would throw off any incidental dust that accumulates on a ceiling fan, particularly on the the blades. But you'd be wrong. Ceiling fans seem to be dust magnets.

Your house or flat, we say without insult, is full of dust. In the hair-raising first chapter of the marvellous *The Secret House*, David Bodanis notes that tens of thousands of skin flakes fall off our body every minute.

'Luckily' for us, there are millions of microscopic mites in our abodes, insects that dine on the skin that we shed. Bodanis estimates that just within the average double-bed mattress, two million dust mites live on our discarded skin and hair. Each mite defecates perhaps 20 times a day; their faecal pellets are so small that they float in the air, circulating around the house. Despite the millions of insects that depend upon our shedding skin for their survival, human skin and hair is by far the largest component in the dust found on ceiling fans and throughout the house. Makes you want to run out and get an air filter, doesn't it?

Ceiling fans create a tremendous amount of airflow, and dust is thrown around the room. But much of it lands on the fan and its blades, and just seems to sit there. Charles Ausburn, of Casablanca Fan Company, pleads guilty, but with an explanation:

> The air always has a great deal of dust in it – particles that you can see and also microscopic ones. Over time, a large volume of the circulating air hits and collects on the blades of the fan. People often ask why spider webs and dust can be seen on the fans. But they must understand that there is a lot of dust in the circulating air.

But the accumulation of dust on a given object is not random. Most dust particles carry an electrical charge and therefore can be attracted to one another (a dust ball is simply an accumulation of charged dust particles that have a fatal attraction). Physicist Chris Ballas, of Vanderbilt University, explains:

> The charged dust particles are attracted and cling to any surface that develops a charge. This can be electrical equipment, which directly carries electric current, or a surface subjected to frictional forces, which result in a static electricity build-up. The latter is the case for ceiling fans. As the blades rotate, they experience frictional forces as they "rub" against the air; this knocks electrons around, causing the blades to build up a net charge. The charged dust particles then stick to the charged areas of the blades.
>
> The leading edge [the edge first cutting the air as the blade spins] of the blades usually develops the thickest layer of dust. That's because the leading edge encounters the most friction and develops the largest charge.
>
> So the dust doesn't collect on the blades simply by "falling" or landing on them. The electrical-attraction effect also plays a large part. This same effect explains why some vertical surfaces also get quite dusty (television and stereo equipment, for example). The dust doesn't just fall off these surfaces – it sticks due to the electrical attraction.

What is one hearing when a house is 'settling' or creaking?

We like to think of a home as a bulwark, a refuge from the vicissitudes and capriciousness of the outside world. The infrastructure of a house consists of elements like beams, pillars and foundations, words that connote steadiness, permanence and immutability.

But architects we talked to soon disabused us of this notion. In fact, talking to an architect about the stability of houses is a little like talking to *Psycho*'s Norman Bates about shower safety. In particular, we were startled by the book *How Buildings Work: The Natural Order of Architecture*, written by Edward Allen, and passed on to us by James Cramer, Executive Vice-President/CEO of the American Institute of Architects. In one chapter, 'Providing for Building

Movement', Allen details the many ways in which buildings move, and if we weren't averse to clichés and bad puns, we would say that the opening rocked us to our very foundations:

> A building, even a seemingly solid, massive one, is never at rest. Its motions are usually very small ones, undetectable by the unaided eye, but most of them are of virtually irresistible force, and would tear the building to pieces if not provided for in some way.

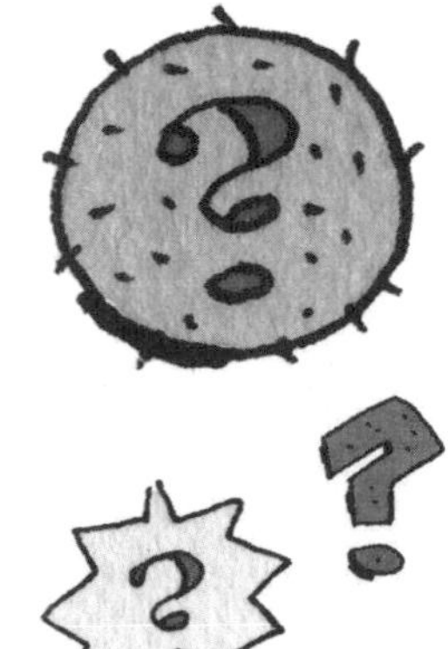

Allen states that in an average house, all of these components can and do move:

1 The soil underneath the foundation buckles under the weight of the new foundation.
2 Materials that are put in place while wet, such as mortar, concrete and lime plaster, shrink as they harden.
3 Some dry materials, such as gypsum plaster, tend to expand and push against adjoining elements.
4 Most timber used in houses is not completely dry when put in place. Wet timber shrinks.
5 Structural elements that carry weight loads, such as beams, pillars and columns, deflect under the weight.
6 Wind and earthquakes cause additional 'natural' deflection.
7 Wood and concrete sag.
8 Wood, in particular, tends to expand when exposed to high humidity and contract in dry conditions. When humidity decreases noticeably, such as when a room is heated in winter, the wood creaks noticeably.
9 Any material adjoining another material with different movement characteristics is in danger of scraping against another or moving away from the other, which can cause movement and noise.
10 All of the above movements can and do cause noise, but the most common noise associated with 'settling' is the actual expansion and contraction of the building. Allen explains:

> Back-and-forth movements caused by thermal and moisture effects occur constantly. A building grows measurably larger in warm weather and smaller in cold weather. A roof, heated by the sun, grows larger in the middle of the day while the cooler walls below stay the same size. At night the roof cools and shrinks.

And so on and so on. The architect's planning compensates for the inevitable movement of these materials. Or at least we hope that it does. Otherwise, the creaking noises might lead us to the same fate as Janet Leigh's in *Psycho*.

Why are men's ties tapered at the bottom?

Ties don't have to be tapered on the bottom. In fact, they weren't until the early twentieth century. Before then, ties were cut straight down from a piece of material. But now, the vast majority of silk ties are cut on a bias (on an angle to the floor). According to fashion writer G Bruce Boyer, there are two main benefits to cutting on an angle: it produces a tie 'more impervious to the rigours of knotting and maximises the natural elasticity of the silk'.

When the end of the tie is finished, it is 'trimmed square' (along the lines of the weave) so that the end forms a natural point. The larger point, the one presented to the outside world, is known as the 'blade' or 'apron' end, and the smaller, covered-up point is known as the 'upper end'.

Have you ever noticed that knitted ties are not tapered on the bottom? You may have figured out the reason already. Knitted ties (whether made out of wool or silk) are cut and seamed straight across the blade end, rather than on a bias – circumstantial evidence that ties are tapered for purely functional rather than aesthetic reasons.

Why aren't shoes laced up when you try them on in shops?

We learned how to tie our shoes when we were four. But no one ever taught us how to lace up a shoe from scratch. Our assumption was that this shoe store practice was simply to annoy and humiliate us, but indeed, the experts we consulted named four reasons for leaving shoelaces unlaced:

1 Lacing shoes is labour-intensive and can't be done by machine. Therefore, it would be an added expense.

2 Different customers have special preferences in lacing techniques. Shoe consultant and historian William A Rossi told us that 'shoes are left unlaced to allow the buyer to choose his or her own lacing "style"'.

3 It allows customers to try on shoes with easy entry. Some buyers interpret any difficulty in putting on a shoe as indicating that the shoe is too small.
4 Perhaps the most important consideration is psychological. Florsheim's NB Albert indicates that, subliminally, the unlaced shoe is 'brand new'. Stan Sterenberg, owner of an Athlete's Foot store in New York City, reports that a few customers refuse to buy any shoes that are already laced. After all, who knows who's been trying on the shoes before you?

Why are socks angled at approximately 115 to 125 degrees when the human foot is angled at about 90 degrees?

Not all socks are angled, of course. Tube socks are so named because they are a straight tube of fabric closed on one end by sewing. The tube sock is constructed by 'full circular knitting' (i.e. the knitting head on the machine knits in a circle).

A tube sock doesn't contain a designated position for the heel, but more conventional socks do. Most socks are knitted with a feature called the 'reciprocated heel'. Sid Smith, President and Chief Executive Officer of the American National Association of Hosiery Manufacturers, told *Imponderables* how the reciprocated heel is made:

> Imagine a full circular knitting machine starting at the top of the sock and knitting in a complete circle all the way down the top of the sock, until it hits the point where the heel is to be knitted in. At this point, the machine automatically enters what is called the "reciprocated function". Instead of knitting in a complete circle, it knits halfway to each side and then back again, until the heel portion is knitted in.
>
> After this is completed, the machine automatically reverts to full circular knitting to finish the sock. This reciprocation is what causes the finished sock to be angled.

The 115- to 125-degree angle of the sock, then, is the result of, rather than the purpose of, the knitting process. The fabrics used for socks will give or stretch to conform to the contours of the foot. Since a 180-degree tube sock can fit comfortably on the human foot, there is no reason why a conventional sock won't.

Why does starch make our shirts stiff?

Starch is a type of 'sizing', a filler used to add body, sheen and lustre to limp clothing. All shirts come off the rack with sizing, but sizing is water-soluble; every time the shirt is washed, sizing comes out of the shirt. The main purpose of adding starch, then, is to restore the original body of a garment.

The main ingredient in starch is wheat or, less frequently, corn. The grain is mixed with water, resins and chemicals. As Bill Seitz, of the Neighborhood Cleaners Association, describes it, the starch is literally absorbed by the fabric. Cotton plus wheat is stiffer than cotton alone.

Norman Oehlke, of the International Fabricare Institute, adds that starch also enhances soil resistance, facilitates soil removal for the next wash and makes ironing easier.

Synthetic fabrics aren't as receptive to starch as all-cotton garments, so extra chemicals are added to the starch, such as polyvinyl acetate, sulfated fatty alcohols, silicones and, our personal favourite, carboxymethylcellulose.

Why does one sometimes find sand in the pockets of new blue jeans?

Conceivably, you might have picked up a pair of jeans returned by a previous customer who went to the beach, but that is highly unlikely. We aren't gamblers by nature, but we would be willing to wager a small sum that the jeans in question were stonewashed.

Stonewashed jeans are softened by rubbing against pumice stones during washing. Don Wofford, a marketing specialist at jeans behemoth Levi Strauss & Co., explains how mighty stones can turn into sand:

> Pumice is a soft white stone that is placed in huge washers along with jeans to be "stonewashed". Pumice stones used in the stonewashing process sometimes disintegrate into tiny particles (or sand) that end up in the pockets of stonewashed jeans.

Obviously, pockets are the one portion of the jeans most susceptible to trapping loose particles of pumice. Any other sand would tend to get rinsed away with the wash water.

What makes cotton shrink more than wool when both of them are washed?

If we had known how complicated this subject was, we might have tried tackling an easier problem, perhaps solving the unresolved issues in quantum physics or conducting an exhaustive search to find either a scintilla of humour or a decent female role in an Oliver Stone movie.

Trade associations in both the wool and cotton industry sent us literature full of equations and formulas, the likes of which we hadn't seen since we glanced at some of those particularly baffling maths textbooks at school. But since we are stuck with the issue at hand, please believe us when we tell you we are simplifying our answer.

All the processes that turn cotton into a finished garment (for example, spinning, weaving or knitting, dyeing and finishing) strain and contract the fabric. Cotton shrinks when this strain is relaxed. Although many factors can contribute to shrinkage, by far the biggest factor is swelling of the yarn when exposed to water.

One might think that swollen yarn would increase the size of the garment. In fact, a greater length of yarn, known as warp yarn, is required to interweave the greater diameter of the swollen filling threads if the fibres are to remain in position. But the knitting process doesn't allow enough extra yarn to interweave, so the filling threads are drawn together. The result is a relaxation of the internal

How did Levi's 501 jeans get their number?

Levi Strauss (yes, there was a real Levi Strauss) was a textile and clothing merchant in California and sold a wide range of products. The original Levi jean was the 501, and this number was simply its arbitrary stock number, according to Levi Strauss & Co. spokesperson Brad Williams. Strauss disliked applying the word 'jeans' to his garment, so he promoted the 501 as 'waist-high overalls'. Just think, if his company kept that name into the 1970s, chances are that high-fashion designers like Gloria Vanderbilt and Calvin Klein wouldn't have foisted 'designer waist-high overalls' on a gullible public at triple the prices of Mr Strauss.

What gives wool its 'distinctive' smell when it gets wet?

'Distinctive', huh? What delicacy of expression.

All sheep manufacture lanolin, a secretion from the sebaceous glands – the equivalent of human perspiration. Lanolin collects in the wool and prevents it from drying out. That's the good news. The bad news is that lanolin helps impart the 'distinctive' smell of sheep when they get wet.

Almost all of the lanolin should be removed in the processing of wool. After wool is sheared and graded, the next step is the washing and scouring of the fibres. The wool runs through a series of rakes that comb out foreign material and a series of tubs filled with a detergent solution. After the wool is cleaned, it passes through several water rinses that remove the lanolin. Then the wool passes through squeeze rolls and is hot-air dried.

If the scouring process is insufficient, too much lanolin may be retained in the wool. Or if the chemicals used in the scouring process are too strong, it may degrade the fibres. Both problems could cause smelly products.

Our guess is that this question refers to a bulky wool jumper rather than, say, a pair of worsted pants. Representatives of the Wool Bureau and the American Wool Council both mentioned 'oil wool' as the likely inspiration for this Imponderable. Oil wool is intentionally not totally scoured in processing because the natural grease makes knitting easier. The famous Aran Island jumpers of Ireland are notorious 'stinkers'. Note that wool overcoats usually don't have a problem when it rains because modern scouring and finishing technology remove virtually all of the wool's lanolin.

strain and shrinkage in length. This shrinkage can occur in the clothes dryer as well as in the washing machine, as anyone who has ever seen an extra-large t-shirt turn into a medium after a prolonged spin can attest. Chemical processes can eliminate all but about 1 per cent of this shrinkage, but the treatment affects the feel and wear characteristics of the cotton.

Despite wool's reputation as a relatively shrink-free material, it is susceptible to the same relaxation of strain problems as cotton, and one more as well: felting shrinkage. Felting shrinkage is why you can't put most wool garments in the washing machine, as the American Wool Council explains:

> Felting shrinkage occurs when wool is subjected to heat, moisture and friction, the kind of friction that takes place in washing agitation. The microscopic scale-like structures of the wool fibre interlock; the fabric becomes thicker and smaller; it shrinks or felts. This kind of shrinkage is irreversible.

So why doesn't wool shrink when exposed to the heat in drycleaning? Because as part of the finishing process of making a wool garment, the wool is preshrunk in a process called 'fulling' or 'milling'. Heat, moisture and friction are applied to the fabric so that it shrinks a specified amount in length and width. Fulling lightens the weave and helps provide the softer texture desired of wool garments. Many chemical processes have been invented to allow treated wool garments to be machine washed and dried.

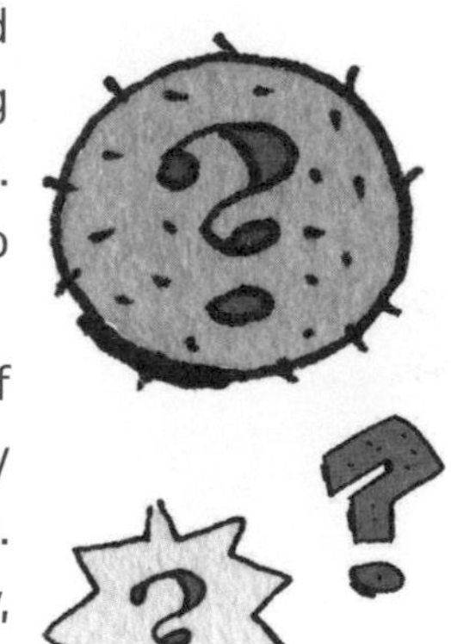

One advantage of wool over cotton is that shrinkage caused by relaxation of fibre strains can often be reversed. We have been testing this hypothesis by bravely, and without regard to our own welfare, gaining weight over the years. We can conclusively state that our old cotton t-shirts, which once fit perfectly, are not capable of expanding to fit our now ampler frame.

Why does rinsing with hot water 'set' a stain? Why is rinsing with cold water more effective in eliminating the stain?

First the good news. As you increase the temperature of the water applied to a stain, the solubility of the stain also increases. Obviously, dissolving the stain is a good first step in eliminating the stain.

Now the bad news. In practice, most of the time, 'dissolving' the stain translates into spreading the stain. Usually, hot water helps break up the stain, but it doesn't lift the stain; rather, it allows stains to penetrate deeper into the fibre. Oily stains, especially on synthetics, have this reaction. Once the stain sets deeply enough in a fabric, detergents or drycleaning are often ineffective.

In other cases, hot water can actually create a chemical change in the stain itself that hampers removal. Protein stains are a good example of this problem, as Lever Brothers spokesperson Sheryl Zapcic illustrates:

> 'If protein is a component of the stain, rinsing with hot water will coagulate the protein. For example, egg white, which is a protein, can be loosened with cold water without coagulating; however, hot water will immediately coagulate the egg white. Technically, this is called denaturation of the protein. In any event, the stain becomes insoluble or set.'

On some stains, it won't matter much whether hot or cold water is used.

Our own rule of thumb on this subject is: nothing works. We have been in fancy French restaurants where our dining companions insist that 'only soda water can get that stain out of your tie'. Of course, we never have soda water at hand. To placate our true believer, we end up ordering a glass. And, *naturellement*, the stain lingers as an enduring testament to our naïve belief that we will one day get a stain out of a garment successfully.

Why does just about everything look darker when it gets wet?

Drop some water on your new cream-coloured blouse and you get a dark spot. Have a buffoon standing near you spill his Perrier on your navy blue blazer and the light liquid somehow manages to make the coat's dark colour even darker. Why is this so?

Elementary physics, it turns out. You lose the true colour of the garment in three ways:

1. Even a thin coating of water will force light coming towards the garment to refract within the water film. The available light is thus disbursed.
2. The reflection on the surface of the water causes incoherent light scattering.

3 A combination of the two points above ensures that there will be less light available on the surface of the jacket to reflect back to your eyes. Thus the spot will appear darker than the rest of the jacket that doesn't have to compete with water in order to reflect light.

Why don't the silver fillings in our mouth rust?

The fillings don't rust because there is no iron or steel in the amalgam, or 'silver' fillings. Without iron, there is no rust.

But we understand the tenor of the question. Combine metal with constant exposure to air and liquid, and you'd think your fillings would be devastated by corrosion. Here's why they aren't. There is silver in silver fillings, but it isn't the dominant component. Most amalgam fillings consist of approximately 50 per cent mercury with the rest silver, tin, copper and zinc. The silver content can range between 2 and 35 per cent, usually on the higher end of the scale.

Why is there more mercury than silver in fillings? Mercury has the ability to alloy with other metals. If you combined, say, silver, copper and tin, you'd end up with a powder without any tensile strength. Mercury helps combine the other liquids to form a solid mass that is strong and yet can be compressed into a cavity and seal it effectively. Although the silver amalgam filling is inexpensive to manufacture and easy to install, the metal does corrode, which is one of the reasons why fillings sometimes have to be replaced. But the corrosion has a positive side, too, as dentist Philip Klein explains:

> When the restoration is inserted, a corrosive layer begins to form at the metal-tooth interface. This layer mechanically seals the restoration and prevents leakage that would ultimately lead to recurrent cavities and failure.

The corrosion actually prevents bacteria and other chemicals from entering the cavity-laden tooth.

All well and good, you might be saying, but isn't mercury a dangerous toxin? It sure is. Many countries in Europe, for example, have outlawed the use of amalgam fillings, yet the British Dental Association, the World Health Organization and most mainstream health organisations maintain that the minimal amount of leakage of mercury from fillings is within acceptable guidelines for risk. Alternative and holistic dentists argue that mercury poisoning from amalgam fillings can cause everything from kidney damage to brain damage. Suddenly, a little corrosion in your mouth doesn't seem like a big deal.

Why do we have to shake deodorant and other aerosol cans before using them?

If you could see inside a can of deodorant, you would see that the ingredients are not arranged uniformly in the can. The propellant is not soluble and so won't mix with the active ingredients in the deodorant.

In many cases, you would see three or four levels of ingredients in a can. The top layer would contain the hydrocarbon gas used as a propellant. Other active ingredients, such as aluminium salt, emollient and fragrance, also might seek their own level. By shaking up the can, you would guarantee spraying the proper proportion of ingredients.

Any effort expended in shaking the can is well worth the appreciation from friends and loved ones. But a stiff spray of hydrocarbon gas simply isn't sufficient to take care of a nasty body odour problem.

Why are most perfumes yellow?

The answer to this Imponderable boils down to the not illogical conclusion proffered by Annette Green, President of the Fragrance Foundation: 'The reason that fragrance is usually yellow is because that is the natural colour of the essential oils [in perfumes] when they are processed.'

Actually, the perfume concentrates, the collection of scores, hundreds or sometimes thousands of raw materials (essential oils) that are later diluted with alcohol to make cologne or perfume, can vary quite a bit in colour. Some of the common essential oils in perfume, such as oak moss, start out with a strong green or brown colour. But many of these oils are amber in colour, and, according to Peter Gesell, Vice-President of Creativity at International Flavor and Fragrances, will take on a yellowish cast when diluted.

If the natural ingredients don't yield a pleasing hue, the perfumer may tint it. According to Gesell, it is difficult to turn an extremely dark mixture light or to make drastic changes, so the end result is usually not profoundly different from the ingredients' natural colour.

Not all perfumes are yellow, of course. Some perfumes with other colours are packaged in opaque bottles, to hide the actual cast. Bright 'designer colours' are trotted out as marketing tools, although one perfumer we spoke to said, off the record, that he thought the 'natural' yellow colour appealed more to the upmarket customer, and that the popularity of perfumes with 'weird' colours was confined mostly to teenagers. These products' popularity tends to be as ephemeral as the fragrance's scent.

Why do coloured soaps and shampoos yield white suds?

Very little dye is put into soap or shampoo to colour them. As College of San Mateo Physics Professor Donald Beaty puts it, 'When it's in the bottle, the light that is used to view the liquid passes through a considerable thickness of colourful shampoo or liquid soap.'

But once you make suds, the water-soluble dye is highly diluted. The percentage of dyed colour contained in the original product is greatly reduced. Beaty adds that nothing magical 'happens' to the colorant in the dye:

> Light that reflects from the surface of each soap bubble will contain the same range of colours as the light used to illuminate the lather. We tend to perceive the reflected light as white light if the incident light is normal room light or daylight.

Sally Miller, a consumer services representative of soap and shampoo behemoth Procter & Gamble, told *Imponderables* that manufacturers could easily put enough colorant into bar soaps or shampoos to yield coloured suds, but their research indicates 'most consumers find white lather preferable for applying to the skin or the hair'.

A high concentration of dye could also stain towels and turn a demure blonde shampoo user into a green-haired Cyndi Lauper look-alike.

Why are clean things squeaky? Why do drinking glasses sometimes squeak and other times remain squeakless when you rub them?

When you rub two substances together, all sorts of interesting things happen. Just ask the birds and the bees, or your local biochemist. Our local biochemist happens to be Dr Donald Graham, of Langara College in Vancouver, British Columbia, who told us that when you hear a good, clean squeak, the glass has overcome the 'coefficient of friction'.

Pardon? The coefficient of friction is simply a forbidding term to describe the force necessary to overcome the friction between two objects. When the coefficient is high, it means greater force is necessary to overcome the friction; when the coefficient is low, there is little friction between the two objects.

When an object, say a drinking glass, is full of dirt or the residue of a beverage, or your fingers are greasy or oily, these impurities act as a lubricant, and your fingers can glide along the surface of the glass. But if the object is free of impurities, it generates more friction between it and your fingers when you rub because the two surfaces come into full contact with each other; the rubbing material keeps sticking for a moment before the force moving it overcomes the friction. It then releases, only to get caught again, ad infinitum.

The force of the friction, and the accompanying catching and releasing, causes the squeaking object to move, or to vibrate (in some cases, both objects vibrate, although not all materials are capable of vibrating); if the vibrations occur at frequencies that correspond to audible sounds, we hear those vibrations as

Why does shampoo lather so much better on the second application?

Even if our hands and hair are already wet, we can't seem to get a healthy lather on the first try when we shampoo our hair. But after we rinse, the shampoo foams up like crazy. Why is lather more luxuriant the second time around?

Evidently, it's because we have greasy hair, according to Dr John E Corbett, Vice-President of Technology at Clairol: 'In the first shampoo application, the lather is suppressed by the oils in the hair. When the oils are rinsed off [by the first application], the shampoo lathers much better on the second application.'

squeaks. Of course, the force of the rubbing surfaces against each other and the kind of motion used during the rub will affect the volume and tempo of the sound.

With some surfaces, very little force is needed to generate a squeak, and glass just happens to be one of them. Another scientist friend, Harold Blake of Zephyrhills, Florida, is so committed to research pursuits that he even works in restaurants, astounding and, we'd guess, occasionally annoying his friends:

> Often, even in a fancy restaurant, I take my beverage goblet, if it's thin and on a stem, and when the liquid is nearly gone, I moisten my finger and slowly glide it along the rim. When I achieve the necessary "drag" on my finger to the glass, my finger sort of jumps rapidly, scuffing along the glass, and the goblet begins to sing. It is usually a high-pitched tone, melodious and penetrating. In one restaurant, no one knew where the sound was coming from. Other patrons started looking around. Even the people at my table refused to believe my finger was making that loud a whine.
>
> What happened, of course, is that friction causes the finger to push against the glass rim, and then added force releases the finger on the rim as it advances to a new spot. This sets up a natural vibration in the glass. It is the same frequency you hear if you "tink" the glass with your finger.
>
> You can do this with dinner china, windowpanes and blackboards [uh-oh, bad vibrations]. You just need to have the right amount of friction to create the series of scuffs and releases. The reason for some squeak-failures is the lack of the right amount of friction, or surface tension, or stickiness.

You might think that both our hands and the glass have smooth surfaces, but you'd be wrong. As Blake puts it:

> The epithelial cells on a finger or edge of a fingernail, the cotton fibres on a towel, the cells in the hairs of a horse's tail, all, under a microscope, look like furrows in a ploughed field, or the cobblestones in the roughest street. Rough!

Blake reminded us that as far back as the Middle Ages, Europeans enjoyed 'musical' or 'tuned' glasses, which eventually were used as concert instruments.

Rims of different glasses of different sizes, tuned in different keys by the amount of water put in the vessel, were played by squeakmaestros, presumably with impeccably clean hands.

The principles of friction and vibration explain the sound generated by all stringed instruments. You can take a violin bow, drag it along a Stradivarius and achieve a resonant, mellifluous vibration. Drag the same bow along a carpenter's saw, and you'll hear a penetrating vibration that only a dog could love.

Why are newspapers so effective in cleaning windows?

If you read most newspapers for more than a few minutes, your hands feel dirty. So why do windows look squeaky clean when you rub the same newspaper against the glass? We asked experts in window cleaning, newspaper printing and inks this very same question.

One potential allure would have to be price. Newsprint, the kind of paper used for newspaper printing, is probably the cheapest paper manufactured – and discarded newspaper the cheapest of all. Still, we couldn't find a single professional cleaner who uses newspapers on the job, although several could see why newspapers could be effective in a pinch. Jim Grady, of Tri-State Window Cleaning in Wappinger Falls, New York, writes:

> I don't use newspaper to clean windows. I use squeegees. When I was a child, my father did tell me that newspapers were an effective way to clean windows, probably because it was free or cheaper than paper towels. But as the good book says, when I became a man I put away my childish ways and I haven't put a piece of newspaper on glass in 25 years.

The first quality that is prized in a drying agent is absorbency, and in this regard newspaper hits the jackpot. Theodore Lustig, at the West Virginia University School of Journalism, told us:

> Newsprint is extremely porous [larger spaces between fibres] and is uncoated [no waxes or fillers]. Therefore, it pretty much acts like a sponge, making it useful in whatever

tasks require sopping up moisture. This may account for its ability to clean windows.

Another proponent of the absorbency theory is Jim Patton, Process Manager at Smurfit Newsprint, in Pomona, California, who adds that newsprint's lack of water repellency is another reason for its success in cleaning windows:

> Newsprint is pretty dam absorbent. Most papers have a sizing applied to them to give them water repellency. Newspapers have a minimum of repellency. At a different newspaper manufacturer I worked for, they used newsprint in the men's room for drying your hands.

Of course, the lack of sizing in newsprint isn't to aid in window cleaning – it's to please newspaper publishers. Bob Cate, Director of Manufacturing Services at newsprint producer Bowater, Inc., agrees that the lack of sizing in newsprint is key to its efficacy in cleaning windows, and explains how:

> You want any ink to soak into the paper, as opposed to standing out on the surface, but you don't want it to soak in so fast that it comes out on the other side. This is why newspaper is absorbent – so that the ink can soak in and not sit on top of the paper when it's applied.

Newspapers are not only cheap and absorbent, but also give the cleaned, dry windows a shine, according to Brent Weingard, of Expert Window Cleaner:

> ... to my knowledge, newspaper is generally never used by professional window cleaners. It's really more of a "home remedy" cleaning tool that actually works surprisingly well. It doesn't have lint, is very absorbent and gives the glass a shiny finish. My theory of what causes that shiny finish is evidenced by looking at your hands after handling newspapers: it's ink! I believe it is a film of ink that is left on the glass surface that gives windows this colourful reflective finish.

So what are the downsides of professionals using newspapers to clean windows? They are few, but they are prohibitive. The first, enunciated by Richard

Fabry, publisher of *American Window Cleaner* magazine, is the killer: 'Sure, newspaper gets the glass clean, but it is s-l-o-w. Get a professional squeegee and it'll go much faster.'

Another problem: what do you do with the newspapers when you are finished with them? Gary Mauer, of Window Cleaning Network in Oconomowoc, Wisconsin, a town with more Os in its name than window cleaners, writes:

> 'Because we clean so many windows, it's simply not practical to use and dispose of bundles of newspaper. For that reason alone, you'll be hard pressed to find a professional window cleaner who uses newspaper.'

Next time you clean your own windows, you might want to give newspapers a try instead of paper towels. The professionals tended to look askance at paper towels – they dry the glass surface well enough, but leave lint. Cloth nappies or tight-knit towels or rags are a better bet. With newer inks, often vegetable-rather than petroleum-based, newspapers tend to streak less than in the past (and for that matter, stain your hands much less when you read them). In years past, amateurs who used newspaper to clean windows tended to dirty white frames around the windows, streaking them with ink.

Why does a newspaper tear smoothly vertically and raggedly horizontally?

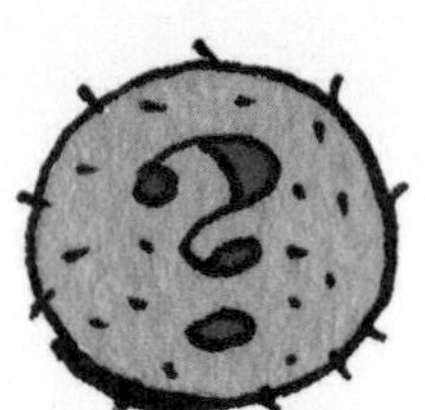

Newsprint is made up of many wood fibres. The fibres are placed on printers in pulp form, consisting of 80 to 90 per cent water – the newsprint dries while in the machine. The printing machines are designed to line up the fibres in a horizontal position to add tear strength to the sheet vertically.

The basic purpose of lining up the fibres in one direction is simply to add stability to the sheet when the press is running. According to Ralph E Eary, National Director of Production and Engineering for the newspaper division of Scripps Howard, 'All standard-size newspapers are printed vertically on an unwound sheet of newsprint.' A rip in one sheet endangers the whole printing process, and at best costs money and time.

In other words, the finished newspaper has a grain, just as a piece of meat or linen has a grain. (Ever notice how hard it is to tear a bedsheet in one direction

How do stamp pads keep moist when they are constantly exposed to the drying influence of air?

The ink used in stamp pads has a glycol and water base, which forms a mixture that actually absorbs moisture from the air. On a humid day, this hygroscopic effect allows the stamp or stamp pad to replenish any moisture lost on dry days.

and how easy in another?) When you rip the newspaper vertically, you are tearing with the grain or, more accurately, between grains.

Why does dog food have to smell so awful?

We always hear about dogs' vaunted sense of smell. The olfactory area in a human is about 3 sq. cm; a dog's is 130 sq. cm. While humans tend to trust their sense of sight more, a dog evaluates food and other living things with its sense of smell. And with this heightened ability, the dog chooses to eat stuff that smells like dog food? Maybe we olfactory ignoramuses cannot savour the scent that is kibble, like children who can't appreciate the bouquet of a fine burgundy. But we're not buying that. We're going to have to agree to disagree with our canine friends.

Pet owners tend to anthropomorphise their dogs, so it's surprising that designer dog foods haven't been developed to make masters want to compete with Fido for the grub, but the pet industry maintains that its focus is on what pleases the pet. Robert Wilbur, of the Pet Food Institute, explains:

> Pet foods (unlike most human foods) provide the sole diet of most pets and the product must be complete and balanced nutritionally. In addition, pet foods must also be appetising and appeal to a pet's sense of smell and taste. This is known as palatability ... Scent and flavour must appeal to the dog and may differ from what would appeal to us.

Ironically, dogs, who will eat just about anything lying on the street, also have sensitive stomachs. Lucille Kubichek, of the Chihuahua Club of America, notes

that efforts to find a scent that humans would like could lead to health issues: 'Dog foods carry the odours of the ingredients of which they are composed. I doubt food odours could be neutralised without adding one or more chemicals, which probably would be harmful to the animal.'

Fat is often the second ingredient listed on pet food nutrition labels, and this is often responsible for that awful dog food smell. In her book, *Food Pets Die For*, Ann N Martin lambastes its quality:

> Fats give off a pungent odour that entices your pet to eat the garbage. These fats are sourced from restaurant grease. This oil is rancid and unfit for human consumption. One of the main sources of fat comes from the rendering plant. This is obtained from the tissues of mammals and/or poultry in the commercial process of rendering or extracting.

While the pet food industry and its critics, such as Martin, wrangle about whether commercial pet food is dangerous to their health, most dogs seem to be quite content to quickly clean their plates. That makes us happy. The faster they eat the dog food, the sooner the smell goes away.

Why doesn't aluminium foil feel hot when it comes out of a roaring oven?

Rest assured, 'if you stuck your finger into a hot oven, the aluminium would be hot', writes James Plumb, Director of Communications for the Aluminum Association. Let's say you put into your 200°C oven a baked potato wrapped in aluminium foil, along with a meatloaf in a ceramic container covered by a glass top. All of the foods and containers will eventually attain the temperature designated on the thermostat, but at varying speeds.

Different metals have varying abilities to spread heat quickly and evenly – those that are best at this task are referred to as having a 'high conduction rate'. One of the reasons why aluminium is used for foil is that it is, as a representative of Alumax Foils put it, 'an excellent conductor of heat'. Only three other metals have a higher conduction rate: gold, silver and copper – all much more expensive commodities.

But why does the aluminium foil cool off so much faster than, say, the ceramic casserole dish or the glass top? Once the foil is removed, it is as responsive to the cooler ambient air as it was to the hot air inside the oven. Aluminium quickly releases its heat into the cooler room.

But one crucial difference between aluminium foil and the glass top or the casserole dish is its thinness, as Jeff Glenning, a materials engineer at Reynolds Metals Company, explains:

> ‘Since the foil is very thin, the heat does not have to travel far in the metal before it is released into the air. If you think about it, aluminium foil is the only metal that is used in cooking that is this thin. Pots and pans are usually made out of much thicker metal, sometimes aluminium. But since they are much thicker than foil, these metallic objects trap heat inside the metal for a longer period of time. Thus, the high heat conduction rate and the shape of the foil allow it to cool before you touch it, giving the illusion that it was never hot.’

Glenning adds that another physical characteristic of aluminium adds to the 'not hot misconception'. While aluminium has high conductivity, it has low emissivity (heat radiated from the aluminium's surface). Put your hand a couple of centimetres above boiling water and the heat will be oppressive; put your hand the same distance above a hotter piece of aluminium and you will not feel intense heat. Glenning says that 'the aluminium would not feel hot until the skin actually comes in contact with the surface of the aluminium'.

Why are paper and plastic drinking cups wider at the top than the bottom?

Reader Charles Lyons writes:

> ‘I have never been able to understand why paper and plastic drinking cups are designed with the wide end at the top. That makes them top-heavy and much easier to tip over. Making

> them with the wide end on the bottom would make the cups more stable and less likely to tip over, with no disadvantage at all that I can see.'

Come to think of it, Charles's suggestion has been used for aeons in the design of bottles. We certainly never found it difficult drinking from a 'bottom-heavy' beer bottle. Most glass bottles and many glass or ceramic drinking cups don't taper at the bottom, so why should disposable cups? What are we missing?

Plenty, it turns out, according to every cup producer we spoke to. John S Carlson, Marketing Director of James River, put it succinctly:

> 'The cups are wider at the top so that they can be "nested" in a stack during shipping, storage on the grocery store shelf and in your cupboard at home. If they weren't tapered slightly, they'd stack like empty soup cans.'

In retailing, not only time but space is money. Better to get more of your product on the shelf and live with the consequences of an extra customer or two tipping over their drink.

Why do straws in drinks sometimes sink and sometimes rise to the surface?

The movement of the straw depends upon the liquid in the glass and the composition of the straw itself. The rapidly rising straw phenomenon is usually seen in glasses containing carbonated soft drinks. Richard Williams, a meteorologist at the US National Weather Service, explains the phenomenon:

> '... the rise occurs as carbon dioxide bubbles form on both the outside and inside of the straw. This increases the buoyancy of the straw and it gradually rises out of the liquid.
>
> The gas is under considerable pressure when the drink is first drawn or poured. When that pressure is released the gas forms small bubbles on the sides of the glass and on the straw. As the bubbles grow the straw becomes buoyant enough to "float" higher and higher in the container.'

Occasionally, though, a straw will rise in a non-carbonated beverage, and we didn't get a good explanation for this phenomenon until we heard from Roger W Cappello, President of straw maker Clear Shield National. We often get asked how our sources react to being confronted with strange questions. The only answer we can give is – it varies. Sure, we like authoritative sources who fawn over us and smother us in data. But we must confess we have a special place in our hearts for people like Cappello, who make us sweat a little before divulging their secrets. Here is his letter to *Imponderables*, verbatim, skipping only the usual pleasantries:

> After pondering your question for a while, I decided to toss your letter as I was too busy for this. I later retrieved the letter and decided I would attempt to give you an answer that is slightly technical, mixed with some common sense and creative licence.
>
> First off, I know the action you were referring to had something to do with "specific gravity". Specific gravity, as defined by Webster, is "the rate of the density of a substance to the density of a substance (as pure water) taken as a standard when both densities are obtained by weighing in air".
>
> Straws today are formed from polypropylene, whereas many years ago they were made of polystyrene, before that paper, and before that, wheat shafts.
>
> Assuming water has a specific gravity of 1, polypropylene is 0.9, and polystyrene is 1.04. A polypropylene straw will float upwards in a glass of water, whereas a polystyrene straw will sink. However, a polystyrene straw will float upwards in a carbonated drink as the bubbles attach themselves to the side of the straw, which will help offset the slight specific gravity difference between water and polystyrene. A polypropylene straw will float higher in a carbonated drink for the same reason. If you put a polypropylene straw in petrol, and please don't try this, it will sink because the specific gravity of petrol is lighter than water.
>
> If you lined up 10 glasses of different liquids, all filled to the same level, the straws would most likely float at all different levels due to the different specific gravities of the liquids and the attachment of various numbers of bubbles to the straws.

I really wish you hadn't brought this up as I'm going to lunch now. I think I'll order hot coffee so I can ponder the imponderables of my business without distraction. Good luck.'

We can use all that good luck you were wishing us. I'm sure you had a productive lunch too. Anyone willing to share information with us can eat (and sleep) with a clear conscience, knowing that they have led to the enlightenment of their fellow humans.

Why do bottles have necks?

Bottles date back to the ancient civilisations of Egypt and Mesopotamia. Historians think that wine consumption started there as far back as 5400 BC, but their bottles didn't resemble ours at all – they were amphorae, clay flasks with short necks. Remains indicate amphorae were stoppered with cloth, pieces of leather or fired clay.

When glassblowing was developed during Roman times, most of the vessels were squat and onion-shaped, probably because these were easier to manufacture. This shape was badly suited for winemakers, in particular, because wine bottles need to be stored on their sides in order for the wine to stay in contact with the cork (dry corks crumble and may allow air to enter the bottle – oxygen is the enemy of ageing wine properly).

Before mass production of glass bottles, there was no uniformity in size, but by the nineteenth century, most wine bottles were 700 to 800 ml, with 750 ml not becoming the standard until well into the twentieth century. The long-necked glass bottle has only been with us for a couple of hundred years, so we were a little surprised when an authority like renowned bottle collector Lieutenant Commander J Carl Sturm replied to our query with: 'This question has never been raised that I know of in my 44 years of collecting old bottles. I can only theorise as I know of nothing in print.'

We spoke to or corresponded with nearly 30 experts on bottles – bottle collectors, glassblowers, bottle manufacturers and winery executives – and we were offered plenty of theories but no smoking-gun answers. We couldn't even gather a definitive conclusion about whether the longish neck was a by-product of the glassblowing process, an aesthetic decision or a utilitarian feature. Steve Fulkerson, General Manager of Saint-Gobain Containers, a company that makes many different kinds of bottles, advocates the by-product theory:

> Early glass containers were hand-blown by inserting a tube into a gob of molten glass and blowing on the tube by mouth. As the bubble expanded, the outside of the bubble was shaped by the use of a wooden paddle. A container with a neck was easier to handle as the inside of the neck surrounded the last few inches of the tube, making it less likely that the gob would fall from the tube as it was being shaped.

Rick Baldwin, Midwest Regional Director of the Federation of Historical Bottle Collectors, adds that:

> A neck, the end of which was tooled to form a heavier lip, afforded a smaller area for a closure/seal. A smaller area would be easier for the glassblower to form a nice, "perfectly circular" sealable lip, and the task could be done faster.

But just as many experts felt that the neck had nothing to do with glassblowing methods. Sturm is in this school: 'There are quite a few containers with wide mouths that were used for food storage, etc. The glassblower had the knowledge and capability of cutting the container so that it didn't have a neck.'

The glassblowers we contacted agreed, and pointed out the same design advantages of necks that most of the bottle historians noted:

1 Bottles with necks are easier and cheaper to seal. Fred Holabird, historical consultant and owner of Holabird Americana auction house, told *Imponderables*:

> My guess is that it's cheaper to have a stopper that's small. If you put the equivalent of a jar lid in a wide bottle, the cost is proportionally higher. So it's cheaper to make an enclosure with a small lid.

John Pritchard, Operations Manager of Simi Winery, notes that the neck of the bottle has always been used to hold the cork. Necks have been 'pretty much' standardised now to a length of 6.25 cm in order to hold a

5 cm cork effectively. The narrow neck decreased evaporation (important when early bottles were used to hold expensive perfume oils) and exposure to air.

2 **Necks provide a handle.** Rick Baldwin, who notes that 'you've already caused me to lose three nights' sleep pondering the question', observes that long necks were long ago applied to large, bulbous flasks 'so that they could be drunk from directly'. Paul Bates, who with son Tom established the Museum of Beverage Containers and Advertising in Millersville, Tennessee, points out a practical advantage to the long neck that was particularly true in the past – in the early days, bottles were much heavier than they are now. Without a neck, these bottles would have been more likely to slip out of one's hands. And for wines, in particular, the neck acts as a handle when grabbing a bottle stored horizontally.

3 **Necks facilitate pouring.** Traffic jams are referred to as 'bottlenecks' for a reason. Rick Baldwin argues that a neck, and its smaller diameter opening, affords a slower and more restricted flow of contents, whether one is decanting a liquid into another vessel or swigging it straight from the bottle.

Bottle manufacturer Steve Fulkerson told *Imponderables* that the neck plays an important part in the 'pourability' of a bottle. He dared us to try to pour wine from a wide mouth jar into a wine glass (no thanks, we have enough problems pouring from a bottle).

We seem to have a love connection with swanlike long necks, whether we are pouring wine, beer or tomato sauce.

Why doesn't glue get stuck in the bottle?

There are two basic reasons:

1 In order for glue to set and solidify, it must dry out. Latex and water-based glues harden by losing water, either by absorption into a porous substrate (the surface to be bonded) or by evaporation into the air. The glue bottle, at least if it is capped tightly, seals in moisture.

2 Different glues are formulated to adhere to particular substrates. If the glue does not have a chemical adhesion to the substrate, it will not stick. For example, John Anderson, Technical Manager for glue maker Elmer's Laboratory, told us that the Elmer's bottle, made of polyethylene, does not provide a good chemical adhesion for the glue.

Even when the cap is left off, and the glue does lose water, the adhesion is still spotty. We can see this effect with the cap of many glue bottles. In most cases, dried glue can and does cake onto the tip after repeated uses. But Anderson points out that the adhesion is 'tenuous', and one can easily clean the top while still wet and remove the glue completely. Likewise, if you poured glue on a drinking glass, it might adhere a little, but you could easily wipe it off with a cloth or paper towel because the glue cannot easily penetrate the 'gluee'.

What's the difference between 'super' and ordinary glues?

The main difference between 'super' glues and merely mortal ones is that Super Glue is fabricated from a polymer called cyanoacrylate, while most other glues are a combination of natural resins in a solvent solution. The different ingredients create a different bonding process, too, as Rich Palin, Technical Advisor to Loctite Corporation, reveals:

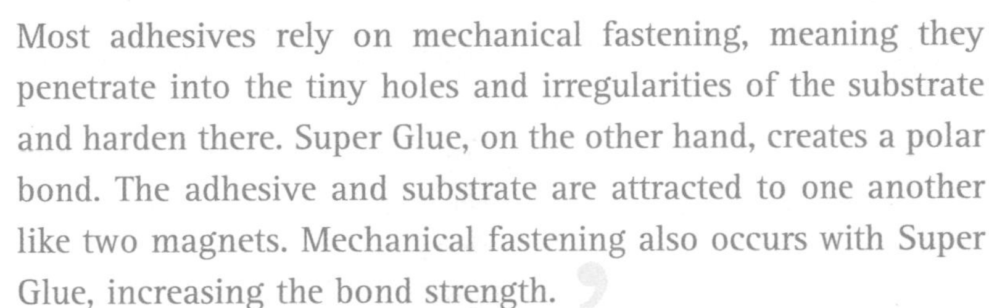

> Most adhesives rely on mechanical fastening, meaning they penetrate into the tiny holes and irregularities of the substrate and harden there. Super Glue, on the other hand, creates a polar bond. The adhesive and substrate are attracted to one another like two magnets. Mechanical fastening also occurs with Super Glue, increasing the bond strength.

Borden Glue's John Anderson adds that because super glues don't rely solely on mechanical fastening, they are much better at bonding dissimilar surfaces than conventional glues.

Why are dress and shoe sizes so arbitrary (10 is quite a small dress, but quite a big shoe)? Why aren't they related to measures such as inches or centimetres?

It is certainly odd that when a man tries on a jacket, he goes for one that corresponds to the known size of his chest in inches; whereas when a woman tries on a dress, she goes for an even number that has no apparent relation to any unit of measurement. Shoe sizes are stranger still: 1 to 13, then back to 1 again. But the fact is that neither dress sizes nor shoe sizes are arbitrary at all: they are both results of necessary calculations performed by the craftsmen and craftswomen who once made these items by hand.

To take shoes first, the sizes that are standard in Britain are perhaps the only surviving usage in the modern world of an ancient and rather charming unit of length – the barleycorn. The interesting thing about barleycorns – the dried grains of barley – is that they are extremely uniform in size: all pretty much one-third of an inch long. In medieval times, this made them a really handy way of measuring lengths shorter than an inch, which is the width of a man's thumb, and about the shortest distance that can easily be measured with the human body.

All tradesmen who routinely needed to measure very small lengths – shoemakers among them – knew about the barleycorn and used it. In 1324, this old rule of thumb became a rule of law. King Edward II issued a decree formalising the coincidental relationship between the inch and the barleycorn: it was no longer just a happy fact that it took three barleycorns to make an inch; it was now government policy that a barleycorn should be an official unit of measurement, equal to one-third of an inch.

In theory, King Edward's law made it possible for cobblers everywhere to make shoes in standard sizes. But there was no point in laboriously measuring out the whole length of a shoe in fiddly little barleycorns. Cobblers knew from experience that the smallest practical size for a child's shoe was about the width of a grown man's hand – which is usually four inches. They took this as their starting point – Size 0 – and went up in barleycorn increments until, with the twelfth barleycorn, they reached four inches and another hand's width. At this point they found it convenient to start again from zero, no doubt using the same twelve barleycorns. At some later date, probably when barleycorns

What is the purpose of the **ball** on **top** of a flagpole?

We were asked this Imponderable on a television talk show in Los Angeles. Frankly, we were stumped. 'Perhaps they were installed to make the jobs of flagpole sitters more difficult,' we ventured. Frustrated by our ignorance, we resolved to find the solution.

According to Dr Whitney Smith, Executive Director of the Flag Research Center in Winchester, Massachusetts, the ball may occasionally be combined with a mechanism involved with the halyards that raise and lower a flag, but this juxtaposition is only coincidental. Much to our surprise, we learned that the ball on top of a flagpole is purely decorative.

Actually, the earliest flag-like objects were emblems, like an animal or other carved figure, placed atop a pole. Ribbons beneath these insignia served as decoration. According to Dr Smith, the importance of the two was later reversed so that the design of the flag on a piece of cloth (replacing the ribbons) conveyed the message while the finial of the pole became ornamental, either in the form of a sphere or, as the most common alternatives, a spear or (especially in the United States) an eagle.

George F Cahill, of the National Flag Foundation, believes that a pole just isn't as pleasing to the eye without something on top. Spears don't look good on stationary poles, and eagles, while visually appealing, are more expensive than balls or spears. Cahill adds another advantage of the ball:

> 'On poles that are carried, a spear can be a hazard, not only to individuals, but to woodwork and plaster, and eagles are cumbersome and easily breakable. So, the ball gives the pole a safe and rather attractive topping and finish.'

We speculated that perhaps birds were less likely to perch on a sphere than a flat surface, thus saving the flag from a less welcome form of decoration. But Cahill assures us that birds love to perch on flagpole balls.

We may never have thought of these balls as *objets d'art*, but they are.

were fading from memory, the larger zero-sized shoe was incorporated into the lesser scale and became a Size 13. Apart from that, the system is the same as it was in medieval times. Your size 10s are so-called because they are notionally ten barleycorns longer than a cobbler's two hands, and one barleycorn longer than the next person's Size 9s.

As for dress sizes, they are a far more recent invention, but at the same time somehow more obscure, because the shape of the female body is a far more subtle and complicated thing than the size of a human foot. The numbers have their origin in the charts used by dress-makers and 'pattern engineers' when cutting the pieces for a new dress. These charts, which were universal in the first half of the twentieth century, allowed seamstresses, by doing a few calculations, to make projections of a woman's dimensions based on the few measurements that were usually taken in the dress shop. The charts were numbered for diffferent heights and girths – 8, 10, 12, 14 and so on. Retailers of ready-made clothes borrowed the dressmaker's numbers, but in the process their complex rationale was lost completely. And the real, functional signifance of a Size 10 dress was rendered as defunct as good old King Edward and his royally endorsed barleycorns.

If you dig a hole and try to plug the hole with the very dirt you've removed, why do you never have enough dirt to refill the hole?

After speaking to several agronomists, we can say one thing with certainty: don't use the word 'dirt' casually among soil experts. As Dr Lee P Grant, of the University of Maryland's Agricultural Engineering Department, remonstrated us, dirt is what one gets on one's clothes or sweeps off the floor. Francis D Hole, Professor Emeritus of Soil Science and Geography at the University of Wisconsin-Madison, was a little less gentle:

> What would you do if you were some fine, life-giving soil who is 20,000 years the senior of the digger, and you were operated on by this fugitive human being with a blunt surgical instrument (but without a soil surgeon's

> licence), and if you were addressed as so much "dirt" to boot? I am suggesting that a self-respecting soil would flee the spot and not be all there for you to manipulate back into the hole.

So there's the answer: the soil is offended by you calling it dirt, and has flown the scene of your crime against it.

We promised Grant and Hole we would treat soil with all the respect it was due, and temporarily suppress the use of the 'd' word, if they would answer our question. They provided several explanations for why you might run out of soil when refilling a hole:

1 **Not saving all the soil.** Dr Hole reported one instance where, in their excitement about their work, a team of soil scientists forgot to lay down the traditional canvas to collect the collected soil: 'We had lost a lot of the soil in the forest floor, among dead branches and leaves.'

2 **You changed the soil structure when you dug up the dirt.** Grant explains:

> Soil is composed of organic and inorganic material as well as air spaces and microorganisms. Soil has a structure which includes, among other things, pores (or air spaces) through which water and plant roots pass. Within the soil are worm and other tunnels and/or air spaces. All of this structure is destroyed during the digging process.

Hole notes that stomping on the hole you are refilling can also compact the soil, removing pores and openings, resulting in plugging the hole too tight: 'It sounds like a case of poor surgery to me. You treated the patient (the soil) badly by pounding the wound that you made in the first place.'

3 **Soil often dries during the digging/handling/moving.** Grant reports that the water in soil sometimes causes the soil to take up more space than it does when dry.

Both experts stressed that the scenario outlined by our correspondent is not always true. Sometimes, you may have extra soil after refilling, as Hole explains:

> It is risky to say that "you never have enough soil to refill" because sometimes you have too much soil. If you saved all your diggings on a canvas and put it all back, there could be so much soil that it would mound up, looking like a brown heap of coffee grounds where the hole had been.

… you loosened the soil a lot when you dug it out. When you put the soil back, there were lots of gaps and pore spaces that weren't there before. It might take a year for the soil to settle back into its former state of togetherness. A steady, light rain might speed the process a little bit. ’

How do they keep more than two pieces of a jigsaw puzzle from fitting together? Is every piece unique?

Although you could argue that anyone who embarks upon fitting together a 1000-piece jigsaw depiction of a tomato already has masochistic tendencies, no puzzler wants to be further frustrated by encountering two pieces that fit into the same spot. So it behooves jigsaw puzzle makers to forestall this potential problem.

Milton Bradley's solution to the twin-piece possibility is decidedly low-tech: its designers draw the puzzle freehand. A designer makes a line drawing of a potential puzzle pattern, and blueprints are created. Inspectors then check to make sure that every piece is unique and the right size, and that every piece interlocks, snugly fitting into its adjoining neighbours.

Mark Morris, Public Relations Director of jigsaw giant Milton Bradley, told *Imponderables* that the puzzle is checked by eye for potential duplicate pieces. This is far from foolproof, of course, but the best assurance of keeping out potential twins is that if everything is drawn by hand, duplication is virtually impossible.

Once a design is approved, a die is cut (by laser) from the blueprints. Then the physical die is used to cut the pieces. The scene is printed on a cardboard backing and the die, inside a hydraulic machine, pushes down and cuts the puzzle in one shot. The whole process (including the creation of the box top, the closing of the box and the sealing of the entire contents) takes seconds.

Another insurance policy for the manufacturer is that the same die is used throughout an entire product line. For example, Milton Bradley produces several different lines of puzzles. All the 550-piece Big Ben puzzles for a season will be designed from an identical die – only the image will differ. Morris adds that Milton Bradley changes the dies frequently, though, because 'hard-core' puzzlers will recognise the die pattern 'after a while'.

At least one of Milton Bradley's competitors, Edaron, utilises a comparatively high-tech solution to the duplication threat. You may not recognise the Edaron name because it is a 'contract manufacturer' that makes puzzles sold under the brand names of other companies. Edaron utilises a proprietary computer program that designs the shape of the individual pieces and also checks to assure both that the pieces interlock and that the pieces are unique. The software creates a design from which the die is cut.

Edaron, like Milton Bradley, uses the same die across a given puzzle range. Edaron might have contracts with four different companies for 550-piece puzzles, so a separate die is used for each client, but the same die is used for all the 550-piece puzzles for that client.

One of the big advantages of this high-tech solution is that all the old designs can be saved conveniently as software. At any time, Edaron can recut a die with the same design. Edaron recuts the dies about once a year because the die loses its sharpness and begins to yield dull, unclean cuts. Fuzzy jigsaw borders can lead to just as much frustration among solvers as the scourge of duplicate pieces.

Why does Mickey Mouse have four fingers?

Or more properly, why does Mickey Mouse have three fingers and one thumb on each hand? In fact, why is virtually every cartoon animal's hand beset with one missing digit?

Conversations with many cartoonists, animators and Disney employees confirm what we were at first sceptical about. Mickey Mouse has four

Why is Scotland Yard in England?

The original Scotland Yard, established by Robert Peel in 1829, was placed on the site of the former palace where Scottish kings and queens resided when visiting England to conduct affairs of state or to pay tribute to English royalty. 'Scotland Yard' became known as the name of the street as well as the palace.

Although the Criminal Investigation Department of the Metropolitan Police later moved to the Thames Embankment and then to the Victoria area of London, it retains the name of its original site.

fingers because it is convenient for the artists and animators who have drawn him. In the early cartoons, each frame was hand-drawn by an animator – painstaking and tedious work. No part of the human anatomy is harder to draw than a hand, and it is particularly difficult to draw distinct fingers without making the whole hand look disproportionately large.

The artists who drew Mickey were more than happy to go along with any conceit that saved them some work. So in Disney and most other cartoons, the animals sport a thumb and three fingers, while humans, such as Snow White and Cinderella, are spared the amputation.

And before you ask – no, we don't know for certain which of Mickey's fingers got lopped off for the sake of convenience. Since the three non-thumbs on each hand are symmetrical, we'd like to think it was the pinkie that was sacrificed.

Why were Athos, Porthos and Aramis called the Three Musketeers when they fought with swords rather than muskets?

The Three Swordsmen sounds like a decent enough title for a book, so why did Dumas choose *The Three Musketeers*? Dumas based his novel on *Memoirs of Monsieur D'Artagnan*, a fictionalised account of 'Captain-Lieutenant of the First Company of the King's Musketeers'. Yes, there really was a company of musketeers in France in the seventeenth century.

Formed in 1622, the company's main function was to guard the King (Louis XIII) during peacetime. During wars, the musketeers were dispatched to fight in the infantry or cavalry; but at the palace, they were the *corps d'élite*. Although they were young (mostly 17 to 20 years of age), all had prior experience in the military and were of aristocratic ancestry.

According to Dumas translator Lord Sudley, when the musketeers were formed, they 'had just been armed with the new flintlock, muzzle-loading muskets', a precursor to modern rifles. Unfortunately, the musket, although powerful enough to pierce any armour of its day, was also extremely cumbersome. As long as 2.4 m and weighing more than 10 kg, they were too unwieldy to be carried by horsemen. The musket was so awkward that it could not be shot accurately while resting on the shoulder, so musketeers used a fork rest to steady the weapon. Eventually, the 'musketeers' were rendered musketless and relied on newfangled pistols and trusty old swords.

Just think of how muskets would have slowed down the derring-do of our three heros. It's not easy, for example, to slash a sword-brandishing villain while dangling from a chandelier if one has a musket on one's back.

Why do teddy bears frown?

Considering that the toy business is full of sugarcoated images for children, and the happy face is the default countenance for dolls and most stuffed animals, we've often wondered why teddy bears are so dour. So we contacted teddy bear artists, designers and manufacturers, collectors and people who write about teddy bears for a living to illuminate exactly what is bothering stuffed bears.

Strangely, the first teddy bears were made in Germany and the United States in the same year – 1902. Mindy Kinsey, editor of *Teddy Bear and Friends* magazine, picks up the story. At the beginning, at least, teddy bears were designed to appear realistic:

> In Germany, they were modelled after bears Richard Steiff saw in the zoo and at the circus. In America, teddies were inspired by the bears Theodore Roosevelt hunted (and in a particularly famous instance, failed to shoot) and were named after the president himself.
>
> Early teddies, therefore, had long muzzles, long arms, humped backs and small ears, much like the real thing. Their mouths tended to be straight embroidered lines that might appear to frown, but were only meant to mimic their real-life counterparts.

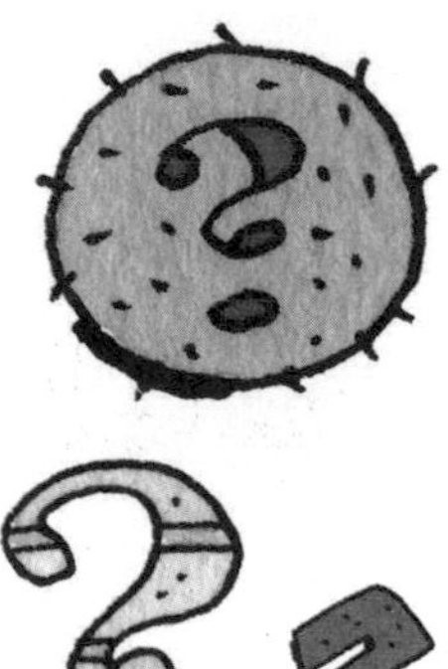

When we called the big teddy bear makers, such as Gund, Steiff and Russ Berrie, the designers couldn't articulate why the expression of most of their bears was sad. Some suggested that they weren't trying to make their bears frown at all. But go to the web sites of these companies, or visit your local toyshop, and we think you'll agree that compared to most other stuffed animals and toys, the classic bears could use a dose or two of Prozac. But not just designers denied the 'frown' premise. Kinsey's response was typical:

> Today's teddy bears, however, can have big grins, wistful smiles, laughing open mouths, puckers and every other mouth

imaginable. Some still have the straight-line mouths, but I like to think of them as wise, contemplative, trustworthy or sincere expressions – not frowns.

Jo Rothery, Editor of the magazine *Teddy Bear Times*, thinks variety is the spice of teddy bear life:

Of course there are some bears that are definitely grumpy and have been designed that way by the bear artist. Some collectors do specialise in the grumpy characters, perhaps because they remind them of someone – fathers, husbands, grandfathers, colleagues, etc. And other collectors, particularly of vintage teds, feel that a sad expression adds to the character of the bear and reflects his age and all the experience he has had over the years.

There are some very "smiley" bears, whose mouths are upturned and instinctively make you want to smile back when you look at them. Again, there are collectors who specialise in such bears, but I think the majority of us like to have a collection that includes lots of different expressions, possibly even some of the open-mouthed variety, although it is hard to get that particular expression right.

Some bear artists succeed in capturing that "wild" natural look very well without making the bears look at all scary.

Rothery adds that it is just like when one dog in a litter stirs your heart, even though 'they all look alike'.

Even when you see a line-up of identical teddies, each one will have a slightly different expression, and there is one that will appeal to you more than any of the others and demand that you take him home with you.

We were shocked when three Gund designers couldn't articulate why they drew bears' expressions the way they did, but one creator, Linda McCall, describes it as an almost mystical process:

Some of my bears' mouths smile, some frown and some look really, really grumpy! It just depends on the "feel" I get from the bear. I know it sounds strange to someone who probably has never made a bear. You stitch the darn thing together and you let it sit overnight. Then you look at it again and you just know if it should be a happy bear, a thoughtful bear or whatever mood it seems to convey. That's why if you look at all artist-made bears, no two would ever be alike. ’

McCall, and several other sources, think the tradition of the 'frowning bear' stems from an attempt to mimic how a real bear's mouth looks. After all, bears in the wild aren't known for their grins. The 'realistic' theory, perhaps the favoured one among our sources, contends that most bears aren't frowning, but merely exhibiting a neutral emotion.

If you look carefully at the faces of teddy bears, you'll see that the mouths of many are shaped like an upside-down capital Y. Teddy bear artist Cherri Creamer, of Alive Again Bears, says that the inverted Y is used to align the face so that the nose and eyes conform to the mouth. Whatever reason, the inverted Y provides a downward cast to bears' mouths. So this 'convenient' method of aligning the bear might be responsible for what we interpret as a frown.

We're partial to a psychological theory to explain the 'frown' of the teddy bear. Jo Rothery comments that the inverted Y:

‘ gives teddy bears a contemplative, relaxed look, an expression that makes them seem only too willing to sit there, "listen" and absorb their owners' emotions, whether those emotions happen to be sad or happy. ’

If the emotions of a teddy bear are opaque, a child can pour his emotions into his plush toy, and the bear becomes an instant empathiser.

Stars, clouds, trees – they can drive you crazy if you try to understand all their puzzling quirks. Here we tackle some of the grand questions of nature and science: Why don't you ever see stars in photos of astronauts in space? Why are the oceans salty? How did Romans do calculations using Roman numerals?

science and nature

If heat rises, why does ice form on the surface of lakes and ponds?

Anyone who has ever filled an ice-cube tray with water knows that room temperature water decreases in density when it freezes. We also know that heat rises. And that the sun would hit the top of the water more directly than water at the bottom. All three scientific verities would seem to indicate that ice would form at the bottom, rather than the top, of lakes and ponds. 'What gives?' demand *Imponderables* readers.

You may not know, however, what Neal P Rowell, retired Professor of Physics at the University of South Alabama, told us: water is most dense at 4°C. This turns out to be the key to the mystery of the rising ice.

One of our favourite scientific researchers, Harold Blake, wrote a fine summary of what turns out to be a highly technical answer:

> As water cools, it gets more dense. It shrinks. It sinks to the bottom of the pond, lake, rain barrel, wheelbarrow or dog's water dish. But at 4°C, a few degrees above freezing, the water has reached its maximum density. It now starts to expand as it gets cooler. The water that is between 4°C and 0°C (the freezing point of water) now starts to rise to the surface. It is lighter, less dense.
>
> Now, more heat has to be lost from the water at freezing to form ice at freezing. This is called the "heat of fusion". During the freezing process, ice crystals form and expand to a larger volume, fusing together as they expand, and using more freezing water to "cement" themselves together. The ice crystals are very much lighter and remain on the surface.
>
> Once the surface is frozen over, heat dissipates from the edges and freezing is progressive from the edges. When the unfrozen core finally freezes, there is tremendous pressure exerted from the expansion, and the ice surface or container sides yield, a common annoyance with water pipes.

Once the top layer of the lake or pond freezes, the water below will rarely reach 0°C; the ice acts effectively as insulation. By keeping the temperature of the water below the ice between 0°C and 4°C, the ice helps some aquatic life survive in the winter when a lake is frozen over.

If water is heavier than air, why do clouds stay up in the sky?

What makes you think that clouds aren't dropping? They are. Constantly. Luckily, cloud drops do not fall at the same velocity as a water balloon. In fact, cloud drops are downright sluggards: they drop at a measly 3 mm per second. And cloud drops are so tiny, about 0.1 mm in diameter, that their descent is not even noticeable to the human eye.

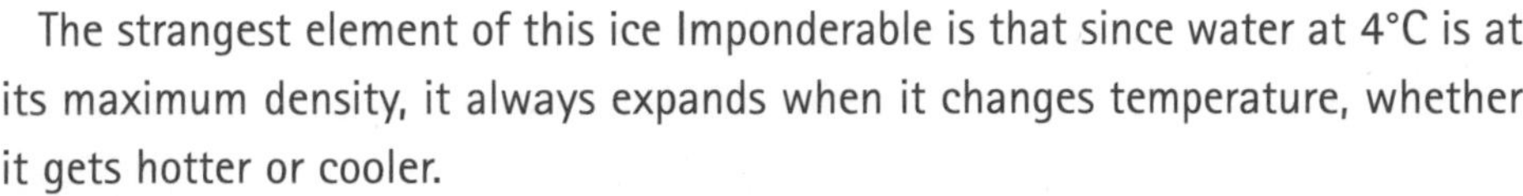

The strangest element of this ice Imponderable is that since water at 4°C is at its maximum density, it always expands when it changes temperature, whether it gets hotter or cooler.

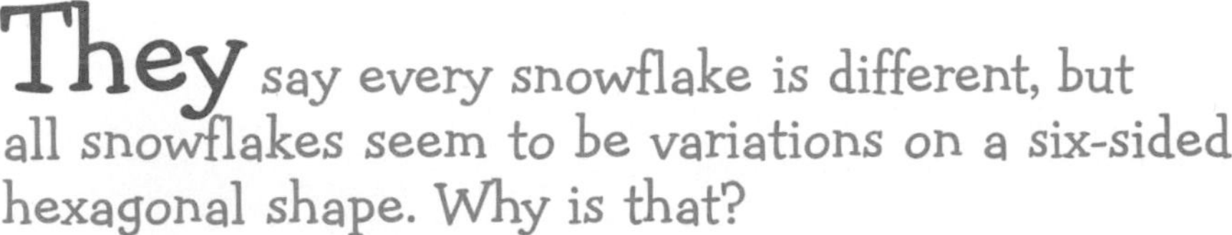

They say every snowflake is different, but all snowflakes seem to be variations on a six-sided hexagonal shape. Why is that?

First things first: it is not a fact that every snowflake is different. There is no reason why two snowflakes could not be identical. But there are billions of forms that a snowflake can take on, so you are about as likely to find a matching pair as you are to spot a grain of sugar in the midst of an avalanche.

It is also not entirely true that all snowflakes are hexagonal. They also occur as needles and as hollow columns, to name but two of the possibilities. We are familiar with the flat, lacy type of snowflake because they are aesthetically the most appealing, and so get the all the good press.

It *is* true, though, that the deep structure of snowflakes is six-sided. This is because they are made from frozen water – and water, formless though it appears to us – is made up of entirely hexagons. The two atoms of hydrogen and the single atom of oxygen that make up a water molecule bind together with other molecules to make a six-sided lattice, like microscopic chicken wire. The structure of H_2O is invisible to us, but it manifests itself when water freezes inside clouds: ice crystals naturally form a perfect hexagon.

A simple hexagon is at the centre of every snowflake. But certain conditions inside clouds – temperature above all – make the corners of these cold crystals more 'sticky' than the straight edges, with the result that the crystal grows more quickly at the corners and so puts out 'branches'. The branches grow other branches, proliferating beautifully as they do. And since all six sides are subject to the same conditions, these six branches tend to be the same. The result is a tiny work of art, sculpted by nature for us to enjoy and wonder at.

Why are rain clouds dark?

Rain is water. Water is light in colour. Rain clouds are full of water. Therefore, rain clouds should be light. Impeccable logic, but wrong.

Obviously, there are always water particles in clouds. But when the particles of water are small, they reflect light and are perceived as white. When water particles become large enough to form raindrops, however, they absorb light and appear dark to us below.

Why does lightning have a zigzag pattern?

We're always pleased to meet a source who is enthusiastic about his work. Matt Bragaw, the lightning specialist at the National Weather Service Forecast Office in Melbourne, Florida, is such a man. He shares his passion about lightning on his corner of his office's web site (at www.srh. noaa.gov/mlb/ltgcenter/whatis.html). Matt was kind enough to answer some of our incessant follow-up questions. He warned us that although lightning was one of the first remarked-upon natural phenomena, it is one of the least understood, with many of the major discoveries about it made only in the past 15 years.

Although there are other kinds of lightning, such as heat lightning and Saint Elmo's fire, the familiar zigzag lightning we're talking about here is cloud-to-ground lightning (lightning inside a cloud, also known as cloud-to-cloud lightning, is actually more prevalent). Before we see any sign of lightning on the ground, turbulent wind conditions send water droplets up the cloud while ice particles fall downwards. The top of the cloud usually carries a strong positive charge and the bottom a negative one. During the movement of the ice and water droplets within the cloud, electrons shear off the rising droplets and stick to the falling ice crystals. The opposite charges attract until a tremendous electrical charge occurs within the cloud. When the cloud can no longer hold the electrical field, sometimes a faint, negatively charged ladder channel, called the 'stepped leader', materialises from the bottom of the cloud.

While it might look as if the bolt of lightning strikes the earth instantaneously, in one zigzag strike, what you are really seeing is a whole series of steps, which are only about 50 m in length each. Bragaw elaborates:

> In what can be described as an "avalanche of electrons", the leader's path often splits, resplits and re-resplits, eventually taking on a tendril-like appearance. Between each step, there is a pause of about 50 microseconds, during which time the stepped leader "looks" for an object to strike. If none is "seen", it takes another step, "looks" for something to strike, etc. This process is repeated until the leader "finds" a target.
>
> It is this "stepped" process that gives lightning its jagged appearance ... Studies of individual strikes have shown a single leader can be comprised of more than 10,000 steps!

Once the leader hits the ground, all of the other branches of the stepped leader's channel stop propagation towards the earth.

We mentioned that the stepped leader is faint as it leaves the cloud and heads towards the ground. If so, then why is lightning usually so bright? The negatively charged stepped leader repels all negative charge in the ground, while attracting all positive charge, which sends energy back from the ground to the clouds. This 'return stroke' occurs in less than 100 microseconds, which is why we can't differentiate cloud-to-ground movement from ground-to-air. But this upward process, according to Bragaw, 'produces almost all the luminosity' that we see when we think we are observing cloud-to-ground lightning strikes.

Twenty to 50 milliseconds (thousandths of a second) after the initial return stroke stops flowing up the channel, 'leftover' electrical energy in the cloud often sends more leaders down to the earth in the same channel. Because these 'dart leaders' use an already-established channel, they discharge continuously instead of in steps. Even though these subsequent dart leaders don't need to stop to look for places to hit, as their route is the same as for the first leader, you'll still see the familiar zigzag. As Bragaw puts it: 'Because the stepped leader initially burns a jagged path, all lightning takes on a jagged appearance.'

What is the technical definition of a sunset or sunrise? How is it determined at what time the sun sets or rises? Why is there natural light before sunrise and after sunset?

The definitions are easy. A sunrise is defined as occurring when the top of the sun appears on a sea-level horizon. A sunset occurs when the top of the sun goes just below the sea-level horizon.

But how do scientists determine the times? No, they do not send meteorologists out on a ladder and have them crane their necks. No observation is involved at all – just maths. By crunching the numbers based on the orbit of the Earth around the sun, the sunrise and sunset times can be calculated long in advance. Richard Williams, a meteorologist at the US National Weather Service, explains that published times are only approximations of what we observe with the naked eye:

> 'The time of sunrise and sunset varies with the day of the year, latitude and longitude. The published sunrise and sunset times are calculated without regard to surrounding terrain. That is, all computations are made for a sea-level horizon, even in mountainous areas. Thus the actual time of sunrise at a particular location may vary considerably from the "official" times.
>
> When we observe sunset, the sun has already gone below the horizon. The Earth's atmosphere "bends" the sun's rays and delays the sunset by about three minutes. Likewise with sunrise, the sun makes its first appearance before it would on a planet with no atmosphere. We actually get five to ten minutes of extra sunlight due to this effect.'

Why do the clearest days seem to follow storms?

Our correspondent wondered whether this phenomenon was an illusion. Perhaps we are so happy to see the storm flee that the next day, without battering winds, threatening clouds and endless precipitation, seems beautiful in contrast.

No, it isn't an illusion. Meteorologists call this phenomenon 'scavenging'. The rainwater that soaks your shoes also cleans away haze and pollutants from the atmosphere and sends it to the ground. At the same time, the wind that wrecks your umbrella during the storm diffuses the irritants that are left in the atmosphere, so that people in surrounding areas aren't subjected to those endless days of boring, pollution-free environments.

Of course, where the pollutants end up depends upon the direction of the prevailing winds. If you are living in a community with generally bad air quality, the wind is your friend anyway. Chances are, the wind is carrying in air from a region with superior air quality.

Why is it that what looks to us like a half-moon is called a quarter-moon by astronomers?

An intriguing Imponderable, we thought, at least until Robert Burnham, Editor of *Astronomy*, batted it away with the comment, 'You picked an easy one this time!'

Much to our surprise, when astronomers throw lunar fractions around, they are referring to the orbiting cycle of the moon, not its appearance to us. *Sky & Telescope*'s Associate Editor Alan MacRobert, explains:

> The moon is *half* lit when it is a quarter of the way around its orbit. The count begins when the moon is in the vicinity of the sun (at "new moon" phase). "First quarter" is when the moon has travelled one-quarter of the way around the sky from there. The moon is full when it is halfway around the sky, and at "third quarter" or "last quarter" when it's three-quarters of the way.

Robert Burnham adds that 'quarter-moons' and 'half-moons' aren't the only commonly misnamed lunar apparitions. Laymen often call the crescent moon hanging low in the evening sky a 'new moon', but Burnham points out that at this point, the moon is far from new: 'In fact, by then the crescent moon is some three or four days past the actual moment of new moon, which is the instant when the centre of the moon passes between the Earth and sun.'

Why is the moon sometimes visible during the day?

This Imponderable would be so easy to answer if the sun, moon and Earth would get together and agree on a uniform schedule. But they refuse to do so, keeping astronomers and astrologers in business, and making it hard for us to provide a simple answer.

Here's the simple answer, anyway. The moon does not shine by its own light. When we see the moon, it's only because we are seeing the reflection of sunlight bouncing off its surface. You can see the moon in the daytime when the sun and the moon are located in the same direction in the sky. As the moon proceeds on its (approximately) 29-day orbit around the Earth, at times it's on the opposite side of the Earth from the sun.

Although we may remember this only when we've been indulging in too many recreational substances, the Earth is also spinning on its axis once every 24 hours, a much shorter time than it takes the moon to revolve around us or for the Earth and moon together to orbit around the sun (a year). Though we perceive the moon as rising and setting as it 'moves' across the sky, it's really the Earth rotating on its axis ('underneath' the moon) that causes this effect. In one day, the moon doesn't move much relative to the sun or to the Earth, even though during these 24 hours, we see a complete cycle of day and night because of our planet's spinning.

Viewing of the moon is also contingent on the state of the Earth's atmosphere. The stars are 'out' during the day, but we can't see them because the scattered light from the sun is bright enough to drown out the relatively dim light from the stars. But the moon is the second brightest object in the sky, next to the sun, so even though it appears pale, we can usually see it during the day if it is close in direction to the sun. But on days with excessive glare or cloudiness, the moon may not be visible, especially just before and after a new moon.

Even though the moon and sun often appear to be close together, the sun is always about 400 times farther away from Earth than the moon is. We can see the moon during the daytime when the sun and moon are relatively close in direction, but not too close! When they are aligned too closely, we can't see the moon because the sun is directly behind it and can't light up the side of the moon facing us. When they are in opposite directions, in the daytime, the sun is overhead but the moon is on the opposite side of the Earth.

When the moon is overhead, you do see it, but it is night because the sun is on the other side of the Earth. It's when the moon and sun are at right angles, or close to it, that you can best see the moon during the day – the sun, moon, and Earth form a big triangle, and the sun is 'in front' of the moon to light up the side of the moon that is visible to us, and it's daytime because the sun is up in the sky above us.

Still confused? Maybe this analogy from Tim Kallman, an astrophysicist at the Laboratory for High Energy Astrophysics at NASA, will help:

> ‘It might be useful to think of the sun as a large light bulb, and the moon as a large mirror. There are situations where we can't see the light bulb, but we can see the light from the bulb reflected in the mirror. This is the situation when the moon is out at night. We can't see the sun directly because the Earth is blocking our view of it, but we can see its light reflected from the moon. However, there are also situations where we see both the light bulb and the mirror, and this is what is happening when we see the moon during the day.’

Why does the moon appear bigger at the horizon than up in the sky?

This Imponderable has been floating around the cosmos for aeons and has long been discussed by astronomers, who call it the moon illusion. Not only the moon but the sun appears much larger at the horizon than up in the sky. And constellations, as they ascend in the sky, appear smaller and smaller. Obviously, none of these bodies actually changes size or shape, so why do they *seem* to grow and shrink?

Although there is not total unanimity on the subject, astronomers, for the most part, are satisfied that three explanations answer this Imponderable. In descending order of importance, they are:

1. As Alan MacRobert of *Sky & Telescope* states, 'The sky itself appears more distant near the horizon than high overhead.' In his recent article in *Astronomy* magazine, 'Learning the Sky by Degrees', Jim Loudon explains:

> Apparently, we perceive the sky not as half a sphere but as half an oblate [flattened at the poles] spheroid – in other words, the sky overhead seems closer to the observer than the horizon. A celestial object that is perceived as "projected" onto this distorted sky bowl seems bigger at the horizon.

Why? Because the object appears to occupy just as much space at the seemingly faraway horizon as it does in the supposedly closer sky.

2 When reference points are available in the foreground, distant objects appear bigger. If you see the moon rising through the trees, the moon will appear immense because your brain is unconsciously comparing the size of the object in the foreground (the tree limbs) with the moon in the background. When you see the moon up in the sky, it is set against tiny stars in the background.

Artists often play with distorting perception by moving peripheral objects closer to the foreground. Peter Boyce, of the American Astronomical Society, adds that reference points tend to distort perception most when they are close to us and when the size of the reference points is well known to the observer. We know how large a tree limb is, but our mind plays tricks on us when we try to determine the size of heavenly objects. Loudon states that 11 full moons would fit between the pointer stars of the Big Dipper, a fact we could never determine with our naked eyes alone.

3 The moon illusion may be partially explained by the refraction of our atmosphere magnifying the image. But even the astronomers who mentioned the refraction theory indicated that it could explain only some of the distortion.

A few sceptics, no doubt the same people who insist that the world is flat and that no astronaut has ever really landed on the moon, believe that the moon really is larger at the horizon than when up in the sky. If you want to squelch these sceptics, here are a few counterarguments that the astronomers suggested:

1 Take photos of the moon or sun at the horizon and up in the sky. The bodies will appear to be the same size.

2 'Cover' the moon with a fingertip. Unless your nails grow at an alarming rate, you should be able to cover the moon just as easily whether it is high or low.

3 Best of all, if you want proof of how easy it is to skew your perception of size, bend over and look at the moon upside down through your legs. When we are faced with a new vantage point, all reference points and size

comparisons are upset, and we realise how much we rely upon experience, rather than our sensory organs, to judge distances and size.

We do, however, suggest that this physically challenging and potentially embarrassing scientific procedure be done in wide-open spaces and with the supervision of a parent or guardian. *Imponderables* cannot be held responsible for the physical or emotional wellbeing of those in search of astronomical truths.

When you are driving at night, why does it seem that the moon is following you around?

As we discussed in the previous Imponderable, the moon looks larger on the horizon than up in the sky, even though the moon remains the same size. Clearly, our eyes can play tricks on us.

Without reference points to guide us, the moon doesn't seem to be far away. When you are driving along a road, objects closest to your car go whirring by. Barriers dividing the lanes become a blur. You can discern individual houses or trees by the side of the road, but, depending upon your speed, it might be painful to watch them go by. Distant trees and houses move by much more slowly, even though you are driving at the same speed. And distant mountains seem mammoth and motionless. Eventually, as you travel far enough down the road, you will pass the mountains, and they will appear smaller.

If you think the mountain range off the road is large or far away, consider the moon, which is 384,000 km away and bigger than any mountain range (more than 3300 km in diameter). We already know that our eyes are playing tricks with our perception of how big and far away the moon is. You would have to be travelling awfully far to make the moon appear to move at all. Jeff Kanipe, of *Astronomy* magazine, concludes that without a road or expanse of landscape to give us reference points, 'this illusion of nearness coupled with its actual size and distance makes the moon appear to follow us wherever we go'.

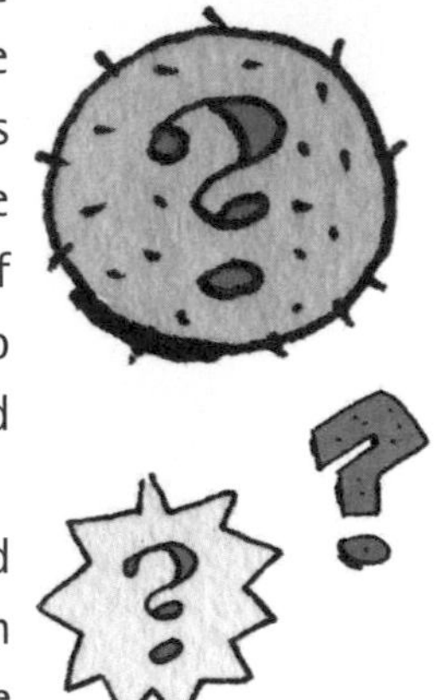

This phenomenon, much discussed in physics and astronomy textbooks, is called the parallax and is used to determine how the apparent change in the position of an object or heavenly body may be influenced by the changing position of the observer. Astronomers can determine the distance between a body in space and the observer by measuring the magnitude of the parallax effect.

But then again, maybe the moon really is following you.

Why can't you see stars in the background in photos or live shots of astronauts in space?

There actually are people out there who believe that NASA pulled off a giant hoax with the 'so-called moon landings'. Often, the lack of stars in the background of photos of the astronauts is cited as startling evidence to support the conspiracy. The answer to this Imponderable has more to do with photography than astronomy. If you take a photo of the sky on a starry night with a trusty old point-and-shoot camera or camcorder, guess what? The background will be dark – no stars will appear in the background.

The stars don't show up because they are so dim that they don't produce enough light on film in the short exposures used to take conventional pictures. But you have seen many photos of stars, haven't you? These were undoubtedly time-lapse photographs, taken with fast film and with the camera shutter left open for at least 10 to 15 seconds. Without special film and a long exposure time, the camera lens can't focus enough light on the film for the image to appear. Jim McDade, former Director of Space Technology for the University of Alabama at Birmingham, elaborates:

> Even if you attempt to take pictures of stars on the "dark side" of the Earth during an EVA [an extra-vehicular activity involving astronauts leaving the primary space module, such as a spacewalk] in low-Earth orbit, a time exposure from a stable platform of about 20 seconds is necessary in order to capture enough stellar photons to obtain an image showing stars, even when using fast films designed for low-light photography.

The same problems occur with digital cameras, film and video cameras, as McDade explains:

> A digital camera, a film camera and the human eye all suffer similar adaptability problems when it comes to capturing dimmer background objects such as stars hanging behind a space-walking astronaut in the foreground. The human eye is still much more sensitive than the finest digital or film camera.
>
> Photographic film is incapable of capturing the "very bright" and the "very dim" in the same exposure. The lunar surface is

brilliant in daylight. The photos taken by the *Apollo* astronauts used exposure times of a tiny fraction of one second. The stars in the sky are so dim that in order to capture them on film, it requires an exposure time hundreds of times longer than those made by the *Apollo* astronauts.'

Those of us who live in the city have had the experience of going into the country on a clear night and being amazed at the number of stars we can see when there are no lights on the ground. You can create the same effect inside your house. On a clear night, turn off the lights in a room and look out the window. Depending upon the atmospheric conditions, a star-filled sky may be visible to you. Switch on the lights inside the room, look outside, and the stars have disappeared.

Why? Light from a bright object near us can easily dwarf light emanating from distant objects, such as stars. In the case of astronauts, the lights attached to the space vehicle or space station or even the lights on an astronaut's helmet can wash out the relatively dim light from the stars in the background.

Even if sensitive film is used, astronauts' outfits reflect just too much light. The glare from the astronauts themselves will provide contrast from the dark sky background and faint stars. Any light emanating from the stars is unlikely to be exhibited when cameras are geared towards capturing clear shots of a space walker.

Perhaps the space conspiracists would stifle themselves if the *Apollo* astronauts had taken time-exposure photographs that could display the stars in all their glory, but they never did. As McDade puts it: 'After all, they went to the moon to explore the moon, not to stargaze.'

Why don't planets twinkle at night?

What causes a heavenly body to twinkle? Alan MacRobert, of *Sky & Telescope* magazine, explains:

'Twinkling is caused by light rays being diverted slightly – jiggled around – by turbulence where warm and cool air mixes in the upper atmosphere. One moment a ray of light from the star will hit your eye; the next moment, it misses.'

Our eyes fool our brains into thinking that the star is jumping around in the sky.

Stars are so far away from us that even when viewed through a sophisticated telescope, they look like single points of light. Even though planets may at first appear the same size as stars to the naked eye, they are actually little disks in the sky. Jeff Kanipe, Associate Editor of *Astronomy*, told *Imponderables* that 'the disks of planets like Venus, Mars, Jupiter and Saturn can be easily seen by looking at them with a pair of binoculars or a small telescope'.

How does this difference in size between stars and planets affect their 'twinkling quotient'? We've already established that stars appear to the eye as single points. Kanipe explains how that one point turns into a twinkle:

> When starlight passes through about 200 miles [360 km] of Earth's atmosphere, the light-bending properties of the different layers of air act like lenses that bend and jiggle the rays to such an extent that the star's position appears to jump about very slightly, causing it to twinkle.

MacRobert contrasts the effect of refraction upon our view of a planet:

> The disk of a planet can be regarded as many points packed close together. When one point twinkles bright for a moment, another may be faint. The differences average out and their combined light appears steady.

Kanipe phrases it a little differently:

> A planet's light comes from every part of its disk, not just a single point. Thus, when the light passes through the atmosphere, the shift in position is smaller than the size of the planet's disk in the sky, and the twinkling isn't as pronounced.

Still don't get it? Let's use a more down-to-earth analogy, supplied by Kanipe:

> From the vantage point of a diving board, a coin on the floor of the swimming pool appears to shift violently about because the water acts like a wavy lens that continuously distorts the rays of light coming from the coin. But a submerged patio table, say, looks fairly steady because the water can't

distort the light rays coming from its greater surface area to the point that the table appears to shift out of position.’

Does the moon have any effect on lakes or ponds? If not, why does it only seem to affect oceans’ tides? Why don’t lakes have tides?

If there is any radio show that we fear appearing on, it’s Ira Fistel’s program in Los Angeles. Fistel, a lawyer by training, has an encyclopaedic knowledge of history, railway lore, sports, radio and just about every other subject his audience questions him about, and is as likely as we are to answer an Imponderable from a caller.

So when we received this Imponderable on his show and we proceeded to stare at each other and shrug our shoulders (not particularly compelling radio, we might add), we knew this was a true Imponderable. We vowed to find an answer for the next book (and then go back on Fistel’s show and gloat about it).

Robert Burnham, of *Astronomy* magazine, was generous enough to send a fascinating explanation:

‘Even the biggest lakes are too small to have tides. Ponds or lakes have no tides because these bodies of water are raised all at once, along with the land underneath the lake, by the gravitational pull of the moon. (The solid Earth swells a maximum of about 18 inches [45 cm] under the moon’s tidal pull, but the effect is imperceptible because we have nothing that isn’t also moving by which to gauge the uplift.)

In addition, ponds and lakes are not openly connected to a larger supply of water located elsewhere on the globe, which could supply extra water to them to make a tidal bulge. The seas, on the other hand, have tides because the water in them can flow freely throughout the world’s ocean basins ...

On the side of Earth nearest the moon, the moon’s gravity pulls sea water away from the planet, thus raising a bulge called high tide. At the same time on the other side of the planet, the moon’s gravity is pulling Earth away from the water, thus creating a second high-tide bulge.

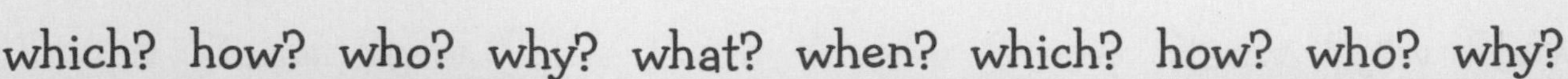

Low tides occur in between because these are the regions from which water has drained to flow into the two high-tide bulges. (The sun exerts a tidal effect of its own, but only 46 per cent as strong as the moon's.)

Some landlocked portions of the ocean – the Mediterranean or the Baltic – can mimic the tideless behaviour of a lake, although for different reasons. The Mediterranean Sea, for example, has a tidal range measuring just a couple of inches [5 cm] because it is a basin with only a small inlet (the Strait of Gibraltar) connecting it to the global ocean. The Gibraltar Strait is both narrow and shallow, which prevents the rapid twice-a-day flow of immense volumes of water necessary to create a pronounced tide. Thus the rise and fall of the tide in the Atlantic attempts to fill or drain the Med, but the tidal bulge always moves on before very much water can pour in or out past Gibraltar. ’

Alan MacRobert, of *Sky & Telescope*, summarises that a body of water needs a large area to slosh around in before tidal effects are substantial, and he provides a simple analogy:

‘ Imagine a tray full of soil dotted with thimbles of water, representing a landmass with lakes. You could tilt it slightly and nothing much would happen. Now imagine a tray full of water – an ocean. If you tilted it just a little, water would pour out over your hands. ’

What precisely is sea level? And how do they determine exactly what it is?

Painstakingly. Obviously, the sea level in any particular location is constantly changing. If you measure the ocean during low tide and then high tide, you won't come up with the same figure. Wind and barometric shifts also affect the elevation of the seas.

But the oceans are joined and their height variation is slight. So geodesists (mathematicians who specialise in the study of measurement of the Earth) and oceanographers settle for an approximation. Because the cliché that 'water seeks its own level' is true, geodesists worry more about sea level variations over time than between places. Measurements are taken all over the globe; there is no one place where sea level is determined. One sea level fits all.

The US National Geodetic Survey defines 'mean sea level' as the 'average location of the interface between ocean and atmosphere, over a period of time sufficiently long so that all random and periodic variations of short duration average to zero'. The US National Ocean Service has set 19 as the appropriate number of years to sample sea levels to eliminate such variations; in some cases, measurements are taken on an hourly basis. Geodesists simply add up the 19 years of samples and divide by 19 to arrive at the mean sea level.

The mean sea level rose throughout most of the twentieth century – on average, over 1 mm a year. On a few occasions, sea level has risen as much as 5 or 6 mm in a year, not exactly causing flood conditions, but enough to indicate that the rise was caused by melting of glaciers. If theories of the greenhouse effect and global warming are true, the rise of the global sea level in the future will be more than the proverbial drop in the bucket.

What's the difference between an ocean and a sea?

The standard definition of an ocean, as stated in the United States Geological Survey's Geographic Names Information Service, is 'The great body of salt water that occupies two-thirds of the surface of the earth, or one of its major subdivisions'. Notice the weasel words at the end. Is the Red Sea a 'major subdivision' of the Indian Ocean? If so, why isn't it the Red Ocean? Or simply referred to as the Indian Ocean?

Most, but by no means all, seas are almost totally landlocked and connected to an ocean or a larger sea, but no definition we encountered stated this as a requirement for the classification. Geographical and geological authorities can't even agree on whether a sea must always be saline. The United States Geological Survey's Topographical Instructions say yes; but in their book *Water and Water Use Terminology*, Professors JO Veatch and CR Humphrys indicate

Why are the oceans salty? What keeps the oceans at the same level of saltiness?

Most of the salt in the ocean is there because of the processes of dissolving and leaching from the solid earth over hundreds of millions of years, according to Dr Eugene C LaFond, President of LaFond Oceanic Consultants. Rivers take the salt out of rocks and carry them into oceans; these eroded rocks supply the largest portion of salt in the ocean.

But other natural phenomena contribute to the mineral load in the oceans. Salty volcanic rock washes into them. Volcanoes also release salty 'juvenile water', water that has never existed before in the form of liquid. Fresh basalt flows up from a giant rift that runs through all the oceans' basins.

With all of these processes dumping salt into the oceans, one might think that the seas would get saturated with sodium chloride, for oceans, like any other body of water, keep evaporating. Yet, according to the Sea Secrets Information Services of the International Oceanographic Foundation at the University of Miami, the concentration of salts in the ocean has not changed for quite a while – about, oh, 1.5 billion years or so. So how do oceans rid themselves of some of the salt?

First of all, sodium chloride is extremely soluble, so it doesn't get concentrated in certain sections of the ocean. The surface area of the oceans is so large that the salt is relatively evenly distributed. Second, some of the ions in the salt leave with the sea spray. Third, some of the salt sticks to particulate matter that sinks below the surface of the ocean. The fourth and most dramatic way sodium chloride is removed from the ocean is by the large accumulations left in salt flats on ocean coasts, where the water is shallow enough to evaporate.

Thus the level of salt in the ocean, approximately 3.5 per cent, remains constant.

that 'sea' is sometimes used interchangeably with 'ocean': 'In one place a large body of salt water may be called lake, in another a sea. The Great Lakes, Lake Superior and others, are freshwater but by legal definition are seas.'

The nasty truth is that you can get away with calling most places whatever names you want.

What keeps the water in lakes and ponds from falling below ground?

Let's say you happen to spill a drink on your kitchen floor. The liquid remains on the floor's surface, doesn't it (unless you happen to have a dog handy to lap it up)? Spill it on your front yard, though, and the earth will absorb it.

The same principle applies when it rains. Gravity carries the raindrops down, and the precipitation 'wants' to soak into the ground, and will, unless something prevents it. Assuming the rain goes below ground level, it will continue its progress downwards until it hits something that stops it. Most commonly, the moisture encounters bedrock, which can consist of basalt, shale, slate and many other substances that water simply cannot permeate. Eventually, if enough water collects on the bedrock, the soil starts to fill up like a sponge. When the soil becomes saturated with water, the upper surface is referred to as the 'water table'.

But the water table is not a static line; it is a dynamic and ever-shifting entity, as physical oceanographer Karl Newyear explains:

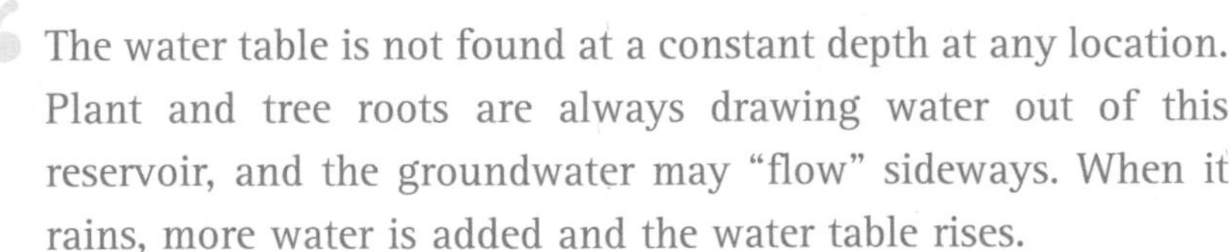

> The water table is not found at a constant depth at any location. Plant and tree roots are always drawing water out of this reservoir, and the groundwater may "flow" sideways. When it rains, more water is added and the water table rises.
>
> Sometimes the soil layer is very thin or lots of precipitation has fallen. Then the water table may actually be at or even above the ground surface: this is when puddles form. The water stands on top of the mud because all the ground beneath is saturated.
>
> The water table is not necessarily a horizontal surface. When the water table is tilted, you would expect the water to "flow downhill". This is indeed the case, but usually it happens quite slowly. To move in any direction, water needs some sort of pathway: earthworm holes or empty spaces between clumps of

> dirt. Different soil types have different porosities – soils with large particle sizes, like sand, have high porosity, while soils with small particle sizes, like clay, have low porosity. The higher the porosity, the easier it is for water to flow through it.

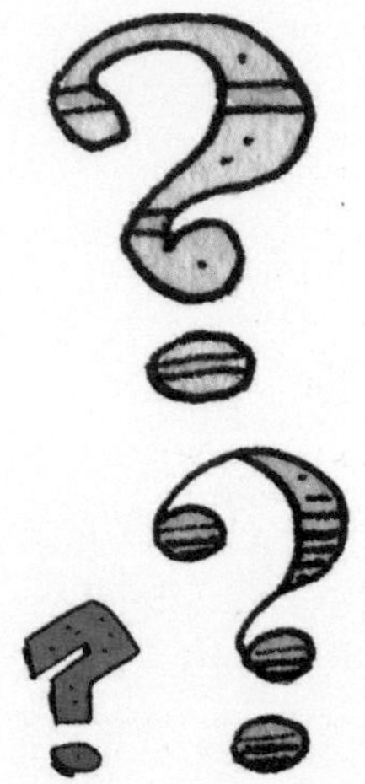

As Arved Sandstrom, of the Physical Oceanography Group of Memorial University of Newfoundland, puts it: 'Ponds and lakes don't permeate because the space is already occupied by other water.' In this sense, the presence of the lake or pond is a manifestation no stranger than the puddles found on a bathroom floor when the tub has overflowed with water.

But as all the oceanographers we spoke to insisted, the accumulation of water in lakes and ponds is more complicated. In some cases, bodies of water are simply the exposed portions of the local water table. But a pond can appear well above the water table if rain is falling faster than it permeates the ground, a natural manifestation of 'standing water' not unlike the bathwater that refuses to leave the basin because of a 'slow drain'.

If water is composed of two parts hydrogen and one part oxygen, both common elements, why can't droughts be eliminated by combining the two to produce water?

We could produce water by combining oxygen and hydrogen, but at quite a cost financially and, in some cases, environmentally.

Brian Bigley, Senior Chemist for Systech Environmental Corporation, says that most methods for creating water are impractical merely because 'you would need massive amounts of hydrogen and oxygen to produce even a small quantity of water, and amassing each would be expensive'. Add to this the cost, of course, of the labour and equipment necessary to run a 'water plant'.

Bigley suggests another possible alternative would be to obtain water as a by-product of burning methane in an oxygen atmosphere:

> Again, it's a terrible waste of energy. Methane is a wonderful fuel, and is better used as such, rather than using our supply to produce H_2O. It would be like giving paper money to people to be used as facial tissue.

Why is the Earth's core still hot?

We know that the Earth's core is hot, but not how hot. Actually, even geologists don't know exactly what the temperature is, either, but they know it is almost as hot as the sun. That's hot.

Luckily for us, the surface of the Earth is considerably cooler. After all, the surface is losing heat by being in contact with cooler air. But the core is continually heated by the decay of radioactive elements. Scientists believe that the original heat from the formation of the Earth is still being played out in these transformations. The sun is likely to expand and burn us before the core of our planet cools off.

The rule of thumb has traditionally been that for every 33 m in depth, the temperature of the Earth increases by 1°C. But this old approximation was based on distances that scientists could measure by drillholes. If this ratio held true all the way to the core of the Earth, its temperature would be 100,000°C. Most geologists agree that the actual temperature is closer to a still unfrosty 5000°C.

Why are we more worried about future global warming when our own core is so incendiary? The amount of heat that reaches the Earth's surface is not enough to affect it drastically, and what heat there is quickly radiates to outer space. In their book, *Physical Geology*, Brian J Skinner and Stephen C Porter emphasise that the heat transfer is not uniform:

> ‘The heat loss is not constant everywhere. Just as the geothermal gradient varies from place to place, so does the heat flow, which is greatest near young volcanoes and active hot springs, and least where the crust is oldest and least active.’

Of course, the Earth's crust helps insulate the core from losing more heat. These cracks in the crust, like volcanoes and springs, are the few venues that allow us to glimpse the heat trapped in the sizzling core below.

In recent years, scientists have developed the ability to measure radioactivity more precisely through measuring particles called 'antineutrinos'. Scientists have long suspected that radioactivity might be responsible for all the heat generated at the Earth's core, and geologists are optimistic that eventually they will be able to map exactly where the energy is being generated. Even more recently, two scientists from the University of California, Berkeley, discovered that potassium can form an alloy with the iron in the Earth's core. Although Dr Kanani Lee found that potassium might make up only 0.1 per cent of the Earth's core, 'it can be enough to provide one-fifth of the heat given off by the Earth'.

The University of California, Berkeley, announcement of the potassium discovery presents the current consensus:

> The Earth is thought to have formed from the collision of many rocky asteroids, perhaps hundreds of kilometres in diameter, in the early solar system. As the proto-Earth gradually bulked up, continuing asteroid collisions and gravitational collapse kept the planet molten. Heavier elements – in particular iron – would have sunk to the core in 10 to 100 million years' time, carrying with it other elements that bind to iron.
>
> Gradually, however, the Earth would have cooled off and become a dead rocky globe with a cold iron ball at the core if not for the continued release of heat by the decay of radioactive elements like potassium-40, uranium-238 and thorium-232, which have half-lives of 1.25 billion, 4 billion, and 14 billion years, respectively. About one in every thousand potassium atoms is radioactive.

As you have seen, scientists tend to take the long view. Although biophysicist Joe Doyle later reiterated the 'radioactive theory', his first response to why the Earth's core is still hot was: 'There hasn't been enough time for it to cool yet.'

Why are ancient cities buried in layers? And where did the dirt come from?

This Imponderable assumes two facts that aren't always true. First, not all ruins are the remains of cities. Many other ancient sites – such as forts, camping sites, cave dwellings, cemeteries and quarries – are also frequently buried. Second, not all ancient cities are buried; once in a while, archaeologists are given a break and find ruins close to, or at the surface of, the ground.

Still, the questions are fascinating, and we went to two experts for the answers: George Rapp, Jr, Dean and Professor of Geology and Archaeology of the University of Minnesota, Duluth, and Co-editor of *Archaeological Geology*; and Boston University's Al B Wesolowsky, Managing Editor of the *Journal of Field Archaeology*. Both stressed that most buried ruins were caused by a combination of factors. Here are some of the most common:

1 Wind-borne dust (known to archaeologists as 'Aeolian dust') accumulates and eventually buries artefacts. Aeolian dust can vary from wind-blown volcanic dust to ordinary dirt and household dust.

2 Water-borne sediment accumulates and eventually buries artefacts. Rain carrying sediment from a high point to a lower spot is often the culprit, but sand or clay formed by flowing waters, such as riverine deposits gathered during floods, can literally bury a riverside community. Often, water collects and carries what are technically Aeolian deposits to a lower part of a site.

3 Catastrophic natural events can cause burials in one fell swoop, though this is exceedingly rare, and as Dr Rapp adds, 'In these circumstances the site must be in a topographic situation where erosion is absent or at least considerably slower than deposition.' Even when a city is buried after one catastrophe, the burial can be caused by more than one factor. Wesolowsky notes that although both Pompeii and Herculaneum were buried by the eruption of Mount Vesuvius in 79 AD, one was buried by mudflow and the other by ashflow.

4 Man-made structures can collapse, contributing to the burial. Sometimes this destruction is accidental (such as floods, earthquakes, fires), and sometimes intentional (bombings, demolitions). Humans seem incapable of leaving behind no trace of their activities. Says Rapp: 'Even cities as young as New York City have accumulated a considerable depth of such debris. Early New York is now buried many feet below the current surface.'

5 Ancient civilisations occasionally did their own burying. Wesolowsky's example:

> 'When Constantine wanted to build Old St Peter's on the side of the Vatican Hill in the early fourth century, his engineers had to cut off part of the slope and dump it into a Roman cemetery (thereby preserving the lower part of the cemetery, including what has been identified as the tomb of Peter himself) to provide a platform for the basilica.
>
> When Old St Peter's was demolished in the sixteenth century to make way for the current church, parts of the old church were used as fill in low areas in the locale.'

Rapp points to the example of tels, ancient mounds found in Central Europe, the Middle East and as far east as Pakistan:

> Often they are several metres high. Each "civilisation" is built over the debris of the preceding one. The houses were mostly of mud brick, which had a lifetime of perhaps 60 years. When they collapsed, the earth was just spread around. In 2000 or 3000 years, these great habitation mounds (tels) grew to great heights and now rise above the surrounding plains. Each layer encloses archaeological remains of the period of occupation.

While we self-consciously bury time capsules to give future generations an inkling of what our generation is like, the gesture is unnecessary. With assistance from Mother Nature, we are unwittingly burying revealing artefacts – everything from chocolate wrappers to beer cans – every day.

How does aspirin find a headache?

When we get a minor headache, we pop two aspirin and, voilà, the pain diminishes within a matter of minutes. How did those little pills find exactly what ailed us instead of, say, our little right toe or our left hip?

We always assumed that the aspirin dissolved, entered our bloodstream and quickly found its way to our brain. The chemicals then persuaded the brain to block out any feelings of pain in the body. Right? Wrong.

Willow bark, which provided the salicylic acid from which aspirin was originally synthesised, had been used as a pain remedy ever since the Greeks discovered its therapeutic power nearly 2500 years ago. Bayer was the first company to market aspirin commercially in 1899 (Aspirin was originally a trade name of Bayer's for the salicylic acid derivative, acetylsalicylic acid, or ASA). The value of this new drug was quickly apparent, but researchers had little idea how aspirin alleviated pain until the 1970s. In their fascinating book *The Aspirin Wars*, Charles C Mann and Mark L Plummer describe the basic dilemma:

> Aspirin was a hard problem ... It relieves pain but, mysteriously, is not an anaesthetic ... And it soothes inflamed joints but leaves normal joints untouched. How does aspirin "know" ... whether

> pain is already present, or which joints are inflamed? Researchers didn't have a clue. They didn't even know whether aspirin acts peripherally, at the site of an injury or centrally, blocking the ability of the brain and central nervous system to feel pain. ’

The breakthrough came more than 70 years after the introduction of the best-selling pharmaceutical in the world, when researcher John Vane discovered that aspirin inhibited the synthesis of prostaglandins, fatty acids manufactured by virtually every cell in the human body. They resemble hormones, insofar as they secrete into the bloodstream, but unlike most hormones, they tend to stay near their point of manufacture. Prostaglandins serve many biological functions, but the particular ones that cause headache pain, usually known as PGE 2, increase the sensitivity of pain receptors. So prostaglandins seem to serve as an internal warning system by producing discomfort, inflammation, fever and irritation in areas of the body that are not functioning normally. According to Harold Davis, Consumer Safety Officer with the US Food and Drug Administration, prostaglandins dilate blood vessels, which can also produce headaches.

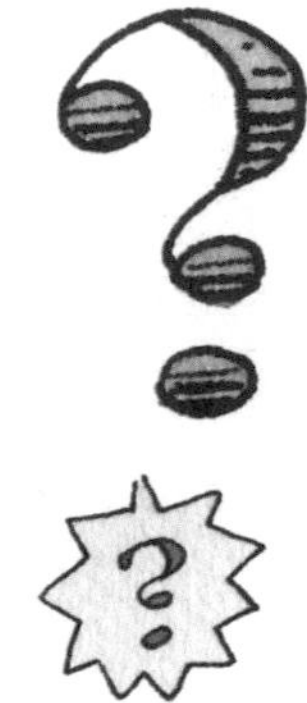

The discovery of the role of prostaglandins in producing pain explains why aspirin works only on malfunctioning cells and tissues; if aspirin can stop the production of prostaglandins, pain will not be felt in the first place. Still, aspirin doesn't cure diseases; it can alleviate the symptoms of arthritis, for example, but it doesn't stop the progress of the condition.

In all fairness, scientists still don't know exactly what causes headaches or all the ways in which aspirin works to relieve pain. Unlike morphine and other mind-altering drugs, aspirin works peripherally. The key to the success of any peripheral painkiller is in reaching the pain receptors near the irritation or inflammation, not simply in reaching sufficient concentrations in the bloodstream. In the case of aspirin, the ASA is connected to the bloodstream; the bloodstream's connected to the prostaglandins; the prostaglandins are connected to the receptors; and the receptors are connected to the headache.

Why does a horrible drug like heroin have a ‘heroic’ name?

Yes, *heroin* derives from the same Greek word, *heros*, that gave us the English *hero* and *heroine*. Although heroin's manufacture and distribution have long been outlawed around the world, the morphine derivative was developed as a legitimate painkiller.

Heroin was originally a legitimate trademark taken by a German pharmaceutical company, so the brand name was consciously designed to evoke only positive associations. Not only was heroin effective as a painkiller, it also had the 'bonus' of giving patients a euphoric feeling, and as we now know, delusions of grandeur. Although these side effects can be deadly in an illicit drug, it was at first a distinct selling point in marketing heroin to doctors as a painkiller.

Why do we have a delayed reaction to sunburn? Why is sunburn often more evident 24 hours after we've been out in the sun?

It's happened to most of you. You leave the house for the beach. You forget the sunscreen. Oh well, you think, I won't stay out in the sun too long. You do stay out in the sun too long, but you haven't burned too badly. Still, you feel a heaviness on your skin. That night, you start feeling a burning sensation.

The next morning, you wake up and go into the bathroom. You look in the mirror. You are bright red. Don't you hate it when that happens?

Despite our association of sunburn and tanning with fun in the sun, sunburn is, to quote US Army dermatologist Colonel John R Cook, 'an injury to the skin caused by exposure to ultraviolet radiation'. The sun's ultraviolet rays, ranging in length from 200 to 400 nanometres, invisible to the naked eye, are also responsible for skin cancer. Luckily for us, much of the damaging effects of the sun is filtered by our ozone layer.

Actually, some of us do redden quickly after exposure to the sun, but dermatologist Samuel Selden told us that this initial 'blush' is primarily due to the heat, with blood going to the surface of the skin in an effort to radiate the heat to the outside, reducing the core temperature.

This initial reaction is not the burn itself. In most cases, the peak burn is reached 15 to 24 hours after exposure. A whole series of events causes the erythema (reddening) of the skin, after a prolonged exposure to the sun:

1 In an attempt to repair damaged cells, vessels widen in order to rush blood to the surface of the skin. As biophysicist Joe Doyle puts it, 'The redness we see is not actually the burn, but

rather the blood that has come to repair the cells that have burned.' This process, called vasodilation, is prompted by the release of one or more chemicals, such as kinins, setotonins and histamines.

2 Capillaries break down and slowly leak blood.
3 Exposure to the sun stimulates the skin to manufacture more melanin, the pigment that makes us appear darker (darker-skinned people, in general, can better withstand exposure to the sun and are more likely to tan than burn).
4 Prostaglandins, fatty acid compounds, are released after cells are damaged by the sun, and play some role in the delay of sunburns, but researchers don't know yet exactly how this works.

All four of these processes take time and explain the delayed appearance of sunburn. The rate at which an individual will tan is dependent upon the skin type (the amount of melanin already in the skin), the wavelength of the ultraviolet rays, the amount of time in the sun and the time of day.

Once erythema occurs, your body attempts to heal you. Peeling, for example, can be an important defence mechanism, as Dr Selden explains:

> ‘The peeling that takes place as the sunburn progresses is the skin's effort to thicken up in preparation for further sun exposure. The skin thickens and darkens with each sun exposure, but some individuals, lacking the ability to tan, suffer sunburns with each sun exposure.’

One dermatologist, Joseph P Bark, told us that the delayed burning effect is responsible for much of the severe skin damage he sees. Sunbathers think that if they haven't burned yet, they can continue sitting in the sun, but there is no way to gauge how much damage one has incurred simply by examining the colour or extent of the erythema.

To Bark, this is like saying there is no fire when we detect smoke. Long before sunburns appear, a doctor can find cell damage by examining samples through a microscope.

Why do bombs create mushroom-shaped clouds?

Before we can explain the reason for the shape of these clouds, two common misconceptions have to be cleared up. Many people believe that bombs are dropped from planes, hit the ground and explode in part because of the contact with the earth. Actually, bombs are designed to detonate in the air before they hit the ground.

And the 'mushroom' is not composed of ingredients contained in the bomb. Rather, the cloud is a conglomeration of dirt, dust and debris from the ground.

We talked to Todd A Postma, a nuclear engineer at the Advanced Nuclear Engineering Computational Laboratory, who explained the formation of the menacing mushroom:

> In an atomic blast, such as the bombs dropped on Hiroshima and Nagasaki, the mushroom cloud develops because the blast lifts a tremendous amount of debris from the ground into the air.
>
> The bomb blast is directed downward and reflects off the Earth's crust. As a result, much soil is carried upward into the air. Initially, most of this soil motion is straight up [creating the "stem" of the mushroom]; however; once the soil is up in the air and the vertical kinetic energy is spent, the horizontal wind force takes over and spreads the cloud out. Then gravity takes over and the soil begins to drift downward [accounting for that weird phase when the cloud appears to be imploding].
>
> The mushroom shape can be distorted somewhat if there is a strong prevailing wind at the time. Also, once the soil has had time to disperse, the cloud looks less and less like a mushroom.
>
> Conventional explosions [such as TNT] create mushroom clouds too. It's just that the effect is magnified with nuclear explosions because of the magnitude of the blast. There's nothing inherent in a nuclear blast, as opposed to a conventional blast, which causes the mushroom cloud.

The 'horizontal wind force' that helps disperse the 'cap' of the mushroom is to a large extent created by the blast itself rather than ambient weather conditions. When the bomb detonates, a fireball spreads out in all directions. Because this fireball is a hot gas, it tends to rise, creating a suction effect underneath that helps 'suck' up the debris from below in a vacuum effect.

At the top of the fireball, the expansion meets some air resistance and tends to flatten out, creating the 'flat top' associated with the cap of a mushroom, rather than the roundish top you might expect to see. If there were no gravity or air resistance (for example, if you set off the bomb in space), a

bomb would presumably expand equally in all directions, creating a huge, inflating sphere.

When the blast hits the earth, a parabolic-shaped crater is usually formed (a parabola is the shape of satellite dishes and the reflectors below the bulbs in torches). The parabolic shape is crucial to the formation of the cloud, because no matter in what direction an incoming object hits a parabolic shape, be it a television wave in the case of a satellite dish, a light wave in the case of a reflector or debris from a bomb, the reflected objects are sent back perpendicularly – all parallel to one another. In the case of the bomb, since the crater is located on the ground, the debris moves straight up, perpendicular to the ground, which results in what appears to be a perfectly straight, vertical 'stem' on the mushroom.

When a smaller 'conventional' bomb is set off, you often don't see the mushroom shape because of the smaller scale and blinding speed of the blast. An atomic bomb's speed might be just as great, but the cloud is so much larger that it takes longer to unfold.

And what happens if a bomb does not detonate until it hits the ground? The results are unpredictable – no consistent pattern is formed. The shape of the 'cloud' would depend on the content of the target hit. It is likely to look more like a turbulent mess than any vegetable.

How did the Romans do the calculations necessary for construction and other purposes using Roman numerals?

Our idea of a good time does not include trying to do long division with Roman numerals. Can you imagine dividing CXVII by IX and carrying down numbers that look more like a cryptogram than an arithmetic problem?

The Romans were saved that torture. They relied on the Chinese abacus, with pebbles as counters, to perform their calculations. In fact, Barry Fells, of the Epigraphic Society, informs us that these mathematical operations were performed in Roman times by persons called '*calculatores*'.

They were so named because they used *calcule* (Latin for pebbles) to add, subtract, multiply and divide.

Why do we call our numbering system 'Arabic' when Arabs don't use Arabic numbers themselves?

The first numbering system was probably developed by the Egyptians, but ancient Sumeria, Babylonia and India used numerals in business transactions. All of the earliest number systems used some variation of 1 to denote one, probably because the numeral resembled a single finger. Historians suggest that our Arabic 2 and 3 are corruptions of two and three slash marks written hurriedly.

Most students in Europe, Australia and the Americas learn to calculate with Arabic numbers, *even though these numerals were never used by Arabs.* Arabic numbers were actually developed in India, long before the invention of the printing press (probably in the tenth century), but were subsequently translated into Arabic. European merchants who brought back treatises to their continent mistakenly assumed that Arabs had invented the system and proceeded to translate the texts from Arabic.

Why is balsa wood classified as a hardwood when it is soft? What is the difference between a softwood and a hardwood?

Call us naive, but we thought that maybe there was a slight chance that the main distinction between a softwood and a hardwood was that hardwood was harder than softwood. What fools we are.

It turns out that the distinction between the two lies in how their seeds are formed on the tree. Softwoods, such as pines, spruce and fir, are examples of gymnosperms, plants that produce seeds without a covering. John A Pitcher, Director of the Hardwood Research Council, told *Imponderables* that if you pull one of the centre scales back from the stem of a fresh pine cone, you'll see a pair of seeds lying side by side: 'They have no covering except the wooden cone.'

Hardwoods are a type of angiosperm, a true flowering plant that bears seeds enclosed in capsules, fruits or husks (e.g. olives, lilies and walnuts). Hardwoods also tend to lose their leaves in temperate climates, whereas softwoods are evergreens; but in tropical climates, many hardwoods retain their leaves.

While it is true that there is a tendency for softwoods to be softer in consistency (and easier to cut for commercial purposes), and for hardwoods to be more compact, and thus tougher and denser in texture, these rules of thumb are not reliable. Pitcher sent us a booklet listing the specific gravities of important commercial woods. He indicates the irony: 'At 0.16 specific gravity, balsa is the lightest wood listed. At a specific gravity of 1.05, lignumvitae is the heaviest wood known. Both are hardwoods.'

Why does wood 'pop' when put on a fire?

Once again, John Pitcher, of the Hardwood Research Council, was kind enough to help us out:

> 'Wood pops when put on a fire because there are little pockets of sap, pitch [resin] or other volatiles that are contained in the wood. As the wood surface is heated and burns, heat is transferred to the sap or pitch deeper in the wood.
>
> The sap or pitch first liquefies, then vaporises as the temperature increases. Gases expand rapidly when heated and put tremendous pressure on the walls of the pitch pocket. When the pressure gets high enough, the pocket walls burst and the characteristic sound is heard.'

Why does a fire create a crackling sound? Is there any reason why a fire cracks most when first lit?

Of course, 'pops' are not unrelated to 'crackles'. John Pitcher, of the Hardwood Research Council, explains that the larger the sap or pitch pockets in the wood, the bigger the pop; but if there are smaller but more numerous pockets, the wood will crackle instead.

The reason most fires crackle most when first lit is that the smaller pieces of wood, used as kindling, heat up quickly. The inside sap pockets are penetrated and crackle immediately. Big pieces of wood burn much more slowly, with fewer, intermittent, but louder pops.

For any, pardon the expression, 'would-be' connoisseurs of timber acoustics, Pitcher provided *Imponderables* readers with a consumer's guide:

> There are distinct differences in the popping characteristics of woods. High on the list of poppers is tamarack or larch. Most conifers are ready poppers. On the other hand, hardwoods, such as ash, elm and oak, tend to burn quietly, with only an occasional tastefully subdued pop. You might call them poopers rather than poppers.

Why don't trees on a slope grow perpendicular to the ground as they do on a level surface?

Trees don't care if they're planted on a steep hill or a level field. Either way, they'll still try to reach up towards the sky and seek as much light as possible. Botanist Bruce Kershner told *Imponderables*:

> This strong growth preference is based on the most important of motivations: survival. Scientifically, this is called "phototropism", or the growth of living cells towards the greatest source of light. Light provides trees with the energy and food that enable them to grow in the first place.
>
> There is also another tropism (involuntary movement towards or away from a stimulus) at work – geotropism – the movement away from the pull of gravity (roots, unlike the rest of the tree, grow towards the gravitational pull). Even on a hill slope, the pull of gravity is directly down, and the greatest source of average light is directly up. In a forest, the source of light is only up.
>
> There are, however, cases where a tree might not grow directly up. First, there are some trees whose trunks grow outwards naturally, but whose tops still tend to point upwards. Second, trees growing against an overhanging cliff will grow outwards on an angle towards the greatest concentration of light (much

like a houseplant grows towards the window). Third, it is reported that in a few places on earth with natural geomagnetic distortions (e.g. Oregon Vortex, Gold Hill, Oregon), the trees grow in a contorted fashion. The gravitational force is abnormal, but the light source is the same.'

John Pitcher, of the Hardwood Research Council, adds that trees have developed adaptive mechanisms to react to the sometimes conflicting demands of phototropism and geotropism:

'Trees compensate for the pull of gravity and the slope of the ground by forming a special kind of reaction wood. On a slope, conifer trees grow faster on the downhill side, producing compression wood, so named because the wood is pushing the trunk bole uphill to keep it straight. Hardwoods grow faster on the uphill side, forming tension wood that pulls the trunk uphill to keep it straight.

Why softwoods develop compression wood and hardwoods develop tension wood is one of the unsolved mysteries of the plant world.'

If nothing sticks to Teflon, how do they get Teflon to stick to the pan?

'They', of course, is DuPont, which owns the registered trademark for Teflon and its younger and now more popular cousin, Silverstone. GA Quinn of DuPont told us that the application of both is similar:

'When applying Silverstone to a metal frying pan, the interior of the pan is first grit-blasted, then a primer coat is sprayed on and baked. A second layer of polytetrafluoroethylene (PTFE) is applied, baked and dried again. A third coat of PTFE is applied, baked and dried.

'About the only thing that sticks to PTFE is PTFE. So, the three-coat process used in Silverstone forms an inseparable bond between the PTFE layers, and the primer coat bonds to the rough, grit-blasted metal surface.'

How do the trick birthday candles (that keep relighting after being blown out) work?

Michael DeMent, Product Spokesperson for Hallmark, told us that the wicks of their Puff Proof Candles are treated with magnesium crystals. The crystals retain enough heat to reilluminate the wick after candles are blown out.

Because the magnesium-treated wicks retain heat so well, Hallmark recommends extinguishing the candles permanently by dipping them in water.

DeMent shocked us (and in this job, we're not easily shocked) by telling us that practical jokers aren't the only customers for trick birthday candles. Some penurious types view them not as trick candles but as reusable candles. After the candles are blown out for the first time, they gather the candles and pinch the wicks with their hands or surround them with a paper towel or other material so that the heat is allowed to radiate around the other object. They then rebox the candles and use them another time.

Will Super Glue stick to Teflon?

We were wary of contacting Loctite, which manufactures Super Glue, and DuPont, which markets Teflon, about this almost metaphysical Imponderable, for it would be like prying a confession from the immovable object (Teflon) and the unstoppable force (Super Glue) that one of their reputations was seriously exaggerated. But we are worldly wise in such matters.

So first we contacted DuPont about Teflon, a registered trademark for polytetrafluoroethylene (which, for obvious reasons, we'll call PTFE). As we expected, Kenneth Leavell, Research Supervisor for DuPont's Teflon/Silverstone division, took a hard line. He firmly holds the conviction that Super Glue won't stick to Teflon, at least 'not very well and certainly not reliably'. Here are some of the reasons why not:

1. The combination of fluorine and carbon in PTFE forms one of the strongest bonds in the chemical world and one of the most stable.
2. The fluorine atoms around the carbon-fluorine bond are inert, so they form an 'impenetrable shield' around the chain of carbon atoms, keeping other chemicals from entering. As Leavell puts it, 'Adhesives need to chemically or physically bond to the substrate to which they are applied. PTFE contains no chemical sites for other substances to bond with.'

3 Adhesives need to wet the substrate directly or creep into porous areas in the substrate. But the low surface energy of PTFE prevents wetting and bonding. Leavell compares it to trying to get oil and water to stick together.

And then he lays down the gauntlet: 'Super Glue is "super" because of its speed of cure and relatively strong bonds. As an adhesive for PTFE, it's no better than epoxies, polyurethanes, etc., would be.'

So, the immovable object claims near invincibility. How would the unstoppable force react? We contacted Richard Palin, Loctite's Technical Service Advisor. And he folded like a newly cleaned shirt. Yes, Palin admitted, Teflon lacks the cracks necessary for Super Glue to enter in order to bond properly; there would be nowhere for the glue to get into the pan. Yes, he confessed, the critical surface tension is too low for the adhesive to wet the surface. Yes, he broke down in sobs, Super Glue would probably just bead up if applied to a Teflon pan.

Just kidding, actually. Palin didn't seem upset at all about Super Glue's inability to stick to Teflon. By all accounts, there isn't much demand for the task.

What happens to the tread that wears off tyres?

The tread gradually wears off our tyres. After a few years of heavy driving, it eventually becomes bare. But we don't see bits of tread on the road (except from premature blow-outs, of course). Roads are not discoloured with blackened tread bits. Does tyre tread disappear along with our socks?

The car industry, the tyre industry and some independent pollution experts have long been concerned about what may seem to be a trivial problem. Two specialists in the chemistry department of the Ford Motor Company have estimated that 600,000 tonnes of tyre tread are worn off US vehicles every year. The possibility was more than remote that all of this material might remain in the air, in suspendable particles, which could be dangerous to humans. So they sought a way to measure what happens to the disappearing tread.

Tests to determine the presence of tyre tread were held at three sites, all of which presented some problems. First, indoor tests were designed to simulate driving wear on a tyre. Unfortunately, without ambient weather conditions, worn rubber simply tended to stick to the simulated road surface. Scientists knew this wasn't what happened under real conditions, for the second type of test, on real roads, indicated that virtually no rubber stayed on the road, due to wind, rain and movement of surrounding traffic. Additionally, surface areas around roads were sometimes cleaned by maintenance crews, hindering efforts to measure long-term accumulation of tyre tread. The third type of test, in tunnels, might be thought to show the maximum possible build-up of tyre tread, except that road surfaces in tunnels tend to wear tyres less than surface streets, and the lack of natural wind and rain in the tunnel made any extrapolation difficult.

Still, the combined results of these experiments did provide quite a lot of information about exactly what happens to tyre tread. Whereas the most common substance in exhaust fumes is dangerous lead, the most plentiful tyre debris is in the form of styrene-butadiene rubber (SBR), the most common rubber hydrocarbon in treads. Most of the tread debris is not in the form of gas, but rather in microscopic particles that are heavy enough to fall to the ground.

All road and tunnel tests seem to confirm that particle debris found along roadsides accounted for at least 50 per cent of the total missing tyre tread, and possibly much more. One study indicated that 2 per cent of all roadside dustfall consisted of worn tread material. Another study, in Detroit, found that of the total particulate loading in the air, only 1 per cent was tread dust. Even in tunnel tests, tyre tread comprised only 1 to 4 per cent of the total airborne particulate matter generated – a percentage far less than that of the exhaust emissions of petrol- and diesel-powered vehicles.

All the tests concur, then, that the vast majority of worn tread in particle form falls on the ground instead of staying in the air.

Why do glasses sweat when filled with cold beverages?

It's elementary physics, dear readers. The answer is 'condensation'. The 'sweat' doesn't sneak from the liquid inside of the glass to the outside; rather, it immigrates from the ambient air.

The cool liquid (and ice) in the glass cools the glass itself, in particular the outside of the glass, and this slightly cools the air just outside the glass. Cooler air cannot hold as much water vapour as warmer air, so the water vapour in the cooled air immediately surrounding the glass condenses into liquid form. The water molecules in the air surrounding the glass lose thermal energy to the cool surface and convert from a gas to a liquid.

Condensation is thus the opposite process of evaporation, in which water is absorbed into the air. We see the same principle at work in nature, as Chris

When **glass** breaks, why don't the **pieces** fit back together perfectly?

We received a wonderful response to this Imponderable from retired engineer Harold Blake. The key point he makes is to remember that while glass appears to be inflexible, it does bend and change shape. If you throw a ball through a plate glass window, the glass will try to accommodate the force thrust upon it; it will bend. But if bent beyond its limits, glass shatters or ruptures.

At the point that the glass breaks, the glass's shape is distorted but the break is a perfect fracture – the parts would fit back together again. But as soon as the glass shatters, the parts begin to minimise their distortion and return to the unstressed state.

When the pieces return to their unstressed state, the fracture is no longer 'perfect'. Like a human relationship, things are never quite the same after a break-up.

Blake points out that other seemingly inflexible materials show the same tendencies as glass. Ceramics, pottery and metals, for example, also distort and then return to a sightly altered 'original' configuration.

Ballas, a doctoral candidate in physics at Vanderbilt University, explains: 'Dew forms for essentially the same reason, so in a way the "sweat" on the glass is a miniature dew. You may notice that the "sweat line" on the glass forms precisely at the cold beverage line.'

Dr Tom LeCompte, Research Assistant Professor of Physics at the University of Illinois, told *Imponderables* that the colder the outside of the glass gets from the ice or drink inside, the more condensation occurs:

> The [amount of] cooling depends on the material of the glass. An aluminium can, a good conductor of heat and cold, filled with cold drink, will sweat more than a Styrofoam cup. [Styrofoam is a poor conductor of heat and cold, which is why it is slow to change temperature whether containing scalding-hot coffee or the coldest beer.] It is possible to get a Styrofoam cup to sweat but it takes effort – filling the cup with liquid nitrogen (at –196°C) will do the trick.

No thanks, Tom. We'll stick to coffee and Diet Coke.

The only other significant variable in determining the quantity of sweat is the relative humidity in the air. The more humid the ambient air is (i.e. the more water vapour there is in the air), the more the glasses will sweat. This explains why glasses, as well as humans, tend to sweat more in summer.

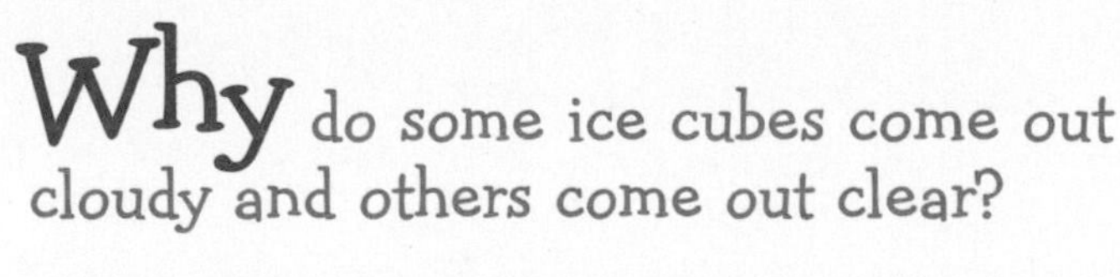

Why do some ice cubes come out cloudy and others come out clear?

A caller on a Cleveland, Ohio, radio show first confronted us with this problem. We admitted we weren't sure about the answer, but subsequent callers all had strong convictions about the matter. The only problem was that they all had *different* convictions.

One caller insisted that the mineral content of the water determined the opacity of the cube, but this theory doesn't explain why all the cubes from the same water source don't come out either cloudy or clear.

Two callers insisted the temperature of the water when put into the freezer was the critical factor.

Unfortunately, they couldn't agree about whether it was the hot water or the cold water that yielded clear ice.

We finally decided to go to an expert who confirmed what we expected – all the callers were wrong. Dr John Hallet, of the Atmospheric Ice Laboratory of the Desert Research Institute in Reno, Nevada, informed us that the key factor in cloud formation is the temperature of the freezer. When ice forms slowly, it tends to freeze first at one edge. Air bubbles found in a solution in the water have time to rise and escape. The result is clear ice cubes.

The clouds in ice cubes are the result of air bubbles formed as ice is freezing. When water freezes rapidly, freezing starts at more than one end, and water residuals are trapped in the middle of the cube, preventing bubble loss. The trapped bubbles make the cube appear cloudy.

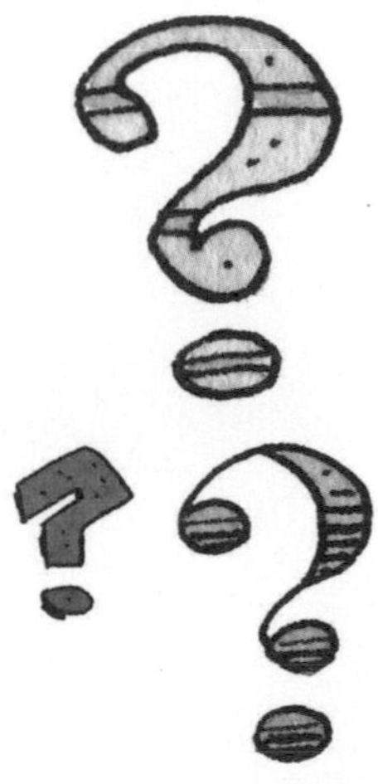

All our favourite pastimes seem so perfectly simple and clear – that is, until you try to explain the game to a newcomer. So, Mr or Ms Sports Expert, tell us: Why are there 18 holes in golf? Or why are tennis balls fuzzy? And where did the Olympic torch relay come from? You'll enjoy the answers.

sport

Why are there 18 holes on a golf course?

In Scotland, the home of golf, courses were originally designed with varying numbers of holes, depending on how much land was available. Some golf courses, according to United States Golf Association Librarian Janet Seagle, had as few as five holes.

The most prestigious Scottish golf club, the Royal and Ancient Golf Club of St Andrews, originally had 22 holes. On 4 October 1764, the course was reduced to 18 holes in order to lengthen each fairway and make play more challenging. As a desire to codify the game grew, 18 holes was adopted as the standard after the St Andrews model.

Why do golfers yell 'fore' when warning of an errant shot?

This expression, popularised by former US President Gerald Ford, actually started as an English military term. When the troops were firing in lines, the command ''ware before' (short for 'beware before') indicated that it might be prudent for the front line to kneel so that the second line wouldn't blow their heads off.

'Fore' is simply a shortened version of the 'before' in ''ware before.'

Why do golf balls have dimples?

Because dimples are cute? No. We should have known better than to think that golfers, who are known to wear orange trousers, would worry about appearances.

Dimples provide greater aerodynamic lift and consistency of flight than a smooth ball. Jacque Hetric, Director of Public Relations at Spalding, notes that the dimple pattern, regardless of where the ball is hit, provides a consistent rotation of the ball after it is struck.

Janet Seagle, of the United States Golf Association, says that other types of patterned covers were also used at one time. One was called a 'mesh', another the 'bramble'. Although all three were once commercially available, 'the superiority of the dimpled cover in flight made it the dominant cover design'.

Although golfers love to feign that they are interested in accuracy, they lust after power: dimpled golf balls travel farther as well as straighter than smooth balls. Those cute dimples will stay in place until somebody finds something better.

Is netball just a girls' version of basketball?

Netball is indeed a women's version of basketball, which was invented by a Canadian teacher named James Naismith in 1890. Netballing legend has it that the women's game came about in 1895 when Clara Baer, a PE teacher at Newcomb Girls' College in New Orleans, wrote to Naismith asking for a copy of the rules. He drew her a sketch of a basketball court showing the 'zones' which, as a matter of tactics, certain players ought to patrol. Baer supposedly misunderstood Naismith's sketch, taking it to mean that players were confined to those areas. Thus was invented 'zoning', the key difference between basketball and netball.

But that story is not entirely true. Baer did write to Naismith – but to ask permission to publish her own set of rules for girls' basketball. As for the zoning rule, it was invented as early as 1891 by another American educationalist named Senda Berenson as a way of making basketball less boisterous, and more ladylike. This was the key requirement for girls' sports in the late-Victorian era: that they provide females with a form of exercise to be enjoyed with grace and gentility – and also watched with total decorum. This requirement was most strongly insisted upon in Britain. American-style women's basketball developed into the autonomous sport of netball only after it was exported to English schools at the turn of the twentieth century.

Why is the scoring system in tennis so odd?

Tennis as we know it today is barely more than 100 years old. A Welshman, Major Walter Clopton Wingfield, devised the game as a diversion for his guests to play on his lawn before the real purpose for the get-together – a pheasant shoot. Very quickly, however, the members of the Wimbledon Cricket Club adopted Wingfield's game for use on their own under-utilised lawns, empty since croquet had waned in popularity in the late eighteenth century.

Long before Wingfield, however, there were other forms of tennis. The word 'tennis' first appeared in a poem by John Gower in 1399, and Chaucer's characters spoke of playing 'rackets' in 1380. Court tennis (also known as 'real' tennis) dates back to the Middle Ages. That great athlete Henry VIII was a devotee of the game. Court tennis was an indoor game featuring an asymmetrical rectangular cement court with a sloping roof, a hard ball, a lopsided racket and windows on the walls that came into play. Very much a gentleman's sport, the game is still played by a few diehards.

Lawn tennis's strange scoring system was clearly borrowed from court tennis. Although court tennis used a 15-point system, the scoring system was a little different from modern scoring. Each point in a game was worth 15 points (while modern tennis progresses 15-30-40-game, court tennis progressed 15-30-45-game). Instead of the current three or five sets of six games each, court tennis matches were six sets of four games each.

The most accepted theory for explaining the scoring system is that it reflected a preoccupation with astronomy, and particularly with the sextant (one-sixth of a circle). One-sixth of a circle is, of course, 60 degrees (the number of points in a court tennis game). Because the victor would have to win six sets of four games each, or 24 points, and each point was worth 15 points, the game concluded when the winner had 'completed' a circle of 360 degrees (24 x 15).

Writings by Italian Antonio Scaino indicate that the sextant scoring system was firmly in place as early as 1555. When the score of a game is tied after six points in modern tennis, we call it 'deuce' – the Italians already had an equivalent in the sixteenth century, a *due* (in other words, two points were needed to win). Somewhere along the line, however, the geometric progression of individual game points was dropped. Instead of the third point scoring 45, it became worth forty. According to the *Official Encyclopedia of Tennis*, it was most likely dropped to the lower number for the ease of announcing scores out loud, because '40' could not be confused with any other number. In the early 1700s, the court tennis set was extended to six games, obscuring the astronomical origins of the scoring system.

There have been many attempts to simplify the scoring system in order to entice new fans. The World Pro Championship League tried the table-tennis scoring system of 21-point matches, but neither the scoring system nor the league survived.

Perhaps the most profound scoring change in the past century has been the tie-breaker. The United States Tennis Association's Middle States section, in 1968, experimented with sudden-death play-offs, which for the first time in modern tennis history allowed a player who had won all of his regulation service games to lose a set. The professionals adopted the tie-breaker in 1970, and it is used in almost every tournament today.

Why are tennis balls fuzzy?

The core of a tennis ball is made of a compound consisting of rubber, synthetic materials and about 10 chemicals. The compound is extruded into a barrel-shaped pellet that is then formed into two half-shells.

The edges of the two half-shells are coated with a latex adhesive, then put together and cured in a double-chambered press under strictly controlled temperature and air-pressure conditions. The inner chamber is pressurised to 13 psi (pounds per square inch), so that the air is trapped inside and the two halves are fused together at the same pressure.

Once the two halves have been pressed together to form one sphere, the surface of the sphere is roughened so that the fuzz will stick to it better. The core is then dipped into a cement compound and oven-dried to prepare for the cover application.

The fuzzy material is felt, a combination of wool, nylon and Dacron woven together into rolls. The felt is cut into a figure-eight shape (one circular piece of felt wouldn't fit as snugly on a ball), and the edges of the felt are coated with a seam adhesive. The cores and edges of the two felt strips are mated, the felt is bonded to the core, and the seam adhesive is cured, securing all the materials and for the first time yielding a sphere that looks like a tennis ball.

After the balls are cured, they are steamed in a large tumbler and fluffed in order to raise the nap on the felt, giving the balls their fuzzy appearance. Different manufacturers fluff their balls to varying degrees. The balls are then sealed in airtight cans pressurised at 12 to 15 psi, with the goal of keeping the balls at 10 to 12 psi.

The single most expensive ingredient in a tennis ball is the felt. Many other sports do quite well with unfuzzy rubber balls. In the earliest days of tennis, balls had a leather cover and were stuffed with all sorts of things, including human hair. So why do tennis ball manufacturers bother with the fuzz?

Before the felt is added, a tennis ball has a hard, sleek surface. One of the main purposes of the fuzz is to slow the ball down. The United States Tennis Association maintains strict rules concerning the bound of tennis balls. One regulation stipulates, 'The ball shall have a bound of more than 53 inches and less than 58 inches [1.35–1.47 m] when dropped 100 inches [2.54 m] upon a concrete base.' The fluffier the felt, the more wind resistance it offers, decreasing not only the bound but also the speed of the ball. If the felt were too tightly compacted, the ball would have a tendency to skip on the court.

A second important reason for fuzzy tennis balls is that the fluffy nap increases racquet control. Every time a tennis ball hits a racquet the strings momentarily grip the ball, and the ball compresses. With a harder, sleeker surface, the ball would have a tendency to skip off the racquet and minimise the skill of the player.

A third contribution of fuzz is the least important to a good player but important to us refugees from hardball sports like racquetball and squash. When you get hit hard by a fuzzy tennis ball, you may want to cry, but you don't feel like you're going to die.

Why don't football players suffer long-term brain injuries from heading the ball?

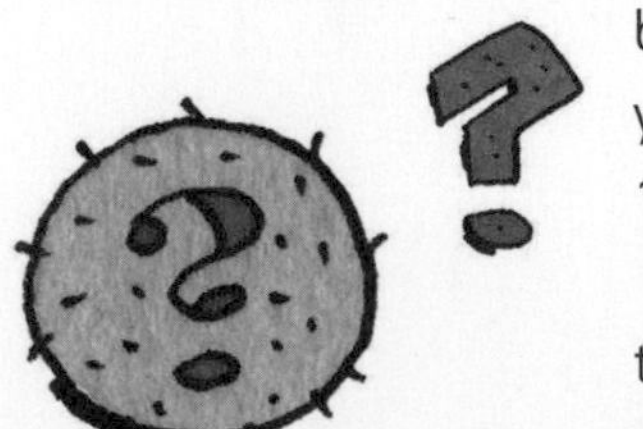

One of the basic skills of football is the header, which is often used to play a ball that has been kicked high into the air. Heading seems counter-instinctive to us because we usually try to avoid a flying object coming for our head. And when you consider that a ball kicked by a highly skilled player can travel up to 100 km/h, it seems downright dangerous.

Numerous studies of professional players, who may head the ball thousands of times during their careers, have been inconclusive, but the issue occasionally makes headlines. In 1998, Billy MacPhail, a former Glasgow Celtic player, lost a legal battle to claim benefits for dementia that he said was due to heading old-style leather balls.

Then there was the case of Jeff Astle, who played for England in the 1960s and was known for scoring goals with his head. When Astle died suddenly in 2002 at the age of 59, the coroner ruled the cause of death was an 'industrial disease', suggesting that repeated heading of balls during his professional career was the cause of his subsequent neurological decline.

According to the experts, good technique is the essential to heading the ball safely. Rehabilitation psychologist Michael J Asken told *Imponderables*:

> Proper heading technique involves use of the frontal bone to contact the ball, the neck muscles to restrict head motion and the muscles of the lower body to position the torso in line with the head and neck to increase the resistant mass and decrease acceleration of the head.

Surprisingly, there has been little research on the effects of heading the football on children, but the Florida Institute of Technology is working to fill the gap. Dr Frank Webbe, a sports psychologist at the university, says it's too early for a definitive answer to the question, but he already has reached some conclusions:

> *First*, children should not be using their heads (and the brain inside) as a tool until and unless the supporting structures have sufficient mass and strength to withstand such treatment. Exactly when a child will develop sufficient underlying support varies with age, gender and individual factors. A few might be ready by age 12, many won't be ready until after age 15.
>
> *Second*, in most leagues the size of players varies tremendously. Some 11-year-olds are as big as adults; some are very small and petite. When a very large child kicks a ball with full force and a very small child with poorly developed neck musculature attempts to head it, a concussive injury could ensue.
>
> *Third*, anyone who heads should receive good technical instruction from a knowledgeable coach. Proper technique can prevent many injuries.

Webbe, a former football referee and coach, also has a personal opinion:

> Children under 14 should not be heading the ball in league games. Many will learn and practise the technique, but practice headings are rarely of the intensity and with the prospect of injury that occurs in games.

Just in case you do find a football flying towards you and you can't resist the urge to head it, Dan Metcalfe, an English football coach, offers this helpful tip:

> Look at the line of the eyebrows and then move the point of contact one finger width higher than the eyebrows in the middle of the head. This is the hardest part of the head and also allows the player to keep their eyes on the ball as it approaches.

Why are so many football teams called United?

There are actually fewer teams called United than you might think. In the four divisions of the English league there are just ten, and there are two United teams in Scotland. But though the United suffix applies only to a small fraction of top-flight teams, the word is nevertheless indelibly associated with professional football. Everyone knows you are talking about football when you say that you support United – even if they are not certain which United gets you excited.

This is surely because the most famous and widely supported football team in the world is a United. Manchester United has a long and distinguished history – and it is to Mark Wylie, curator of the Manchester United Museum and Tour Centre, that *Imponderables* turned to discover more about the origin of the strange term. Is it just that, in football's infancy, several teams got together to make a better squad? Not exactly, says Mr Wylie:

> Manchester United was founded in 1878 and was then called Newton Heath. It was a club for the coach and wagon workers of the Newton Heath depot of the Lancashire and Yorkshire Railway Company. We often get letters from people who have heard that their grandfather or great-grandfather played for Newton Heath, but there were other teams with similar names. There was a side called Newton Heath Local, and another one called Newton Heath Athletic. They had nothing to do with the Newton Heath that became Manchester United; they did not unite with them to make a bigger Manchester side, or anything like that.
>
> So Manchester United is a bit of an odd one. The word United does not signify that the team is an amalgamation of two or

more teams. Whereas Newcastle United, for example, did indeed come about when two separate clubs – Newcastle West End and Newcastle East End – merged to form a unified Newcastle side. Lots of teams amalgamated with others at the end of the 19th century, partly in connection with the formation of the Football League in 1888.

Manchester United took its present name in 1902. By the turn of the century it had cut its links with the rail company, and was no longer based in Newton Heath, so a name change seemed appropriate. Many names were considered, among them Manchester Central and Manchester Celtic (though the club had no Scottish or Irish associations at all). Everyone agreed that Manchester United was the best name – but we were not the first United. I'm not sure who was, but I can tell you that in our case the word "united" does not mean anything at all. ’

So Man U borrowed its suffix arbitrarily from an already established team simply because it sounded good. But if a catchy name was all the club was looking for, why not plump for the dash and romance of, say, 'Manchester Rovers' or 'Manchester Wanderers'? Mr Wylie has an answer for that one:

‘ Most of the early teams in the League were northern. Though the game started in public schools, it was enthusiastically taken up by workers in the heavy industries, once they got their Saturday afternoons off. Many teams have their roots in the "muscular Christianity" of the late-Victorian era. Vicars would start a football club as an alternative to the Scouts or the Boys' Brigade. It was a way of keeping lads out of pubs and out of trouble, a way of saving the working classes from themselves.

So, in the early days of organised football, there were many such teams that had no regular ground to play on. They played on a different pitch every week, even when they were at home. Because they moved around, they got nicknamed "the wanderers" or "the rovers". It was a way to distinguish them from some other local team that had a fixed abode. But over time the name stuck – hence Blackburn Rovers, Bolton Wanderers. Newton Heath always had a ground of their own – though they wandered in the sense that, being a railway team,

> they could easily travel to matches in other parts of the north. They often played Crewe Alexandra, also a railway team – founded at a meeting in a Crewe hotel called the Alexandra. ’

Very interesting. But the question remains: which was the first team to call itself United? *Imponderables* has looked into it, and it turns out that the original is not Newcastle – though their East End and West End adopted the name ten years before Manchester, in 1892. In fact, the first United is not even a football team. The first ever sporting organisation to use the word in its title was the Sheffield United Cricket Club. This institution came about in 1854, when a member of the Sheffield Cricket Club proposed that several clubs get together and lease a ground away from the city centre, at a place that had 'the advantage of being free from smoke'. Three cricketing fraternities joined the venture: Sheffield itself, Hallam and the Wednesday Cricket Club, so called because that was the day the club generally played. They leased some real estate from the Duke of Norfolk at Bramall Lane, on the rural southern fringe of the city.

The players of the summer game then wanted a sport that would suit the winter months – and the backers of the new ground needed to put on games so that they could pay the lease. Regular winter football was the obvious way to fulfill both needs. So it was that both Sheffield United and Sheffield Wednesday football clubs emerged from the Sheffield United Cricket Club. The first football match to be played at the new ground took place as early as 1862, which makes Bramall Lane (now the home of Sheffield United) the oldest major football stadium in the world. And as for the rest of the round dozen Uniteds in the football leagues of England and Scotland – Manchester, Newcastle, West Ham, Leeds, Colchester, Southend, Carlisle, Rotherham, Scunthorpe, Dundee and Ayr – all of them are paying a small homage to Sheffield United, the first team to proclaim oneness in its name, and one of the most venerable football clubs in the land.

What do the names of other football teams signify?

Modern football began as a middle-class game. The first clubs were associations of old boys from the public schools and the colleges, or were formed on a regimental basis by army officers. All those teams – Royal Engineers, Old

Etonians, Oxford University – are now extinct so far as professional football is concerned. Most of the professional clubs we know today have working-class origins, and many have their roots in scratch teams put together by factory workers. Arsenal is the only one whose name preserves that connection: it was founded by young foundry workers (most of them from the north of England) at the Royal Arsenal in Woolwich, south London. For a while the team was called Woolwich Arsenal but became simply Arsenal when the club moved to north London in 1913. West Ham United, which was nurtured in the Thames Iron Works, preserves the fact like a fossil in its punning nickname 'The Hammers'.

The name of Derby County contains in 'county' a clue that it started as a cricket club. Tottenham Hotspur began in the same way, playing on ground belonging to the descendants of Sir Henry Percy – Shakespeare's 'Harry Hotspur'. Some resonant names, such as West Bromwich Albion, are purely geographical – but how much more fun it would have been had the team kept the name West Bromwich Strollers. Queen's Park Rangers, on the other hand, was probably right to lose its association with the institution that gave it birth: the Droop Street Board School.

Why do basketballs have fake seams? Do they have a practical purpose or are they merely decorative?

A caller on a radio chat show asked this question indignantly, as if the ball industry were purposely perpetrating a fraud, at worst, and foisting unnecessary decoration on a ball, at best. Before you accuse basketball manufacturers of making a needless fashion statement, consider that most basketball players need all the help they can get manipulating a basketball. A basketball is too big for all but a few players to grasp with their fingers. Those 'fake' seams are there to help you grip the ball.

Basketball manufacturers make two kinds of seams, narrow and wide. US National Basketball Association professionals prefer the narrow-channel seams, while many amateurs, particularly young people with small hands, use wide-channel seams.

What is the origin of the Olympic torch relay?

The torch relay is one of the most prominent symbols of the Olympic Games, and it fairly crackles with the grandeur and ideals of ancient Greece. In truth, its origins were considerably more modern and less high-minded – the relay began as a Nazi propaganda stunt in 1936, when the Games were held in Berlin.

Chancellor Adolf Hitler told Dr Carl Diem, the President of the Olympic Organising Committee, that he wanted to impress the world with the magnificence of the Third Reich. One of Diem's ideas, seconded by Propaganda Minister Joseph Goebbels, was to have the Olympic flame in Greece carried by torch relay to Berlin.

With Goebbels' publicity machine broadcasting glowing radio reports all along the route, the flame was carried by 3075 runners, from Greece to the Olympiastadion in Berlin, where it was used to light a colossal brazier. Among the 100,000 spectators cheering the fiery spectacle was the Führer himself.

The torches, which were supposed to signify unity and cooperation among nations, were made by Alfried Krupp, the German munitions manufacturer that helped arm Germany for both world wars.

In his book *The Naked Olympics*, Tony Perrotte writes:

> The "revived" 1936 torch race perfectly fit the Nazi design for the Olympics as a showcase for the New Germany. With its aura of ancient mysticism, the rite linked Nazism to the civilised glories of classical Greece, which the Reich's academics were arguing had been an Aryan wonderland.

Why is the javelin pointed at both ends?

The javelin throw is one of the oldest of athletic endeavours, going back at least 3000 years to the Mycenaeans. The ancient javelins were pointed at only one end – as befit their original use as weapons for hunting and warfare.

It wasn't until 1954 that the tail end got a tip. In that year, Dick Held, an American engineer, began experimenting with javelin design. 'When I first started designing and building javelins, the rules were quite simple and the javelin was little more than a wooden stick with a grip and a metal point,' Held, who is now retired, told *Imponderables*.

He gave the javelin a tapered tail to improve its aerodynamics, giving it less drag and more lift during flight. The changes were wildly successful. Suddenly javelins were flying huge distances. For some perspective, at the 1908 Olympic Games in London, the winning throw was about 50 m. At the 1956 Games, the gold medal toss was 86 m.

Ominously, athletes were throwing javelins the entire length of sports stadiums to the point that spectators were endangered. The International Association of Athletics Federations stepped in and ordered a redesign so that the javelin would under-perform. This was achieved by moving the centre of gravity forward and making the tail section thicker.

Dr Nathan Schneeberger, a javelin enthusiast and coach from St Paul, Minnesota, told *Imponderables* that the javelin is a unique blend of new and ancient design:

> ‘We owe the metal point on the tail end of the javelin to the quest for distance by modern-day engineers, and we owe the metal point on the front end to the quest for functionality of our ancestors. Nevertheless, a carbon fibre javelin is one of the few objects from the twenty-first century that could be transported back a few thousand years in time and still make perfect sense. My iPod would be a novel curiosity (especially after the battery died), but my javelin would be instantly understood and valued.’

In track events with staggered starts, why do the outside runners cut to the inside immediately rather than follow a more gradual, straight line?

In middle-distance track events, such as the 800 m, the athletes start the race in lanes. Because the runners in the outside lanes must travel a greater distance than those on the inside, the starting lines are staggered, with those closest to the inside farthest back at the start. At the 'break point', usually right after a full turn and at the beginning of the straightaway, runners in the other lanes have the opportunity to break to the inside to save running distance.

But sharp-eyed reader Dov Rabinowitz wrote to us:

> ‘The outside runners always seem to start moving towards the inside at the beginning of a long straight section, and by the

time they are about one-quarter to one-half of the way along, they have moved completely to the inside of the track, so that the runners are nearly single file.'

Rabinowitz theorises that runners waste extra steps to break to the inside prematurely, and that a sharper turn wastes some of the runner's forward momentum.

We posed Dov's Imponderable to four full-time running coaches and even more runners. All of the coaches agreed with Greg McMillan, a coach, runner and exercise scientist, who preaches simple geometry:

'The question is a good one and the situation drives many coaches crazy. Every track athlete is taught that once you are allowed to "break for the rail", the athlete should run at a gradual diagonal to the inside lane. Since the point where the athlete may break from running in lanes is usually after the first curve (as in the 800 m race), the best thing to do is run in a straight line towards the rail at the far end of the back stretch (around the 200 m mark on most tracks). This will create the shortest distance around the track.'

Running extra metres is an obvious hindrance to winning. So why do runners do it? McMillan thinks that the fly in the ointment is often psychological:

'[The straight-line approach] sounds easy and every athlete will agree with it. But in the real world, this guideline goes out the window when the race starts. Most athletes will agree that it's the "safety in the pack mentality". The runner wants to get near the competition and feels vulnerable out on the open track. So while it doesn't make logical sense to make a drastic cut towards the rail, the emotions of the athlete often cause this to happen. Some runners are better at controlling this urge than others.'

Roy Benson, President of Running Ltd, based in Atlanta, Georgia, has coached professionally for more than 40 years, and says that most runners have strategy rather than mathematics on their minds: 'Those in the outer lanes are usually trying to cut off runners on their left and take the lead as soon as possible.'

But you can find yourself in traffic problems if you stay on the inside too. Gordon Edwards, a coach and runner from Charlotte, North Carolina, wrote about the tactical dangers of breaking to the inside too soon:

> It would be impossible and hazardous to cut immediately to the first lane as you might impede other runners or bump into them. If you watch distance races, many runners run in the second or third lanes at times, even on the curves, for strategic reasons. Yes, they will run farther doing this, but sometimes it is a necessary tactic.

One of the reasons why runners might not break to the extreme inside is so that they can draught behind the lead runner, just as racing car drivers 'leech' on the lead car. Rather than risk clipping the heels of the lead runner, it can be safer to be on the side. McMillan says that draughting is especially effective on windy days, and the benefits of running in the slipstream of another runner can outweigh the extra few metres the racer on the outside must complete.

We couldn't entice any of the runners to admit that they scooted to the inside prematurely for psychological reasons. All of them understood the merits of the gradual drift to the inside, and several chided other runners for darting to the inside prematurely:

> Every coach I ever had hammered home the distance-saving value of taking a tangent rather than cutting in; there's plenty of time ... to make a cut, if the traffic pattern dictates it, but the farther away from the break point you are, the better, particularly because so many runners have a sheep-like mentality and break all at once; let them stumble all over each other fighting for the rail.

But the runners were afraid of traffic problems. One used a road analogy:

> [This problem is] not dissimilar from merging onto a road ... Although the straight diagonal line is slightly shorter, a quick analysis of the runners you are merging with might make one

decide to cut in a bit quicker to avoid a potential bump, or to wait a bit, then cut in, also to avoid someone. In theory, if everyone is exactly even when they all go to cut in, and they all take the straight diagonal line to the pole, well, then that's one big jam up!'

Some runners, draughting be damned, prefer racing from the front. If the runner feels he is in the lead, but is on the outside, he might want to cut over 'prematurely' to get to the inside immediately and force competitors to try to pass him on the outside. But runners realise that it is possible to be 'boxed-in' too – stuck in the inside lane, in a pack, with runners in front and outside of them, preventing acceleration.

Many a horserace has been lost because the jockey couldn't keep his mount from veering wide. Peter Sherry, a coach and former medallist at the World University Games, disagrees somewhat with the premise of the Imponderable. He thinks that the incidence of 'elite' runners cutting to the left prematurely is lower than we're implying, and that it's more typical of high school races or races with less experienced athletes. He argues that if an elite runner darts to the inside quickly, there's usually a good reason – usually:

'that a runner wants to make sure he gets a position on the rail before the race gets to the first turn. If you get caught on the outside of the pack during the turn, you will be running farther than someone on the inside rail.'

For more information about the configuration of running tracks in general and staggered starts in particular, go to www.trackinfo.org/marks.html.

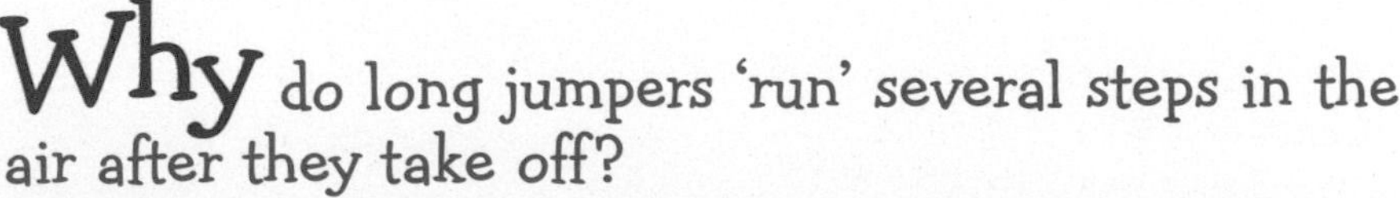

Why do long jumpers 'run' several steps in the air after they take off?

This motion is called the 'hitch-kick', and it is employed by long jumpers to cut down on the body's natural tendency to rotate sideways while in flight.

It will help if you picture a long jump in your mind. There is the dazzling sprint down the runway, then the abrupt planting of one foot on the board. That leg stops suddenly for an instant, but the other leg and the upper body continue moving. The effect is to twist the body sideways, which is known as forward rotation.

Ed Luna, the long jump coach for the University of California at Riverside, told *Imponderables* that jumpers want to remain facing forward so they can extend their legs as far as possible before they hit the sand:

> "The purpose of inflight arm and leg action is to counteract forward rotation, maintain balance, and put the jumper into the optimum position at landing with the feet extended well beyond the athlete's centre of mass. The hitch-kick fights forward rotation by creating counter rotation through the cycling of the arms and legs."

Why is English cricket traditionally organised on county lines rather than city by city?

Cricket, unlike football and rugby, is a pre-industrial game, played in England before the rise of the large conurbations such as Manchester and Leeds. It has its roots in the rural byways of southern counties, where villagers played their cricket in open fields, with no boundaries and often no fixed location for the game at all. It was always a countryman's sport.

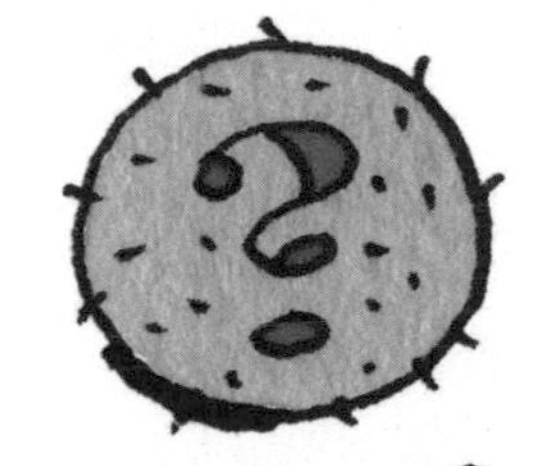

For more background on the county origins of cricket, we went to Dr Andrew Hignell, the secretary of the Association of Cricket Statisticians and Historians as well as the archivist of Glamorgan County Cricket Club:

> "The county as the organisational unit for cricket begins as far back as the 18th century. Wealthy aristocrats would set a wager on a game, and raise an eleven from their rural estates. The teams formed in this way might describe themselves as "Eleven Gentlemen of Kent" or "Eleven Gentlemen of Sussex".
>
> The rise of county cricket was also given a boost by the phenomenon of "country house cricket", whereby landowners in mid-to-late Victorian times would gain social kudos by having a cricket match as part of the entertainment. Let's say the Duke of Beaufort is staging a game at Badminton House against a team all of whom were drawn from Bedfordshire. That team

> might very well call itself simply Bedfordshire. Even when a county club had not yet been formed, the county was important as what you could term the "catchment area". That is not to say that there were no city-based teams. Dr WG Grace, for example, put together a team in London that played at Crystal Palace – but even then he called it "London County".

The first mention of a 'county championship' occurs in a report in a Maidstone newspaper in 1837, in connection with a three-way competition between teams from Sussex, Kent and Nottinghamshire. Such events became more common and more feasible after the spread of railways made it possible for players and spectators alike to travel further afield. These early inter-county tournaments were money-making events. Entrepreneurs hired the teams and provided the cash to build permanent venues such as Lord's and Edgbaston. It made commercial sense to site the grounds in urban centres of population, also to hire the best players in any given county – people wanted to see a good game, after all. The business rationale of it all meant that a Kentish team, say, would no longer be just eleven keen fellows who hailed from Kent, but eleven paid players who were the best Kent had to offer. From here it was short step to a fully fledged county cricket championship. As Dr Hignell elaborates:

> The official County Championship was constituted in 1889, and first played in 1890. Eight counties were initially involved: Gloucestershire, Kent, Lancashire, Nottinghamshire, Middlesex, Sussex, Surrey and York. Cricket was organised into classes, like old-fashioned train carriages. First-class matches were those involving the teams in the County Championship. Second-class cricket was made up of teams in the "Minor County Championship". Some of those were over time promoted to the first-class game: Somerset in 1891; my own county, Glamorgan, in 1921 and Durham in 1992. Third-class cricket is all the rest.

The county-based system was reinforced by the rules on recruitment. Until well after the Second World War, an up-and-coming player could not play for a county other than one in which he was born without written permission from that county's cricket club. In other words, every county had first refusal on its native talent. This tradition helped to preserve the geographical structure of the game of cricket, even as British governments redrew and reorganised the counties, undermining the very idea of a county as a territory towards which a person might have feelings of patriotism or loyalty. There are surely many cricket fans who passionately support Leicestershire or Hampshire, but who would be hard put to draw its boundaries on a map – and spare a thought for the followers of Middlesex, a county that exists now as little more than a postal district.

Why are cricket bats traditionally made of willow?

In the early days of cricket, when bowlers rolled the ball along the ground and the batsman's tool resembled a hockey stick, all kinds of timber were used to make the bat. Willow emerged as the best wood for the job in the 18th century, when the rules of the game were codified and bowlers were allowed to toss the ball through the air. This development meant that batsmen needed to be armed with something that was light enough to swing, but at the same time heavy enough to give some oomph when it struck the ball. Willow is not a dense wood, and so is light; it is tough and, once treated and 'knocked in', unlikely to split or splinter. Willow is, in short, the ideal bat-making material. It became almost universal by 1800.

But not just any willow will do. The timber used for the best blades is a cultivar of one particular species, *Salix alba* var. *caerulea*. The trees are grown commercially, and carefully managed. Each sapling has to be set dead straight in the ground; while young, the saplings need to be protected from the rasp-like teeth of rabbits and deer. And each spring all buds must be rubbed off the trunk so that it produces no branches, and the timber it yields has no knots. It takes 15 years to grow a cricket bat willow – not all that long when one considers that the finest bats will make many a century.

Why are there six balls in an over?

There is no reason why an over has to consist of six balls, and this is one aspect of the game of cricket that has been remarkably fluid until very recently. In the first days of organised cricket, at the beginning of the 18th century, four balls was the norm. But the norm was no more than a custom: there was no hard and fast rule. One of the first recorded instances of the six-ball over in a top-flight game was a match between Eton and Harrow, played at Lord's in 1827. As cricket became more of a spectator sport there was a pressing reason for increasing the number of balls in an over: four deliveries between changeovers meant that too much time was expended on the dull business of repositioning the field.

In 1884 the custodian of the game's laws, the Marylebone Cricket Club or MCC, decreed a standard five-ball over for first-class cricket. But this nod to the decimal system seemed oddly continental, and an over was increased to six balls in 1900. Australia adopted an eight-ball over in the first decade of the 20th century; New Zealand followed suit in 1924, and South Africa in 1937. England decided to try out the colonial eight-ball over in 1939, but the experiment was cut short by the outbreak of war and never revived. Eight-ball overs continued to be legal, and were common in Australia and New Zealand (depending on conditions of play), until 1980. It was only in 2000 that the six-ball over was enshrined, finally and immutably, in the laws of the game.

How did the rugby ball get its distinctive shape?

When the boys of Rugby School first devised their own version of football, they turned to a local bootmaker, William Gilbert, to supply the ball. Tradition says that its ovoid form was dictated by the shape of the pig's bladder used to make it. But inflated pigs' bladders were also contained within the balls used for the 'kicking game', and these needed to be as spherical as possible. So the shape of the balls used in rugby must have come about primarily as a result of the design of the leather casing.

Gilbert used long curved panels of leather, which lent the ball a 'plum' shape – rounder and less pointy than a modern ball, but definitely not spherical. This shape naturally suited Rugby School's 'carrying game', because the ball could be firmly gripped or tucked under the arm. An oval ball was standard by 1835, if a passing reference in *Tom Brown's Schooldays* is to be believed: '... the new ball you may see lie there, quite by itself, in the middle, pointing towards the school goal'.

The invention of vulcanised rubber in the 1860s made it much easier to standardise the shape of a ball. Richard Lindon, another Rugby bootmaker, became the principal supplier of both spherical soccer balls and oval rugby balls. The shape of the rugby ball became more definitely pointy as proponents of the game strove to differentiate their game from Association Football, and a rule that insisted a rugby ball be oval was finally adopted by the Rugby Football Union in 1892. The best balls still bear the name of Gilbert, the cobbler who made balls as a sideline when not mending the shoes of the privileged boys in the nearby school.

In chess, why is the queen more powerful than the king? Given the ancient roots of the game, shouldn't the king be the strongest piece?

Chess, as most people play it, is a gentle, cerebral pursuit – a pastime fit for the senior common room or a park bench on a sunny afternoon. But at its root chess is a wargame, a battle between two armies.

In ancient India (where most authorities think chess originated) the earliest form of the game was known as *chaturanga*, which means 'four regiments'. The pawns represented the infantry; the knight the cavalry (naturally); the bishop the war elephants (to this day, the Russian word for the bishop is *slon*, which means 'elephant'); and the rook or castle represented the chariots. In this scheme, the king, or *raja*, stood at the back, like a general directing the movements of his armies. The piece by his side was not his queen but his *mantri*, which means minister. It could only move one diagonal space at a time.

In this form the game came first to Persia, then to the Arab world. The word *raja* was translated into Persian as *shah*. Though it does not look much like it, the Persian *shah* is the origin of the English word chess. The Sanskrit word *mantri*, meanwhile, was rendered *farzin* in Persian, then as *firz* in Arabic. It still denoted a king's right-hand man (rather than woman): *firz* is the root of the English word 'vizier'. The Moors took the game of chess with them into Spain when they invaded in the 8th century. It was enthusiastically taken up by the Spanish nobility, and was quickly adopted as an aristocratic pastime throughout Europe.

For centuries, Europeans played the game in the slow Arabic manner: players spent many moves deploying their forces, more or less regardless of their opponent. It was only well into the game that the battle really got under way. But there was something rather tiresome about this, and in the early Middle Ages players began to look for ways to liven up the contest. New versions arose: chess was played in conjunction with dice to introduce an element of chance; in some places it became the custom always to play for money; elsewhere, two-handed games were abandoned in favour of books of chess problems.

Sometime in the mid-1400s – probably in the Spanish city of Valencia – someone had a revolutionary idea. Give the *firz* new powers to move around the board: backwards and forwards, along rows and columns as well as diagonally, and as few or as many spaces as desired. This was a brilliant innovation because it did not alter the fundamental nature of the game, but made chess much faster – and much better. Now one could begin attacking almost from the first move. The new version of the game spread as rapidly as had the Arab original.

At the same time, the 'identity' of the *firz* had been changing. There was a natural tendency to see the piece next to the king as a queen: the term *regina* (queen in Latin) was used to describe the piece in a Swiss manuscript that dates as far back as the 10th century. In France, the word *firz* was sometimes rendered as *fierge*, which is close to *vierge* – 'virgin' or 'maiden'. To a medieval mind, this piece of popular etymology would have suggested Mary, mother of Jesus. And the association of the *firz* with the Queen of Heaven would have made it easier to accept the newly empowered piece as the mightiest on the board.

It has also been pointed out that Spain had a real-life model for a forceful, formidable queen in the person of Isabella of Castile, who, with her husband, Ferdinand II of Aragon, was engaged in unifying the country at the very time that the chess queen acquired her special potency. Perhaps Isabella inspired the new version of the game, in which a halting royal adviser became a swift-footed consort, a warrior queen, the guardian of the king's person.

Why is water polo so called, when it bears little resemblance to the equestrian game of polo?

Water polo grew out of a Victorian fondness for swimming exhibitions. In 1879 the London Swimming Association drew up a set of rules for an entertainment it termed 'Football in the Water'. The game was an immediate hit with the British

Where did the **butterfly** swimming **stroke** come from?

The butterfly, which is competitive swimming's newest stroke, was developed in the mid-1930s, but it wasn't allowed in the Olympics until 1956. The story of the butterfly is a good illustration of how coaches and swimmers are constantly searching for ways to improve stroke efficiency.

During the 1920s, the Japanese Olympic coaches used underwater photography to research stroke mechanics, and their efforts paid off when Japanese competitors won five of the six men's swimming gold medals at the 1932 Games in Los Angeles. It was a wake-up call to the rest of the swimming world, and one of the top US coaches – David Armbruster at the University of Iowa – began doing his own filming.

Armbruster was seeking to make the breaststroke faster. He knew that the action of bringing their arms forward underwater slowed breaststrokers down, so he came up with a method of bringing the arms forward over the water. The revised stroke (Armbruster kept the breaststroke kick) brought great improvements in speed.

The following year, Jack Sieg, an Iowa swimmer, developed a technique involving swimming on his side and beating his legs in unison similar to a fish tail. As Armbruster later explained in the book *Weissmuller to Spitz: The History and Background of the Olympic Games*:

> ‘Sieg tried the same leg action while swimming face down. Sieg synchronised his leg action with the butterfly arm action using two leg beats to each arm pull. Sieg showed the stroke speed potential by swimming 100 yards [91 m] in 60.2 seconds, but the dolphin kick was ruled illegal because the legs moved in the vertical plane.’

Within a few years, nearly every breaststroker was using this overarm butterfly action without the dolphin kick. The pure butterfly wasn't legalised for some two decades, but at the 1956 Olympics in Melbourne 'the fly' – one of swimming's most demanding and beautiful strokes – became an official event.

public, but proponents and spectators of the new sport were hard put to find a snappier, more satisfying name for it. The 'football' that the London Swimming Association had in mind was not what we regard as football, but rugby – and the expression 'water rugby' was current for a time. 'Water baseball' was also used, though the game bears even less of a resemblance to that than it does to equestrian polo. A newspaper report of a game that took place in the sea off Bournemouth in 1876 described the sport as 'aquatic handball' – an accurate label that for some reason did not stick.

In 1887 William Wilson, a pioneer of competitive swimming, codified the rules of the game for Scotland, and called it 'aquatic football'. About this time, Scottish associations began independently to use the term 'water polo'. The word 'polo' had found its way back to the mother country from India; it comes from the Balti word *pulu*, which simply means 'ball'. Who first yoked 'water' to 'polo', nobody knows. But, for the first time, the game had a name that was not derived from an established land-based sport, which must have looked like a good thing. Probably none of the Scottish swimmers knew of the equestrian game, which takes its name from the same Indian word but was only just becoming established in Britain at the time.

Wilson had made a good job of writing the rules, and in time the Scottish version of the game became the international standard. The name 'water polo' rapidly became standard too, and was the usual term by the time the game was played in the Paris Olympics of 1900.

Why does the leader in the Tour de France bicycle race wear a yellow jersey?

There is a clue on the jersey itself – the letters 'HD'. They're the initials of Henri Desgrange, who founded the Tour de France in 1903. At the time Desgrange was the Editor and owner of *L'Auto*, a daily sports newspaper, and his plan was to use the race to promote his publication.

The French specialty newspaper market was highly competitive at the turn of the last century, and to distinguish themselves from each other, dailies were printed on different-coloured newsprint. *L'Auto* appeared on bright yellow paper.

As the Tour de France grew in popularity, a problem arose for spectators. The competition was spread over some 20 days, and at any given moment it was hard to pick out the overall leader from the crowded pack of cyclists.

Complaints multiplied, and finally, in the middle of the 1919 competition, Desgrange had an entrepreneurial brainstorm: give the leader a yellow jersey – the same distinctive colour as the pages of *L'Auto*.

On 19 July 1919, the Frenchman Eugene Christophe became the first race leader to don the yellow jersey. Voilà! The yellow jersey (also known as the *maglia gialla, gelbes Trikot* or *maillot jaune*) entered the international language of cycling – and one of the sports world's oldest and most revered uniform traditions was born.

How were the various coloured belts in judo, karate and the other martial arts assigned, and what do they signify?

Although the martial arts have existed for at least 4000 years, and in structured disciplines for several centuries, the belt system originated in judo, a modern style developed by Dr Jigoro Kano in 1882, about the same time basketball was invented in the United States. Kano, a Japanese educator, had studied the older jujitsu and other martial arts for more than 20 years and wanted to create a competitive sport that emphasised athleticism rather than combat.

'Judo' stems from *ju*, which means 'gentle' or 'to give way', and *do*, the Japanese word for 'way' or 'principle'. 'Jujitsu', sometimes spelled 'joujitsu', means 'gentle practice', while 'judo' is usually translated literally as 'the gentle way'.

What's so gentle about judo? Remember that the early martial arts were used for actual combat, and the participants had considerably more to worry about than the colour of their belts: the loser of a kung fu fight often lost his life. The sport of judo, from its inception, emphasised self-defence and turning the attacker's force against the opponent. Kano also stressed the health and philosophical side of the martial arts, including morality, diet, social interaction and, of course, physical fitness. Kano promoted his beliefs in his Kodokan school, which opened in Japan in 1882.

Before Kodokan, the traditional Japanese martial arts student wore a *gi*, a loose-fitting robe, usually tied around the waist with a cloth belt. The gi was all-white, including the belt. Kano hit upon the idea of differentiating the experience and skill levels of his students by awarding different belt colours. This not only enabled students to find suitable sparring partners and to differentiate teachers from students but also introduced a tangible status symbol, a recognisable 'trophy' of accomplishment.

Kano's original belt system was relatively simple. The beginner wore a white belt and advanced to green, brown and finally black.

Within each of these rankings were various degrees of achievement. For example, there were 10 *dans* (categories) within black belt, ranging from the first to the tenth degree, but all wore the same black belt.

Kano's belt scheme eventually spread to many of the other martial arts, and to the profusion of sub-schools of judo. No overseeing body or federation mandated any consistency in colour schemes, so that variations from Kano's model were common. There is still no international organisation that specifies universal colour schemes or any exact measure of proficiency necessary to achieve any belt colour.

In some schools, a promotion of belt colour can be achieved only in competitions. In others, demonstrations of technique are emphasised. One teacher can award a promotion in some schools, while others employ committees to judge progress.

The lack of consistency in the awarding of belts has led to strange anomalies, even among serious judo practitioners. Some schools have lax standards, essentially allowing students to 'buy' a black belt. The Olympic Games judo committee has tried to monitor different schools, in order to make competitions fair, but it isn't always possible, as *Bruce Tegner's Complete Book of Judo* illustrates:

> The Olympic Games judo committee recognises a number of judo associations whose members are permitted to wear their rank belts in contest; other players must wear the white belt of the novice ... The recognition of an organisation means only that there is a formal relationship, but it does not mean the judo clubs or groups without "official" recognition are incapable of producing tournament judo players.

Several martial arts students we contacted indicated that their particular school employed eccentric colouring schemes. One mentioned that the founder of his school did not like black, so that dan belts in Tang Soo Do are midnight blue, instead; another, a practitioner of Northern Shaolin (a Chinese style), indicated that all students wear a black sash, except for the grandmaster, who wears a saffron (yellow) sash. In some schools, only the tip of the belt is coloured.

Swiss Master Zurg Ziegler (the 'Lightning Fist'), a lofty eighth-dan black belt who specialises in kung fu (Chinese) and hapkido (Korean) and owns several martial arts academies throughout the world, told *Imponderables* that before the advent of judo, belt colouring schemes were unnecessary:

> In the olden days, there was no grading at all: there were only students and teachers/masters. Your title was [given] according to your "age and generation" in martial arts, and your name was upheld with your skill. There was no belt level or colour differentiation. It just wasn't necessary because most styles were only taught to a very few – often within a single family.

If we have established that there is no consistency or uniformity in the awarding of belt colours, most judo and karate schools have a scheme not dissimilar to that used by Raymond L Walters, President of the USA-Korean Karate Association and proprietor of the Jade Dragon Martial Arts Academy in Great Falls, Montana. Here is the summary of belts used in Walters' school:

White – No knowledge
Yellow – Learning the basics
Orange – Building on the basics
Green – Developing your skills
Purple – Testing your skills
Blue – Reaching for knowledge
Brown – Refining new knowledge
Red – Understanding yourself
Red over Black – Guided self-direction
Black – Now a true student

How were these colours chosen to represent the various skill levels? Perhaps the most common explanation is that before judo was invented, martial-arts students were issued an all-white robe. According to Ziegler, in those days a student was expected to fold his uniform in a precise way after each class, forming a small, tight package tied with the belt. The perspiration of the student started discolouring the belt, but students were not allowed to wash their uniforms:

> After some time, your belt started to have a different colour, yellow-greenish at first. Then you started working on throwing techniques and ground fighting so your belt/uniform became slowly green-brownish coloured ... After some months of intensive training, the colour of your brownish belt slowly turned into some blackish shade – that's how these colours came along.

Others, such as martial arts student Gary Donahue, emphasise the spiritual meaning behind the colours:

> White is the pure state of being. You have no knowledge of any martial abilities. When you have a black belt, your soul is stained with the knowledge of how to maim and kill. You must constantly practise and achieve higher understanding of your art, thus achieving a point at which you will never need to use your art, for you are at peace with the universe.
>
> By the time this point is reached, you have so worn your old black belt, that it starts to fray and become discoloured yet again, attaining the original white colour. At this point, the circle is complete, and you again return to pure innocence.

Several martial arts practitioners employ metaphors about nature to explain the meanings of the belt colours. Raymond Walters writes about how his school of tae kwon do views the colour scheme: 'A student in tae kwon do is considered to be a constantly growing individual much like a tree grows from a seed that is planted in the ground ...'

For example, the white belt signifies the potential growth of a seed before it is put into the ground; the yellow belt indicates the seed has sprouted and can see the sun for the first time; a brown belt means that the tree's roots have spread in the soil to give it strength and stability; and a black belt signifies that the seed that was planted is now grown and has the potential to start new trees of its own.

But some of our sources claim that these spiritual and poetic explanations for the belt colours are nothing but nonsense. The most vocal is John Soet, Editor of *Inside Karate* magazine:

> The myth is "the old belt starts white and gets dirtier with practice, and so the belts turned black after time and became a symbol of proficiency". However, the reality is much more mundane. Mr Kano, the developer of modern judo, was a teacher. He was looking for a way to distinguish (symbolise?) the level of achievement his various students had attained. He hit upon the idea of using various belt colours to denote the various levels of achievement. He simply borrowed from what he was already familiar with.
>
> In the athletic programs of the Chinese schools at the time, students at various class levels wore uniforms of different colours to indicate what year they were in. In particular, swimming students wore the following colours: white – first year; green – second year; brown – third year; black – fourth year. Mr Kano simply borrowed those colours to develop his original four-colour belt system, ranging from white for a beginner, through green and brown, and finally black for a master.
>
> Many disciplines have modified and embellished the coloured-belt system. The US added the myriad of colours you see now; this stems from Ed Parker of Hawaii [a karate teacher], who developed the first American styles in the late 1950s and 1960s.

Our favourite response to this Imponderable came from Jim Coleman, the Executive Editor of *Black Belt* magazine, who advanced the 'belt gets black from years of use' theory. When we asked him if he thought this story was true, he replied: 'Well, it's as good as anything.'

Why is a square boxing area called a 'ring'?

Even a punch-drunk fighter can work out that his workspace is a square. Where did 'ring' come from?

The answer is that 'ring' was first applied not to the boxing area, but to the spectators who formed a ring around the combatants, according to *Brewer's Dictionary of Phrase and Fable*. Although hand-to-hand combat was probably invented by the first two-year-old boy to discover he had a younger sibling, the first public boxing matches took place in early eighteenth-century England. These were bare-knuckled, no-holds-barred affairs with no time limits, no ropes and no referees. The winner was the last man standing. The ring of bloodthirsty fans formed a permeable enclosure for the pugilists.

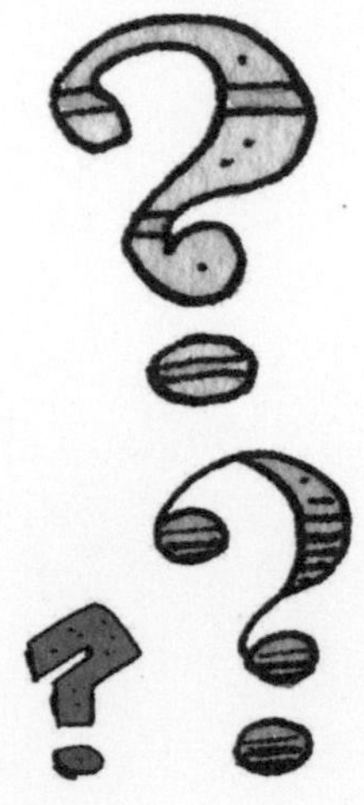

Eventually, as boxers started to make more money for their efforts, small arenas were built that featured rings demarcated by wooden barriers or heavy ropes. The current ring, with four (or occasionally three) ropes tied to turnbuckles on corner posts, is the descendant.

Although sanctioning bodies mandate the size of boxing rings, professional wrestling has no such requirement. In many venues, the same rings are used for boxing and wrestling. Amateur wrestling is done on mats laid across a floor. Ironically, the action in amateur wrestling is demarcated by a circle, yet it isn't called a ring.

None of this makes much sense without the historical perspective. That's probably why the most common slang term for the ring in professional wrestling is 'the squared circle'.

What is that sniffing noise boxers make when throwing punches?

Listen carefully to any boxing match, or to any boxer shadow-boxing, and you will hear a sniffing sound every time a punch is thrown. This sound is known to many in the boxing trade as the 'snort'.

A 'snort' is nothing more than an exhalation of breath. Proper breathing technique is an integral part of most sports, and many boxers are taught to exhale (usually, through their nose) every time they throw a punch. Scoop Gallello, President of the International Veteran Boxers Association, told *Imponderables* that when a boxer snorts while delivering a punch, 'he feels he is delivering it with more power'. Gallello adds: 'Whether this actually gives the deliverer of the punch added strength may be questionable.'

Robert W Lee, President and Commissioner of the International Boxing Federation, remarked that the snort gives a boxer:

> 'the ability to utilise all of his force and yet not expend every bit of energy when throwing the punch. I am not sure whether

> or not it works, but those who know much more about it than I do continue to use the method and I would tend to think it has some merit. ’

The more we researched this question, the more we were struck by the uncertainty of the experts about the efficacy of the snorting technique. Donald F Hull, Jr, Executive Director of the International Amateur Boxing Association, the governing federation for worldwide amateur and Olympic boxing, noted: ‘While exhaling is important in the execution of powerful and aerobic movements, it is not as crucial in the execution of a boxing punch, but the principle is the same.’

Anyone who has ever watched a Jane Fonda aerobics video or DVD is aware of the stress on breathing properly during aerobic training. Disciplines as disparate as weightlifting and yoga emphasise the need for consciousness of inhalation and exhalation. But why couldn't any of the boxing experts explain why, or if, snorting really helps a boxer?

Several of the authorities we spoke to recommended we contact Ira Becker, the doyen of New York's fabled Gleason's Gymnasium, who proved to have very strong opinions on the subject of snorting:

> ‘ When the fighter snorts, he is merely exhaling. It is a foolish action since he throws off a minimum of carbon dioxide and some vital oxygen. It is far wiser to inhale and let the lungs do [their] own bidding by getting rid of the carbon dioxide and retaining oxygen. ’

The training of boxing, more than most sports, tends to be ruled by tradition rather than by scientific research. While most aspiring boxers continue to be taught to snort, there is obviously little agreement about whether snorting actually conserves or expends energy.

Why are downhill ski poles bent?

Unlike the slalom skier's poles, which must make cuts in the snow to negotiate the gates, the main purpose of the downhill ski poles is to get the skier moving and into a tuck position – and then not get in the way.

According to Tim Ross, Director of Coaches' Education for the United States Ski Coaches Association, the bends allow the racer 'to get in the most aerodynamic position possible. This is extremely important at the higher speeds of downhill.' Savings of hundredths of a second are serious business for competitive downhill skiers, even when they are attaining speeds of 100 to 120 km/h.

If the bends in the pole are not symmetrical, they are designed with careful consideration. Dave Hamilton, of the Professional Ski Instructors of America, reports that top-level ski racers have poles individually designed to fit their dimensions. Recreational skiers are now starting to bend their poles out of shape. According to Ross, the custom-made downhill ski poles may have as many as three to four different bend angles.

Funny. We haven't seen downhill skiers with three to four different bend angles in their bodies.

How do you steer a luge around curves?

The obvious answer is 'very carefully'. Lugers rocket down an ice chute at speeds up to 135 km/h, on their backs, 8 cm from the ice, without any braking devices. The tiniest lapse in form or concentration can lead to a bone-crunching crash.

Luge experts agree that the most perilous part of this perilous sport is steering around turns. It's also a critical element in competitive racing. Good steering can add up to a tremendous amount of saved time over the course of 14 curves during a 50-second run. Yet, to the uninitiated, lugers (they're also called 'sliders') don't seem to be steering at all.

Walter Corey, High Performance Director for Luge Canada, told us that the steering action is so subtle it is all but imperceptible to the casual observer. 'It's very much like skiing. In fact, we find that skiers make a good transfer to luging,' he says. The luge is steered mainly with the feet by applying pressure on the runners. Corey explains that this requires a precise mix of shifting body weight, pressing down with the shoulders and rolling the head.

Aiding in this process are the kufens, mechanisms attached to the curved steel runners at the front of the luge that help the slider to steer with his or her feet. These body movements, combined with the gravitational force exerted in curves, actually increase speed. 'It's all very well to talk about this,' Corey observes, 'but the only way to really understand it is to experience it. It's quite a thrill.'

We'll just have to take your word for it.

How do figure skaters keep from getting dizzy while spinning? Is it possible to eye a fixed point while spinning so fast?

Imponderables readers aren't the only ones interested in this question. So are astronauts, who suffer from motion sickness in space. Carole Shulman, Executive Director of the Professional Skaters Guild of America, explains:

> Tests were conducted by NASA several years ago to determine the answer to this very question. Research proved that with a trained skater, the pupils of the eyes do not gyrate back and forth during a spin as they do with an untrained skater. The rapid movement of the eyes catching objects within view is what actually causes dizziness.
>
> The eyes of a trained skater do not focus on a fixed point during a spin but rather they remain in a stabilised position focusing on space between the skater and the next closest object. This gaze is much like that of a daydream.

So how are skaters taught to avoid focusing on objects or people? Claire O'Neill Dillie, a skating coach and motivational consultant, teaches students to see a 'blurred constant', an imaginary line running around the rink. The imaginary line may be in the seats or along the barrier of the rink (during layback spins, the imaginary line might be on the ceiling). The crucial consideration is that the skater feels centred. Even when the hands and legs are flailing about, the skater should feel as if his or her shoulders, hips and head are aligned.

Untrained skaters often feel dizziest not in the middle of the spin but when stopping (the same phenomenon experienced when a tortuous amusement park ride stops and we walk off to less than solid footing). Dillie teaches her students to avoid vertigo by turning their heads in the opposite direction of the spin when stopping.

What surprised us about the answers to this Imponderable is that the strategies used to avoid dizziness are diametrically opposed to those used by ballet dancers, who use a technique called 'spotting'. Dancers consciously pick out a location or object to focus upon; during each revolution, they centre themselves by spotting that object or location. When spotting, dancers turn their head at the very last moment, trailing the movement of the body, whereas skaters keep their head aligned with the rest of their body.

Why won't spotting work for skaters? For the answer, we consulted Ronnie Robertson, an Olympic medallist who has attained a rare distinction: nobody has ever spun faster on ice than he has.

How fast? At his peak, Robertson's spins were as fast as six revolutions per second. He explained to us that spotting simply can't work for skaters because they are spinning too fast to focus visually on anything. At best, skaters are capable of seeing only the 'blurred constant' to which Claire O'Neill Dillie was referring, which is as much a mental as a visual feat.

Robertson, trained by Gustav Lussi, considered to be the greatest spin coach of all time, was taught to spin with his eyes closed. And so he did. Robertson feels that spinning without vertigo is an act of mental suppression, blocking out the visual cues and rapid movement that can convince your body to feel dizzy.

He explains that the edge of the blade on the ice is so small that a skater's spin is about the closest thing to spinning on a vertical point as humans can do. When his body was aligned properly, Robertson says that he felt calm while spinning at his fastest, just as a top is most stable when attaining its highest speeds.

While we had the greatest spinner of all time on the phone, we couldn't resist asking him a related Imponderable: why do almost all skating routines, in competitions and skating shows and exhibitions, end with long and fast scratch spins? Until we researched this Imponderable, we had always assumed that the practice started because skaters would have been too dizzy to continue doing anything else after rotating so fast. But Robertson dismissed our theory.

The importance of the spin, to Robertson, is that unlike other spectacular skating moves, spins are sustainable. While triple jumps evoke *oohs* and *aahs* from the audience, a skater wants a spirited, prolonged reaction to the finale of his or her routine. Spins are ideal because they start slowly and eventually build to a climax so fast that it cannot be appreciated without the aid of slow-motion photography.

Robertson believes that the audience remembers the ending, not the beginning, of routines. If a skater can pry a rousing standing ovation out of an audience, perhaps supposedly sober judges might be influenced by the reaction. Robertson's trademark was not only a blindingly fast spin but a noteworthy ending. He used his free foot to stop his final spin instantly at the fastest point. Presumably, when he stopped, he opened his eyes to soak in the appreciation of the audience.

What is the thinking behind the strange names of racehorses?

To answer this question, *Imponderables* consulted Owen Byrne. He is an official of the British Horse Racing Authority, which took over the administration of racing from the Jockey Club in 2006. Every day, as part of his job, Owen Byrne sits down with two colleagues, a cup of tea and a packet of biscuits, and goes through all the new names that have been submitted for up-and-coming British racehorses. These three officials process 40 names a day on average – about 10,000 every year.

> The rules of racing govern the names that you can give a horse. There are three principles: you have to protect the heritage of the sport; you have to make sure that no horse receives a name that could cause confusion; and you have to watch that no racehorse gets a name that is rude or likely to offend.
>
> Protecting heritage means that the names of certain famous horses can never be re-used inside Britain: you can't call your horse Desert Orchid or Best Mate. There's also an international authority that rules that the names of winners of certain races can't be re-used globally – such as Red Rum and Hurricane Run.
>
> When I say that we aim to eliminate confusion, I mean that you wouldn't want two horses with very similar names in the same race. So before the daily lists come to us, all the names submitted are run through a computer program that checks for phonetic similiarities with other racehorse names. If a new name sounds like one that's already registered, then it's not allowed. We also don't allow names that would be confusing in commentary, so you can't call a horse "Hitting the Front", because that's a phrase often used by commentators. And you can't call a horse "Number Four", because more often than not some other horse will have that number.
>
> When my two colleagues and I go through new names, one of the things we're looking out for is "rudies" – that is names that might be offensive in some way. Names of trademarks are allowed so long as the trademark holder has said it's okay. You also need permission to use the names of public personalities. Footballers' names are popular, but you can't call your horse

David Beckham, for example, unless you ask him first. The name Rooney is very protected. But there *are* racehorses called Van Nistelrooy and Bobby Charlton.

Foreign words and phrases are allowed, but we always insist on knowing their literal meaning before we grant it, in case it's rude. The French authority once allowed a horse to be given the English name Big Tits. Either they didn't realise what it signified or didn't care – but that horse is not allowed to race in Britain.

Finally, there are some other technical rules. The names of racehorses can't be longer than 18 characters, including spaces. And they have to start with a letter of the alphabet rather than a number or a punctuation mark – so you couldn't, for example, call your horse 'Appy Days, with a cockney accent. ’

Apart from that, you can call your horse anything you want. But it is all the restrictions taken together that account for the bizarre and abstruse names that many racehorses end up with. You have to be creative, and sometimes a little weird, to come up with something new. Every owner has his or her own way of going about it. Back to Owen Byrne:

‘ Lots of Arab owners use Arabic names, and there's one gentleman who always gives his horses names consisting of seven letters, because seven is lucky in Dubai. The mare Heltornic [winner of the 2006 Gold Cup at Haydock] took her name from the first syllables of the names of the owner's children. There's one owner who advertises his own company by always making it part of his horses' names. There's another chap whose horses all include a Welsh placename; he's Welsh himself, of course. In Germany, racehorses' names are influenced by a rule that says that the first letter has to be the same as that of the dam. ’

The names of the dam and the sire – a horse's mother and father – are a rich and traditional vein of ideas. It is common for a horse to be christened with a name linked to one or the other. There was a mare called Casualty, for example, that gave birth to foals who were named Traumatic, Accident and Traction. A horse called Leg Warmer was the dam of Hot Wax; and Kangaroo was the sire of Hopalong.

But the most satisfying names are those that manage to combine both parents in such a way as to yield something new and original – which is, after all, what happened to produce the horse itself. Red Rum, for example, took three letters, like chromosomes, from the name of each parent: Quorum and Mared. Splicing names is a game that any horse owner can play, as Owen Byrne points out:

> Her Majesty the Queen is an owner who has a reputation for witty and inventive names. Among her horses have been Rash Gift, which was by Cadeaux Genereux out of Nettle. And then there was Whitechapel, which was by Arctic Tern out of Christchurch.

'By' – by the way – indicates the sire, and 'out of' is shorthand for the dam. One such name that might have raised a small eyebrow with the officials of the British Horse Racing Authority, had it been registered there, was an Australian foal that was by Proud Knight, out of Please A Lady. It was ingeniously named Once A Knight.

Is there any logic to the arrangement of numbers on a dartboard?

The dartboard known as the 'clock' board (occasionally known as the 'London clock' or 'English clock') is today the international standard for all darts tournaments. The board itself is 45 cm in diameter, with a scoring diameter of 34 cm. The centre of the board contains two small circles: the inside bull, called a 'double bull' or 'double bull's-eye' is worth 50 points; the outer bull, called simply a 'bull's-eye', scores twenty-five.

Each wedge is worth the number of points indicated on the board, but the outer circumference of the scoring pie contains a concentric ring, about 1 cm wide, the double zone, that allows you to double the value of the wedge in which it is hit. The triples ring, located halfway between the centre of the board and the outside circumference, allows you to triple the value (so hitting the triple ring on a 20 gives you more points than landing on the double bull's-eye).

Why are there **two** red **stripes** around the thinnest part of tenpin **bowling pins?**

Their purpose, according to Al Vanderneck, of the American Bowling Congress, is to look pretty. Part of Vanderneck's job is to check the specifications of tenpin bowling equipment, and he reports that without the stripes, the pins 'just look funny'. The area where the stripes are placed is known as the 'neck', and evidently a naked neck on a bowling pin stands out as much as a tieless neck on the wearer of a dinner jacket.

Actually, we almost blew the answer to this Imponderable. We've enjoyed the occasional bowling match in our time, and we always identified the red stripes with pins made by the AMF company; the other major manufacturer of bowling pins, Brunswick, used a red crown as an identification mark on its pins. So we assumed that the red stripes were a trademark of AMF's.

AMF's Product Manager, Ron Pominville, quickly disabused us of our theory. Brunswick's pins have always had stripes, too, and Brunswick has eliminated the red crown in its current line of pins. A third and growing presence in pindom, Vulcan, also includes stripes on its products.

We haven't been able to confirm two items: who started the practice of striping the necks of bowling pins? And exactly what is so aesthetically pleasing about these stripes?

Dartboard patterns and numbering schemes were not always so uniform. Undoubtedly, darts were originally used as weapons rather than as game equipment. Legend has it that the first darts were made for a Saxon king who was too short to use a bow and arrow. He solved the problem by sawing off the ends of arrows, leaving projectiles about 30 cm long.

The sport of darts dates back to England in the fifteenth century, when military men sawed off arrows and threw them against the ends, or butts, of wine casks. The game was called 'the butts', and the shortened arrows were called 'dartes'. Henry VIII was an aficionado of the sport, and Anne Boleyn gave her king a set of jewel-encrusted darts as a birthday gift.

As the sport grew in popularity, warriors looked for better targets than wine casks. They began using round slices from fallen trees, particularly elm trees. The concentric rings of the trees formed natural divisions for scoring purposes (they looked not unlike an archery target's rings), and the cracks that appeared when the wood dried out provided radial lines for more scoring areas.

The passage of time saw a proliferation of new patterns on boards, and various regions of England claimed their own patterns. By the early twentieth century, some boards featured as many as 28 different wedges; some as few as ten.

Eventually, standardisation of the boards became inevitable, if only because of the affinity between beer and darts. Darts became the popular game in English pubs during the late nineteenth century. The elm dartboards had to be soaked overnight to keep them from drying out and developing cracks. Often, the boards were soaked with the most available liquid, beer, so the boards tended to drip all over the floor, creating a smelly mess.

To the rescue came Ted Leggett, an analytic chemist, who just after the First World War created a modelling clay that had no scent, unlike other clays of that time. He called his product (and company) Nodor (a compressed version of 'no odor') and quit his job to market the clay. According to Leggett's daughter, Doris Bugler, one day the chemist threw some darts at a lump of his clay, and the darts held. Eureka!

The Nodor dartboard was first marketed in 1923; it sported today's 'clock' pattern but also incorporated other regional patterns. As darts increased in popularity, Leggett decided that a ruling body should be formed to regulate interdistrict competitions – Leggett became the first President of the National Darts Association in 1935. It was at this point that the 'clock' pattern became standard.

Was there any particular reason for the ascendancy of the 'clock' board? *Imponderables* contacted many experts to find out who invented the clock board, but to a person, they repeated the sentiments of Barry Sinnett, of

Anglo-American Dartboards, who has worked in the darting business for more than 30 years:

> No one seems to know. It's known to be unknown. I have taken a couple of trips to England and talked to several of the old-timers from the English dartboard companies. No one knew (and that includes people at Nodor).

Even a casual glance at the numbers on the dartboard indicates that there is some method to the numbering scheme on a dartboard. Note that high and low numbers alternate around the board. So why not always aim for the 20 to score the most points possible? There are two good reasons why one might not, as Mike Courtenay, a devoted darter and Manager of Darts and Things, a store in Van Nuys, California, points out:

> Many people just try to throw at the 20 segment because it's the highest score on the board besides the bull's-eyes. But that's often a mistake. The numbers on either side of the 20 are only 1 and 5 – a higher scoring area is near the bottom left, where 16, 7, and 19 are adjacent.

The clock board constantly forces players to make strategic decisions. After all, it might occur to the neophyte always to aim for the double bull's-eye. The problem with this approach is that when you miss, as you usually will, you have no idea what wedge you will land in – you are just as likely to land in 1 as twenty.

Why do females tend to throw 'like a girl'?

Not only do girls (and later, women) tend not to be able to throw balls as far as boys, but their form is noticeably different. If you ask the average boy to throw a cricket ball as far as he can, he will lift his elbow and wind his arm far back. A girl will tend to keep her elbow static and push forward with her hand in a motion not unlike that of a shot putter.

Why the difference? Our correspondent says he has heard theories that females have an extra bone that prevents them from throwing 'like a boy'. Or is it that they are missing one bone? We talked to some physiologists (who assured us that boys and girls have all the same relevant bones) and to some specialists in exercise physiology who have studied the underperformance of girls in throwing.

In their textbook, *Training for Sport and Activity: The Physiological Basis of the Conditioning Process*, Jack H Wilmore and David L Costill cite quite a few studies that indicate that up until the ages of ten to 12, boys and girls have similar scores in motor skills and athletic ability. In almost every test, boys barely beat the girls. But at the onset of puberty, males become stronger, possess greater muscular and cardiovascular endurance, and outperform girls in virtually all motor skills.

In only one athletic test do the boys far exceed the girls before and after puberty: the softball throw. From the ages of five to 16, the average boy can throw a softball about twice as far as a girl.

Wilmore and Costill cite a fascinating study that attempted to explain this phenomenon. Two hundred males and females from ages three to 20 threw softballs for science. The result: males beat females two to one when throwing with their dominant hand, but females threw almost as far as males with their non-dominant hand. Up until the ages of ten to 12, girls threw just as far with their non-dominant hand as boys did.

The conclusion of Wilmore and Costill is inescapable:

> ‘Major differences at all ages were the results for the dominant arm ... the softball throw for distance using the dominant arm appears to be biased by the previous experience and practice of the males. When the influence of experience and practice was removed by using the non-dominant arm, this motor skill task was identical to each of the others.’

All the evidence suggests that girls can be taught, or learn through experience, how to throw 'like a boy'. Exercise physiologist Ralph Wickstrom believes most children go through several developmental stages of throwing. Boys simply continue growing in sophistication, while girls are not encouraged to throw balls and stop in the learning curve. As an example, Wickstrom notes that most right-handed girls throw with their right foot forward. Simply shifting their left foot forward would increase their throwing distance.

When forced to throw with their non-dominant hand, most boys throw 'like a girl'. The loss in distance is accountable not only to lesser muscular development in the non-dominant side, but to a breakdown in form caused by a lack of practice.

Index

F

G

J

K

L

M

N

O

P

Q

R

S

T

U

V

W

X

Y

Z

About the Author

David Feldman grew up in Mar Vista, California. From an abnormally early age, Dave was fascinated by popular culture. He loved rock 'n roll and the 1950s and 60s US television sitcom *Leave It to Beaver*, and tried to analyse why and how they were successful commercially and artistically. In university, he studied literature, with a special interest in Russian writers, but he was also busy convincing sympathetic professors at Grinnell College (yes, an accredited institution of higher learning) to allow him to undertake independent studies in popular culture.

After winning a Watson Fellowship to study popular culture in Europe, Dave ditched Dostoevsky and went to Bowling Green State University, at that time the only school in the world with a postgraduate degree in popular culture. There he taught the first-ever university course on soap operas.

After moving to New York, Dave was a consultant for the American ABC television network but took a job in the programming department of the NBC network, where he worked in both daytime and prime-time programming. He was and is obsessed with television, but wasn't cut out to be a TV programmer. So he saved up his money with the intention of embarking on a writing career. A trip to the supermarket triggered the 'Imponderables' idea (see introduction). The rest, if not history, has been Dave's work for more than 20 years.

Dave lives in New York. He's single but has many interests besides work to occupy him: tournament duplicate bridge, listening to his massive music collection, searching for good food anywhere, reading, annoying his friends, indulging in all facets of popular culture and writing autobiographical sketches in the third person.

Imponderables

Project Editor
John Andrews

Art Editor
Conorde Clarke

Designer
Kate Harris

Illustrator
Elwood Smith

Additional Research
Jonathan Bastable

Proofreader
Cécile Landau

Indexer
Diane Harriman

Reader's Digest General Books

Editorial Director
Julian Browne

Art Director
Anne-Marie Bulat

Head of Book Development
Sarah Bloxham

Managing Editor
Nina Hathway

Picture Resource Manager
Sarah Stewart-Richardson

Pre-press Account Manager
Dean Russell

Product Production Manager
Claudette Bramble

Production Controller
Katherine Bunn

Origination
Colour Systems Limited, London

Printing and binding
China

The material in this book originally appeared in the following books, all published by HarperCollins Publishers, Inc.: *Why Do Pirates Love Parrots?*; *Do Elephants Jump?*; *How Do Astronauts Scratch an Itch?*; *What Are Hyenas Laughing At, Anyway?*; *How Does Aspirin Find a Headache?*; *Are Lobsters Ambidextrous?*; *Do Penguins Have Knees?*; *Why Do Dogs Have Wet Noses?*; *When Do Fish Sleep?*; *Why Do Clocks Run Clockwise?*; and *Why Don't Cats Like to Swim?*

Imponderables is published by
The Reader's Digest Association Limited
11 Westferry Circus, Canary Wharf, London E14 4HE

This special deluxe edition was compiled and published by The Reader's Digest Association Limited by permission of JET Literary Associates, Inc.

We are committed both to the quality of our products and the service we provide to our customers. We value your comments, so please do contact us on 08705 113366 or via our website at **www.readersdigest.co.uk**

If you have any comments or suggestions about the content of our books, email us at **gbeditorial@readersdigest.co.uk**

ISBN: 978 0 276 44419 7
Concept code: US4918IC/OP
Book code: 400-319 UP0000-1
Oracle Code: 250010344H.00.24